MW01283770

GLOBAL PERSPECTIVES ON THE OLD TESTAMENT

GLOBAL PERSPECTIVES
ON THE OLD TESTAMENT

EDITORS

Mark Roncace
Wingate University

Joseph Weaver
Wingate University

Boston   Columbus   Indianapolis   New York   San Francisco   Upper Saddle River
Amsterdam   Cape Town   Dubai   London   Madrid   Milan   Munich   Paris   Montréal   Toronto
Delhi   Mexico City   São Paulo   Sydney   Hong Kong   Seoul   Singapore   Taipei   Tokyo

Editor in Chief: Ashley Dodge
Publisher: Nancy Roberts
Editorial Assistant: Molly White
Director of Marketing: Brandy Dawson
Executive Marketing Manager: Kelly May
Marketing Coordinator: Jessica Warren
Managing Editor: Denise Forlow
Program Manager: Mayda Bosco
Operations Supervisor: Mary Fischer
Operations Specialist: Eileen Corallo
Art Director: Jayne Conte
Cover photo: Shutterstock, Inc.
Cover design: Bruce Kenselaar
Director of Digital Media: Brian Hyland
Digital Media Project Manager: Tina Gagliostro
Full-Service Project Management and Composition: Integra Software Services, Pvt. Ltd.
Printer/Binder: RRD/Harrisonburg
Cover Printer: RRD/Harrisonburg
Text Font: 10/12, Times LT Std

Credits and acknowledgments borrowed from other sources and reproduced, with permission, in this textbook appear on appropriate page within text (or on page 242).

Copyright © 2014 by Pearson Education, Inc. All rights reserved. Printed in the United States of America. This publication is protected by Copyright and permission should be obtained from the publisher prior to any prohibited reproduction, storage in a retrieval system, or transmission in any form or by any means, electronic, mechanical, photocopying, recording, or likewise. To obtain permission(s) to use material from this work, please submit a written request to Pearson Education, Inc., Permissions Department, One Lake Street, Upper Saddle River, New Jersey 07458 or you may fax your request to 201-236-3290.

Many of the designations by manufacturers and seller to distinguish their products are claimed as trademarks. Where those designations appear in this book, and the publisher was aware of a trademark claim, the designations have been printed in initial caps or all caps.

Library of Congress Cataloging-in-Publication Data
CIP information not available at time of publication.

10 9 8 7 6 5 4 3 2 1

ISBN 10: 0-205-90921-3
ISBN 13: 978-0-205-90921-6

BRIEF CONTENTS

CONTENTS

PREFACE

This book is a lot like the Bible itself in that it is a diverse collection of writings emanating from a variety of geographic, social, cultural, political, economic, and religious contexts. But wait—that first sentence has already indicated a great deal about us (the editors) and about our views of the Bible. Maybe we've already revealed more about us—our background, education, life experiences, and so on—than about the Bible itself. To us, the Bible—and specifically the Old Testament—is indeed an eclectic anthology, much like this book. However, if someone else were to have written that first sentence, they might have started by introducing the Bible as the infallible Word of God, a book that provides moral and ethical guidelines for everyday life and God's plan of salvation. Another person might have opened with the claim that the Bible is one of the most toxic texts ever produced and that its continuing influence in our world is one of the great mysteries and tragedies of our day. Incidentally, neither of these two potential perspectives is incompatible with our statement that the Bible is an eclectic anthology. The point is this: It's all about perspective. People are different. They approach the Bible with their own various ideas, beliefs, and assumptions, which means there are a myriad of possible ways to write that first sentence. Nobody can say anything without saying something about themselves.

But you may have already known that. Most people living in our postmodern world—or whatever we are supposed to call it now (that's also a matter of perspective)—realize that there is no neutral, objective perspective from which to assess things, no position that is unencumbered by a specific life setting. Everyone comes from somewhere. Everyone is born in a certain time and place to certain parents and has had certain experiences that shape how we see the world. All those "certainties," to which many more could be added, make up who you are; they define your specific context and perspective. They also mean that you can be certain that your interpretation of a given biblical text is not the only way that it can be interpreted. While the idea of varied perspectives is hardly new, you may not be aware of the extent and nature of some of those different readings. Hence this book.

FORMAT OF THE BOOK

Herein we have gathered four essays around 28 Old Testament texts. Our intention is for you to read the given portion of the Bible and then to consider what four people from various contexts and backgrounds have written about it. In doing so, you will see the biblical text in a new light; you will learn something about the various interpreters and their particular location; and you will discover something about yourself. Put differently, when we encounter views that are different from our own, we have the wonderfully enriching experience of learning about (1) the Old Testament and (2) other interpreters and the places from which they come, which in turn (3) helps us see our own lives and views in a new way. We are thus engaging the Old Testament, each other, and ourselves. It's a dynamic, interactive triangle.

But all three corners of the triangle must be present. The importance of your corner bears emphasizing: You must read the Old Testament for yourself. This is absolutely indispensible. You must read carefully and develop your own insights and analyses. This will not only help you "hear" the biblical voice (filtered through your own context, of course), but it will also enable you to appreciate the four different perspectives. We instructed the authors of the essays not to summarize the biblical passage; there is no sense in using valuable space on something that you can do for yourself. So, you must uphold your end of the deal: You must read the Old Testament! Yes, you are reading a translation of the Bible and a translation is already an interpretation; but, still, it's crucial that you experience the text on your own.

To encourage you to do this, we have not included any of our own introductory material to each Old Testament passage, as it would inevitably reflect our own perspective, which would defeat the book's purpose of including as many different points of view as possible. Furthermore, you should read the essays with a Bible in hand; many times the authors include only the biblical reference (not the full quotation), which you would do well to look up in order to help you interact thoughtfully with the essay.

To facilitate further your engagement with all three corners of the triangle, we have included four questions at the end of each set of essays (one question for each essay). Use the questions to prompt your critical interaction with the various essays. If the question could occasionally be answered "yes" or "no," don't simply leave it at that. Assume that "Why or why not?" or "Explain your answer" follows—we just thought it unnecessary to write it out for you. Yes, our questions inevitably reveal our own interests and ideas, so please feel free to add your own questions and to question our questions. In fact, if you don't, you probably aren't thinking hard enough.

There are a mere 112 essays in this book; this, needless to say, is a pittance of the possible number. A book titled *Global Perspectives on the Old Testament* should not be a book at all, but rather a multivolume encyclopedia. But if that were the case, you would have had a much harder time buying it and carrying it around. Think for a moment about how this book barely scratches the proverbial surface of global perspectives on the Old Testament. If there are approximately 7 billion people in the world and if only 1 in every 1,000 has something to say about the Bible, then our 97 authors represent only about 0.000014 percent of perspectives on the Bible. We make this point—odd as it may seem—because we hope this collection of essays encourages you to seek out many more interpretations of the Old Testament, whether they be from scholarly books and commentaries or friends and family over lunch. These essays are intended to start conversations, not end them. It's a big world, and this book is terribly small. We are hoping you will create the rest of the encyclopedia.

We have done our best to assemble a wide range of views. Nevertheless, the book should probably be titled *Global* Perspectives* on the Old Testament**. With the first asterisk we call attention to the fact that as English speakers we could only accept essays written in English. We also solicited submissions via e-mail. As such, by requiring contributors to write in our native language and to have Internet access, we have by necessity precluded a majority of the world's population. Furthermore, we live and work in the United States. Most of our personal and professional connections are here; therefore, there are far more contributors from the United States than any other single country. Because of this, we feel as though we should iterate that we mean "global" in more than simply the geographic sense. There is religious, ethnic, ideological, political, and socioeconomic diversity in the essays, and those elements, of course, are not bound by particular geographic location. We also assembled contributors from various walks of life; this book is much more "global" than a typical collection of professional academic papers.

The second asterisk shows that, while limiting our fingerprints as much as possible, the essays were proofread and minimally edited. We made the decision to standardize spelling and punctuation, and even to capitalize the word "Bible." Beyond that, we did little else. We did not standardize, for example, the style of referring to eras (B.C.E., C.E., B.C., A.D.); we did not change inclusive or non-inclusive language or capitalization for pronouns referring to deity. The third asterisk denotes that the term "Old Testament" reflects a Christian perspective; it implies that something "New" fulfills it. We have, however, decided to follow the order of the books in the Hebrew Bible (rather than the Christian Old Testament). Furthermore, although we did not begin with a prescribed list of 28 Old Testament texts for which to solicit essays, we did, of course, ultimately determine which texts the book would address.

Let's mention one more asterisk-worthy matter. You will notice that each set of essays opens with a page featuring a map locating each of the four authors in that set. But where on the map should we put each author's dot? Where the author was born? Where they have spent most of their life? Where they went to school? Where they were when they wrote the essay? Where they reside now? The place about which they write? It's not that easy. We live in a transient world. We have decided to put the dot in the place, or places, about which they are writing. Or if geographic location or context is not central to their essay, then the dot is located in the place of their primary current residence. Hence all the dots should have an asterisk to that effect too.

In short, this is only one of many possible ways to assemble a book called *Global Perspectives on the Old Testament*. Despite its limitations and the inherent difficulty of producing a book of this nature, we are confident that you will find these perspectives to be enlightening and engaging. There are many additional introductory and hermeneutical issues that we could explore at the outset, but we won't. So let us limit ourselves to two final thoughts. First, the Old Testament is the sacred literature of the Jewish and Christian traditions, but the influence and impact of the Old Testament have extended beyond those two religions. People who are not Christian or Jewish read or are familiar with the Old Testament. In our effort to offer as many global perspectives as possible, we have included views by those who do not treat the Old Testament as Scripture. We fully understand that some people with a faith commitment to the text may feel that those outside the tradition do not have anything to offer. We respectfully disagree, and both of us—for the record—are in the Christian tradition.

Our world is too big and complex to ignore thoughtful and intelligent readers simply because they approach the text without a set of traditional religious lenses—or because they come from a tradition other than Judaism or Christianity. We sincerely appreciate all of the authors of these essays for allowing their work to be published in a book that includes approaches with which they may strongly disagree.

Second, if the essays are eclectic, then so too are the biblical texts that they interpret. You will notice that some sets of four essays deal with only one chapter from the Bible (Genesis 22), some with part of a book (Genesis 37–50, Exodus 1–15), and others with whole books. Much of this has to do with the nature of the Old Testament—it's not a tidy collection, and some parts have garnered more attention than others. As a result, sometimes the essays in a chapter are in direct dialogue over the same specific text or topic, while other times they address different portions of the passage. Hopefully, every set of essays will draw you into the discussion.

The Old Testament has a sort of "unevenness" to it, and so do the various sets of essays that follow, which in turn reflects the complex nature of the world in which we live. And thus, we end this short Introduction where it began: If the perspectives herein feel somewhat scattered—all over the place—then we say, "Yes, exactly, and so is both our global world and the Old Testament." Hence a book with our title will inevitably be a bit messy. And yes, this view again reflects our particular perspective as white, Western-educated, middle-class, heterosexual men in the Christian tradition. From where we stand, the following essays offer fresh, compelling readings of the Bible from a variety of perspectives. Tell us what you think from where you stand.

STUDENT AND TEACHER RESOURCES

This text is available in a variety of formats—digital and print. To learn more about our programs, pricing options, and customization, visit www.pearsonhighered.com.

MySearchLab with eText

A passcode-protected website that provides engaging experiences that personalize learning, MySearchLab contains an eText that is just like the printed text. Students can highlight and add notes to the eText online or download it to an iPad. MySearchLab also provides a wide range of writing, grammar, and research tools plus access to a variety of academic journals, census data, Associated Press news feeds, and discipline-specific readings to help hone writing and research skills.

Instructor's Resource Manual and Test Bank (0-205-92572-3)

This valuable resource provides chapter outlines, lecture topics, and suggested media resources. In addition, test questions in short essay formats are available for each chapter.

MyTest (0-205-95460-X)

This computerized software allows instructors to create their own personalized exams, to edit any or all of the existing test questions, and to add new questions. Other special features of this program include the random generation of test questions, the creation of alternative versions of the same test, scrambling question sequences, and test previews before printing.

ACKNOWLEDGMENTS

As the editors, not the authors, of this book, the list of people we gratefully acknowledge can be found in the Table of Contents. Indeed, the 97 contributors deserve more thanks than we can offer. Their timely and insightful work made this project a reality. We offer our sincerest gratitude to each and every one of them.

We also express appreciation to our wonderful colleagues at Wingate University for designing and implementing a new core curriculum, which was the impetus for this textbook. Without their vision and support, this book never would have happened. We are so grateful to the reviewers who took the time to assess this text prior to its publication: Wayne Brouwer, Hope College; Steven Godby, Broward College-South Campus; Warren Johnson, East Texas Baptist University; and Jeff Tillman, Wayland Baptist University. We also thank Maggie Barbieri for expert editorial guidance and Nancy Roberts for her willingness to take on such an unwieldy project.

Mark Roncace

Joseph Weaver

CHAPTER 1

GENESIS 1–3 (PART I)

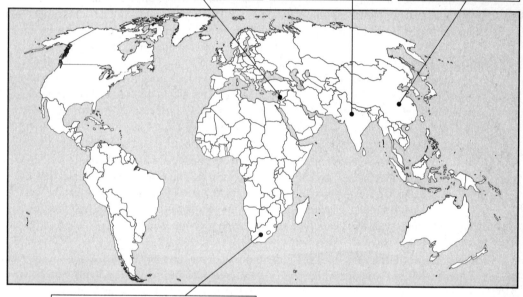

Meir Bar-Ilan outlines six differences between the two creation stories in Genesis, beyond the ones that are typically noted.

M. Aravind Jeyakumar compares the interpretation of the Hindu *Purusa-Sukta* creation accounts with traditional readings of the biblical text.

Sonia Kwok Wong compares the biblical text to Chinese creation myths, with attention to how one accounts for the similarities found in various creation myths.

David T. Williams explains the challenges of reading the biblical creation stories in African cultures and the greater appreciation of human community that it brings.

READINGS

Chinese and Biblical Creation Myths
Sonia Kwok Wong

The *Purusa-Sukta* Compared to Biblical Texts
M. Aravind Jeyakumar

The Concept of Human Community in African Creation Stories
David T. Williams

Six Differences between Two Creation Stories in Genesis
Meir Bar-Ilan

CHINESE AND BIBLICAL CREATION MYTHS

Sonia Kwok Wong (China)

Creation is a common theme in mythologies worldwide. In China alone, there are six separate creation myths. In spite of geographical distance and cultural divergence of the countries in which they are attested, creation myths display striking resemblances. As a Chinese biblical scholar, I am intrigued by the similarities that I find between the biblical and the Chinese creation myths. In this essay, I will compare one of the earliest versions of the Nüwa creation myth of China with the biblical one (Gen. 1–3), demonstrating that the methodological lens in reading Chinese myths could be applied to the biblical creation story.

The earliest versions of the Nüwa myth are found scattered fragmentarily in the Chinese literature of the Warring States era (c. fourth century B.C.E.), although the myth is dated to a much earlier time. Nüwa is often depicted as a goddess with a human face and serpent body in ancient texts and grave paintings. She has been esteemed and worshipped as the creator of the universe, the great progenitor of humankind, the supreme matchmaker, and the patron of marriage by many people in China.

The Nüwa myth is nonstatic and malleable. It has undergone a complex process of oral and textual transmission. Consequently, numerous versions of the myth have been engendered. To quote (my translation) an early Han-dynasty version in *Fengsu tongyi* (*Penetrating Customs*), as cited in *Taiping yulan* (*The Imperial Readings of Taiping Era*):

> It is said that when heaven and earth were separated, there was no humankind. Nüwa created human beings by kneading yellow earth. The task was so arduous that she was too exhausted to complete it. So she flicked the sludge with her cord and lifted it to form humankind. The ones kneaded with yellow earth became the rich aristocrats and those made by flicking the sludge the poor commoners.

In contrast to Genesis 1–3, the Nüwa myth does not mention any divine reason for the creation of humankind, and, of course, the gender of the creator is different. It is not difficult, however, to notice the striking similarities, such as the motifs of the separation of heaven and earth and molding humankind from earth. These motifs are by no means limited to Chinese and biblical creation myths. In fact, they also appear, for instance, in the folk literature of Ireland, Greece, Babylonia, Siberia, Indonesia, Australia, and India.

If I expand my comparison to other Chinese creation myths, more parallels to Genesis 1–3 emerge. For instance, it is said that the mythological figure Pangu created the universe out of chaos (cf. Gen. 1:2) and that Yilou enlivens humans by blowing air into them (cf. Gen. 2:7). How do we account for the similarities found in the creation myths of cultures that are so different and so far apart geographically?

One way to account for them is by conjecturing a common ancestry. In the mid-nineteenth century, some scholars, such as Max Müller, who believed in the common ancestry of Indo-European languages, postulated a protomythology of Indo-European folktales. The monogenetic theory has now been dismissed and regarded as a "myth" itself, because it fails to explain the similar and even identical motifs found in folktales of non-Indo-European languages. It is possible that similar myths found in geographical proximity might have developed from a "proto-myth"; however, it is extremely hard to prove genealogical link of those found in remote places with independent language systems.

Another possible explanation is to attribute the similarities to the parallel development of cultures. Anthropologists once had assumed that all human cultures undergo the identical process of cultural evolution. Cultures in the same developmental stage, irrespective of their geographical distance, would produce folklores that converge in thematic elements because of the commonality in the way that the "primitive" people perceive the world and express themselves. Myths, in this sense, are polygenetic and regarded as remnants of the "primitive" culture in the contemporary world. This view presupposes that all human societies progress in the same sequence and number of stages, and thus it fails to acknowledge that cultures evolve and develop differently based on contextual constraints.

Societies need not follow the same developmental path. Similarities in myths could be attributed to similar concerns, customs, beliefs, values, and circumstances shared by cultures, even if they do not follow a programmed path of development. Similar, or even identical, ideas could be genealogically related or have originated separately (each case must be assessed independently). Also, independent myths could subsequently exert influence on each other through the process of dissemination. In the case of the similarities in the Chinese and the biblical creation myths, it would be far-fetched to postulate a common ancestry because of the geographical distance and cultural divergence between ancient China and Palestine.

The construction of many myths reflects an urge to find explanations on how the world came to be in its present form (an etiology). While the urge might be a spiritual concern, its ideological dimension cannot be overlooked. The Nüwa myth quoted above is conspicuously a product of a stratified society. The last line, likely a later addition to the original version, is an etiology of social stratification. The distinction between the rich and the poor is said to have been preestablished by the goddess Nüwa in primeval time. The implication is that social stratification is a divine mandate, predestinated and unalterable. The myth serves to perpetuate social inequality through the rhetoric of divine legitimation. Ancient myths were often produced or reappropriated by ruling elite for their own interest and agenda, be it for the purpose of maintaining social status quo, inducing social transformation, or forging a sense of group identity.

This methodological lens can also be applied to the stories in Genesis 1–3. What are the ideologies embedded in the biblical creation story? Who benefits from these ideologies? Is it a rewritten version of an earlier myth for ideological purposes? Has it been reappropriated subsequently as a means to legitimate certain social structures? By reading the biblical text as an ideologically charged myth, new insights will be gleaned.

Sonia Kwok Wong (M.Div., Chinese University of Hong Kong) is a Ph.D. candidate in Hebrew Bible at Vanderbilt University, Nashville, Tennessee, United States.

THE *PURUSA-SUKTA* COMPARED TO BIBLICAL TEXTS

M. Aravind Jeyakumar (India)

Every culture of the world has creation stories which attempt to trace the origin of the universe and its components with special reference to human beings. These stories are conditioned by the religious, cultural, social, and political context from which they originate. The same is true of the interpretations of these narratives: they derive from a particular location. As such, creation stories may be used to explain and justify certain political, religious, and social realities that are oppressive and discriminatory. Such is the case with the Genesis creation narratives and the Hindu *Purusa-Sukt*a creation accounts. Here I will first explain the traditional reading of each text which has fostered inequity and repression through the centuries. Then I will explore an egalitarian rereading of both accounts.

There is not one Hindu creation story. Numerous cosmogonies can be found in almost all of the important Hindu scriptures and there are many interpretations for those creation myths. They are all representations of the main principle of Brahman, which is described as being "everywhere and nowhere, everything and nothing." Creation came from Brahman's thought, or the actions of the god Brahma, who is the representation of Brahman as a man.

According to the *Purusa-Sukta* creation hymn (*Rig-Veda* Book: X. Hymn: 90), creation is the result of the sacrifice of *Purusha* (Man), the primeval being, who is all that exists, including "whatever has been and whatever is to be." When *Purusha*, who had "a thousand heads, a thousand eyes, and a thousand feet," was sacrificed, the clarified butter that resulted was made into the beasts which inhabit the earth. From the dismemberment came also the animals, plants, rituals, sacred words, and the Vedas. This same sacrifice produced the gods, *Indra* (the menacing king of gods), *Agni* (Fire), *Vayu* (Wind), as well as the Sun and Moon. From *Purusha's* navel the atmosphere was born; his head produced the heaven, his feet produced the earth, his ear the sky, his mind the moon, his eye the sun, his breath the wind, his feet the earth, and his belly button the atmosphere. The four *varnas* were also born from *Purusha*: the mouth was the Brahman (priest), the arms the *Kshatriya* (warrior), the thigh the *Vaishya* (general populace), and the feet the *Sudra* (servant). For centuries the *sudras* and the outcastes (Dalits) have been treated as lesser humans by the so-called upper dominant castes. This creation hymn is understood in all later Hindu scriptures to sanction the caste system as divine ordination. Thus India follows a social caste structure based on this ancient narrative.

Traditional interpretations of the Genesis narratives have also been used to support hierarchical social structures. Here God is seen as the ruler over the whole creation; God alone commands and controls. God is over the whole creation and the creatures have to submit to the creator. Man is created first and then woman is formed from the rib of the man; therefore woman is subordinate to man. This interpretation, then, establishes God as superior to human beings, and man as superior to woman. It has been used to oppress women folk and to propagate man's superiority over woman.

But different, egalitarian readings of both Genesis and *Purusa-Sukta* can be offered. A liberating reading of the Genesis creation account presents the following insights: God is the source of all creation. God is creator, but at the same time God's re-active and re-creative aspects in the process of creation are emphasized. While the image of the deity as transcendent in Genesis 1 detaches God from humanity and nature, the anthropomorphic picture of God in Genesis 2–3 emphasizes God's activity in the creative process and humankind's active role along with God. Creatures participate with God in creation by separating, ruling, developing, and reproducing; this emphasizes their involvement as cocreators along with God. God does not place Himself above all else but rather works alongside the rest of creation. This reading dismantles the traditional and colonial idea of God as king or ruler and establishes a smooth nexus between God, humans, and the natural world.

Moreover, both male and female are created in the image and likeness of God. Here, both man and woman have the freedom to think and express themselves without fear; both have self-dignity and self-respect. The creation of woman after man from his rib does not imply hierarchy, but rather it brings completion and wholeness. Their physical oneness, commonality of concern, and loyalty and responsibility to one another are emphasized. The spirit of God breathed into human beings highlights that both man and woman share divine life and breath.

An egalitarian rereading of *Purusa-Sukta* focuses on the fact that every human being is from the cosmic person, Brahma, the Supreme Being, so there should not be any inequality among human beings in the name of caste. Brahma is the source of all creation. Everything originates from Him and into Him all is absorbed. Since all the four groups of people originated from the same flesh, there are no hierarchical differences. All groups originated from parts of the body that are divine and thus there is no issue of pure and impure or purity and pollution in the name of caste. The diversity of all creatures—humans, plants, and animals—originated from the same substance, indicating their ultimate unity within the diversity of God's creation.

The heterogeneous creation concept highlights differences in creatures created by Brahma, but rejects hierarchical social structures in which one group dominates and oppresses another. Different people with different skills are necessary for the smooth functioning of society. But superiority or inferiority is not the purpose here; every human being must be given equal respect irrespective of his or her occupation. Occupational skills should not be designated in terms of caste. The idea is that all *varnas* are contained in every individual instead of every individual being comprised within one of the four *varnas*; no one should be humiliated at any cost because everyone is created from the same Brahma (same substance).

Furthermore, the anthropomorphic account of *Purusa-Sukta* exposes God in human form and God sacrificing His own body to create the human and natural world. It is thus a creation story of love and peace. Through the sacrificial love of Brahma, the whole world and humanity was formed. This narration proclaims a message of peace between diverse creatures and humankind created from the "same substance" of Brahman.

In sum, our rereading the Genesis and *Purusa-Sukta* creation stories has undermined the traditional understanding of them as sanctioning hierarchical structures. Creation means differences, plurality in creatures, and diversity in skills or tasks assigned to the creatures. But no one is inferior or superior to another because all are created by God and from God. Even God is not superior since he is cocreator (Gen. 2–3) and sacrificially offers his own body (*Purusa-Sukta*). The created order demands the plurality of creatures with interdependence; it requires participation without dominance or hierarchical structures for peaceful coexistence. Thus discrimination in the name of gender, caste, class, or any such form is against the created order.

M. Aravind Jeyakumar (B.D., M.Th., Gurukul Lutheran Theological College and Research Institute, Chennai, South India) is Lecturer in the Department of Biblical Studies at Leonard Theological College, Jabalpur, Madhya Pradesh, India.

THE CONCEPT OF HUMAN COMMUNITY IN AFRICAN CREATION STORIES

David T. Williams (South Africa)

Europe and its offspring in other parts of the world have had a tradition of treating Genesis 1–3 as literally true, an historical account of primal events which set the scene for the development of all human history. Although this view has begun to change somewhat in recent years—for example, the belief that God created the world in six 24 hour days has waned—the tradition still persists among many Christians around the world.

African Christians, however, are much less likely than those in the United States and other places to accept a literal explanation of Genesis. There are a number of reasons. First, Africa has a far shorter history of writing, and therefore much less respect for the authority of the written word. While a written signed document is treated as authoritative among Europeans, this is not the case in Africa. Second, whereas European religious and literary history did have a variety of stories to explain the origin of the world, these have long since generally been forgotten, partly because they were regarded as just stories. In contrast, while the old stories of origins in Africa, explaining such things as why palms of black people are not pigmented, may not be believed, they are still widely known. The natural reaction for African Christians, then, is to treat the Genesis accounts in the same way, namely, as "white" myths. Indeed, the Bible itself is still commonly regarded as a "white" book, so not really a part of Africa; therefore it can readily be rejected, which it is in many cases.

Africa is pervaded by spirituality. Indeed, Africa tends to be much more religious than the modern West. But this spirituality is not in relation to God, which is yet another reason that it is difficult to identify with the creation stories in Genesis. It is common in Africa to stress the separation of God from the world rather than a connection between the two. This is so strong that many early missionaries did not see any belief in God at all. The belief was always there, but it was in a God who is clearly transcendent—a God who made the world, but has minimal involvement with it thereafter (much like European deism and the "absent watchmaker" God). In Africa, people do not relate to God directly, leading to what is perhaps the most characteristic religious belief in Africa, namely, that people can interact with the dead and with their ancestors, and that only through their mediation is any approach to God possible. It is in this belief that African spirituality resides. The absence of this crucial element from the Genesis stories contributes to its lack of relevance for many Africans.

Interaction with ancestors is part of a view of humanity which complements the belief in the absence of God. Without a direct individual relationship with God, interpersonal human relationships are more important. In contrast to the excessive individualism in the West is what we might call "communitarianism" in Africa. This, again, makes the Genesis stories—at least as they have been presented to Africans—not particularly meaningful. For example in the story of the Fall, the human couple are portrayed as individually responsible and individually guilty. But in a culture where the emphasis is on the community, there is little sense of personal guilt. This means that there is little felt need for individual salvation—certainly not salvation in the afterlife. Indeed, the African view is that people will naturally survive after death as ancestors. The whole notion of the separation of righteous people from wicked people is difficult to accept where the unity of the community is paramount.

There are, however, a couple of ways in which an African context does connect nicely with Genesis 1–3. First, the phrase "these are the generations" in 2:4 does put individuals firmly into the context of the group. More important, though, is that the story of the Fall indicates the effect of sin not just on individuals but on the group as well. Paul develops this in Romans 5, where he explains his notion of "original sin," which applies to all of humanity, the human community we might say. Here the unity of humanity is significant in an Africa that has felt the brunt of racism, where people have sometimes been treated as subhuman. For Paul and Christian theology, all humans are affected by events in the Garden. Furthermore, the African emphasis on community finds a point of contact with Genesis in that humans are created in the image of God (1:26–27). Although exactly what it means to be created in the image of God has been much debated, it seems clear enough that all people—regardless of gender, race, ethnicity, or any other factor—have a special significance which separates them from the animals and bonds together all of humanity.

Notably, however, an African reading of the text does not resonate with the fact that the passage describes the creation of a single couple—one man and one woman. That is, in the biblical story the richness of community does not extend beyond the model of a monogamous, nuclear family—husband, wife, and children. In African culture, the extended family is much more important, not to mention the practice of polygamy—neither of which are in the purview of Genesis 1–3.

Here we might argue that if the God-given monogamy of the Genesis account were practiced more diligently in Africa, our continent might not have the highest prevalence of HIV/AIDS in the world—a problem which is not disconnected from a celebration of community. Indeed, Genesis flows quickly from the description of the creation of humanity to its perversion. The story of the Fall is a reminder that the ideal for human behavior is not humanity, but God's norms. Indeed, the essence of the serpent's primal temptation is the elevation of humanity as a norm. Where this is done, disaster follows. The one thing that comes over so strongly in the story of the Fall is that there are norms set by God, and disobedience to them has serious consequences.

An African reading of Genesis 1–3—and of Scripture in general—brings greater appreciation of human community, an emphasis that has tended to be overshadowed elsewhere. It also makes a valuable contribution to the key questions concerning the nature of humanity and how humans should behave toward each other. This fits beautifully with the uniquely African philosophical concept of *ubuntu*. Literally translated as "humanity," Archbishop Desmond Tutu explained *ubuntu* this way in his book *No Future Without Forgiveness*: "A person with Ubuntu is open and available to others, affirming of others, does not feel threatened that others are able and good, for he or she has a proper self-assurance that comes from knowing that he or she belongs in a greater whole and is diminished when others are humiliated or diminished, when others are tortured or oppressed." There is no doubt that the world stands in great need of this ethic, as long as it is seen in the context in which Genesis puts it: as something given through God and in relationship to him.

David T. Williams, originally from the United Kingdom, has served as a missionary in Southern Africa since 1971; he is currently Professor of Systematic Theology at the University of Fort Hare, South Africa.

SIX DIFFERENCES BETWEEN TWO CREATION STORIES IN GENESIS

Meir Bar-Ilan (Israel)

It has been well known for centuries that Genesis 1–3 contains two different stories: one in 1:1–2:3 and a second in 2:4–3:24. Originally scholars stressed the fact that in the first story the deity is named Elohim (God), while in the second story he is called Yahweh-Elohim (Lord God). While there is no need to underestimate this difference, it should be noted that the change of the divine name is not essential, but rather technical (just like the difference in the number of

Hebrew words: 469 in the first story and 640 in the second). The aim of this paper, therefore, is to analyze the essential differences between the two stories. There are six such differences:

THE AIM OF THE STORIES   In the first account there is only one protagonist: God. Given that His deeds are so tremendous, with no precedent, it is clear that the aim of the first story is to glorify God (as creator). However, in the second story there are several protagonists, each of them is doing or saying something in his or her turn. The bottom line of this second story is that man has to toil hard for his living, woman has to suffer, and wild animals will threaten man's existence. That is, it is an etiological story, explaining the destiny of human beings, why the world is the way that it is. The differences between the stories become evident by looking at statistics of words and their dispersion. In the first story, man appears after 317 words (63 percent of the text), and he is mentioned in 102 words, that is 20 percent only. However, in the second story, man is mentioned after 29 words (4 percent of the text) and he takes up more than 80 percent of the text. In short, one story is God oriented while the other is man oriented.

TIME VERSUS SPACE   Time governs the first story (day one, day two, and so forth). Moreover, the luminaries were created to enable man to reckon times (not for warming or ripening fruits, for example). There are different types of times: linear (1:1–7), cyclical (evening, morning), and secular time of the working days and the holy time (day seven), a "quality-time" according to religious perspective, not a social one. Other than God himself, time governs the world, and there is no specific space. The second story is by contrast space oriented. The narrator depicts the Garden of Eden, the venue of the story, by giving it geographical dimension aided by four rivers (and lands). Moreover, the importance of the location is augmented by the fact that man is expelled from his congenital territory, marking the importance of realm in one's life. While holy times mark the life of religious persons, territory marks the more mundane man (who ignore God's ruling).

THE POWER OF THE WORD   In the first story, the word of God is His tool to create the world. The power of speech is evident. Speech is a divine tool that preexisted the world. Names that were given by God to His deeds, such as "day" or "sky," marked the end of their creation. With this power of the word, God blessed His creatures—fish, fowl, man, and the seventh day— showing that the existence of the world is word dependent. And only God speaks. Unlike the first story, in the second God does not use His speech ability as a tool of creation; rather man uses it to impose his own supremacy. The word has no divine merit and God brings forward the animals to man waiting for man to name them. In other words, the first story implies that language is divine, denoting it is part of the creation, while in the second story language is a man-created phenomenon.

ORDER AND LAW   The first story is marked by the order of numbers (one, two, three) and comes to its culmination in the seventh day. Order is also implied in the creation of the luminaries and stars, as in the "rules of Heaven" (cf. Jeremiah 33:25; Job 38:33), and in the "laws" necessary for creation (cf. Proverbs 8:27–29). So although the terms "law" and "order" do not appear in the first story, it is clear they were there from the very beginning. Stars have laws and order, and God, their Creator, is not only the Lord of time but also the Lord of order. However, in the second story there is no order (even not implied) and there is no law. As a matter of fact, God decreed a law (not to eat from the Tree) but after a short while this law is transgressed and chaos seems to dominate the world. In brief, God goes together with time and order, while man goes together with space and disorder.

THE ROLE OF NUMBERS   In the first story, numbers are the spine of the story and their appearance at the end of each passage denotes the tempo, or dynamics, of the story. In the first story there are 469 words and among them there are 10 number-words, in this order: *one, two, three, two, four, five, six, seven, seven,* and *seven.* The percentage of number-words is 2.016. In the second story, there are 640 words and only six are number-words (*four, one, two, three, four, one*), which means a percentage of 0.937. This difference in the use of numbers, part of what is called "stylometry," reflects attitude toward science (and order). While God did not create numbers, He did something to them: He bestowed quality on quantity. The number seven is related to God as well as to blessing and nonactivity, which exemplifies holiness. Thus the number seven was transferred from being quantity only to become a symbol of quality. The number seven accompanies God from primordial till the end of times; seven means divine.

SERMON VERSUS STORY   The structure of the two stories is very different. The first story is full of formulas. Each and every passage begins and ends with a formula (and God said, let there be, and God saw that it was good, etc.). As a matter of fact, roughly 20 percent of the text is formulaic. Thus it has a clear, special, and "tight" structure. The second story, by contrast, is "loose"—it has no specific structure (but like any story there is an exposition, a change, and an end). Therefore, it is assumed that the first story originally began as a sermon, probably to mark a new year, while the second story was nothing but a story. The second story is the craft of a narrator, but the first one is a speech made by a speaker, a preacher (a priest and a prophet).

Meir Bar-Ilan is Professor of Jewish History and Talmud at the Bar-Ilan University, Israel; he is the author of more than 100 learned papers and five books.

QUESTIONS

1. What if, for the sake of discussion, it could be proven that the biblical tradition was in fact influenced by the Chinese stories or vice-versa? How, if at all, would that influence your understanding and interpretation of the texts?

2. Jeyakumar notes how both Genesis 1–3 and the *Purusa-Sukta* have been used to sanction hierarchical social structures. Are such interpretations distortions of the text? Or does the text lend itself to such interpretations?

3. In addition to the ways that African "communitarianism" resonates with Genesis 1–3, identify several additional aspects of the text that might also lend themselves to a "group-oriented" perspective.

4. In addition to the ones that Bar-Ilan mentions, identify some reasons for viewing Genesis 1–3 as two separate stories.

CHAPTER 2

GENESIS 1–3 (PART II)

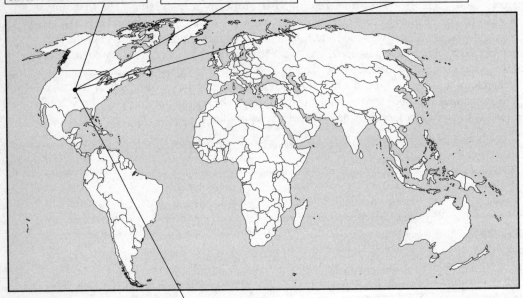

Patrick Gray presents a theistic evolutionist perspective, with a list of questions that surface in the encounter between the Bible and modern science.

Keith Megilligan argues for a literal reading of Genesis 1—God created the world in six 24-hour days—based on an acceptance of divine revelation.

Jonathan Merritt proposes that a proper reading of Genesis 1:28 and 2:15 requires that humans treat the natural world with care and benevolence.

Phillip Sherman considers how biblical texts, specifically Genesis 1:26–28 and the Garden of Eden story, understand animals and our relationship to them.

READINGS

Theism, Evolution, and Reading Genesis
Patrick Gray

A Literal Reading of Genesis
Keith Megilligan

Genesis and the Treatment of the Natural World
Jonathan Merritt

Animals and Our Relationship to Them
Phillip Sherman

THEISM, EVOLUTION, AND READING GENESIS

Patrick Gray (United States)

Jews and Christians have studied the opening chapters of Genesis for centuries without pausing to think about Charles Darwin, but it is increasingly difficult for many Western readers to do so at the turn of the twenty-first century. Many readers assent to the idea that evolution in some form has in fact taken place over the course of the history of plant and animal life. Of this group of readers, many also believe in God. It is therefore not inaccurate to label them proponents of theistic evolution.

For some of these readers, the Bible and biology are apples and oranges. Contradictions between the account in Genesis 1–3 and the findings of biologists, geologists, and astronomers do not bother them because they see them as belonging to two very different literary genres. In this approach, it is misguided to try to harmonize the biblical account with the theory of evolution because the author(s) had neither the intention nor the capacity to provide a scientifically accurate explanation of the origin and development of life on earth. It is important to note that this position has ancient roots. Philo, a first-century Alexandrian Jew, and Origen, the most learned Christian scholar of the third century, believed that it was a mistake to read the Bible only literally and never allegorically or symbolically. Augustine in the fourth century agreed, remarking (in *The Literal Meaning of Genesis* 1.19.38–39) that Christians sometimes make fools of themselves by insisting on specific scientific explanations of statements such as "And God said, 'Let there be light' " (Gen. 1:3).

Other proponents of theistic evolution hold that Genesis and modern science are compatible, or at least not incompatible. Read in a certain way, a number of texts provide a basis for this position. For example, the sequence of events in the first chapter of Genesis—though not the second chapter—more or less corresponds to the scientific understanding of the order in which life on earth developed, beginning with aquatic animals and proceeding to land-based mammals and, finally, human beings. Different species emerge at different stages of creation.

More than offering positive, specific evidence for compatibility with evolutionary theory, however, it is more accurate to say that certain aspects of Genesis are sufficiently vague as to leave the door open for such a reading. Whereas the six-day creation would seem to rule out the timeline proposed by biologists for the first appearance of living organisms, the Hebrew term *yom*, like its English equivalent "day," can denote an "age" and not simply a period of 24 hours. The verbs translated "make," "create," and "form," likewise, do not imply any specific duration. Biblical narrative can be notoriously uneven and imprecise when it comes to chronology, and some readers have proposed a "gap" between Genesis 1:1 and 1:2 into which one might fit the millions or billions of years required for natural selection to produce the biodiversity witnessed today.

Apart from the story of Eve's creation from Adam's rib, the Bible is mostly silent about the precise mechanism by which God created. Exactly how or when God intervened to produce various species is not stated. (This leads Gary Larson, in his *Far Side* comic strip, to imagine the possibilities. One strip depicts God telling an assembly of animals, "Well, now I guess I'd better make some things to eat you guys.") Proponents of theistic evolution argue that the laws of nature described by Darwin and his descendants are the unstated means by which God brought the various species into existence. There are differences of opinion as to the extent and frequency of any divine intervention this required, and it is too simplistic to try to fit everyone into a few neatly defined categories. To be sure, Basil of Caesarea speaks for many when he says in the fourth century that "those who think that all that exists is without government or direction, but borne about by chance, are…infected by the deceit of atheism" (*Hexaemeron* 1.2). Yet Alfred Russel Wallace, Darwin's contemporary who independently formulated a theory of natural selection, still saw a "directive mind" and a sense of purpose manifested in evolutionary processes even as he rejected Christianity.

It is undeniable that one's presuppositions about creation and evolution can have a distorting effect when reading. At the same time, certain theological and scientific biases can frequently promote close, careful interpretation as readers are keenly attuned to what, exactly, the text of Genesis says and does not say, as well as to what Darwinian theory entails and does not entail. Attentive, invested reading can bring to the surface critical questions which are only implicit in the encounter between the Bible and modern science. Such questions include the following:

> Has the history of the human race consisted of "rising" from more primitive life forms or "falling" from an original state of grace, as the traditional interpretation of Genesis 3:1–19 suggests? Or perhaps both?

> Can the human mind or soul evolve in the same way that anatomical and physiological structures evolve? Or is any talk of nonphysical "evolution" (as in social Darwinism or evolutionary psychology) fundamentally different in kind from what biologists study?

> If God "creates" by means of natural selection, should he be seen as a "sloppy" creator for tolerating all the death and extinction that is a natural part of this lengthy process? By contrast, is he a "deadbeat" creator for calling the universe into existence and then abandoning it, stepping back and allowing it to unfold without intervening to guide it with his providential hand?

> What is a human being? And how does it differ from other humanoid forms? Is it a matter of genetics or anatomy or is it something intangible? Can something like the soul or "the image of God" (1:27) emerge via chance mutations or does it require a supernatural touch? Does the dignity accorded to humans in Genesis 1–3 depend on a particular understanding of their emergence?

> Does Genesis support the idea of creation *ex nihilo*, "out of nothing"? This is technically a matter of astronomy or physics or metaphysics, but it is a useful reminder that Darwin wrote *On the Origin of Species* and not on the origin of whatever raw materials gave rise to living organisms that grew into various species. Evolution is about development and change, not about ultimate origins.

Patrick Gray (Ph.D., Emory University) is the Albert Bruce Curry Professor of Religious Studies at Rhodes College, Memphis, Tennessee, United States.

A LITERAL READING OF GENESIS

Keith Megilligan (United States)

The Hebrew of the Old Testament has an emphasis upon form and function, not necessarily flowery prose. That is, the language is concise and purposeful. Its expressions attempt little by way of "logic" or sophisticated argumentation. The prose portion of the Old Testament is pretty straightforward. So when the text starts with a somewhat flat, yet very profound, interjection, "In the beginning, God created...," it is not laying the basis for an argument. The Bible *assumes*, even presupposes, the existence of God; it is not interested in trying to prove such a claim. That being said, anything that God does is therefore not only noteworthy, but it is also considered fact. And so this language of form and function gives the creation event to us straightforwardly, with an emphasis upon action: God created.

Further, the Bible also assumes that God's existence is eternal because it is He that is responsible for chronological events. He is, in fact, responsible for time. Once again, the text is pretty simple in its assertion, "In the beginning...." Such a declaration about time and its *genesis* (pardon the pun) shows us that whenever the beginning was, God was already there, and that we, humanity, needed some help with time–space continuum, not God. So, God is presented not only as being present when "time" began, but He also was/is responsible for its construction for our benefit.

The evidence for this in the text is fairly clear. Using the Hebrew/Jewish historical notation of what constitutes a "day," the text then states what God did within each day. In order for God to give us such "timing," He establishes a light source in the heavens as a verification point for measuring evening and morning. Without any fanfare or explanation, God weaves creation (of a light source) together with "time" so that the two become inseparable for mankind. His means for accomplishing such a feat is simply His powerful spoken word (cf. Psalm 33:6, 9).

An additional notation about time is critical to the acceptance of the biblical account of creation. The descriptive phrase about evening and morning is presented as a modifier of the daily events of creation, and the numeric notation associated with each day is likewise critical. For example, "And there was evening and there was morning, a third day" (1:13). While some have argued for extremely lengthened periods of time in order to help coordinate the biblical account of creation with "modern scientific data," the question of time related to creation is an exegetical one, not a scientific one. Quite simply, and I realize that I set myself up for target practice at this point, one either accepts the Word of God's presentation about creation or one does not.

The Hebrew word for "day" as it is used in Genesis 1 is *yom*. The normal understanding for the translation of this word is "day," as in one 24-hour period. Not only does the previous reference to a light source and planetary rotation validate and support this view but so too does the use of a numeric adjective (first, second, etc.). Thus, the normal, natural way of understanding "day" in Genesis 1 is the 24-hour period. But lest such a normal/natural understanding escape our grasp, the Lord provides additional support for such an understanding when He gave the Ten Commandments: "For in six days the Lord made the heavens and the earth, the sea and all that is in them, and rested on the seventh day; therefore the Lord blessed the Sabbath day and made it holy" (Exodus 20:11). This passage illustrates in a couple of ways that "day"/*yom* in Genesis should be understood as a 24-hour period. First, the adjectives "six" and "seventh" declare a simple/normal way of viewing a "day" in the Genesis account. Second, since the Lord blessed the seventh/Sabbath day by making it holy, it defies exegetical logic to understand that God (and thus man) should be resting for more than a 24-hour period. Much less should we be expected to understand it as, for example, an extended geological age of any significant duration.

Correspondingly, it would follow that if the "days" of Genesis are 24 hours in length, then the cumulative effect upon time (following creation) would be similarly impacted. That is, the days that accumulate into weeks which accumulate into months and then years would mean that the total time since creation would be much less than the eons of time proposed by evolutionary models. By "much less" is meant a universe and world that has been in existence for only thousands (possibly tens of thousands) of years rather than millions or billions. The Bible helps demonstrate this by providing two genealogies later in Genesis 5 and 11, which provide for a briefer time continuum of historical portions.

The coordination of God establishing "time" with the event of creation becomes a theological and practical necessity for man. The theological/exegetical evidences presented above speak to the first necessity. The practical necessity is evidenced each "day" of our lives. Mankind has been created as creatures of time. Time to us has become necessary for so many things—from baking a cake to running a race to the duration of holding an elected office. The focus of such necessity is further confirmed by our emphasis upon validating our individual existence: with a birth certificate and a death certificate. It is hard to imagine that either one of those items would be important if time were not created by God as a "birthright" to humanity. Our struggle with understanding creation and cosmogony is not as much a scientific one as it is a spiritual one. By God's Spirit we are either graced with the ability to accept the biblical record of creation or we are not (see 1 Corinthians 2:12–16).

When one attempts to understand the meaning of the Old Testament, one either has the humility and grace to accept the revelation of Scripture or one does not. Natural minds, those who are bereft of the presence of the Spirit of God, cannot understand such revelation. Scientists attempt to explain creation in rational terms, whereas God has given it to us by divine revelation. Principally, from the time of Darwin onward, disciplines of science have impacted "modern" thinking to the extent that we have been left with only one perspective on history, an evolutionary one. By definition and implication, evolution must have huge measures of time. If it does not, then the theory is weakened if not completely compromised. But God does not have that "problem" for at least a couple of reasons. First, if we accept that creation is a biblical issue and not exclusively a scientific one, our answers rest with the Creator, not scientists. And second, in order to accept and even value the biblical viewpoint, we need the author's (Creator's) assistance to comprehend the evidence that He has presented. To do that, we need His Spirit to bear witness with our spirit (Romans 8:9–17) that we are children of God and have the ability to understand what our Heavenly Father would teach us about His creation.

Keith Megilligan (B.A., John Brown University; Th.M., Grace Theological Seminary; D.Min., Westminster Theological Seminary) has served as pastor and teacher for more than 30 years.

GENESIS AND THE TREATMENT OF THE NATURAL WORLD

Jonathan Merritt (United States)

In 1843, Ludwig Feuerbach proclaimed, "Nature, the world, has no value, no interest for Christians. The Christian thinks only of himself and the salvation of his soul" (*The Essence of Christianity* [New York: Harper and Row, 1957], 287). Feuerbach wasn't the only one to claim such a thing. In the 1967 issue of *Science*, Lynne White Jr. released his now-infamous paper "The Historical Roots of Our Ecological Crisis." In it, he labels Western Christianity "the most anthropocentric [human-centered] religion the world has ever seen."

It's hard to dispute that Feuerbach's and White's claims are at least partially grounded in reality. Many pastors and congregants today don't understand the importance of a biblically grounded, historically informed theology of nature. According to a 2009 study by LifeWay Research, about half of all Protestant pastors in the United States say they speak to their church about creation care "rarely" or "never." Most seem to grasp the importance of soul salvation, but far fewer—especially those in fundamentalist circles—express sincere interest in nature and environmental issues.

Why is this? To what can we ascribe this discrepancy? It seems that at least part of the blame lies with our misunderstandings, misinterpretations, and misapplications of critical passages in the opening chapters of Genesis. We are able to properly frame our theology of nature and role as creation's stewards when we understand critical passages in the opening book of our sacred text.

The creation account in Genesis 1 is one of the most widely known passages in the entire Bible. Unfortunately, this passage has become so embroiled in scientific debates about the origin of life that few are mining the theological truths hidden within the text. In the poetic rhythm of this 31-verse chapter, we find several repeated actions that greatly inform a theological conversation about creation and stewardship. Both actions come from God and both actions speak volumes about nature.

First, we encounter the act of creation. Over and over God creates and forms matter into land and water and life. And each time God purposes to create, the text simply says, "It was so." This teaches us that God has a powerful purpose for his creation. Indeed, the very fact that God created it tells us that it is meaningful and purposeful. Additionally, we encounter the act of commentary. God doesn't see fit to merely create; God shares his perspective about his creation: "God saw...it was good." Notice that God didn't call it useful or beautiful. He called it good, ascribing to creation intrinsic value and worth. And the writer includes the phrase repeatedly. Why? Because he is emphasizing and underscoring the pleasure God feels. It is an expression of delight or, one might say, the seal of divine approval. But it is also more than that. For modern readers, it is a warning that we dare not treat the object of God's pleasure with wanton disregard. Properly read and understood, the creation narrative teaches us about a God who made all things, imbued these things with value, and takes great pleasure in the natural world. This passage bolsters the idea that creation is a special treasure of God, and one worthy of our attention and care.

Although the creation narrative itself sets us in the right direction, many great Christian thinkers throughout history have stumbled when they interpret "the dominion passages" (1:28; 2:15). These verses are perhaps the biggest textual influencers driving Feuerbach's and White's conclusions. The idea that humans have dominion over creation has shaped the so-called "instrumentalist" view of nature: that the natural world exists solely to meet human needs.

The immediate problem we encounter is the seeming contradiction between 1:28 and 2:15. In the former, we find the seemingly harsh command to "subdue" the earth and "have dominion" over it. In the latter, we find a softer command to "keep" and "care for" the earth. When used selectively and in isolation, either of these passages can be effective in debate. But a proper understanding of the divine plan must bring these passages into harmony to synthesize a biblically informed definition of "stewardship" or "dominion."

The Hebrew word for "subdue" in 1:28 literally means to take control of something. It is usually found in a political context in scripture. Genesis 1 is the only place in the entire Old Testament where the object of this verb is the earth. The Hebrew word for "rule over" or "dominion" literally means to exercise a given authority over something. Unfortunately, many Christians perceive the word "dominion" to mean "domination." But a closer look reveals a different understanding. This word can be used to describe priests executing their duties or shepherds taking care of their sheep, but it is most often used to refer to the power of kings over their subjects. We can infer, then, that 1:28 gives humans a monarch-like role over nature.

What was the role of a monarch in the Old Testament context? An Israelite king was unique. He was not to be a ruler like those the other nations had. In 1 Samuel 8:6, the Israelites ask for a "king to judge us like all the nations." This apparently disappointed God and Samuel because Israel wasn't like all the other nations. Their ultimate ruler was God, and their earthly rulers weren't given carte blanche authority. An Israelite king was not to rule oppressively or be greedy. He was to remain a servant and subject of Almighty God (see Deuteronomy 17:16–20). When an Israelite king abused his dominion—when he got greedy, oppressed the people, or enslaved his subjects—God would judge and punish him.

As God gave "dominion" to Israelite kings, we have been given limited authority over the natural world. After all, "the earth is the Lord's and everything in it" (Psalm 24:1). We do not have license to treat animals cruelly and use the earth however we wish so long as humans benefit from it. We do not have carte blanche power, but rather the privilege of responsibly managing the earth's many benefits and resources as servants of the Lord.

In Genesis 2, God has just placed the first human in a garden that God himself has planted and cultivated. In verse 15, we learn why God placed him there: "to work it and take care of it" (translations vary on the two verbs, but all contain the idea of showing concern for the earth). The command to Adam—as a representative for all mankind—is really a charge for us all to care for the world. And nowhere in scripture is it ever revoked. The passage is clear and is reiterated in the chapter that follows (3:23): Humans are commanded by the Creator to care for His creation.

In this way, then, we can synthesize God's command to Adam to take care of the earth (2:15) with the instruction to subdue and have dominion over it (1:28) into a single understanding of biblical stewardship. We can conclude that humans are given the task of ruling the earth as "benevolent kings."

The words of Feuerbach and White haunt contemporary Christians with the same ferocity they did when they were first spoken. In fact, one might argue that they are even more damning today in light of contemporary ecological developments. But where Feuerbach and White get it wrong is in the true witness of the scriptures. The Bible is not the enemy of ecological responsibility, but one of its greatest assets. If we rediscover what the text actually teaches about nature, we will see the world as God sees it and care for it as he has commanded.

Jonathan Merritt (M.Div., Southeastern Baptist Theological Seminary; Th.M., Emory University) is author of Green Like God: Unlocking the Divine Plan for Our Planet; *his work has appeared in* USA Today, The Atlanta Journal-Constitution, Christianity Today, *and* The Washington Post.

ANIMALS AND OUR RELATIONSHIP TO THEM

Phillip Sherman (United States)

Several years ago I read the book *Animal Liberation* by the moral philosopher Peter Singer. In this (now-famous) work, Singer argues that the majority of human beings fail to treat animals in an ethical fashion and that humanity ought no longer to act as though the pain and suffering of animals is morally inconsequential. He advocates for a vegetarian diet and strict limitations on animal-based experimentation. Many who agree with Singer hold that human antipathy toward animals flows naturally from a profound cultural misunderstanding of the relationship between human beings and other forms of animal life. I have remained somewhat ambivalent with regard to Singer's argument. I do not, for example, eschew the eating of meat. But I was troubled. There is a tendency for many advocates of animal rights to claim that biblical texts were partly responsible for current attitudes toward the lives of animals. I realized, however, that I had never thought systematically about the presence of animals in the Hebrew Bible. "Biblical" animals were largely invisible to me. I was also troubled by the truth I perceived in Singer's work. The modern food industry has reduced animals to objects. Their pain and suffering is less important than the financial bottom line and the need to supply meat to a voracious public at a low cost. We bring countless millions into existence only to slaughter them. As someone who studies ancient Israelite texts, I found myself increasingly asking this question: "How do biblical texts understand animals and our relationship to them?"

The Hebrew Bible has a great deal to say about the lives of animals. There is scarcely a book in the Hebrew canon which does not make at least a passing reference to animals. It has even been suggested that upwards of 120 species of animals populate the pages of the Hebrew Bible. It is curious, therefore, that contemporary readers of the Bible, broadly speaking, often seem oblivious to this ubiquitous animal presence. This is curious as animals and their lives were clearly important, indeed essential, to the lives and well-being of the peoples responsible for the production and transmission of biblical texts. The marginalization of animals amongst readers of the Bible—both critical and devotional—can arguably be connected to a foundational passage from Genesis 1.

Genesis 1:26–28 (in)famously contains a divine blessing on *homo sapiens* and commands only one type of animal to exert dominion and rule over the created order and over all other forms of life. This passage has encouraged and continues to encourage countless readers to view animal life as subordinate to the lives of human beings. Accordingly, the lives of animals carry less moral and ethical value. Various advocates for the ethical treatment of animals have adopted the term "speciesism" to describe a common human tendency to marginalize or fail to recognize the moral considerations owed to animals. (Singer himself makes ample use of the term.)

Such an ideology is not without its attractions. Human beings, male and female, are said to be created in the divine image and, according to one dominant interpretation of that phrase, are to function as the divine's coregent on earth. Many interpreters have seized on the claim that humanity is created in the divine image to assert a biblical foundation for the "rights" of human beings or to claim human dignity as a biblically grounded concept. Such dignity, however, is purchased at a price. The special status accorded human beings is inseparable from their superiority to all other classes of living beings. Indeed, their vocation is fulfilled in their rule over the other creatures. The very idea of "humanity" is dependent upon the control and suppression of the "animal." The distinctive, semidivine status of human beings and (therefore) the nondivine, subhuman status of other forms of life are presented as a function of creation itself, built into the very structure of the created world and closely linked to the divine, primal blessing. That this ideological program remains largely invisible to modern readers of the Bible who relate to animals (wild and domestic) in radically different ways from the producers of biblical literature is a testament to its persuasiveness. An effective ideology is an invisible ideology.

To name an ideology is not to dismiss it outright. Every ideology served a purpose for the culture that created it. It is not my goal to claim that such an ideology was without use to the earliest readers of the Hebrew Bible who lived, simultaneously, in greater community and in heightened tension with the animal world. Perhaps such an ideology was even necessary. My goal, rather, is to suggest that readers of biblical texts ought to attend to the full range of views concerning animals and their lives contained within the pages of the Hebrew Bible. Most biblical scholars would hold that 1:26–28 was produced by elite, Priestly scribes writing during or shortly after the Babylonian exile of the people of Judah—that is, Genesis 1 may have been one of the last written texts in the Hebrew Bible, even though it appears first in the Bible. Some scholars would also assert that the work of these Priestly scribes included a reevaluation of many of the sacred traditions of the people of Israel. Such reevaluation was the result of life in a radically new social and political context. In addition, much biblical scholarship is devoted to tracing the chronological development of central ideas throughout the literary history of ancient Israel. We should, accordingly, be more critical in our reading of this ideology of human dominion and seek to contextualize the emergence of such a viewpoint in Israel's long history with animals. Readers have too often allowed what is admittedly a rather chronologically late and theologically sophisticated reflection on the nature of the relationship between human beings and the rest of the animal world (i.e., 1:26–28) to serve as the dominant model by which all other biblical texts concerning animals ought to be read.

But where else might we look to determine ancient Israelite views concerning animals and their lives? What other models for the human/animal relationship might we find? A major counterbalance to the ideology of 1:26–28 can be found close at hand in the creation story located in Genesis 2–3, which most scholars would assert was written prior to Genesis 1. In this account, the human male is created before the animals. The Israelite deity, noting Adam's isolation, brings all of the animals before Adam to see what he will name them (2:19). While this passage has traditionally been read as an example of human domination—Adam imposing various names upon the animal kingdom—a less anthropocentric reading is possible. The deity seems to believe that a suitable companion for the first human being might be found among the animals. The fact that none of the animals are found to be an appropriate associate for Adam does not place humanity in a superior position to them. A gulf of some sort certainly separates them. As the serpent will prove, however, the gulf is not unbridgeable and is not defined by hierarchy. Commentators have noted that both Adam and the animals are created from the same substance (the ground/*adamah*) and are infused with the same animating presence (life-breath/*nephesh*). Human animals and nonhuman animals are not two kinds of beings, demarcated by reason or linguistic ability, but rather very similar kinds of being. There is no sharp break between the two. Alienation and animosity do eventually threaten the relationship between human beings and animals outside of Eden. The second creation account, however, recalls a time before the origin of such animosity and alienation, a time before the origin of speciesism.

That modern readers seldom attend to the animals that populate the pages of the Hebrew Bible is an indication of the little respect we grant animals in our own collective lives. Reading the Hebrew Bible looking for the lives of animals is one way to ensure that we are attending to the animals in our own culture.

Phillip Sherman is Assistant Professor of Religion at Maryville College, United States.

QUESTIONS

1. What is the importance for Gray of referring to early commentators on the Bible such as Philo and Augustine?

2. Assess Megilligan's last paragraph. Is he essentially rejecting science and reason? If so, what are the implications of such a move?

3. What would one have to do or know in order to assess Merritt's arguments about the proper understanding of the word "dominion" in Genesis 1:28? What are the potential benefits and pitfalls of looking at how a specific word is used in other contexts?

4. Reflect more fully—Sherman only makes one passing comment—on the role and portrayal of the serpent (the most prominent animal in the text). Does the serpent help or hinder Sherman's argument?

CHAPTER 3

GENESIS 12–21

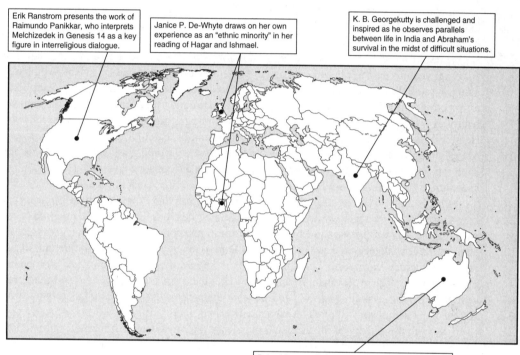

Erik Ranstrom presents the work of Raimundo Panikkar, who interprets Melchizedek in Genesis 14 as a key figure in interreligious dialogue.

Janice P. De-Whyte draws on her own experience as an "ethnic minority" in her reading of Hagar and Ishmael.

K. B. Georgekutty is challenged and inspired as he observes parallels between life in India and Abraham's survival in the midst of difficult situations.

Roland Boer reads the story of Sodom and Gomorrah in Genesis 18–19 in light of the world-famous Sydney (Australia) Gay and Lesbian Mardi Gras.

READINGS

Life in India and Abraham's Trials
K. B. Georgekutty

Raimundo Panikkar's Interpretation of Melchizedek in Genesis 14
Erik Ranstrom

An "Ethnic Minority" Interpretation of Hagar and Ishmael
Janice P. De-Whyte

Sodom and Gomorrah and the Sydney Gay and Lesbian Mardi Gras
Roland Boer

LIFE IN INDIA AND ABRAHAM'S TRIALS

K. B. Georgekutty (India)

When I was a young child attending Sunday classes, I held the idea that Abraham was a man who had everything together. I considered Abraham to be a great man who enjoyed God's never-ending provision. The trouble, however, is that we tend to overlook the details in the Abraham stories. There is a tendency to dwell on the mountain-peak experiences of the lives of great men and miss many great lessons that need to be learned from other aspects of their lives. The praiseworthy experiences must be observed in the context of their entire lives. Now when I look at the stories in Genesis 12–21 as an Indian who lives among uncertainties and diversities, it challenges me.

First of all, the life under the divine mission is not easy, but uncertain. Abraham's story is not one mainly of faith but of a struggle in the midst of poverty and survival. Abraham was a migrant to Palestine, a sparsely populated and poor region. His descent to Egypt and Philistia affirms this perception of Palestine. The general background of the Ancient Near East knows the reality of migration all too well. The Code of Hammurabi, Egyptian laws, and the laws of the Hebrew Bible acknowledged the existence of migration in search of food. Abraham moves into a very strange country. Moving into new areas is always intimidating. New territory is always daunting. Abraham settled in Moreh at Shechem among a strange people with a strange language and strange gods who required the sacrifice of their children as an act of worship.

In the midst of those uncertainties, a famine comes and Abraham must go to Egypt. In Egypt Abraham's struggle was a struggle for life over death. So he starts the tough task of net-working his way all the way to Pharaoh's throne. Then follows struggle after struggle, battle after battle. It challenges me as one who lives among the uncertainties of life: natural disasters, poverty, illiteracy, corruption, black money, child labor, dowry, prostitution, and women battering. To me, the story of Abraham is calling us to boldness and confidence and trust in the face of difficulty and uncertainty. The story teaches that the proper response to the uncertainties of life is generosity demonstrated in relationships with others.

Second, it is a story of diversity and pluralism as in my country. It is amazing to notice that Abraham lived among and interacted with people of diverse cultures and religious traditions— Babylonians, Canaanites, Philistines, and Egyptians. It is astonishing to see how a man of Abraham's stature would move (back) to a place where people did not share his religious beliefs. Indeed, if Abraham's neighbors had no respect for Abraham's God, then he was in danger. He lived in the heart of a hostile country. Likewise, India is among the most diverse societies in the world. It has people from all the major world religions—Hindus, Muslims, Christians, Sikhs, Buddhists, Jains, and Zoroastrians (Parsis). Religious diversity is coupled with enormous linguistic and cultural diversity. Although India has no official or established state religion, Hindus are the majority. In such a context, it is always a big challenge for a Christian to live as a member of a minority group where one feels alienated and insecure.

Third, the story continues with the traditions of Hagar and Ishmael. Hagar has been driven out from her home to safeguard the interest of her oppressor Sarah. Hagar does not have her own independent voice. More precisely, Hagar represents the women of India, many of whom suffer from poverty and social exclusion. They are often the target of family violence, which is a par-ticularly acute problem in India. Both Hagar and Ishmael faced the same circumstances as Indian lower-caste people and communities that were excluded from the rest of society and denied access to social and economic goods. They both remain as the model of resistance and rebellion in the midst of unjust circumstances. Thus we have the responsibility to support the weak and silent voices of the text in order to make them audible.

Fourth, I am forced to confront one of the most difficult questions: How do we evaluate the views of the writers of the Abraham story? Their attitudes were exclusive and hostile to poor people. This was articulated clearly in the affliction and expulsion of Hagar in Genesis 16 and 21. And still, the writers also represented the positive understanding that God is the one who helps those who are in trouble and who are oppressed. If these ideas are brought together they create an obvious tension between exclusive social actions and an inclusive theological understanding of God. How is it possible that the same deity contains such a strong contradiction? God is the one who takes care of those who are excluded by the people guided by the very same God. In the story, the deity is on both the side of the oppressed and the oppressors.

In sum, Genesis 12–21 reflects the life situation of the majority of Indians. It is a story of resistance and survival in the midst of diverse and hostile situations. Although the stories are written from the perspective of the rulers/oppressors, the story offers inspiration and challenges in new contexts where people are still in danger of poverty, being (ab) used, and being dealt with harshly and unjustly.

K. B. Georgekutty is Lecturer in Old Testament at Faith Theological Seminary, under Senate of Serampore College, Kerala, India.

RAIMUNDO PANIKKAR'S INTERPRETATION
OF MELCHIZEDEK IN GENESIS 14

Erik Ranstrom (United States)

Raimundo Panikkar (1918–2010) was one of the leading theological proponents of Christian interreligious dialogue in the twentieth and early twenty-first century. From an early age, Raimundo wondered about the relationship between Christianity and Hinduism, not from a detached, academic perspective but from within the very crucible of identity formation. Born to a Spanish Catholic mother and Indian Hindu father, Panikkar was ordained into the Catholic priesthood in 1946 and traveled throughout India in the 1950s. Panikkar returned to Europe almost a decade later, and famously quipped: "I 'left' Europe a Christian, 'found' myself a Hindu, and I 'return' a Buddhist, without having ceased to be a Christian" (*The Intrareligious Dialogue* [New York: Mahwah/Paulist Press, 1978], 2). For the remainder of his career Panikkar extolled the virtues of interreligious encounter to the point where some called him the "apostle of interreligious dialogue." Panikkar believed that being a Hindu made sense within his Catholic Christian identity and even contributed to its depth. Here, I will examine these themes in just one of Panikkar's many scholarly works, "Meditacion sobre Melquisedec" (*Nuestro Tiempo*. Pamplona IX 102 [1962]: 575–595; all translations are mine). Here Panikkar offers a way of viewing the convergence of the world's religions, including Hinduism, in the person of Jesus Christ and Christian faith.

The main biblical character in Panikkar's theology of world religions is the mysterious, enigmatic Melchizedek. Melchizedek appears only three times in the entire Bible, including

Genesis 14:18–24. In this story, Abram is moving into the land God had promised him and encountering the destabilizing conditions of territories divided by factions of all kinds. After rescuing Lot from the hands of one of these forces, Abram is approached by a Melchizedek, King of Salem. Melchizedek, a Canaanite priest-king, blesses Abram and praises God for his protection of Abram and his kin. Abram in turn gives to Melchizedek the tithe, a tenth of everything. In many apocryphal stories about Abraham in Judaism, Christianity, and Islam, he is imagined as rejecting his "pagan" past so as to prepare himself for the revelation of the one God. Genesis 14:18–24, however, paints a much different picture. Here a "pagan" priest thanks God on behalf of Abram, who acknowledges the priestly status of Melchizedek and defers to him. And Melchizedek's story does not end in Genesis 14. In Psalm 110, Melchizedek is proclaimed an eternal priest, and Hebrews 7 sees Melchizedek as foreshadowing Christ. Panikkar works with all these elements to construct a Christian theology of world religions and to point the way to an interreligious vocation in the Church.

Christians typically read the Old Testament in light of Jesus Christ. The story of salvation moves toward Christ as the fulfillment of God's promises to the world and the hope of its peoples. Panikkar contributes something significant to this christocentric hermeneutic. He stresses that not only Israel but also the world's religions find completion in Jesus Christ. Christ did not come to destroy the Law and the Prophets, nor the world's religions, but to fulfill them. God promised the world a Savior through the covenantal promise God made with the entire creation. This cosmic covenant, oriented toward Christ, is for Panikkar the true spiritual meaning of the world's ancient religions. Insofar as the people of various religions of the world through their prayers and spiritual desires are implicitly awaiting the fulfillment of their hopes for God in the world, that is, the manifestation of Jesus Christ ("God-with-us"), Panikkar says, "in a certain sense, Christianity has existed since the beginning of creation" (589). Therefore, Panikkar's Christian faith does not alienate him from Hinduism, but unites him with it at its very core, its deepest longings and intentionality.

Panikkar continues to tease out the implications of this fulfillment theology by introducing the idea of a "physical continuity" between Christ and the religions of the world. The meaning of this phrase is very suggestive. Christ's very person exists in deep solidarity with the bodiliness and history of the world's religious traditions. Though Jesus Christ represents "something new and unknown," it must also be affirmed that "history never commences newly and absolutely" but is always marked by an intimate relatedness with what has gone on before (590). God entering into history in the person of Christ consummates this relatedness and fulfills the religions, according to Panikkar, by assuming the priestly order of Melchizedek (Hebrews 5:6). Melchizedek, who represents the priesthood of the religions of the world, anticipates the hope of the God who would come into their midst by offering the eucharistic elements of bread and wine.

Panikkar was unique in his articulation of this fulfillment theology not because he demonstrated how Christ's redemption fulfilled the histories of the world's religions and Israel, as other Catholic Christian theologians in the mid-twentieth century were also advancing similar theses. But what sets Panikkar apart from these thinkers was how he inverted the fulfillment thesis in a way that opened Christianity up to dialogue. Usually this theology emphasizes how much the religions need Christ. Panikkar does not deny this. But he also avoids what could be a stance of arrogant superiority by emphasizing how much Christians need the religions to understand Christ. If Christ is the fulfillment of the religions, then the religions have much to tell us about who this Christ is. As relative newcomers to God's story of salvation, Christians have much to learn from these traditions about this Christ.

Another way in which Panikkar went beyond the simple appreciation of the world's religions was by eschewing a gradualist approach to the order of salvation history. Such an approach usually explains God's involvement in the world as comprising three increasingly intensifying movements from lesser to greater divine presence and manifestation: cosmos, Israel, and Christ. The upshot of this is usually to overlook the world religions of the cosmic covenant because the entire movement is toward a greater intensity and fullness of what the previous epoch lacked (i.e., the third and final movement is all that matters, Christ). Panikkar's thinking essentially rearranges this order by presenting Christians with a mandate to learn from and honor the religions of the cosmic covenant. Panikkar points to Melchizedek's superiority over Abraham and the Jewish levitical priesthood as a way of giving more weight to the religions. Thus, he opens a space for reconsidering the world religions as holding a privileged place in God's salvation history—though in the process he is unfortunately influenced by a strain of anti-Judaism. Panikkar interprets Melchizedek's blessing of Abram in Genesis 14:17, following Hebrews 7:7, as a sign of "the greater blessing the lesser" (581). Christ's priesthood is better understood in reference to the world's religions than to Israel, for Melchizedek's priesthood is "a fruit of the Word and not of the Jews" (579).

Not all of Panikkar's early reflections on Christ and Melchizedek work for us anymore. We are more sensitive to the fact that the world's religions are not primarily about the promise and expectation of a foreseen Savior. We know that the New Testament's interpretation of the Old Testament, which Panikkar took for granted, is both dangerous in light of anti-Semitism as well as ignorant of the fundamental Jewishness of Christianity in general. Yet, there is much to learn from Panikkar's journey into the scriptures, into the world's religions, and into his very identity, for he found the Christ in all those places. Panikkar disrupted the way Christians normally think about revelation, encouraging Christians to contemplate Melchizedek and the world's religions in order to understand who the God of Jesus Christ really is. Once one internalizes this contemplation, the distinctions between "Christians" and "non-Christians" begin to blur. Hindu and Christian are no longer two separate realities, but cohere together, even within one's very self.

Erik Ranstrom is a Teaching Fellow in the Department of Theology at Boston College, United States.

An "Ethnic Minority" Interpretation of Hagar and Ishmael

Janice P. De-Whyte (Ghana, England)

I am a Ghanaian woman. My people are matrilineal; thus I belong to my mother's family and to her tribe, the Ashanti. I am also a British woman. Once, I won an academic award called "The Ethnic Minority Excellence Award," given by the government to a few secondary school students in London, England. I have lived under the designation of "ethnic minority" for most of my life.

I read cultural and religious practices in the Old Testament and I resonate with them because of they are similar to practices of my heritage. I read Scripture with an intuitive sensitivity toward the "minority"—those women and men whose stories are far less told in sermons and popular religious literature. I've heard numerous sermons on the faith of Sarah and Abraham, in which Hagar is a byword, an incidental character to be passed over. Yet, Hagar's story reveals to contemporary society the God who is able to engender spirituality despite social disadvantage and dysfunction. Such a cultural reading flows out of a deep respect for Scripture and a belief that the Holy Spirit must be the guide of all interpretation, whether Western or African. Scripture interpretation for the "minority" is in focus here.

The Ashanti of Ghana prize the gift of children. Traditionally a woman does not inherit the property or material wealth of her family; thus children are the means through which she may build her own legacy. The matrilineal nature of the Akan and the importance placed on the bond between mother and child is highlighted through the proverb *wo na awu a, wo abusua asa* (when your mother dies, you have no relatives left). Sarah knew that to be considered a true wife in the Ancient Near East was to have children who would carry on her legacy. It is understandable then that Sarah would go to any lengths in order to be "built up" (Gen. 16:2).

Ultimately, Sarah's surrogacy plan turns sour. Instead, the mistress' desire to be "built up" by her maidservant results in her "being small" in Hagar's eyes (16:4). The dynamics of honor and shame are as central to Ghanaian culture as they were to the Ancient Near East. An Ashanti woman or man strives to bring *animonyam* (honor) and not *animguase* (shame) to their family name. What Sarah and Abraham did with their authority challenges us; do we use our authority in line with the promises and revelation of God or do we go our own way? In due course, it is God's plan, not our own schemes, which will bring honor.

Yahweh's encounters with Hagar communicate his interest in those labeled as "ethnic minority" or any other minority group. After she has seen the angel of the Lord, Hagar is surprised that she has seen God in angelic form and lived. The young Egyptian maid is the first to name God, as she calls him *El Ro'i*, "the God who sees me" (16:13). As a young woman who often finds herself in religious and professional contexts in which I am the minority, I can sometimes identify with the feeling of being unseen and unheard. Hagar's comfort came in her realization she was neither irrelevant nor disposable to God.

Throughout the biblical tradition, God gives promises of many offspring only to the males, the Patriarchs. Interestingly the African Hagar is the only woman to whom Yahweh directly promises many descendents (16:10). Furthermore, the same promise which Yahweh gives to Hagar is that which the Angel Gabriel gives to Mary hundreds of years later, "You will bear a son and you shall call him..." (Gen. 16:11; Matthew 1:23).

Through Hagar's son a great nation will emerge (Gen. 21:18). We are told concerning Ishmael that "God was with the lad and he grew" (21:20). Significantly, this same notice of divine presence and favor during childhood is given in the stories of Samson, Samuel, John the Baptist, and Jesus (Judges 13:24; 1 Samuel 2:21, 26; 3:19; Luke 1:80; 2:40, 52). Ishmael is placed in the same company with these other special children and even the Messiah himself.

Notably, even before there were the twelve sons of Jacob, there were the twelve princes of Ishmael (Gen. 17:20; 25:16). Ishmael had favor and blessing in his life as he died at the ripe old age of 137. In the Ashanti worldview, growing old to meet one's grandchildren and great-grandchildren is the ultimate blessing from God.

As I read the narrative, I cannot help but think of the many children who grow up in single-parent families, as Ishmael did. Often, such children are made to bear the brunt of their parents' decisions by the religious community. Whether a child of a divorcee or an unwed teenager, children of single-parent homes are sometimes ignored and neglected by the faith community. Through Hagar's narrative we see that God cares as much for Ishmael as he does for Isaac, the heir of a nuclear family. Furthermore, while the decisions of the parents made it impossible for all to live under the same roof, God made provisions for Ishmael just as he did for Isaac. Our faith communities must embrace and provide for the Ishmaels and not just the Isaacs of our time.

I am a British woman. I am a Ghanaian woman. Living in two worlds results in constant dialogue between my Western education and Ghanaian heritage. Such dialogue sensitizes me to the actions of God on behalf of the young and voiceless, thus encouraging readings which high-light the "minor" as well as "major" characters of the Bible.

Janice P. De-Whyte is a Ph.D. candidate at McMaster Divinity College, Canada; she also serves as a Youth Pastor.

SODOM AND GOMORRAH AND THE SYDNEY GAY AND LESBIAN MARDI GRAS

Roland Boer (Australia)

The twin cities of Sodom and Gomorrah (Gen. 18–19) have become watchwords for the "sins of the flesh," for sex between men and between women, and for every other wanton sexual vice imaginable and indeed unimaginable. Arguably, the infamy of Sodom and Gomorrah has grown with the retellings over millennia. But I wish to read this text in light of the world-famous Sydney (Australia) Gay and Lesbian Mardi Gras. Why? On more than one occasion, opponents of the Mardi Gras have described it as the Sodom and Gomorrah of our day.

But what is the Gay and Lesbian Mardi Gras? Today it is the largest event of its kind in the world, with hundreds of thousands of people attending and participating. Running over two weeks in late February and early March, it includes intellectual events, films, plays, art displays, cabarets, comedy, literary readings, concerts, a fair day, the pool party, the grand parade, and then the postparade party (for which 20,000 tickets are often sold). Needless to say, the Mardi Gras is one of the largest annual tourist boosts for Sydney.

Is Sydney, then, a sin city to rival Sodom and Gomorrah, or perhaps San Francisco? This might be the initial impression, especially if one were to visit during the Mardi Gras. But two items suggest it is not so. First, the Mardi Gras was not always this way. At the first event, on June 24, 1978, the police revoked permission for the celebration, which was then a protest march in commemoration of the Stonewall Riots (in Greenwich Village, New York, 1969). The march of about 1,000 people was broken up by police, with 53 of the marchers arrested. Those arrested were later named publically in the *Sydney Morning Herald*. Given that homosexuality was still a crime in the state of New South Wales (until 1984), and given that many had not come out as homosexuals to employers and friends, the publication of names led to many losing their jobs.

Second, Sydney is generally a conservative city, with arguably the largest conservative religious groups in Australia. It is a stronghold of the conservative evangelical wing of the Anglican Church; the right-wing Cardinal Pell of the Roman Catholic Church is based in Sydney; the Pentecostal mega-church "Hillsong," now a transnational ecclesial corporation, has its base in Sydney; many smaller conservative religious groups (including Muslims and Jews) find fertile ground in that city. Each of them is opposed to the Mardi Gras, although they express that opposition in different ways. Indeed, one might argue that the strength of the Mardi Gras operates in an inverse ratio to the strength of conservative religion in Sydney.

Perhaps the most consistent and well-known opponent is Reverend Fred Nile, known variously as Uniting Church minister, leader of the Sydney City Mission, radio-show host, founder of political organizations known as the Festival of Light, the Christian Democratic Party, and the Fred Nile Group, and long-standing member of the Upper House in the New South Wales Parliament.

From the beginning, Nile has consistently declared the Gay and Lesbian Mardi Gras a blight on Sydney. Indeed, Sydney is the Sodom of his imagination. Not only does filth reign on television, not only do brothels and casinos boom, not only do children avidly pursue pornography on the Internet, not only does abortion flourish, but the Mardi Gras goes from strength to strength.

Each year Nile and his fellow Christian Democrats organize a protest march against the Mardi Gras parade. They begin with a prayer for rain on the parade and, when the heavens invariably fail to open, they hand out leaflets to any Mardi Gras reveler willing to take one. Many leaflets usually make it from one year to the next. In contrast to the hundreds of thousands at the Mardi Gras, usually no more than 100 turn out for Nile's protest—this in response to a call for "10,000 warriors" to bring the Mardi Gras to a halt. Ultimately, of course, it is in God's hands. And that is what Nile fears: Should Sydney continue on its wanton path, it too may be destroyed for "homosexual immorality," just like Sodom and Gomorrah. For Nile, Sydney and its Mardi Gras directly provoke God, since the parade blatantly celebrates homosexuality, which is worse than sex shops, brothels, and strip shows.

At one such protest (in 2010), Nile and his supporters handed out "pieces of brimstone" from Sodom and Gomorrah to warn against what may happen: "Hold them in your hands just for a minute and let the reality of the curse that comes upon the land because of sexual immorality…We do not want Sydney to be another Sodom and Gomorrah," they said.

But let us see how well this effort to read the Mardi Gras in terms of Genesis 19 holds up. The men of the city, young and old, who gather at Lot's house and demand sex with the visitors, may easily be connected with the multitudes of gay men (and presumably women) who both live in Sydney and gather at the Mardi Gras. Further, the destruction meted out by God on Sodom and Gomorrah—the fire and brimstone, or burning sulfur and dense smoke (depending upon one's translation)—is just as easily connected with God's anger against the "wickedness" and "grievous sin" of any other place.

After this, the parallels begin to break down. What role, for instance, does Fred Nile play? Is he one of the "messengers" who arrive in Sodom to warn Lot and his family to flee? Given the elision between these "messengers" and God, that would bring Nile dangerously close to an identity with God. Or is he Lot, bidden to leave the city at the last minute? That would render Nile less as a messenger of warning and doom than as a potentially innocent bystander. Perhaps Lot and his immediate family stand in for Sydney's 5 million residents. If so, then the majority of Sydney is not given over to the pleasures of the flesh and thereby the comparison with Sodom loses its effect.

And what about me as an erstwhile resident of Sydney? Am I one of the residents engaged in all manner of fleshly pursuits, blithely ignoring the warnings of the raining sulfur? Or am I a Lot, a relatively innocent bystander about to be caught in the mayhem? I am certainly not a self-appointed angel of the Lord, or even God himself, about to destroy an evil city.

In closing, it is worth pointing out that the Gay and Lesbian Mardi Gras has taken Fred Nile and other opponents to heart. He is often featured—in parody—in at least one float in the Mardi Gras parade. For instance, one year the Sisters of Perpetual Indulgence carried Nile's head—as a massive roast surrounded by vegetables—on a platter like that of John the Baptist's. Nile threatened prosecution. And while Nile rages against a parade with men dressed as Catholic nuns, or men dressed as church bishops wearing large crosses on their dresses, or other men almost naked wearing only leather straps and other "unfavorable material," he is often depicted as a member of precisely one of these groups.

Roland Boer is a cyclist, ship-voyager, and research professor at the University of Newcastle, Australia.

QUESTIONS

1. Identify all the places in the biblical text where Abraham has "nonpeak experiences."

2. Does Melchizedek demonstrate that other people were in fact worshipping the God of Abraham before Abraham? Does Panikkar draw a legitimate interpretation of Melchizedek?

3. What cultural practices in Genesis 12–21 do you resonate with, if any? Which ones are strikingly hard to connect with? How does the Ashanti's view of children compare to the views of your cultural tradition?

4. Based on a careful reading of the text, is the story of Sodom and Gomorrah about God's disapproval of homosexuality? How would you personally respond to Fred Nile?

CHAPTER 4

GENESIS 22

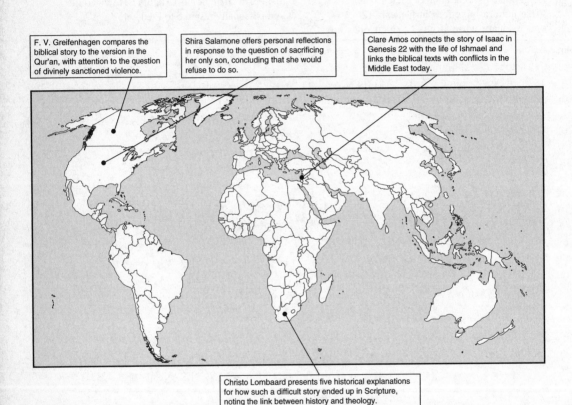

F. V. Greifenhagen compares the biblical story to the version in the Qur'an, with attention to the question of divinely sanctioned violence.

Shira Salamone offers personal reflections in response to the question of sacrificing her only son, concluding that she would refuse to do so.

Clare Amos connects the story of Isaac in Genesis 22 with the life of Ishmael and links the biblical texts with conflicts in the Middle East today.

Christo Lombaard presents five historical explanations for how such a difficult story ended up in Scripture, noting the link between history and theology.

READINGS

Genesis 22 and Conflict in the Middle East
Clare Amos

A Comparison of Genesis 22 to the Qur'an
F. V. Greifenhagen

A Personal Reflection on the Sacrifice of a Son
Shira Salamone

Five Explanations for the Inclusion of Genesis 22 in Scripture
Christo Lombaard

GENESIS 22 AND CONFLICT IN THE MIDDLE EAST

Clare Amos (Lebanon)

In the early years of our marriage my husband and I lived and worked in Beirut and Damascus, where he was the Anglican chaplain. On the walls of our apartment was a cloth print we had bought in the *suq* (marketplace) in Damascus. It depicted a rather grisly looking scene—a man about to sacrifice a young boy is being prevented by the last-minute intervention of a fierce angel. Visitors to our apartment naturally assumed it was a depiction of the biblical story of the near-sacrifice of Isaac. We enjoyed correcting them: It was in fact the sacrifice of Ishmael, for in many Muslim sources it is Ishmael rather than Isaac who is the son that Abraham is apparently instructed to slaughter.

Whenever I read Genesis 22 I remember that confusion between Isaac and Ishmael. Why do the Judaeo-Christian tradition and the Muslim tradition differ regarding who is the intended sacrifice? And does this confusion perhaps offer a hint that is worth exploring in Genesis itself, a hint that perhaps might have something important to offer in the context of the modern Middle East?

Genesis 22 has been described as a text which is "central to the nervous system of Judaism and Christianity." It resonates with Jewish theologies of the Holocaust and Christian understandings of the death of Christ. Its sparse and understated telling, yet one that, as Erich Auerbach put it, is "fraught with background," leaves the reader with a sense of horror mingled with frisson.

But Genesis 22 needs to be read in the context of Genesis 21. This is the account of the expulsion by Abraham of Ishmael and his mother Hagar into the wilderness, apparently with the expectation that they would perish. That the two stories are connected is indicated by several parallels which are central to both: the expression "early in the morning"; the motifs of the delivering angel; the bush; the importance of seeing; two sons of Abraham, one apparently sentenced to death because of internal family strife, the other suffering a similar sentence at God's demand; and two brothers, both rescued from their respective fates by divine intervention at the last minute. Notice too how the narrative of Genesis 22 is introduced by the phrase "After these things," which encourages the reader to see the interconnections between the two chapters. Indeed Abraham's actions in Genesis 21 toward Ishmael and his mother could be said to offer a sort of "rationale" for the seemingly monstrous demand in Genesis 22 that he should sacrifice his other son Isaac. Although the expulsion of Hagar and Ishmael is sanctioned by God even if at Sarah's behest (21:12), we can wonder whether Abraham was perhaps using God simply as a convenient way of sorting out a family quarrel. We can all hear God speaking to us when it is opportune to do so, and Abraham's loyalty to God goes through many twists and turns. So now in turn with the demand for Isaac God seeks to discover just how pure Abraham's faith really is. The "sacrifice" of one son has led to the demand for the sacrifice of the second.

There is one other motif that circles these chapters and entwines them together. It is the theme of the *ger*, which has a major place in the Abraham stories. The Hebrew word *ger* is difficult exactly to capture in translation; it is variously rendered as "alien," "resident alien," "migrant," and "sojourner." It normally spoke of someone without land rights, who in a real sense did not belong in a particular land or country, who was therefore vulnerable and whose existence and well-being depended on the generosity of the settled people of that land. In the law codes of Exodus, justice for the *ger* is one of the touchstones that God requires of his people. Note how the root *ger* as both a noun and a verb occurs several times in Genesis 20, 21, and 23 (20:1; 21:34; 23:4). But the verbal root seems also to be used in the form of a pun on the name of the Philistine city "Gerar" (20:1). Even more significantly, it is also there in the name "Hagar"—the consonants of whose name in Hebrew could simply mean "the alien." Perhaps it is as though she is being pictured as the archetypal *ger*.

Thus, one way of reading these chapters is to suggest that they explore what it means for Abraham and Sarah to be *gerim*—dependent upon the hospitality of people such as Abimelech, who treats them with generosity and good will. But in turn it also raises questions about the treatment by Abraham and Sarah of others such as Hagar. Is the way they behaved toward her in accord with how God's people should treat others who are vulnerable? The writers of Genesis do not provide an easy answer, but they do at least seem to raise the question.

Whether it is through the Muslim tradition that the sacrificial son was Ishmael rather than Isaac or through the way that Genesis entwines the stories of Isaac and Ishmael, it is clear that somehow the fates of the two brothers are "bound" together. Is not this of possible significance for the destiny of the current Middle East, where the spiritual heirs of both Isaac and Ishmael live with hostility between them? It is fascinating that the author of Genesis refuses to write Ishmael out of the biblical story, even though Isaac is seen as the more favored brother. For example, there is a genealogy given for Ishmael in 25:12–18. The way that the two brothers stand together to bury their father near Hebron (25:9) offers a poignant contrast to the way that the site of Abraham's tomb has become a modern flashpoint of hostility and hatred.

Writing with an awareness of the significance of these stories for the life and well-being of the modern Middle East, it is relevant to note that respect for the *ger* is a model that could also have modern-day applications. When the birth of Ishmael is announced to Hagar by the divine messenger in 16:12, the comment is made that he "shall live at odds with all his kin." However, the underlying Hebrew could also be translated another way to read, "He shall live alongside all his kin." The destiny of the Middle East, and perhaps of our world, lies between those two possible meanings.

There is a well-known poem by the Israeli poet Shin Shalom, with verses spoken as from the mouth of Isaac, which is used in some Jewish traditions during the celebration of the New Year, and which reflects on the biblical interweaving of the figures of Isaac and Ishmael. Isaac asks poignantly, "Ishmael, my brother, How long shall we fight each other?" The final lines of the poem stand as aspiration and goal for all who care for the destiny of the Middle East today: "Time is running out, put hatred to sleep. Shoulder to shoulder, let's water our sheep."

Clare Amos served as Director of Theological Studies in the Anglican Communion Office before recently joining the World Council of Churches in Geneva, where she is responsible for Christian–Muslim and Christian–Jewish relations.

A COMPARISON OF GENESIS 22 TO THE QUR'AN

F. V. Greifenhagen (Canada)

Would you kill for God? This question is raised by one of the paradigmatic stories for Jews and Christians: the poignant narrative of Abraham's near sacrifice of his son, found in Genesis 22:1–19. The same story also occupies a paradigmatic place for Muslims, and a version of the story appears in Qur'an:

Surah 37 *Al-Saffat* ("Those Ranged in Ranks") 99–113.

[99]He (Abraham) said: "I will go to my Lord! He will surely guide me!" [100]"O my Lord! Grant me a righteous (son)!" [101]So we gave him the good news of a boy ready to suffer and forbear. [102]Then, when (the son) reached (the age of) (serious) work with him, he said: "O my son! I see in a vision that I offer you in sacrifice. Now see what is your view!" (The son) said: "O my father! Do as you are commanded; you will find me, if Allah so wills, one practicing patience and constancy!" [103] So when they had both submitted their wills (to Allah), and he had laid him prostrate on his forehead (for sacrifice), [104]We called out to him, "O Abraham!" [105]"You have already fulfilled the vision!" And thus indeed We reward those who do right. [106]For this was obviously a trial. [107]And We ransomed him with a momentous sacrifice. [108]And We left (this blessing) for him among generations (to come) in later times: [109]"Peace and salutation to Abraham!" [110]Thus indeed do We reward those who do right. [111]For he was one of Our believing servants. [112]And We gave him the good news of Isaac, a prophet, one of the righteous. [113]We blessed him and Isaac, but of their progeny are (some) that do right and (some) that obviously do wrong, to their own souls. (Translation by 'Abdullah Yusuf 'Ali, 2001)

The Qur'an here generally follows the biblical account: the command to Abraham to sacrifice his son, the aborting of the sacrifice at the last minute, the characterization of the event as a trial, and the commendation of Abraham's faith and obedience. However, the qur'anic version presents a unique perspective on the story. It does not mention many of the details of the biblical account, such as the place of sacrifice; the journey to and from it; or the knife, the wood, the servants, the donkey, the altar, or the binding of the son. The Qur'an seems to assume that its hearers are already familiar with the story, and so it focuses on the particular meaning of the story rather than its details.

Noticeably, the son is not identified in the qur'anic version, and yet he plays a much more active role in the story than he does in the biblical version. In the biblical account, besides carrying the wood and initiating a short conversation with his father, Isaac plays a rather passive role. It is unclear whether he is a willing participant; the fact that his father binds him (22:9) seems to suggest that he was not. And yet postbiblical Jewish and Christian literature transformed Isaac into a willing victim (e.g., Judith 8:26–27; 4 Maccabees 13:12).

The Qur'an continues this interpretive trajectory, portraying the father as consulting with the unnamed son, who is made aware of what God has commanded his father to do. In fact, the son urges his father to obey the command. Father and son are both depicted as willingly submitting to the divine will (37:103). The test in the qur'anic account applies not just to the father but also to the son, and both pass with flying colors.

By omitting the son's name, the qur'anic version has released the story from its context within the sibling rivalry between Ishmael and Isaac as depicted in the Bible, and enabled it to become a general paradigm of faithful obedience to God for believers. While the Bible presents a sacred history in which a choice must be made as to which son will continue the covenantal relationship that leads to the creation of the people Israel, the Qur'an focuses on abstracted models of morality and piety. Both Ishmael and Isaac can be a model of faith and so it is inconsequential which son was almost killed by his father.

Although the identity of the son is not the Qur'an's concern, Muslim and non-Muslim interpreters have argued over whether it was Ishmael or Isaac. At stake in this debate is which religious community can lay legitimate claim to the heritage of Abraham. Isaac appears by name in the qur'anic version only after the sacrifice, seeming to imply that he could not have been the intended sacrificial victim; rather, the victim was his older brother Ishmael. However, the reference to Isaac at the end of the story (37:112) could be a summary statement linked with Abraham's plea for a righteous son at the beginning of the story (37:100), thus implying that Isaac was the intended sacrificial victim. And so the qur'anic version of the story is dragged back into the sibling rivalries, from which it had originally extricated itself.

This religiously sanctioned and revered story of a father's intended violence against his own child raises acute questions for us today about divinely sanctioned violence, child abuse, and patriarchy, questions that are obscured by religious rivalries or mitigated by portrayals of the son as a willing victim. Bruce Feiler, tellingly a journalist and not a professional biblical or qur'anic scholar, writes in his popular book *Abraham: A Journey to the Heart of Three Faiths* (New York: William Morrow, 2002, 108, 110):

> Abraham, I was discovering, is not just a gentle man of peace. He's as much a model for fanaticism as he is for moderation. He nurtured in his very behavior—in his conviction to break from his father, in his willingness to terrorize *both* of his sons—the intimate connection between faith and violence. And then, by elevating such conduct to the standard of piety, he stirred in his descendents a similar desire to lash out, to view pain as an arm of belief, and to use brutality to advance their vision of a divine-centered world…No wonder the story of the binding is so central to Jews, Christians, and Muslims, I thought. It's the part of Abraham's life that cuts closest to our veins and poses the question we hope never to face: Would I kill for God? For many of Abraham's descendents, of course, the answer throughout history has been yes.

This is the question that Jews, Christians, and Muslims would do well to struggle with together as they read this story of Abraham. For the story easily evokes the ancient patriarchal framework, in which fathers, or male authority figures, have the right to sacrifice their offspring on the altar of war. Noticeably absent in both versions of the story is the boy's mother; whether Sarah or Hagar, she is invisible. What would she say or do if given voice and agency? Perhaps she would echo Julia Ward Howe's Mothers Day Proclamation of 1870:

> Our sons will not be taken from us to unlearn
> All that we have been able to teach them of charity, mercy and patience.
> We, the women of one country,
> Will be too tender of those of another country
> To allow our sons to be trained to injure theirs.

Certainly, Muslims, Christians, and Jews, while standing in awe of Abraham's submission to God, in general, do not feel called to emulate him specifically by literally sacrificing their children. Perhaps, just as the ram was substituted for the human sacrifice, the story also powerfully sublimates the terrifying willingness to sacrifice one's own kind by transforming it into a recital of that act as necessarily or divinely unfulfilled. The awesome energy of the impetus to kill is thus not dissipated but rather channeled into self-giving piety.

F. V. Greifenhagen is Associate Professor of Religious Studies at Luther College, University of Regina, Canada.

A PERSONAL REFLECTION ON THE SACRIFICE OF A SON

Shira Salamone (United States)

I've heard the story of the *Akédah*, the Binding of Isaac (and of his near-sacrifice), read in synagogue twice every year for 32 years. It's read on the second day of *Rosh Hashanah* (Jewish New Year) and during the regular cycle of weekly *Torah* (Bible) readings. My husband and I have discussed it many times. We've concluded that G-d (we avoid writing the word *G-o-d* lest we accidentally take G-d's name in vain, which is forbidden) wanted to see whether *Avraham Avinu* (Abraham our Patriarch) would show as much devotion to Him as a pagan would have shown to a pagan god, who, in that era, would have demanded child sacrifice. The difference, of course—and it's a huge one—is that G-d didn't allow *Avraham* to go through with the sacrifice of his child.

To speak of this on an intellectual level is one thing. But to speak of it on a personal level is another. For so many years, I've tried to ignore this question, but, somehow, when it's put to music, it reaches out past my defenses and goes straight to my heart:

> Would you take your only son?
> Would you lay your answer down?
> Would you bind him to the stone?
> Would you take your only son?

The first time I heard Blue Fringe's song *Hineni* ("Here I am") I almost turned it off. The second time, I listened closely, because, given the way the song had affected me the first time, I knew that I would *have* to write about it. The third time was this morning. I listened so that I could write down the lyrics. I'm not sure I'll ever be able to listen to it again. It's a beautiful song, but I can't bear to hear the words.

> Because I have an only son.
> And the answer is "No."

Ani maamin, be-emuna sh'léma (I believe with perfect faith). I sing these words to honor my ancestors, factual or metaphorical, who died with the *Sh'ma* (biblical quotations affirming that we have only one G-d) on their lips. I sing these words for the martyrs who died *al k'dushat haShem* (for the sanctification of G-d's name) during the wars in which the Temples, first and second, were destroyed. For those who died during the revolts of the Maccabees and Bar Kochba. For the Ten Sages, whose terrible deaths we commemorate during the Martyrology on *Yom Kippur* (Day of Atonement). For the victims of the Crusades, the pogroms, and the *Shoah/* Holocaust. For all those who have died because they were Jews. I sing those words to honor my ancestors. Not because I believe in those words. Like Adam and Eve in the Garden of Eden, I'm hiding, but it's my faith that's naked.

Either you believe that life's misfortunes are random or you believe that G-d has His reasons. Neither can I accept the idea, promulgated by some, that misfortune is a punishment for sin nor can I agree with the idea, supported by others, that we must simply accept misfortune and not question why because G-d's ways are beyond human comprehension.

Avinu haAv haRachamun haM'Rachem (Our Father, Compassionate Father Who has compassion). Does He? If so, why did He deem it necessary to put *Avraham* (and, for that matter, *Iyov*/Job) through such a trial?

Eish u'varad, sheleg v'kitor, ruach s'arah osah d'varo (Fire and hail, snow and mist, stormy wind fulfilling His word) (Psalm 148). Why should I trust a G-d who stands by while thousands die in tsunamis and hurricanes to stay my hand and put a ram in my son's place? *Hineni*? Here I am?

No.

I cannot understand how *Avraham* could have argued repeatedly with G-d not to destroy *Tz'dom* and *Amorah* (Sodom and Gomorrah), but did not say a word of protest when G-d told him to sacrifice his own child. Why is *Avraham* nicer to strangers than to his own family? And this is not the first time. He had already sent his son *Yishmael* packing with nothing but bread and water (Genesis 21:8–21). All G-d said was *Sh'ma b'kolah*, listen to her (Sarah's) voice. G-d never suggested that *Yishmael* and his mother Hagar should be sent off into the desert with limited means of short-term survival and no means of long-term support. Judging by the text, *Yishmael* had to have been over 14 years old at the time of his expulsion. *Avraham* could have given him a parting gift of, for example, a small flock of goats. Why didn't he? So, in one sense, is it any surprise that *Avraham* passively accepts the command to sacrifice Isaac?

It appears that G-d wasn't so thrilled with the fact that *Avraham* assented without protest. For afterward, G-d never spoke to him again. Maybe G-d wanted *Avraham* to protest. At any rate, if the choice were imposed upon me, I would die *al k'dushat haShem* (for the sanctification of G-d's name). But I would not take my only son.

Shira Salamone is a Jewish blogger (http://onthefringe_jewishblog.blogspot.com/) who takes Judaism seriously, but not necessarily literally.

FIVE EXPLANATIONS FOR THE INCLUSION OF GENESIS 22 IN SCRIPTURE

Christo Lombaard (South Africa)

Genesis 22:1–19 is a tall tale, in a different sense. Though told in a few verses, it is an account with huge implications. The idea of God ordering human sacrifice is utterly disturbing to our moral sensibilities and to our religious sense of God as author of life and love. In this immoral drama, Abraham—father of three world religions—actively colludes by deceiving his son when Isaac asks some penetrating questions (22:7–8). Yet, Abraham eventually emerges as a hero of faithful obedience, an example to all believers. The story told in these few verses reads almost like the script of a third-rate psychothriller movie, for late-night television viewing only.

No surprise, then, that throughout its existence this account has been the subject of debate and speculation. How could such a story find a place in the *Good* Book? For…*good* people!? *Good* God!?

A popular recent way of dealing with these difficulties has been circumvention. Focusing on how the parts of the text stick together (structuralism) or on its storytelling techniques (narratological readings) skirts two kinds of questions: the moral problems, summarized in the first paragraph above, and the matter hinted at in the second paragraph: Why on earth would such an account become Scripture? These questions must never be dodged, simply because people keep asking them. Only one kind of answer *can* address these questions: historical explanations. Five such historical proposals have been made.

The oldest historical understanding of Genesis 22 reads it as a rallying cry opposing child sacrifice in ancient Israel. Scholars debate whether sacrificing children as an act of loyalty to God was ever a part of Israel's faith. Some doubt whether it was part of the cultures surrounding Israel. But the fact remains: The people of Israel recognized the *possibility* of killing children to prove religious commitment—the ultimate "giving till it hurts"! Clearly, at some stage, this possibility came up for serious consideration. To counter this possibility, which would be a difficult fit with Israel's religious make-up, action was needed: Something *had* to be said. So a story—Genesis 22—was told which made the point clear: God desires animal sacrifice, not human. The lesson? From the beginning of Israel's faith, with father Abraham, human sacrifice was anathema. God does not want it; Abraham did not do it; for "us" (the later generations) it is a no-no too!

The second of the historical understandings seeks to grasp very small parts of 22:1–19. Now where did *this* snippet of the story come from, they ask? Once we know the answer, we can respond: Ah, so *that*'s how it came to be. That's how the story ended up in Holy Writ, as an explanation for the origin of something, that is, an etiology. Verse 14 offers one such example. Here we see an explanation of the origin of the name of a certain place. The thinking is that there was a place called—following some English Bibles' renderings—"The LORD Will Provide" (New International Version), or "Yahweh provides" (New Jerusalem Bible), or "Jehovahjireh" (King James Version's direct transliteration of the Hebrew). So people asked: Where does this name come from? Then, the story of Abraham's sacrifice was related to this site. "Ah, so *that*'s how it came to be…"

A second snippet which calls forth etiological explanation is in verse 2. The implicit ancient question here was: Why is it specifically *in the Moriah area* that we regularly sacrifice to God? That matter would then be resolved by Abraham's sacrifice story: that is where God sent Abraham, and some very special events happened there, so that is why we (later generations) continue to offer sacrifices in Moriah.

None of the etiological explanations cover all aspects of the text. These cultural-historical questions are just too specific. Yet, none of the other forms of explanation can do without these etiological elements. Without etiology, certain snippets of the story remain inexplicable.

Third, in many religions, initiation ceremonies allow entrance into membership and advancement through various levels. Christianity, for instance, has baptism, which is an "entry ceremony," as well as other rites which induct one into full church membership or leadership positions. In Genesis 22 we see three different levels of cultic initiation. The "two young men" in verse 3 (literally) go on a first religious excursion, but as novices they may only progress halfway. Isaac, somewhat older, is taken to the point of almost dying in his initiation ritual, which means he has now passed into religious adulthood. Abraham, lastly, passes muster as a priest, willing to sacrifice all for God. In this interpretation, the three strands of narrative are ancient initiation myths. Centuries later, these cultural memories became entwined, to form a new story demonstrating obedience.

A fourth approach reads the text in light of the problem of human suffering, which lies at the heart of many religions and philosophies. It remains foundational: Why do we endure hardship? More religiously: Why does God allow, perhaps even cause, heartache? Job is the most renowned Old Testament book dealing with such *theodicy*. Yet, the fourth historical approach holds that Genesis 22's crude, unrefined vision of suffering actually inspired the book of Job as a response. Whereas Job holds that suffering remains a mystery before God, Genesis 22 states that God *causes* misery. Isaac represents the suffering Israel in exile, with Abraham as Babylonian oppressor. Fortunately, just before extinction, that same God saves Isaac/Israel—still, though, without giving reasons.

The last, most recent, of the historical interpretations places Genesis 22 within the conflict between patriarchal supporter groups. Old Testament scholarship has long accepted that Abraham, Isaac, and Jacob were initially independent clan elders. In time, the clans grew closer. To cement such ties their tribal origin stories were intermingled; these three patriarchs thus *became* related. Inharmoniously, the adherents to the different patriarchal groups were vying for power. This is seen in the famous doublets/triplets in the Pentateuch: stories from one group retold to favor another. In Genesis 22:2–14 and 19, we see the final showdown between Abraham's supporters and Isaac's adherents. The Abrahamites have the upper hand. Evidently, the Isaacites should know their place: They have been finally surpassed in the social competition stakes. The Abrahamites would have eliminated the Isaacites were it not for divine intervention.

The theological subservience of the Isaacites is soon emphasized. In the frame-verses 1 and 15–18, the Isaacites should now accept that they will be blessed only *through* Abraham. The initially dominant Isaacites of early scriptural prophetism are vanquished in the late Persian period. Genesis 22:19 clinches the game: Isaac is not even mentioned; Abraham takes over Beersheba, the Isaacites' home field.

In sum, Genesis 22:1–19 remains without final solution. These five attempts have been made, and more should. Already amply clear, though, is this: Only *in* the history of the text can we follow its faith. Or put differently, once we know the history, we can grasp the theology.

Christo Lombaard (Ph.D., Communications; D.D., Old Testament) teaches Christian Spirituality at the University of South Africa.

QUESTIONS

1. Based on a close reading of the biblical text, consider the merits of Amos' suggestion that Genesis 22 is God's punishment on Abraham for his treatment of Ishmael.

2. Greifenhagen quotes Feiler as saying that Abraham was a religious fanatic. Is this a fair assessment of Abraham? Can Abraham rightly be compared to people "who are willing to kill for God"?

3. Who has the stronger/better faith: Salamone or Abraham? Who deserves more admiration and respect?

4. Lombaard observes that Genesis 22 flies in the face of "our religious sense of God as author of life and love." From where do people get that "religious sensibility"—society, religious leaders, the Bible, or an intuitive morality?

CHAPTER 5

GENESIS 25–33

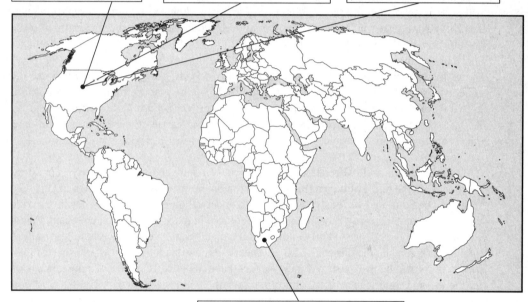

Shirley Phelps-Roper contends that God's treatment of Esau—namely, hating him—is an important text for Christian theology and doctrine.

Arlette Poland, reading as a Jewish feminist, argues that Rebekah is a person of exemplary character, whose actions are based on love, not deception.

Clarence Mitchell shares how the story of Jacob facilitated his own reconciliation with his father, which shows the continuing power of the Bible.

Madipoane Masenya focuses on Leah and the challenges of women in a polygynous partnership, specifically their struggle to enjoy their sexuality.

READINGS

A Jewish Feminist Reflection on Rebekah
Arlette Poland

God's Treatment of Esau
Shirley Phelps-Roper

Leah and the Challenges of Women in Polygynous Partnership
Madipoane Masenya

A Spiritual Reflection on the Life of Jacob
Clarence Mitchell

A JEWISH FEMINIST REFLECTION ON REBEKAH

Arlette Poland (United States)

I approach the women of Genesis as a feminist, a Jew, and a scholar. Here I will show that Rebekah/Rivka is a person of exemplary character and that she acted out of her love for and obedience to God when she supposedly tricked Isaac into blessing Jacob rather than Esau.

We first discover Rivka's model character in Genesis 24, where Abraham's servant has been sent to find a wife for Isaac. In this scene, Rivka acts virtuously by giving water to both the servant and all his camels until they are filled (25:19). In doing so, she goes beyond the expectation of the servant without thought of herself or a reward, and without knowing who the servant was. Some traditional (male) interpretations argue that Rivka acted self-ishly because—through some magical intuition—she knew it was the servant of Abraham searching for a wife for Isaac, but there is nothing in the narrative that logically allows such an interpretation. Later we learn that Isaac truly loves Rivka from the moment he sees her and that she immediately assuages the pain of the loss of his mother, Sarah (24:67). Isaac shows his love by acting proactively on behalf of Rivka, praying for her when she did not conceive some 20 years into their marriage (25:21). This is more than his father, Abraham, ever did for Sarah. Notably, God answers Isaac's prayer before he has finished the prayer. Rivka's value as a wife, lover, and future mother who carries the covenant is validated by God's quick response to Isaac's loving prayer. God's trust in Rivka is now established without question.

Rivka's own positive relationship with God is manifested when she feels pain during her pregnancy. In the midst of her anguish and confusion, her first thought is to turn to God. Genesis 25:22 can be translated variously, but the key to understanding her utterance lies in realizing that this is a woman who is fully aware of her critical role in the success of the covenant. Pain in the course of a pregnancy (particularly in that time) typically indicated the potential loss of the fetus/infant. Further, when there is such pain, it is nearly impossible to speak a whole sentence without being interrupted by the spasms of pain—a fact that male interpreters fail to appreciate. Concern for the life and significance of the child (in terms of the covenant) fueled Rivka's cry. Motherly concern is universal to all women who want to be pregnant and especially where continuation of the family/tribal unit rests on the success of the pregnancy.

God responds instantaneously to Rivka's cry, providing an explanation for the pain—she is having twins—and a prediction of what will become of the twins after their birth (25:23). Interestingly, Rivka alone receives the prophecy concerning the future relationship of the twins. God responds privately to her; Isaac is not included in God's communication. One can speculate why that is so; however, the narrative has established a true love story that must logically lead one to presume that she informed Isaac at some point during the life of the twins. After all, theirs was the first true love story in Genesis and true lovers do not keep secrets. Isaac knows her character and knows of her dedication and love for God. Whatever action is necessary to carry out God's prophecy or command must be done. While it is Rivka who is most active in the so-called trick to gain the blessing of the covenant for Jacob rather than Esau, it is reasonable to assume that Isaac knew of the trick and went along (see below for more on this) with Rivka's plan to keep the secret command/prophecy for the sake of the children and their relationship, and for the sake of the covenant. Further, there was nothing in the command from God to Rivka that required her to keep it a secret from Isaac, only to carry it out and make it a reality.

After the birth of the twin boys, we read that "Isaac loved Esau, because he was fond of game; but Rivka loved Jacob" (25:28). Some commentators assert that Rivka is cunning and manipulative in her apparent favoring of Jacob. It is important to note, however, that there is no clear declaration that Rivka did not also love or favor Esau. Such a conclusion can be drawn because there is no reason stated in the narrative as to *why* Rivka favors or loves Jacob (25:28). Indeed, love of a mother such as Rivka, who is of an exemplary character, as has been firmly established, could not favor one son over another in any way that the relationship between the boys would be damaged or the family unit be torn apart. The love of Rivka for the boys might be expressed differently, because they were such different people, but such difference in her expression of love is not tantamount to ignoring or harming one son over the other.

Here, to my Jewish feminist eyes, Rivka was doing three things—and doing them well. First, she was providing some balance to the household since Esau *was* favored by the father and for a certain stated (and self-gratifying) reason. Second, she was keeping secret from the boys the word from God about the future of her two sons. Third, and most importantly, she was preparing her younger son for the task of carrying the critical covenant. She had to know that he must be of a certain character: obedient, devoted to God, and deeply compassionate. How better can a child learn such qualities than by living with a mother who models them? I posit that Rivka understood her responsibilities as a mother to twins, as a critical lynchpin to the future of the covenant, and as an obedient and devoted servant of God. The simple line that she favored (loved) Jacob fulfills those responsibilities; thus, there are no negative connotations associated with her favoring or special affection.

We now turn our attention to the so-called "trickster" scene, where Rivka arranges for Jacob (the second born) to receive the covenantal blessing, a blessing that normally and automatically would go to the firstborn son. In the course of the scene, there are at least three instances where one could logically deduce that Isaac was quite aware that it was Jacob and not Esau. One is where Jacob presented his father with food (27:18). While this was the food that Isaac loved, the food alone was insufficient to lead Isaac to conclude this was Esau. Next, Isaac noticed that it was indeed the voice of Jacob, not Esau, even though their hands felt the same. Isaac was even prompted to ask one last time if this was indeed Esau (27:24). Jacob responded in the positive, lying to his father as instructed by his mother (who also assured him that any curse from these lies would befall her and not him). Meanwhile, the audience knows that she has been commanded by God to assure this result. And Isaac did not confront Jacob any further.

None of these actions by Rivka were designed for her own self-gratification or the imagined manipulation of her husband for Jacob or against Esau. In fact, it is more likely and more logical that Rivka and Isaac were complicit in this "ruse" and that it was Jacob who was tricked, just as he was later in the narrative by Laban (Gen. 30). Too many interpreters ignore the import of the order or command from God that the younger shall gain the covenant rather than the tradition of the elder son gaining it. Such was not the norm and so it was necessary for Rivka (and Isaac) to trick Jacob in order to comply with God's command. The narrative makes it clear that the scheme is devised by Rivka, but that is to be expected since she is the one who heard the command from God. While Isaac was indeed relatively passive, as many interpreters have argued, he was not tricked. Rather, out of love for Rivka and perhaps fear of God, he complied with her scheme and God's command as he willingly ate the food and drank the wine and then bestowed the sacred covenantal blessing on the younger son.

Arlette Poland (Ph.D., Philosophy of Religion, Claremont Graduate University) practiced law for 20 years before becoming an adjunct lecturer in Judaism, Buddhism, Ethics, and Science and Religion.

GOD'S TREATMENT OF ESAU

Shirley Phelps-Roper (United States)

The story of Jacob and Esau is a simple but amazing story. From this one story God teaches of heaven and hell, obedience and sin, the earthly man and the spiritual man, the hatred of God and the love of God, and the sovereignty and preeminence of God's will. The story is mentioned several times in the New Testament to make key points. It is the very heart of the excellent doctrines of Election (God elects some for eternal salvation) and Reprobation (God condemns others to hell). You cannot have one without the other!

Jacob and Esau were fraternal twin boys born to Isaac and Rebekah. They both have an impeccable bloodline. Their father Isaac and their grandfather Abraham were both Jewish patriarchs and beloved of God. They were both active participants of the covenant of God! From a DNA perspective it is hard to beat a combination like this. If Godly favor was simply a matter of bloodline, both boys would be entitled to it based solely on their gene pool. However, just being related to Godly people is not enough to earn the favor of the Almighty God.

God told their mother Rebekah even before the boys were born that there were two nations and two manner of people in her womb and that the elder, Esau, would serve the younger, Jacob (25:23). And here is the amazing part of this story: God Almighty predetermined and predestinated before they were born and before they had done any good or evil to love Jacob and get this... to *hate* Esau. Yes, you read right. Even though the false prophets of today preach on every corner that God does not hate, his plain revealed word says otherwise. Indeed, those who say that "God loves everyone" ignore this simple fact straight from the Bible.

And moreover, the fact that God hates Esau is repeated not only in several more places in the Old Testament (Malachi 1:2–3 and Jeremiah 49:10) but also in multiple places in the New Testament. In Romans 9:11–15, Paul writes concerning Jacob and Esau:

> For the children being not yet born, neither having done any good or evil, that the purpose of God according to election might stand, not of works, but of him that calleth. It was said unto her, The elder shall serve the younger. As it is written, Jacob have I loved, but Esau have I hated. What shall we say then? Is there unrighteousness with God? God forbid. For he saith to Moses, "I will have mercy on whom I will have mercy, and I will have compassion on whom I will have compassion."

You can spend your whole life arguing about these passages but it does not change them. There is no interpretation required here. The verses are crystal clear. This story blows to pieces the notion that God loves everyone and that he does not hate. God's hatred is not an evil passion as you find in men. It is God's perfect, righteous, and everlasting determination to send the unrepentant sinner to hell for eternity.

That is the right of the Creator. From the council halls of eternity, God created Jacob according to the election of grace and Esau according to the election of damnation. Welcome to election, friends and neighbors! Remember, two nations are represented in Jacob and Esau; one destined for heaven, and one destined for hell. I can already hear the rabble complaining and the attempts to explain away this story. Paul is ahead of you. He anticipates the complaint and asks a rhetorical question: "What shall we say then? Is there unrighteousness with God? God forbid." Every time this generation says that God does not hate, in the same breath they take away the love of God. They are related—you cannot have one without the other. As it is written, Jacob have I loved but Esau have I hated.

Do you want to complain about that, cry and whine about how unfair it is? Paul anticipates that as well in Romans 9:19–22, where he says, among other important things, that we have no right to question God. God created this world as He wanted. He in His infinite wisdom made Jacob to be a vessel of honor. Likewise, He in His wisdom made Esau, before he was born and before Esau had done good or evil, to be a vessel of dishonor to show His wrath. There is no free will here. Esau had zero free will. Esau sold his spiritual birthright for some soup because his tummy was hungry. Esau is the man of the flesh, who despised his birthright (Gen. 25:34). Paul calls Esau a "profane person...who for one morsel of meat sold his birthright" (Hebrews 12:6). Esau despised the spiritual things of God in favor of the devilish and earthly things of this world, just like this generation does. Esau caused his parents great disappointment by marrying the filthy daughters of Canaan, and when he saw it displeased his parents he married another one (Gen. 28:8–9). Esau had murder in his heart for his brother (Gen. 27:41). At all the critical points of life, Esau did wrong.

Here is the essence of this story: Obey God, keep his commandments, and seek after the righteousness of God and you demonstrate yourself to be as Jacob. Seek earthly things, go after strange women, sell your spiritual soul for a morsel of bread, and live a profane life and you demonstrate yourself to be as Esau and receive the fate of Esau.

But if you are Esau, you are damned. Period. Hebrews 12:17 says Esau "found no place of repentance, though he sought it carefully with tears." This verse again destroys the notion that God loves everyone. Not so, Esau even sought repentance from God and never was granted it. Again, Esau had no free will. God hated him from all eternity past and nothing was going to change that. Not his bloodline, not his begging, nothing. You say, again, this is not fair. But who are you, mortal human, to speak against God?

Jacob and Esau represent the two types of people that are born into this earth. You are either one or the other. If you have understanding of these things, lay it to heart, time is running out! The King is at the door! It is the time of the restitution of all things. He that hath an ear, let him hear!

Shirley Phelps-Roper is an attorney and servant of the God of all creation in the last minutes of the last days.

LEAH AND THE CHALLENGES OF WOMEN IN POLYGYNOUS PARTNERSHIP
Madipoane Masenya (South Africa)

Here I will use African love songs to engage the narrative of Leah in Genesis 29–30 with a view to foregrounding the struggles and experiences of women in a polygynous partnership. Specifically, the focus will be on these women's struggles to affirm their sexuality and their right to the enjoyment of fulfilling sexual lives.

In any patriarchal culture—including the ancient Israelite and current African cultures—the sexuality of married women is perceived to be the property of their husbands. Thus a sexually passionate woman is never celebrated. In fact, she might be viewed as either a deviant or an anomaly. Furthermore, there seems to be a general perception among scholars that biblical women did not bother much about their rights to fulfilling sexual rights. However, a gender-sensitive, woman-friendly rehearing of the story of Leah, aided by an African-South African song, will hopefully reveal the fact that married women, particularly those who are part of polygynous marriage relationships, do demand their right to a sexually fulfilling life.

Leah, like many daughters or women who are used by men (fathers and brothers) to achieve male agendas in the book of Genesis, was apparently thrown into marriage unprepared. Getting our cue from the text, no connections between Jacob and Leah were made before the night of their marriage. In the case of Rachel, Leah's younger sister, Jacob's affection is clearly revealed (29:11, 18, 21). The intensity of Jacob's affection for the younger wife compared to that of the older wife (if any) is clearly revealed in 29:30: "So Jacob went in to Rachel also, and he loved Rachel more than Leah." Although Jacob is depicted as having sexual encounters with both wives, there is no mention of his love for Leah after his encounter with her, an omission which would have repercussions on the Jacob–Leah relationship because it marked the onset of Leah's struggle for love and sex.

Could it be that Leah provides one example of a woman who refused to fit into prescribed female sexual roles? A couple of elements in the text suggest so. Leah's demand for love (and sex) from her husband is revealed from her conviction that she *owned* her husband. It is no wonder that Leah uses the possessive phrase "my husband" five times within a span of 29 verses! In 29:32, as Leah named her son *Reuben*, she thought that Jacob her husband would love her ("...surely now my husband will love me"). In naming her second-born son *Simeon* in 29:34, she had hoped to be *joined* to her husband ("now this time my husband will be joined to me..."). The expression "my husband" pointedly and painfully occurs again in 30:15 in the context of cowifely hostility and jealousy as Leah protests against the giving of her son's mandrakes to her sister and cowife, Rachel. The reader is not sure if it was a pattern for Leah to show certain favors toward Rachel in order to "buy" her marital right to sexual pleasure and intimacy to her husband. It is clear, however, that Leah's sexual life was malnourished. Her concerted effort at bearing many sons for Jacob was not helpful in winning her husband's love and intimacy.

As concerned readers of this text, we may rush to put blame on the "possessiveness" of Rachel for Jacob. Should not our critique be leveled against the patriarch Jacob, who in essence agreed to have two wives? Should it not be the responsibility of all marital partners (irrespective of how many such they choose to have) to make sure that all their partners' conjugal needs are catered for satisfactorily? What one finds disturbing, though, is that nowhere in the text do we find Leah addressing her concerns about conjugal deprivation to the right person, that is, to Jacob. The narrator mostly presents her as either speaking to herself or the midwives (cf. the context of the birthing and naming of her sons) or to Rachel, her cowife.

Leah does not hide her sexual craving for Jacob. Her reaction to her sister's request for a fertility "drug?" (mandrakes) in Genesis 30:15 gives the readers a glimpse not only of her sexual craving for her husband but also of her perceived right to sexual pleasure and intimacy. Fittingly, in 30:16 she demands a sexual encounter with her husband. This sexually passionate yet unloved wife's motive for using her reproductive powers to the fullest appears to be inspired more by her sexual desire for Jacob (30:5–16) than her commitment toward the fulfillment of her marital role as mother in a patriarchal society.

One may very well argue that Leah represents one of the neglected, invisible, and perhaps intimidating qualities of womanhood (*bosadi*), namely, a woman's legitimate desire to have her sexual needs met. This quality is also endorsed by the following African-South African

(Northern Sotho) song. The lead male singer of the song is joined by a group of women with the main respondent being his wife (Mokgadi), who responds by singing with a group of women. Here are the lyrics:

(Sepedi)	(English translation)
A re ye nokeng	Let us go to the river (Man and Women)
Wa mpona nala di a rotha (Mokgadi)	Look at me, my nails are falling away (Mokgadi)
A re ye kgonyeng	Let us go to the grinding stone (Man and Women)
Wa mpona nala di a rotha (Mokgadi)	Look at me, my nails are falling away (Mokgadi)
A re ye go šila	Let us go and fetch wood (Man and Women)
Wa mpona nala di a rotha (Mokgadi)	Look at me, my nails are falling away (Mokgadi)
A re ye ntlong	Let us go to the hut (Man and Women)
Ha ha ha, hi, hi, (laughing loudly)	Ha..ha..ha..hi..hi..(laughing) (Mokgadi)
...as the drum goes up higher! (Mokgadi)	

The male singer who is accompanied by female voices exhorts his wife Mokgadi to go to the river to draw water, to go and grind maize, and to go and fetch wood. All three represent ordinary household chores. Mokgadi responds by flatly refusing: "Look at me, my nails are falling away" means that she is lazy, and consequently, she will not engage in those chores. A sharp turn of events, however, occurs in the fourth line when she is invited to the "hut" for a sexual encounter with her husband. She responds positively, with loud laughter supported by the high volume of the drums. Mokgadi, like the biblical Leah, is thus not embarrassed by her legitimate right to a fulfilling sexual encounter with her husband. It is no wonder that Mokgadi's passionate response to the opportunity to engage in sex rather than in ordinary household chores is viewed with distaste by many traditional African listeners of the song.

The response of the woman in the song as well as Leah's craving to be fully loved by her husband throw light on some of the neglected aspects of women's lives either in sacred texts or secular texts. In my view, such negligence continues to render the full humanness of women invisible. It also renders the marginalization of women as irredeemable even as it undermines the fact that women in our patriarchal contexts are not devoid of power. Although women have power, their power is not legitimated. Indeed, Mokgadi and Leah challenge the status quo and its ideology that sexual pleasure in marriage, both monogamous and polygynous, is the luxury of men only.

It is important that marginalized persons should raise *prophetic* voices toward the injustices which they experience. Leah's persistence in exposing her husband's deprivation of his sexual duties toward her serves as an example of women's capacity to protect their sexual needs. Her tendency to address her concerns to the "wrong" people should be challenged, though. Although

Rachel should not be wholly exonerated from the plight in which her sister was thrown, the right person to address was Jacob and the patriarchal structure which privileged men over women. Mokgadi and Leah remind us that women also, even those within polygynous marriage settings, have the right to sexual pleasure. Women as sexual beings thus need to take pride in their sexuality and sex lives.

Madipoane Masenya (ngwan'a Mphahlele) (Ph.D.) teaches in the Department of Old Testament and Ancient Near Eastern Studies at the University of South Africa.

A Spiritual Reflection on the Life of Jacob

Clarence Mitchell (United States)

The story of Jacob and Esau is one of the Bible stories I remember most from my childhood. Jacob running away after tricking his brother only to end up tricked himself was used to encourage me to always be honest and to never run from my problems. I understood it in theory, but it was not until I had to face a real issue in my own life that this story took on a whole new meaning for me: reconciling with my father.

My dad is a loving but rigid and principled man. If you live under his roof, you follow his rules. When I look back at my childhood there was nothing unfair about his rules; but at the time I felt stifled by them. I didn't feel it was fair that I had to live up to his standards. I didn't understand why he wouldn't consider my desires and my perspective. This all came to a head my freshman year of college.

After several weeks at school I still hadn't heard from him. When I finally called, he didn't sound happy to hear from me, but rather, he gave me a hard time about not calling him. He told me that it was my responsibility and my fault for the lack of communication. Again, I was being told that I had to play by his rules. And even worse, I felt that he expected something of me that he didn't expect of himself. I'd had enough. I was determined not to be the one to reach out. If he wanted to talk to me, he could call me.

Thanksgiving break came and we had not talked for many weeks. Even so, I decided that it was only right that I stop by for Thanksgiving dinner. After all, my stubbornness was pretty immature. I wasn't going to miss out on Thanksgiving at my dad's house because I was annoyed with him. When I got there, I knocked on the door. No answer. I looked in the windows to see if anyone was inside but all of the lights were out. Perplexed, I finally picked up the phone to call him; I learned from my stepmom that they were at my stepsister's house in Fresno for the holiday.

They left town for Thanksgiving and hadn't told me. I felt like a fool for having driven over there, but most of all I felt hurt that no one told me about the plan. Once again he hadn't called, and this time I was excluded from a family gathering.

Needless to say I was upset. For years there was an unspoken animosity that I tried to pretend was not there. The more I pretended there wasn't an issue the more resentful I became, and the more estranged our relationship. I ran away, emotionally. I totally disconnected. I lived life on my own, leaving the safety and comforts of Isaac for the uncharted waters of Laban.

Like Jacob, I was emotionally in a foreign land, indentured to my fears, trying to find my way through life without my father. During that time I fell away from my faith in God, other people, pretty much everything. It seemed like I was running as hard as I could but not getting anywhere. It felt similar to how I imagine Jacob felt when he woke up the next morning to discover Leah in his bed instead of Rachel. Several years passed and I was still at square one. I was still in the same job and the same frustrating places in life. I knew that something had to change, but I wasn't exactly sure what it was. Things may have continued this way were it not for a major event that forced us to reconnect. My grandfather died.

During the week of the funeral and for the next several months my Dad and I finally decided to talk openly and honestly. Then, something amazing happened. He told me about what kind of father my grandfather was to him and the things that he tried to do differently with me. He told me how he thought he succeeded and the ways that he felt he fell short. He didn't make excuses, but rather he gave me perspective. For the first time we talked to each other like men, as father and son.

Then my dad apologized. This was the first time that I had ever seen this side of him. Like Jacob, I had to face the fear of coming home to truly see my father as a person instead of this figure that I had created in my mind as a child. I too apologized for my stubbornness. I told him about all of the things that I would have done differently and for the first time in as long as I could remember I told him that I loved him. It was powerful. In that moment we both felt like Jacob as he anticipated his day of reckoning with Esau. We were afraid. But we could no longer let that fear stop us from coming home, from reconnecting, from being free to open ourselves up to the love that we both held dear in our hearts. We were happy to be close again.

Now when I read this story of Jacob and Esau, the words jump off the page in a totally different way. When I see the foolishness of Jacob, I see the foolishness of my youth. When I read how Jacob was stuck for 20 years working for what Laban promised to give him after seven, I see the years that I spent in my own emotional bondage. I was stuck running in place because I refused to receive the guidance that my father was ready and willing to provide. And when I read about how Jacob prepared to come back home, how he sent gifts of livestock ahead of him, how he knelt before Esau with humility, praying for his forgiveness, I see both me and my father during that fateful time. I see how we offered each other gifts of forgiveness and loving communication, and I thank God that those gifts were a strong enough foundation to start a new chapter in our relationship not only as father and son but also as men. Experience has shown me that the words in the Bible truly have a powerful life of their own; we just have to experience life for ourselves in order to hear them speak their truth.

Clarence Mitchell (B.A., Politics, Philosophy, and Economics, Pomona College) is a Christian blogger (www.aconvowithgod.com) and prayer leader at the Pasadena International House of Prayer.

QUESTIONS

1. Assess the strengths and weaknesses of Poland's view of Rivka/Rebekah. How might one offer a counter reading?

2. How does Phelps-Roper use biblical passages outside of Genesis to bolster her argument? Could one agree with her interpretation of the text, but yet not assent to her theological conclusions?

3. Analyze Masenya's interpretation of Leah. Read the text carefully and raise some challenging questions for Masenya.

4. In what ways do Mitchell's reflections help him understand his own life experiences? Do you see any connections between these biblical stories and your own life?

CHAPTER 6

GENESIS 37–50

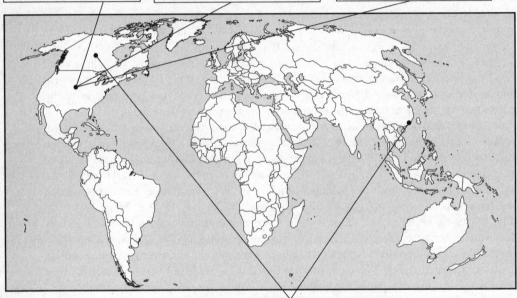

Eric A. Seibert highlights the theme of forgiveness as central to the Joseph narrative, with special attention to the scenes in 45:1–15 and 50:15–21.

Wayne Tarrant employs an economic lens to analyze Joseph's action of saving grain during the years of plenty, which contrasts with policy makers today.

Mona West offers an LGBT reading of the story which shows how garments are used to represent crossing boundaries and to destabilize binary thinking.

Francis G. H. Pang imagines a personal conversation with Joseph about the challenges of moving to a new land and of meeting his family after years of absence.

READINGS

Forgiveness in the Joseph Narrative
Eric A. Seibert

Joseph's Actions and Economic Theory
Wayne Tarrant

An LGBT Reading of Genesis 37–50
Mona West

A Personal Conversation with Joseph
Francis G. H. Pang

FORGIVENESS IN THE JOSEPH NARRATIVE

Eric A. Seibert (United States)

Although the story of Joseph can be read in many different ways, at its core, it is a story about a man who forgave his brothers. The theme of forgiveness, so central to the Joseph narrative, is expressed most vividly in two passages: Genesis 45:1–15 and 50:15–21. This story, with its emphasis on forgiveness rather than retaliation, serves as an especially good example of peace-making and the nonviolent resolution of conflict in the Old Testament.

Early in the narrative, Joseph has a pair of dreams about ruling over his brothers. When he divulges these dreams to his brothers, they are indignant. At an opportune moment, they devise a plan to kill Joseph, though end up selling him instead. Although nothing is initially said about Joseph's reaction to their abuse and hostility, we later learn that Joseph was in "anguish" and plead with his brothers throughout the ordeal, while they turned a deaf ear (42:21).

Two decades later, Joseph sees his brothers again. But now the tables are turned. Joseph is second in command of all Egypt. He has been stockpiling grain for years because God revealed that seven years of famine were coming. When Joseph's brothers come down to Egypt to buy grain, they unknowingly come face-to-face with the brother they had nearly killed. It is only at the end of their second visit that Joseph reveals his identity to them. This dramatic self-disclosure marks the first of two conciliatory scenes between Joseph and his brothers (45:1–15) with the other occurring years later, just after the death of their father Jacob (50:15–21). These two passages contain a number of thematic similarities that emphasize the centrality and importance of forgiveness in the Joseph narrative.

First, both scenes emphasize how Joseph's theological interpretation of events enables him to forgive. When Joseph reveals his true identity to his brothers, he repeatedly claims that his arrival in Egypt was an act of divine providence (cf. 50:20). Although he acknowledges that his brothers *sold* him there, he simultaneously affirms that God *sent* him there. Specifically, Joseph believes he has been divinely dispatched to Egypt "to preserve life" (45:5). Were he to harbor unforgiveness or retaliate against his brothers at this juncture, Joseph might run the risk of being at cross-purposes with God. By framing his circumstances theologically, Joseph is able to forgive his brothers for their outrageous behavior many years prior.

Second, in both passages, Joseph promises to provide food for his brothers and their families on an ongoing basis. This act of kindness demonstrates the depth of Joseph's forgiveness and his determination to care for his brothers despite what they had done to him. After Joseph reveals his identity, he sends a message to his father telling him to resettle the family in Goshen. Joseph says he will provide for their needs and is true to his word (45:10–11; 47:12). Seventeen years later, after his father dies, Joseph's brothers worry that he might finally take his revenge. But Joseph allays their fears by once again promising to provide for them. This makes his forgiveness tangible. It is concrete evidence that his intentions toward his brothers are good. Rather than returning hostility, Joseph extends hospitality. Rather than punishing, Joseph is providing. It seems a striking example of overcoming evil with good (see Romans 12:21).

Third, both passages end with physical and/or verbal assurances that make Joseph's forgiveness visible and personal. While Joseph's emotions are on display at various points throughout the narrative, they are expressed most dramatically when he reveals his identity in 45:14–15. After embracing Benjamin and weeping with him, we are told that Joseph "kissed all his brothers and wept upon them." Joseph also weeps in the final conciliatory scene after which he offers verbal reassurances to his brothers that they need not be afraid. Apparently, Joseph has no intention of retaliating. In both instances, Joseph's behavior reveals the sincerity of his forgiveness as he attempts to assure his brothers that everything is alright between them.

In addition to these two conciliatory scenes, the virtue of forgiving is also apparent when the Joseph narrative is viewed in its broader literary context. It is instructive to note that this narrative is immediately preceded by another story about fraternal strife and forgiveness. Scholars have noted a number of striking similarities between the story of Jacob and Esau in Genesis 25–36 and the story of Joseph and his brothers in Genesis 37–50. Both of these stories include conflict between brothers, the possibility of fratricide, and estrangement leading to decades of separation. Yet both narratives also emphasize the power of forgiveness to resolve fraternal strife, to remove the threat of fratricide, and to reestablish fractured relationships. Stories like these illustrate the enormous value of forgiveness as a way forward.

The importance of forgiveness is further highlighted when the story of Joseph and his brothers at the end of Genesis is compared to the story of Cain and Abel at the beginning. Once again, both stories describe conflict between brothers. But these two stories have very different endings. Cain kills Abel, while Joseph forgives his brothers. Although Joseph easily could have followed the path of Cain, he chooses to forgive instead. By doing so, Joseph's actions demonstrate that violence is neither an inevitable nor unavoidable outcome when dealing with fraternal strife. Other options exist. Reading the Joseph narrative in light of the story of Cain and Abel reminds us that things could have ended very differently for Joseph's brothers. This once again underscores the desirability of forgiveness.

In a sense, Joseph's actions break the cycle of hostility, mistreatment, and violence that appears early in Genesis and continues through much of the book. Joseph's willingness to forgive wrongs committed against him demonstrates how forgiveness functions as an antidote to violence. Forgiveness effectively ends the otherwise endless cycle of violence.

While not everything Joseph does throughout the narrative may be regarded as praiseworthy, his behavior in 45:1–15 and 50:15–21, the two conciliatory scenes discussed here, certainly seems exemplary. These passages represent the kind of texts that can be used to read the Old Testament nonviolently, in ways that do not encourage or endorse contemporary acts of violence. Given the Old Testament's troubling legacy in this regard, as a text that has been used to legitimate various kinds of violence, it seems particularly important to pay special attention to passages like these, passages that emphasize peacemaking, nonretaliation, and forgiveness.

Eric A. Seibert is Associate Professor of Old Testament at Messiah College, Grantham, Pennsylvania, United States; he is the author of Disturbing Divine Behavior: Troubling Old Testament Images of God *and* The Violence of Scripture: Overcoming the Old Testament's Troubling Legacy.

JOSEPH'S ACTIONS AND ECONOMIC THEORY

Wayne Tarrant (United States)

The life of the biblical Joseph could certainly be seen as a series of boom and bust cycles. From being a favored son with all the dreams of a splendid future to being thrown into a pit and sold as a slave, he rose to a position of trust in the house of Potiphar only to be thrown into prison by false testimony. From the depths of prison, Joseph rose to be the overseer of all the inmates, where he used his ability to interpret dreams. Although originally forgotten by the cupbearer for two years, he eventually found a place in the house of Pharaoh. Through the interpretation of Pharaoh's dream, Joseph was able to save an entire country and also his own family. It is this last episode on which I wish to lay an economic viewpoint.

As a reminder, Pharaoh's first dream involves seven fat cows grazing beside the Nile. Seven skinny cows come up to the seven fat cows and devour them. The second dream has seven full heads of grain growing from one stalk. Then seven withered heads of grain grow and swallow the seven good heads. Joseph correctly foretells that this will mean seven years of plenty for Egypt and then seven years of famine.

Joseph takes a series of real economic steps beginning in 41:33. I do not find anything in Pharaoh's dreams that would lead to such an ingenious solution as the one that Joseph proposes. Up to this point in Genesis, I also cannot find a place where someone is asked to save for a rainy day, unless one makes an argument about Noah's plan for the ultimate of rainy days.

Joseph knows that there is going to be an agricultural boom for Egypt for the next seven years. He knows that there will be an abundance of grain during these seven years—even more than the people of Egypt could possible consume will be produced. So Egypt will be left with two choices. The most obvious choice is that Egypt could decide to export the grain to other countries in exchange for some other commodity. Maybe the Egyptians would like grapes and olives from other parts of the world, and so they could exchange their excess grain for the products of another country. In this case the Egyptians could not only consume their fill of grain, but they could also have a variety of items to consume. Or maybe they could choose to exchange for gold, silver, or bronze. There is a great temptation to do just this when you have an excess of an item. But an excess of supply often leads to the realization of lower prices. All the trading partners would have to realize that Egypt has too much grain and needs to dispose of it. Each trading partner could offer less for this grain than during regular production times.

But Joseph knows one additional piece of information. The good years will not last. Although they will have an excess of grain for seven years, there will be a dearth of grain in the seven years that follow. So Joseph devises another plan. We must assume that Joseph undertakes a massive project of building storehouses for grain, as we are told that the grain is stored near the fields that produced it (41:48). He knows that the Egyptians can survive on a fraction of the grain that they will produce in the years of plenty. So he decides to squirrel away 20 percent of the grain each year. In this way they will have grain when the times of famine come. This turns out to be the right solution, because we are told that the entire known world experiences famine. The nice gold, silver, and bronze trinkets they might have had for the grain from the years of plenty would now have to be bartered for grain, likely at a higher price than what they had sold it for during the years of plenty, if grain could even be found.

Further, we are told that Joseph's plan gives Egypt so much grain that he stops keeping a record of what Egypt has stored (41:49). Although some in Egypt might have been discouraged to see grain just piling up, unused, it proves to be a very wise move. In 41:55, we are told that the people of Egypt come to the Pharaoh complaining of hunger and that Joseph's storing of grain allows all of the Egyptians to buy food (41:56). Further, Joseph has stored enough so that he is able to sell to the entire known world (41:57). We do not know if Joseph was a shrewd businessman or not, but the scarcity of food throughout the world could have led to higher prices and greater wealth for Egypt. Or Joseph could have chosen to sell at regular prices and retain allies or allay enemies. In any case, the storing during times of plenty must have made Egypt into a more powerful nation for quite some time. It is notable that this wise solution also leads to Joseph being reunited with his family.

In my mind this is a beginning of Keynesian economics. Keynes's theory says that a government should tax more during times of economic boom. This will alleviate the excess supply of money in the system. During times of economic contraction, the government must step in to supply liquidity, for instance, by fiscal stimulus, so that there is not great suffering. If we can view grain as a form of currency for the Egyptians, then we can apply Keynes's ideas. During the time when there was too much grain, Joseph levied a tax on the produce. One-fifth of the production was to go to the storehouses. During the time of famine, Egypt provided the needed produce so that suffering was alleviated.

Many have claimed that the ongoing destruction of Western economies, particularly the European Union and the United States, is a scathing indictment against Keynesian economics. In truth, if the method of Joseph were used today as then, it is likely that there would be little, if any, problem. The problem seems to be more one of character or of will. During times of recession, governments have been willing to step in to bridge the gap, just as Joseph did and just as Keynes would suggest. However, none of the economic authorities have had the wisdom of Joseph during the times of plenty. Politicians get reelected by promising and delivering to their constituents. This leads to spending more than is collected during times of little but also during times of plenty. The saving that Joseph required of the people during the years of great success is absent. Rather than having a surplus "rainy day fund" from the times of plenty, current governments accrue more debt without regard to the present state of the economy. And this does not lead to saving a country from famine, to being able to sell excess to others at a higher price, or to happy family reunions. While Joseph's position was used responsibly as an opportunity to save lives and appropriate good to his family and among the nations, modern authorities have found themselves in quite another situation altogether.

Wayne Tarrant is a mathematician who has written extensively on risk management as it intersects with economic theory.

An LGBT Reading of Genesis 37–50

Mona West (United States)

The thing most people remember about Joseph is his "coat of many colors" made popular by Andrew Lloyd Webber's *Joseph and the Amazing Technicolor Dream Coat.* Clothing figures prominently in Genesis 37–50. Joseph's coat in Genesis 37—a long robe with special sleeves—angers his brothers because it was actually a woman's garment (2 Samuel 13:18) and is a sign of favoritism from his father Jacob. In Genesis 38 Tamar will take off her widow's garments and put on a prostitute's veil in order to seduce her father-in-law Judah, who later is incriminated by the identifying "clothing" of his signet and cord. Potiphar's wife will use Joseph's garment in Genesis 39 to have him imprisoned because of some perceived impropriety. The Pharaoh makes Joseph an Egyptian in Genesis 41 by giving him his signet and a royal garment. Dressed this way Joseph's brothers do not recognize him when they go to Egypt for food in

42–44. When Joseph reveals his true identity to his brothers, he offers them each a set of garments, and his youngest brother Benjamin gets five sets.

In each of these instances clothing is used to cross rigid boundaries of identity which include gender, ethnicity, and class. The term for this in the Lesbian, Gay, Bisexual, and Transgender (LGBT) community is "cross-dressing." In LGBT culture cross-dressing has been used in powerful ways to disrupt categories of gender. Some gay men, known as "drag queens," will dress and perform as women while still using their male voice. Some lesbians, who are often called "butch," will dress in men's clothes but can still be identified as female because of their breasts. Religious categories have also been disrupted by LGBT people who are "out" as ordained clergy and wear clerical collars and liturgical vestments such as robes, stoles, and chasubles. Of course, not all LGBT people are cross-dressers and we are reminded by the singer Madonna in her performance of "Express Yourself" and the actor Dustin Hoffman who played "Tootsie" that not all cross-dressers are homosexual.

Marjorie Gerber (*Vested Interests: Cross-dressing and Cultural Anxiety* [Routledge: New York, 1992], 10–17) states that cross-dressing is a necessary critique of any kind of binary thinking when it comes to identity: male/female; black/white; Jew/Christian; noble/bourgeois. The cross-dresser or transvestite creates a "third term" which is a "mode of articulation," a space of possibility beyond the either/or of the binary. The function of the cross-dresser in culture is to point to a "category crisis" by being able to cross or make permeable the boundaries of such categories of gender, race, and class, thereby destabilizing the binary.

In the Joseph narrative cross-dressing destabilizes the binaries of youngest/oldest, widow/prostitute, and Hebrew/Egyptian in order to create spaces of possibility for Joseph and his brothers, Tamar and Judah, and the descendants of Jacob as the book of Genesis comes to an end and anticipates the Exodus story.

The theme of the triumph of the youngest son over the oldest weaves throughout the patriarchal and matriarchal narratives of Genesis and we find it in the opening chapters of the Joseph narrative. Jacob, Joseph's father, is one of those who, by cross-dressing as his older brother Esau, steals the birthright (Gen. 27). Now in Genesis 37 Jacob gives a special robe with sleeves to Joseph, one of his youngest sons, as a sign of favor. This coat, especially when Joseph wears it, makes his brothers jealous (not to mention all those grandiose dreams of Joseph's). It will become the sign by which the older brothers declare to their father that Joseph is dead, when in reality he has been sold into slavery.

In this special robe Joseph cross-dresses as a favored son, which destabilizes the binary of youngest/oldest and opens a space of possibility for the brothers to create their identities beyond the rigid boundaries of birthright. We see this at the end of the story when the brothers—especially Judah who is the oldest—attempt to protect Benjamin, who is their father's youngest and favored now that he thinks Joseph is gone.

Tamar cross-dresses as a prostitute in Genesis 38 and seduces her father-in-law, Judah, because he has not fulfilled the law of Levirate Marriage by giving his youngest son to her as a husband in order to raise up male offspring that will insure her place in society as a widow. Her cross-dressing destabilizes the binary of widow/prostitute in order to create a space of possibility in which she becomes the agent of her own destiny. This agency is affirmed by Judah himself, who renders her more righteous than he. He is identified through articles of his own clothing (his signet worn around his neck with a cord) as the one who inseminated Tamar. Interestingly enough when she gives birth to twins, a piece of clothing, a crimson chord, is tied around the wrist of the one who came out first!

The remainder of the Joseph narrative uses cross-dressing to destabilize the binary of Hebrew/Egyptian. There is a tension between Joseph's Hebrew identity and his Egyptian identity once he gets to the house of Potiphar that is sustained until the very end of Genesis and continues on into the Exodus story when Moses struggles with his Hebrew/Egyptian identity.

It is Joseph's "Hebrew garment" that Potiphar's wife uses to accuse him of some impropriety which gets him thrown in prison. But prison winds up being Joseph's passage way into Pharaoh's house and his favor. Because Joseph is able to interpret the Pharaoh's dream and thus prepare the land for a great famine, the Pharaoh sets him over the entire land of Egypt. Moreover, Pharaoh makes Joseph an Egyptian by giving him his signet ring, clothing him in garments of fine linen, and giving Joseph the Egyptian name Zaphenath-paneah and an Egyptian wife, Asenath (41:37–45).

Joseph is really an Egyptian "in drag" and his cross-dressing calls into question these seemingly stable identities. His own brothers do not recognize him when they come before him in Egypt to buy grain, and the blurring of identities continues when Joseph is able to overhear their conversation in Hebrew after accusing them of being spies (42:23). Eventually Joseph "comes out" to his brothers and attempts to cross-dress them as Egyptians when he gives each brother a set of garments while Benjamin, the youngest, gets five sets of garments.

Joseph's cross-dressing as an Egyptian creates a "category crisis" for the larger ancestor narratives that extend into the Exodus story. The boundaries between Hebrew/Egyptian are blurred—Egyptians and Hebrews eat together even though it is an abomination (43:32); the Egyptians sell themselves into slavery to the Hebrew (Joseph) who is an Egyptian in drag (Gen. 47), only to have the Hebrews become the slaves of the Egyptians when a new Pharaoh who did not know Joseph begins to rule (Exodus 1). Joseph's Egyptian sons, Ephraim and Manasseh, are adopted as Hebrews by God in Genesis 48. Cross-dressing Joseph destabilizes the binary of Hebrew/Egyptian in order to open a space of possibility for a *mixed group* to come out of Egypt at the Exodus.

In the same way that Joseph's cross-dressing and "passing" as an Egyptian disrupts the binary of Hebrew/Egyptian, crossing dressing is used in the LGBT community to disrupt the binaries of heterosexual/homosexual and male/female. Effeminate gay men may dress more masculine in order to "pass" as heterosexual—often for their very survival in a sexist, heterosexist culture that is violent toward men who do not look and act like "real men." Lesbians who wear lipstick and dress in feminine ways call into question the heterosexist assumption that all lesbians want to be men. Transgender people cross-dress to identify with the gender they were meant to be when their biological sex is different from that gender identity.

Just like Joseph was able to leverage Egyptian privilege in order for his brothers to survive during a time of great famine, so too LGBT people who pass as heterosexuals are able to leverage heterosexual privilege for their own survival. Even after Joseph "comes out" to his brothers, he remains "Egyptian" to the very end of the story by being buried in Egypt (unlike his father Jacob, who requests to be buried in the land of his ancestors). LGBT people who come out also remain in a heterosexist culture. Just as Joseph's coming out creates a mode of possibility for identities to "blend" as the narrative moves toward the Exodus event, LGBT people who come out also create a mode of possibility for all people to claim the good gift of their sexuality without the need for binary categories—and that is a true Exodus indeed.

Mona West (Ph.D.) is a lesbian, formerly ordained as a Southern Baptist minister, who now serves as Director of Formation and Leadership Development for Metropolitan Community Churches; she is coeditor of Take Back the Word: A Queer Reading of the Bible *and* The Queer Bible Commentary.

A PERSONAL CONVERSATION WITH JOSEPH

Francis G. H. Pang (Hong Kong, Canada)

Twenty years ago I had to leave home for Canada. I asked my mother, "Why do I need to study abroad? Why do I have to leave? Don't we have good schools here?" My mom said, "It's complicated."

"How complicated?" I contested. "After all, you don't want me to live with you; you want me to leave because you want to live with your new husband and new family."

"No! I want you to have a better education and who knows what's going to happen when the government of China takes over us in a few years."

So there I was, sitting in the darkness, alone, couldn't quite speak the language, downright lonely and sacred. Along came this guy who came to me and said, "I know how you feel, my friend."

"You know?" I said, "What do you know? I am forced to come here. My family doesn't want me to be part of them anymore. And they gave me some lame political reason. It is so unfair! I want to go home. I want to go back to my friends and the people I love."

"Yes, it is unfair, I know," he said. "I was sold to be a slave in a foreign country far away from home by my half brothers. I felt betrayed and, of course, very bitter, at the time. I even blamed my dad for not coming to save me. There I was, like you now, a resident alien in a foreign country with a language that I hardly understood. I was pretty lost."

"Oh so it's you, I know you, I've heard the story about you and your eleven brothers. You are Joseph." I said.

"Yes, that's me," he said. "There are always two sides of the coin. On the brighter side, the language barrier actually helped me to improve my communication skills. You see, when you are learning a new language you think twice before you say anything. It is like doing a quick translation in your head before every sentence you say. I used to be a brash kid, badmouthing my brothers and bragging about my dreams, but I learned to be much tactful by the time I stood before Pharaoh. Indeed, I had plenty of time in prison to reflect on my character issues."

"I guess you are right," I nodded, "but I still think it is easy for you to say this in retrospect, cause even you took a long time to finally make peace with your past. Just look at the names of your sons."

"What about it?" he protested.

"You named your firstborn son Manasseh ("forget"), claiming that God had made you forget about your hardship and your family. But by calling him that, every time you utter his name you are actually reminding yourself about your past! In a sense," I continued my little speech, "you are constantly asking yourself to put the past behind you. So that's why I said it takes time to heal. See, even after you have ascended to the top, even after you have settled down and have a family of your own, even a very luxurious lifestyle cannot rescue you from the demons of your past, at least not until after your second son was born. If naming means anything, the name Ephraim ("twice fruitful") tells us that you are looking at the brighter side of things. Even though your past suffering still lingers in your mind, at least you can turn around and focus on the blessings in your life."

"Yes, you are right, it takes time," he said with a smile on his face, "but time is not the antidote to my bitterness toward my past and my family. Time may take the edge off the pain, but the real remedy is from God. You have to look past the surface and see things God's way."

"But how?" I asked.

"It is hard to describe, but to borrow a term from psychology, it is a matter of 'reframing.'"

"Reframing?" I was puzzled. "What is that?"

"Simply put, you have to put things into another perspective, trying to look at the same situation from another angle. I will say it is also an act of divine grace. You see, during my time in Egypt, I was always bothered by the thought that it was my brothers' evil intent that took me to Egypt to suffer, so I always felt bitter, even after I became the vizier of Egypt. But when my brothers came kneeling down before me and begging for food during the famine, it all became clear to me. It gave everything a new meaning—the dream, the famine, everything started to make sense to me. Of course, the revelation of divine intervention and providence did not instantly take away my bitterness. But it provided an impetus for what came after."

"So you are telling me that I will find out in the future why I am here?" I asked.

"Be patient, my friend, it will either come to you or it will become unimportant. Be patient and trust in the Lord."

So we went on and talked about his life in Egypt. I asked him all kinds of questions—what he thought about the comparison between him and the prophet Daniel, and so on.

Time always goes faster than it seems when you look back. And he was right; my perspective on my family and my life in general has changed. After almost a decade, this once very foreign land has turned into familiar territory. I became a diehard Maple Leafs fan and called myself Canadian Chinese. And at the same time I almost forgot about the problem I had with my family. In fact, the idea of going home seems less and less attractive. Thus when I had to go home after my work permit expired, I was devastated and could not shake away the feelings of déjà vu. It was cultural identity crisis all over again. But I had no choice.

So I went back to this crowded city I once called home. My world turned upside down. The language I once spoke with ease all of a sudden seemed so foreign; the friends that were once very close seemed so distant. I was lost, again. Then Joseph came to me.

"So, how are you there? You are finally home," he said with a grin on his face.

"Home? Honestly I am quite confused: Where is home?" I muttered, pondering the question.

"Oh, I see. Having a hard time adjusting to a 'new' place all over again, right?" he asked.

"Yes, it is as if people don't know me anymore. When I talk to them, it seems as if they don't understand me at all. Even though I try to tell people what I have been through in the past ten years, it still seems very hard for them to accept the new me," I said.

"It is hard," he answered, "especially after all these years people can only remember bits and pieces about you from the past. Between now and then, there is a huge gap which needs to be filled. People seem unable to shake away their perception of the old you. The same also happened to me. After I finally made peace with my brothers, they doubted that I'd changed. They did not believe that I was not their brash little brother anymore. They even lied to me about my father, telling me that he asked me to forgive them from his deathbed."

"Yes, I remembered that part." I said. "But you forgave them nonetheless, even took an extra step and reassured them that you would never harm them. God must have really changed your perspective on your past."

"Take heart, my friend, it may take a bit longer for other people to discover this 'new' you, but the most important thing is that God is always with you, no matter where you call home. He is your family and wherever he is, there too is your home."

Francis G. H. Pang, originally from Hong Kong, is a Ph.D. candidate at McMaster Divinity College, Canada.

QUESTIONS

1. Seibert claims that "at its core" the story is about a man who forgave his brothers. What other "cores," that is, central themes, might one identify?
2. Tarrant praises Joseph's economic decisions in Genesis 41. How might Tarrant evaluate Joseph's policies in Genesis 47? What do you think of Joseph's later tactics?
3. Explain the significance of "cross-dressing" for West. What questions might one raise about her general approach and careful textual analysis?
4. Is Pang's presentation of Joseph faithful to the biblical image? Could one imagine Joseph having a different sort of conversation with Pang?

CHAPTER 7

EXODUS 1–15

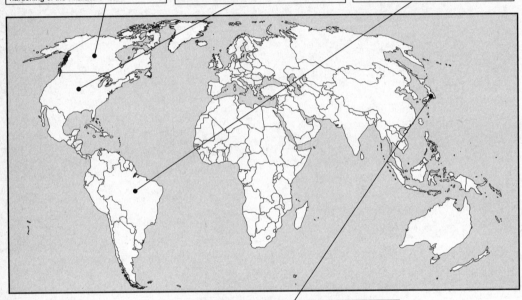

Vanessa R. Sasson reads two aspects of the text through a Buddhist lens: Moses and the Egyptian taskmaster (2:11–15) and the hardening of the Pharaoh's heart.

Megan Bishop Moore reveals the problems of reading the story as accurate history, which leads her to propose that it is better understood as historical fiction.

Gilbert Lozano discusses the policies of the conquistadores and current conditions in Brazil, suggesting the need for a liberationist reading of the biblical story.

Eiko Hanaoka(-Kawamura) compares the revelation of the divine name in 3:14—"I am"—with Japanese philosopher Kitaro Nishida's concept of God.

READINGS

Two Aspects of Exodus through a Buddhist Lens
Vanessa R. Sasson

The Divine Name and Kitaro Nishida's Concept of God
Eiko Hanaoka(-Kawamura)

The Exodus Story as Historical Fiction
Megan Bishop Moore

A Liberationist Reading of the Exodus Story
Gilbert Lozano

Two Aspects of Exodus through a Buddhist Lens

Vanessa R. Sasson (Canada)

Two aspects of the story of Moses and the Exodus can be fruitfully read through a Buddhist lens. The first concerns the scene with Moses and the taskmaster (2:11–15). The Bible tells us virtually nothing about how Moses was raised. His birth story is one of the most famous of the biblical tradition, but beyond that narrative, little is revealed about his early years. He is born an Israelite, but raised as an Egyptian. The question is then, When exactly did Moses discover that he was an Israelite? The text is not clear.

The first time we encounter Moses after his birth is as a young man. According to 2:11, Moses "went out to his people and saw their forced labor. He saw an Egyptian beating a Hebrew, one of his kinfolk." Here it sounds as though Moses is suddenly identifying with the Hebrew slaves, relating to them as his family members. Indeed, he is so overwhelmed by their situation, and by this slave being hit in front of him in particular, that he responds by killing the Egyptian taskmaster (2:12). It is no surprise that so many interpreters assume Moses knew he was a Hebrew before this scene. The story leads the reader in that direction: Moses must have discovered that he was a Hebrew and only then identified with the slaves at his doorstep. He is, moreover, crazed by their suffering and reacts violently—the response of a man who is overwhelmed by new information and has not managed to process it yet.

But what if we were to read the text differently? I have long believed that this is the story not of a man who reacts emotionally to his own people's suffering but rather of a much more universal awakening—a moment that is so powerful, it catapults Moses from one state of being to another and shatters whatever normalcy he had hitherto sheltered himself with. If Moses reacts to the slave only once he knows that he too is an Israelite, then what we have is a man who is moved to action only when his own community is affected. While that may make sense historically and in the context of the Ancient Near East, in which tribal affiliation was paramount, in the realm of mythical heroes and adventures, such a self-centered response would not be very inspiring. Moses must have been greater than that.

The story of the Buddha's awakening may be traced to a number of factors, but one of them is particularly pertinent to this discussion. According to many of the early sources, when the Buddha was a young man, he came across some laborers working in the fields. He watched the beasts of burden toiling the earth; saw the laborers darkened by the sun and covered with sweat; and witnessed innumerable insects, frogs, and snakes being overturned by the plows. His heart was overwhelmed with all of the suffering produced by an ordinary fact of life, and this eventually moved him to leave home to find an answer to the suffering he felt incapable of surmounting. It was a small moment—a picture he must have come across a thousand times before—but for some reason, on that day, the image of labor, suffering, and death pierced his heart and transformed him irrevocably.

I see Moses' story in a similar light. Moses must have come across the slaves on a regular basis. They were surely a fact of his life, something to be expected and ignored much like the homeless people many of us pass on the street. We know they are there, we see them on a daily basis, but we don't really look at them. They are just part of the landscape. But one day, Moses woke up and looked outside and saw the slaves as though for the first time. He saw his "brethren," his fellow human beings, and he could not walk past them blindly again. He looked at them with clear sight and recognized their humanity.

To assume that Moses knew he was an Israelite before this scene limits Moses as a hero. It renders him too self-centered for my Buddhist reading to accommodate. As a universal hero, Moses must have seen the slaves as his fellow human beings, and not simply as his fellow tribesmen. The challenge presented by the Buddhist parallel, however, has to do with his relationship to the oppressors. The Buddha watched men plowing the fields and was overwhelmed with compassion for all the creatures affected: the animals, the men, and the insects. The Buddha did not distinguish one group from another in his emotive response; he did not strike down the men for the suffering they were causing the animals and insects, but appears to have felt compassion for everyone's suffering equally. Moses may have woken to a common humanity when he looked at the slaves, but the taskmaster he killed remained outside his purview. His compassion flowed in only one direction. The question I am therefore left with is whether Moses ever came to see the taskmasters as his brothers too.

The second issue in the Exodus story that can be read through a Buddhist lens concerns one of the most difficult themes of the Hebrew Bible: the hardening of the Pharaoh's heart (7:5, 22; 8:11, 15, etc.). When Moses receives his instructions at the burning bush, God tells him (long before he even returns to Egypt), that he (God) will "harden Pharaoh's heart, and he will not let the people go" (4:21).

What are we to make of this? The text seems to be suggesting that the entire story of the plagues and the exodus was a set-up, predetermined long before any of the characters have a chance to make their own decisions. God will harden the Pharaoh's heart—make him stubborn as some translations have it—and will not let the people go. He will therefore battle with the Pharaoh and demonstrate his many wonders, so that the Egyptians may finally know that he is God (7:5).

Does the Pharaoh not have free will then? And what about Moses? Does he have free will? Moses clearly was reticent to take the job. He struggles with a bramble of excuses to be let off the hook, but God will not hear any of it. Moses is required to speak on his behalf, and the Pharaoh is required to say no. The only real actor in the narrative appears to be God, with everyone else connected to puppet strings from above.

I see in this story a problem that all religions struggle with: How much do we control and how much belongs to a power beyond us? There is no easy answer to this question. We would like to believe we have control, and yet at the same time there is something comforting in the idea that we are not responsible, not in control, and possibly even deeply irrelevant in some way. A burden is removed from our shoulders when we place it all on an otherworldly system instead.

Buddhism struggles with this same question, but the language is one of karma. There are certain inescapable realities that are determined by the karma accumulated in previous lifetimes. The Buddha's awakening is an example of this: His accumulated karma leads him to Buddhahood, rendering all potential attempts at obstruction doomed to failure. Whether Mara (a kind of devil) or anyone else tried to get in his way, the fact remained that Siddhartha was destined to achieve Buddhahood in that lifetime. Even if he himself wanted to do otherwise, he could not escape the footprints awaiting his feet. The powers of the universe conspired together to ensure that he made his way to an awakening that would change the world.

The story of the Pharaoh's hardened heart seems to me a kind of inescapable karma. The outcome is already written and it is just a question of time before the Pharaoh and Moses fulfill their roles accordingly. I don't think this story can be made comfortable though. Neither predetermination nor karma is an ultimately comfortable idea. The rabbis traditionally saw in this story a kind of justice in which the Pharaoh becomes the symbol of Egyptian wrongs, required to pay for the hundreds of years of enslavement the Israelites were forced to endure. But from a modern perspective, such a reading is unsatisfactory: Why would one Pharaoh along with one generation of Egyptians be forced to pay for the mistakes of the past? How would we feel if we were suddenly forced to pay for the mistakes we inherited from our own ancestors? Would justice not at least require that the Supreme Judge offer the Pharaoh a genuine opportunity to change his ways first?

We want to be in control of our lives, to believe that somehow our actions will be reflected in the makeup of our life's outcomes. But deep down inside, we wonder if we really are in charge of anything. When God declares that he will harden the Pharaoh's heart, it is to me a window into the question of human significance. It is akin to the Buddha not having a choice about which path to take as a young man: He is bound to Buddhahood just as the Pharaoh is bound to destruction (and Moses is bound to the pains of prophethood). The hardening of the Pharaoh's heart is meant to be uncomfortable, and that is precisely its most subtle wisdom.

Vanessa R. Sasson is Professor of Religious Studies in the Liberal Arts Department of Marianopolis College, Canada; she has authored several books, including The Birth of Moses and the Buddha: A Paradigm for the Comparative Study of Religions.

The Divine Name and Kitaro Nishida's Concept of God

Eiko Hanaoka(-Kawamura) (Japan)

The first original philosopher in Japan, Kitaro Nishida (1870–1945), understood God as the "Absolute Nothingness," which means the negation of the substantialization and the absolutization of all things and standpoints. A similar way of thinking about God is found in Exodus 3:14, where God is named with the Hebrew verb *hayah*, meaning "to be," "to exist," "to become," and is typically translated "I am." Here God is not an onto-theological substantial God. That is to say, God is not substance or essence or being (person). Rather God is the Acting One, who works as one with the events in our daily life.

Likewise for Nishida, God is also not a substantial onto-theological God. Rather God is one who always works to be able to support each of us with *agape* (perfect love). God, then, is better thought of as acting or functioning, rather than as a separate being. This is precisely the understanding of God that the contemporary world needs.

History shows that postulating a substantial onto-theological God has led to nihilism, as Nietzsche predicted. Nihilism argues that life is without any meaning, purpose, or intrinsic value. The Jewish and Christian traditions hold to a concept of God as being. This God is the basis for all morals and values. God provides the objective truth, the objective standard by which all else can be evaluated. But once it is realized that the Judeo-Christian God is a human construction, then that God ceases to be able to offer any objective meaning, purpose, and value to life. Thus, belief in such a God falls apart and nihilism emerges. Hence, Nietzsche's famous aphorism that "God is dead."

But if we follow the lead of Exodus 3 and Nishida, then other ways of thinking about the nature of God open up. It is true that Nishida's term of "absolute nothingness" and the phrase

"I am that I am" as the name of God are not exactly the same idea. However, in both cases, God is understood as an Action. The Hebrew verb *hayah* means not only "to be" but also "to cause to be," "to become," or "to give rise to." For Nishida, God as "absolute nothingness" is God as action or working—and simultaneously as *agape*. The idea is that the self who tries to live out love as *agape* or compassion negates absolutizing his or her own standpoint. That is, the self-less sacrificing of *agape* necessarily negates the will and desires of the self, the ego—becoming absolute nothingness.

In this way, Nishida helps us link the God of Exodus 3 with the New Testament notion that "God is love." If God is not a being, but rather the action of love, then nihilism can be avoided. God is not a being who creates or is the source of objective moral standards and values which give life meaning and purpose. Rather God is the "absolute nothingness" which negates the self (and all else), allowing one to exercise *agape*. This indeed is a concept of God that our world dearly needs to embrace.

Eiko Hanaoka(-Kawamura) is Professor Emeritus at the Graduate School of Osaka Prefecture University, Japan; he is Vice-President and the chief editor of The Japan Society for Process Studies.

THE EXODUS STORY AS HISTORICAL FICTION

Megan Bishop Moore (United States)

The exodus from Egypt and the wilderness wanderings, which are described in Exodus 1–19 and in parts of Numbers and Deuteronomy and which comprise the background for the books of Exodus–Deuteronomy, are the first events in the biblical story where Israel is portrayed as, and acts as, a large, unified group. These descendants of the 12 sons of Jacob, the story reports, were enslaved in Egypt but were freed by God acting through Moses. Their escape from Egypt was a dramatic event, but their lives quickly became more mundane as they camped in the wilderness (or desert) for 40 years. During this time, however, God revealed to them important laws of conduct and social organization. Finally, the Israelites invaded the land of Canaan and conquered it for their own settlement.

Since the eighteenth century C.E., scholars of the Bible have been interested in the historical truth of the Hebrew Bible/Old Testament stories, and the exodus and wandering stories were no exceptions. For the most part, the biblical stories of the Israelites' or Hebrews' presence in Egypt, including their slavery, as well as their escape and wanderings, were believed to be historical fact. Following the decipherment of hieroglyphs in the early nineteenth century (made possible by the discovery of the Rosetta Stone by Napoleon's troops in 1799 and the work of Jean Champillon), historians felt they surely had the tools to confirm these events. However, over two subsequent centuries of research, including advanced Egyptology and archaeology, have failed to provide any proof that the stories accurately reflect events and conditions in Egypt and the desert prior to Israel's emergence in Palestine (between 1100 and 900 B.C.E.). Rather, the stories appear to be plausible historical fiction, written at least a half-century after the events they describe, with their intent having been to tell of Israel's salvation by Yahweh and debt to him, rather than to report history as we moderns understand it.

Applying normal historical analysis to the stories of the exodus and wanderings exposes a number of uncertainties and problems. First, the Bible gives different dates for the exodus, and each of these dates is a relative date; that is, it locates the exodus in relation to another biblical event for which an absolute date is also unknown. The exodus is said to have occurred 480 years before Solomon's fourth year (1 Kings 6:1), but this figure (12 × 40) seems to do more with dating the temple's construction than the exodus (and in another ancient version, 1 Kings 6:1 has 440 years). In any case, with no firm chronological marker for either the temple's construction or Solomon's ascendancy (in fact, we have no evidence of Solomon or his building of the temple outside of the Bible), this information can be interpreted as suggesting a mid-fifteenth-century B.C.E. date for the exodus. Another set of dates describes the exodus in relation to Jacob's family's arrival in Egypt: 430 years (Exod. 12:40), 400 years (Genesis 15:13), or three generations (Genesis 15:16). These claims are not only contradictory, but entirely unhelpful historically, as no historical information about Joseph exists. Interestingly, even conservative biblical historians of the mid-twentieth century were willing to ignore the implications of these biblical dates and press for a thirteenth-century B.C.E. date for the exodus, based on their interpretation of archaeological evidence (that was later debunked).

Another difficulty for scholars attempting to use sound historical methodology to examine the exodus stories is that the relevant biblical stories appear to be a compilation of various sources whose dates and provenance are impossible to know, and whose reports can be contradictory. For instance, the documentary hypothesis recognizes three sources at work in the exodus story, but none of the 10 plagues appears in every one. Recognizing this, scholars of the early and mid-twentieth century searched for the oldest, and therefore, they assumed, most reliable pieces of the exodus story. Some concluded that the poetry was the oldest and therefore potentially the most accurate, including the "Song of Moses" (Exod. 15:1–19) and the "Song of Miriam" (Exod. 15:21b). Of course, there is no way to prove that these particular pieces should be singled out as old and reliable. Other related theories that posited that the exodus stories were written in the second millennium B.C.E. were more soundly refuted, such as the idea that the book of Exodus was based on a treaty form known from around 1200 B.C.E.

Additional problems for historians relate to the lack of connections with the great deal that is known about ancient Egypt. For instance, the Pharaoh of the story is not named (though Rameses II has been a popular candidate for decades, since one of the cities named in the story is "Rameses"). No single Pharaoh fits the bill for this character. Even more tellingly, no evidence of the plagues can be found in Egyptian records. It is highly unlikely that any of them, most especially a tragedy so unique and widespread as the death of all the firstborn sons in Egypt, that would dramatically impact not only Egypt but the entire civilized world at that time would go unmentioned and unanalyzed by Egyptian chroniclers. Moses' relationship to and battle with the unnamed Pharaoh is a great story with compelling characters and a riveting plot, but not one that can be taken at face value as a report of real events that occurred in an advanced civilization that left copious records of its existence.

By normal methods of history, then, no history of the exodus or wilderness period can be written. Nevertheless, some scholars maintain that the biblical stories about them are at least plausible in a thirteenth-century B.C.E. Egyptian context. They point to the Egyptian flavor of the stories, including personal and place names (e.g., Moses, Asenath, and Rameses), the known presence of Semites in Egypt in the Late Bronze Age, and the forms of some of the laws given in the wilderness, which they say have thirteenth-century parallels in form and content. These scholars have been challenged by others who claim that the stories have few details about Egypt, many anachronisms, and such a general portrayal that they could have been written in, or set in, almost any ancient time period. There is also a growing opinion that certain clues point definitively to a Persian Period date of composition (late seventh to mid-fourth century B.C.E.), the time when many scholars now believe a substantial part of the Hebrew Bible/Old Testament was written.

Despite popular interest in the exodus events, and the importance of these stories to Israel's identity, they, like many of the other biblical narratives, cannot be definitively located in any time period. The biblical evidence is problematic, vague, and sometimes contradictory, and no extrabiblical evidence affirms any aspect of the stories. As a literary composition, then, the exodus narrative is a compelling historical fiction that originally told the story of God's power and salvation for Israelites trapped in a foreign land, and has lent itself to reinterpretations and retellings over more than 2,000 years.

Megan Bishop Moore is the author of Philosophy and Practice in Writing a History of Ancient Israel *and coauthor of* Biblical History and Israel's Past: The Changing Study of the Bible and History; *she is affiliated with Wake Forest University.*

A LIBERATIONIST READING OF THE EXODUS STORY

Gilbert Lozano (Brazil)

The book of Exodus derives its name from a Greek word that means *exit*. It refers to the exit or departure of the Israelites from the land of Egypt. Before that story, however, the book tells the story of how the Israelites had grown in number from the first 70 of Jacob's descendants who had gone to Egypt. The family had grown enormously until it had reached a point when their numbers were seen as a threat by the Egyptian king, who then embarked on several unjust policies. Exodus 1 tells how pharaoh had imposed slavery on the Israelites, and also how he had ordered the destruction of male infants as a way of preventing the possibility of rebellion.

This type of genocidal policy is all too well-known throughout the world, and especially in Latin America. The pharaoh of the story of Exodus was not the first, nor will he be the last, ruler to impose it upon a people. In Brazil, as throughout all of Latin America, the European conquistadores upon their arrival imposed harsh slavery on the native inhabitants. So harsh was the treatment of the Indians (as they came to be known by the European conquerors) that just within a few decades, a population of several million had been decimated. In the context of Latin America, the fate of millions of people was often decided thousands of miles away in the royal palaces of Spain and Portugal. In fact, it was often discussed whether the Indians were truly humans, and whether they had souls. There is probably a connection between the way the Europeans treated the natives and what they thought regarding their lack of humanity. In other words, because the Indians were considered mere creatures of nature, they did not enjoy the same treatment given to those considered to be full human beings. When the Indian populations had been reduced by exploitation, overwork, and death, the Europeans resorted to African slaves in order to provide the labor necessary for the maintenance of the enormous sugarcane estates that supplied the sugar consumed in the European metropolis. Slavery was officially abolished in Brazil in 1888, but not before millions of Indians had been worked to death and millions of Africans had been forcibly removed from their lands and taken to a new continent thousands of miles from their ancestral homes.

Sadly, today we still speak of slave-like working conditions in many parts of Brazil. Just in the year 2010 more than 3,000 persons were found living in such conditions in Brazil. The situation is aggravated by the high concentration of land in the country—the second highest in the world. Latin America, in fact, wins the unfortunate title of being the continent with the largest concentration of land in the hands of the fewest people. The masses do not have access to arable land because it is concentrated in huge estates owned by corporations or rich businessmen, who often live in cities. The working conditions in many of those estates are comparable to slavery. People work for meager wages—if they are paid at all—or for the food they eat and the clothes they wear, and they incur debts which they can never pay back.

The book of Exodus tells that when the pharaoh ordered the annihilation of the male infants, his orders were challenged by the midwives who delivered the Hebrew babies. Moreover, Hebrew mothers also engaged in similar acts of civil disobedience. One of them, Jochebed, refused to obey the law to kill her baby. Probably like many other mothers, she saved her baby, who, by a curious and ironic twist, was raised in the imperial palace, and eventually became the leader of the Israelites. This slave population cried to their God (2:23–25), Yahweh (the Lord), who heard their cries and sent Moses to deliver them. It was the suffering of the Israelites which had moved Yahweh to action in the first place. Though Moses was raised within the Egyptian court and enjoyed a life of privilege, the text points out that Moses is incensed by injustice (2:11–13, 17). The pharaoh, however, stubbornly refused to allow the people to leave, facing, then, God's punishment upon him and his nation.

The story of the liberation of the Israelites from their slavery in Egypt served as one of the most important stories in Latin American liberation theology. For more than three decades (from the mid-1960s to the mid-1990s), the story of the Exodus was used in popular church communities organized in many parishes, especially in northeastern Brazil. This story served to animate the peasants, many of whom identified with the characters in the story because they too were oppressed and cried out for help to the same God who had freed the Israelites many centuries ago. The story was then a favorite among the people, but it was also used by those theologians who were working within this context. Thus, names like Gustavo Gutiérrez, Juan Luis Segundo, Leonardo Boff, and others used the story of the Exodus of the Israelites from Egypt to show that the basic thrust of the Bible is the liberation of the oppressed and that throughout history God has made a preferential option for the poor. Seeing that the God of the Exodus hears the cry of the oppressed, appoints a leader to lead the people out of their conditions, and punishes the system that had oppressed his people, liberation theologians pointed out that the whole thrust of the Bible moved in a similar direction. Thus, in their reading, history inexorably advances toward the liberation of all oppressed people and the removal of oppressive structures.

It is somewhat unfortunate that liberation theology, at least in this part of the world, has lost a great deal of its appeal. The main articulators of that theology have grown old, most have retired, and others have died. The newer theologians here don't have the same interests as previous generations—not that the pressing concerns that plague this continent have gone away. On the contrary, the story of liberation, as told in the book of Exodus, still resonates powerfully in our context, especially since the issues of slavery, economic oppression, inequality, human rights abuses, government corruption, and similar troubles continue to afflict millions of people in this vast continent. The story of a God who hears the cry of the poor and sides with them bringing about their freedom is one that Latin Americans and people everywhere still need to hear.

Gilbert Lozano (Ph.D.) taught at Fidelis, the Mennonite School of Theology, Curitiba, Brazil, and is currently Associate Professor of Biblical Studies at Anderson University, United States.

QUESTIONS

1. Based on the biblical text, make a case both for and against Moses coming to see the taskmasters as his brothers.

2. Explain how Hanaoka connects the revelation of the divine name in Exodus 3:14 with the New Testament concept of God as love.

3. Hypothesize as to why people, prior to important discoveries, assumed that the stories were historical fact. In your experience, does this belief persist among many people? If so, why?

4. Compare and contrast the situation of the Israelites in Egypt and the "Indians" with the conquistadores. Are the differences important?

CHAPTER 8

EXODUS 20

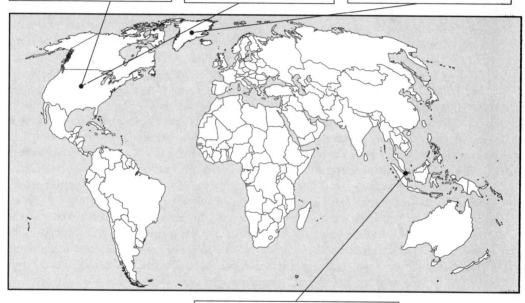

Febbie C. Dickerson explains how the Ten Commandments are understood by her African-American community as a means for establishing right relationships.

Jonathan Redding argues that the Ten Commandments are not applicable in the United States today in light of separation of church and state.

Flemming A. J. Nielsen details the challenges of European missionaries who translated the Ten Commandments into the native language of Greenland.

Maggie Low explains the challenges of honoring God and honoring parents in a Confucian context, where honoring parents supersedes all other duties.

READINGS

The Ten Commandments in an African-American Community
Febbie C. Dickerson

The Ten Commandments and the Separation of Church and State
Jonathan Redding

Confucius and the Fifth Commandment
Maggie Low

The Ten Commandments in Greenland
Flemming A. J. Nielsen

THE TEN COMMANDMENTS IN AN AFRICAN-AMERICAN COMMUNITY

Febbie C. Dickerson (United States)

The Ten Commandments are the words of God spoken directly to the mixed multitude liberated from slavery in Egypt. These commandments provided directions for right relationship with God and neighbor, and they also provided order and stability to a group attempting to find its new identity as free people on the way to the Promised Land. For many African-Americans living with the legacy of slavery, the Ten Commandments were not only moral and theological mandates, they were also assurances of a liberation from social and economic discrimination.

Both the gateway to the South and a notch in the Bible belt, Atlanta distinguishes itself by its welcoming of African-American communities. Along with its vibrant African-American churches, this cosmopolitan city is a center of African-American political success, educational aspirations, and economic prosperity. Atlanta has elected an African-American mayor for the past 38 years. It is the only U.S. city with five historically black colleges and universities. The Atlanta Thrashers has the largest percentage of African-American players in the National Hockey League. Economically, Atlanta has one of the largest concentrations of black affluent and middle-class populations. Atlanta also remains a major hub of the Civil Rights movement and home to the Southern Christian Leadership Conference.

Nevertheless, this shining legacy of Atlanta was born out of the Jim Crow south—the era of racial segregation. My grandparents and parents suffered the indignation of the so-called "separate but equal" system. When I was a young girl, my grandmother showed me the separate entrances for blacks at Atlanta's landmarks. Although bolted shut now, the entrance for African-Americans at the "Fabulous Fox Theater" is still visible. The legacy of Jim Crow continues to permeate our lived experiences—in the voice of my then seventh-grade classmate who called me a nigger, in the eyes of my now 10-year-old niece who perceived that her teacher wanted a white student to be academically superior, and from the perspective of African-Americans still trapped in the grip of poverty with limited access to education. Even more pernicious, the legacies of Jim Crow become internalized; like the Israelites in the desert, we live in free bodies, but our minds and our spirits still feel the shackles.

I am an heir to the histories of Atlanta's progress and oppression. I was born and raised in Atlanta and I grew up in a suburban neighborhood with a mixture of black and white families. Eventually the phenomenon of "white flight" gripped some of our neighbors and the neighborhood became an African-American community. Along with seeking diversity in our living space, my parents endeavored to provide me with diversity in my education. Consequently, in my primary school years I was a part of a group of minority students who integrated more fully one of the public schools. Given the complexity of living in a thriving African-American culture but in some instances still viewed as second class, my church was the place that helped me to live within my racially and culturally mixed society. The Bible and the church were necessary foundations for peaceful living.

The Bible, specifically the Old Testament, is central to many African-American religious communities. African-Americans have historically viewed Israel's Exodus from Egypt as a model for African-American liberation. As the enslaved Africans and their descendents read themselves into the stories of Exodus, they laid claim to an identity as Israel, God's people. Pharaoh was the slave master and Moses was the title given to anyone deemed a freedom fighter. Because we identified with Israel, a main understanding from my context was that the Ten Commandments were a sacred reminder of God's presence in our lives. The older folks in my church understood the commandments to be God's requirements for us to "Remember the Sabbath and keep it holy." Complete the housework and schoolwork by Saturday evenings because Sundays were the time to rest just as God rested. Honor your mom and dad, don't murder, don't steal, and don't tell lies against your neighbor were viewed less as prohibitions than as the way in which the divine presence was experienced. If one followed the commandments, one's life was in order. Therefore, we tried our best to adhere to the commandments. In doing so, we viewed the success of our city, our church, and our families as blessings and rewards for the faithful adherence to God's words.

The Ten Commandments were more than just moral guidelines: They offered theological hope. The opening of the Decalogue cannot be separated from its requirements. The mighty works of God provided for our needs. "I am the Lord your God who brought you out of the land of Egypt; out of the house of slavery." We internalized the text, and so we heard, "I am the Lord your God who brought your ancestors out of Jim Crow. I am the Lord your God who has provided you quality jobs so that your families may prosper. I am the Lord your God who has sustained your health. I am the Lord your God who has watched over your children. I am the Lord your God who has spared you from danger. Therefore, you shall have no other gods before me. You shall not make for yourself idols, for I the Lord your God am a jealous God." We understood those idols to be any material possession that took precedence over our reverence for God.

While the accounts of the Exodus and the Decalogue are about a people liberated less because of the evils of slavery than because God remembered the covenant with Abraham, we chose to see that story as our story and we chose to read it as proclaiming a God who liberated as an act of justice. One may point to other factors impacting the success of African-Americans in Atlanta, but we choose to see our success as related to our biblical values, our concern for right relationships between ourselves and our neighbors, and ourselves and God. We kept the Ten Commandments because we wanted to keep them. The commandments allowed us to live in hope and to see God as our eternal equalizer.

Febbie C. Dickerson is a Ph.D. candidate at Vanderbilt University, Nashville, Tennessee, United States.

THE TEN COMMANDMENTS AND THE SEPARATION OF CHURCH AND STATE

Jonathan Redding (United States)

Having been raised in the American South, I experienced a plethora of children's sermons, Vacation Bible School stories, and Sunday school lessons on the Ten Commandments. But what has surprised me as I have grown up is the arguments and legal battles over the legality of displaying the Ten Commandments on public buildings. Such controversy still seems to arise every few years with varied results and resolutions. But the continual presence of these fights testifies to the fact that many people, especially in the American South, still think that the Ten Commandments are a suitable set of laws for us in the United States today. They seem to think that if only people followed the Ten Commandments, everything would be so much better. To my mind, this reflects the deeply misguided belief that the Bible and/or Protestant Christianity is the panacea for what ails the world.

These 17 verses are etched into the psyche of many Southerners, most of whom could name more commandments than local past state senators. Yet few of these very same people go a single day, or perhaps a week, without breaking a commandment—and they do so with no remorse or compunction. The most obvious such example is the fourth commandment: To do no work on the Sabbath day. Never mind that the Sabbath is the seventh day of the week (Saturday), and not the first day of the week (Sunday), few Christians set aside a whole entire day (Sunday) of rest dedicated to God. Sure, they may not actually go to their place of employment, but they prepare meals, take care of household duties, and participate in other activities which constitute work. (The Jewish tradition has developed a complex set of regulations that outlines what constitutes "work" on the Sabbath.) There are other commandments, too, which many Christians seem to violate. For example, I've been taught that Jesus is God and yet I've seen many images of Jesus—pictures of him with little children, paintings of him on the cross, and so forth. Isn't this a violation of the second command: You shall not make any graven images? Or what about, "Thou shall not murder." Is capital punishment or going to war not a form of murder? Indeed, there is a deep irony in someone who cuts their grass on Sunday, wears a crucifix, and supports the death penalty and, at the same time, wants the Ten Commandments displayed in courthouses and school buildings.

Would anyone, then, seriously advocate an implementation of the Ten Commandments in America today. I think not, for several reasons. First, the verses have a clear audience: ancient Israelites and not current societies. Their ancient intended addressees undercut any argument for using the commandments in modern legal issues, much less positioning them as the foundation for every regulation and decree. Second, 20:2–3 says that the Israelites should follow the Lord God because God brought them out of Egypt. Though Christians utilize this text in modern practice, to claim a connection to the Israelites freed from Egyptian bondage is a stretch for any faith group except contemporary Jews. Therefore, the justification for worshipping God within these verses is irrelevant to American Christians. Removing the commandments from their original specific context discredits and relegates their intended purpose while it accommodates American agendas.

Conservative political pundits often lambast Muslim states that utilize Sharia Law. American Republicans and Democrats alike demonize the Islamic practice, saying that it destroys the wall between Church and State or that powerful corrupt leaders misconstrue and abuse the Islamic law code's statutes. Yet the very same people fail to see the striking similarities between criticisms of Sharia Law and unavoidable dangers of implementing biblical Law. Religious and social freedom become jeopardized when one religion gains legalized superiority, and deifying the Ten Commandments only threatens the fickle stability binding the United States together. Indeed, blending politics and religion risks massive loss of life, as history shows us. Nazi Germany had an "official" state church and all others were outlawed upon penalty of imprisonment and death. Corrupt Muslim extremist countries legalize beating and mutilating women. Isn't the separation of church and state one of America's wonderful redeeming merits?

Though it may appear otherwise, I respect and admire the Ten Commandments within their context. These laws were the first strides the Israelites made as they attempted to separate themselves from their enslaved past. The intentions of the commandments were never to oppress or subjugate anyone; in fact, the opposite is true. The Ten Commandments, in short, are an appropriate, admirable even, set of laws for the ancient Israelites. Not for us as Americans. The Bible has an appropriate place in our world, but it cannot simply be transported wholesale from one place to another. Removing Exodus 20 from its biblical context is a dangerous practice that threatens the Bible's place in contemporary society.

Jonathan Redding is a student at Wake Forest School of Divinity and a parttime Minister with Youth and Families at Peace Haven Baptist Church in Winston-Salem, North Carolina, United States.

CONFUCIUS AND THE FIFTH COMMANDMENT

Maggie Low (Singapore)

Obeying the Fifth Commandment in a Confucianist context can be a dilemma. Conversion to Christianity or to any other religion may be seen as a breach of filial piety because loyalty to one's parents is being challenged by allegiance to Another. Confucius taught in his *Analects* (or Sayings) that duty to the family supersedes all other duties because filial piety and fraternal duty are the roots of humaneness (13:18; 1:2, *Analects*). In fact, the veneration of ancestors occupies a more important place in Chinese life than do the gods, for one may choose one's gods but not one's ancestors. How, then, can the Christian in a Confucianist society keep both the First and Fifth Commandments?

For a start, it must be highlighted that there are many similarities between the biblical concept of honoring parents and the Confucianist principle of filial piety. The Hebrew word for honor (*kabed*) means, literally, to treat someone as weighty, and a word study reveals that honor is shown in three ways that are also consistent with Confucianist teachings: through pecuniary (financial), practical, and public expressions.

In Matthew 15:4, Jesus rebuked the Pharisees for breaking the commandment to honor parents by declaring that the support due to father or mother is "corban," that is, designated for God. One of the primary meanings of honor, therefore, has to do with giving pecuniary support to one's parents. In fact, the Chinese pictogram for filial piety is *xiao,* which consists of the element of *lao* (old person) above and *zhi* (child) below, depicting that the child supports the elderly. Giving tithes to God should never be used by the Christian as an excuse to give less to parents. For dependent parents, this is a matter of grave concern, and even if they are financially independent, Chinese parents would consider even a token sum of money (usually enclosed in an auspicious red packet) as an act of honoring them. This is especially meaningful during special occasions such as Lunar New Year celebrations and birthdays.

Second, honor also carries nuances of caring for others in practical ways. Psalm 91:15 says that God honors his people by rescuing them, and one of the last things that Jesus did at the cross was to entrust the care of his mother to his beloved disciple (John 19:26–27). Confucius urged children not to be ignorant of their parents' ages because it is a cause both for rejoicing and for anxiety (4:21, *Analects*). Thus, to honor parents is to care for them in times of physical or emotional needs. This can take many forms such as attending to them when they are sick or doing household chores, especially for single or married children who are living with their parents, as is common in Asian communities.

Third, cultural anthropologists have pointed out that honor also has a public dimension, or in Chinese terms, to honor someone is to "give face," that is, to let that person be able to show his face in public without shame, or better still, with pride. Respect is to be shown both privately and publicly so that children do not cause parents to "lose face." An important aspect of public esteem is posthumous honor. In 2 Samuel 10:3, David sent a message of condolence to a foreign king upon the death of his father, and this is described as an act of honoring the dead, no doubt eulogizing the former king. Filial piety is defined as serving one's parents when they are alive as well as sacrificing to them when they are dead (2:5, *Analects*). The issue of Chinese funeral rites and ancestral veneration is too complex to discuss in detail, but instead of an outright rejection of all such rituals, Chinese Christians seek acceptable ways to demonstrate honor for deceased ancestors.

Having noted the similarities between the Fifth Commandment and the Confucianist rule of filial piety, it is undeniable that there is fundamental difference between the two. From the scriptural perspective, although honoring parents is a sacred duty, the first and highest commitment is to the Lord, as expressed in the first four commandments. It might be said that the biblical view of filial piety is essentially theocentric (God-centered), while the Chinese view is anthropocentric (human-centered). Conversion to Christianity, therefore, involves an unavoidable clash of worldviews and loyalties.

Interestingly, the Fifth Commandment does not enjoin obedience (Hebrew, *shema*) but rather, honor (*kabed*) to parents. The promulgation of the Ten Commandments was addressed, first of all, to adults and particularly, to the male heads of households. Therefore, the commandment is not meant primarily for keeping young children in line; rather it is directed toward the care of elderly parents. In fact, the narrative of Ruth shows that honoring parents may require one to disobey their expressed wishes, just as Ruth refused her mother's-in-law advice to return to Moab and insisted on following her to Israel in order to take care of her (Ruth 1).

Obedience to parents is certainly commanded in the book of Proverbs, but such instructions are based on the presumption that parents are giving godly training in accordance with the fear of the Lord (Proverbs 9:10). What of parents who fail to demonstrate or impart moral teachings and behavior? While Confucius allows a child to gently dissuade his parents from doing wrong, he tells the child to obey even if his advice is ignored (4:18, *Analects*). Though the Ten Commandments make it clear that obedience to God comes first, the Fifth Commandment is not conditional, that is, children are to honor parents irrespective of parental flaws, in obedience to God. At the same time, within the context of the Ten Commandments, parents are also held accountable to God for what they teach and do. Thus, the theocentric view of filial piety safeguards the well-being of both parents and children, while the anthropocentric framework of filial piety poses the danger of becoming oppressive (as children are enjoined to obey their parents regardless).

Furthermore, the concept of filial piety could be used to explain the priority of loyalty to God. Although Confucius has little to say about the spiritual realm, he does make reference to the ancient belief in one sovereign Being addressed as *Shangdi* (Heavenly Emperor). Like the biblical God, *Shangdi* is not represented by any images and is worshipped as the creator and judge of humanity. The idea, therefore, that one should be filial to the Supreme Being as the divine father may be better accepted by the Confucianist mind-set.

In conclusion, though conversion from Confucianism to Christianity may seem like a betrayal of filial piety, it would be better thought of as a willingness to suffer for the sake of one's family, just as Jesus suffered rejection and crucifixion for those whom he loved. Mary Yeo Carpenter ("Familism and Ancestor Veneration: A Look at Chinese Funeral Rites," *Missiology* 24 [October 1996]: 516) cites the example of Buddhism, which entered China initially as a foreign religion from India but became widely assimilated by the Chinese populace: "The Buddhists teach that the highest form of filial piety is to become a Buddhist monk or nun and so earn merit for the parents. The Christian should teach that the highest form of filial piety is to reach parents for Christ." Buddhism believes that merit accumulated by good deeds gives one a better existence in this or the next life, and such merit may also be transferred to a deceased loved one, such as one's parents. Becoming a monk or nun is considered to be the highest form of good deed, and thus, this renunciation of family ties is reframed as an act of filial piety. In the same way, while conversion to Christianity means a change in loyalty, Christians should see their faith and testimony as the means by which God's gracious salvation can reach their parents.

Maggie Low is Lecturer in Old Testament at Trinity Theological College, Singapore.

The Ten Commandments in Greenland

Flemming A. J. Nielsen (Greenland)

Greenland is geographically situated in North America, but historically, politically, economically, and culturally this huge and sparsely populated island is closely connected to Europe. Christianity came to Greenland in 1721 when the Norwegian missionary Hans Egede arrived. Nobody in Europe knew that the Norsemen had disappeared from Greenland and that the Inuit were the sole people there when Hans Egede set out in search of the lost Scandinavian tribe. Instead of finding his kinsmen, he was confronted with a language and a purely oral Inuit culture that were utterly foreign to him. But he stayed for 15 years as representative of the Danish king, learnt an exotic language that had not been described before, developed a written language, invented words for the foreign religious concepts that he wanted to introduce into the native tongue, and taught his audience to read. And he began to produce a number of Greenlandic religious texts for use by his fellow missionaries and the converts. Those texts, the first of which were produced in very broken Greenlandic in 1723, are the earliest texts written in any Eskaleut language.

Although the first Greenlandic translation of the book of Exodus was not printed until 1832, the Decalogue (Ten Commandments) became well known in Greenland from the very outset of Christian presence in the country. But there were many translational problems.

Prior to the coming of the Europeans and their Christianity, the Inuit world—encompassing coastal areas of Chukotka, Alaska, Canada, and Greenland—knew of no god resembling the Christian one. Vast differences between a European religion emanating from the well-established agricultural societies of the ancient Near East and the shamanism of a nomadic Inuit subsistence economy based on sealing, whaling, and hunting hampered the communication of central Christian concepts. In the pre-Christian Greenlandic religion there was behind the visible world an unseen one that could be approached by the shamans, the so-called *angakkut*. Everything visible had its own spirit, *inua*. Important *inui* ("possessed" plural) were the Man in the Moon, Sila—the unpredictable *inua* of the weather—and the Woman of the Sea. But none of them were supreme gods or the leader of a pantheon. In the language of his day, Hans Egede even called his Greenlandic audience "a people without religion and worship" whose language did not "possess words that are applicable to our religion and worship."

Thus, such words and expressions had to be invented, or as Egede said, it was "necessary to borrow words from our own language and naturalize them in theirs." This strategy can be seen in the rendering of the first commandment where "God" was "translated" by the Danish word *Gud*, which Hans Egede had introduced into Greenlandic very early. This word is still used today, though partly Greenlandized: *Guuti*. Once the word "God" had been naturalized in Greenlandic, it was not difficult to insist that this God should be held in respect according to the second commandment and to forbid every kind of traditional sorcery, magic, and necromancy.

Every shaman had his (or—rarely—her) own favorite helping spirit, *toornaarsuk*. Two Greenlandic word lists had been published in Denmark in the seventeenth century, and from one of those lists Egede had learnt that *toornaarsuk* meant the Devil. When he heard the shamans refer to their *toornaarsuk*, he therefore misinterpreted the concept and believed that there was only one *toornaarsuk* and that the Greenlanders were worshippers of the Devil. However, he did not believe that the shamans themselves were really in contact with the Devil. He rather regarded them as con men who were able to seduce their audience and make *them* believe in the

Devil. The shamans were his main rivals, and he fought them by all possible means out of pity for a people led astray, as he saw it. If the Greenlanders would not cease practicing their sorcery, Egede even said that they would be killed and exterminated from the earth, for God has commanded "us" to kill shamans and liars. His threats, fortunately, were empty and mostly testify to his desperation.

It was more difficult to explain the concept of Sabbath, let alone weeks. In the pre-Christian Inuit society, the days had no names and thus there were no weeks. Even in our time the days are designated by numbers only in Greenland, except for Sunday, which is called *sapaat*, from Hebrew *šabbāt*, and a week is *sapaatip akunnera*, "the Sunday's interval." Moreover, it proved difficult to explain why in a subsistence economy work should be forbidden every seventh day even if the weather was perfect for hunting and the country was teeming with prey. If the Almighty God wanted his people to stay home and listen to the missionaries on a Sunday, why would he let the sun shine so alluringly?

Cultural differences led to other problems in translation. For instance, the traditional Inuit society was polygamous, which was practical if only because men were in a minority since their work was dangerous and caused many fatal accidents. Nobody can survive on their own in traditional Arctic societies, and widowed women had no choice but to become members of new extended families that would appreciate their working skills.

Another problem was the concept of private property in the ninth and tenth commandments implying that man can own house, wife, servants, and livestock. Traditional Arctic societies are nomadic. In Greenland people lived in half-buried houses built of stone and roofed with driftwood, whale bones, and sod during the winter. In the summer half they were nomads living in tents. In early spring, the roofs were removed from the houses to leave only the walls upright, and when the time came again to overwinter, new constellations of extended families were formed and the houses were reroofed and reused by the first groups to arrive at them. The next groups had to search for other houses or build for themselves. Nobody owned such houses permanently. Likewise, nobody owned his own bag or catch. Every hunter had to share what he had according to detailed customary rules. If he refused to do so, his kinsmen would exclude him or ridicule him by satirical songs.

However, in spite of all the problems and immediate setbacks to the missionaries, the traditional society and beliefs faded away fairly quickly as the indigenous people embraced Christianity and its rites, scriptures, and pictures. In the course of time, a Greenlandic nation was built and an imagined Christian community established. Today Greenland is a proud autonomous Christian nation within the Danish national community. The Danish and Norwegian missionaries' insistence that the Gospel should be preached in the vernacular—though it caused all but insurmountable difficulties to themselves—saved the Greenlandic language for posterity, unlike so many other languages in the American hemisphere.

Flemming A. J. Nielsen (Ph.D.) is Associate Professor in the Department of Theology and Religion at University of Greenland.

QUESTIONS

1. Dickerson acknowledges that the biblical story of the Exodus is not primarily about God's liberating people from slavery; but yet her community chose to read it that way nonetheless. Is this problematic? Is it laudable that Dickerson acknowledges how her community is handling the biblical text?

2. In addition to the commandments that Redding mentions, are there others of the Ten which Christians in your culture seem to break regularly?

3. Like the fifth commandment in a Confucian context, what other commandments might be difficult to follow in certain social and cultural settings? Are there any particular such ones in your context?

4. Was Egede's work benevolent and beneficial to the native Inuit? Or was it manipulating their language and culture in an attempt to control them?

CHAPTER 9

LEVITICUS

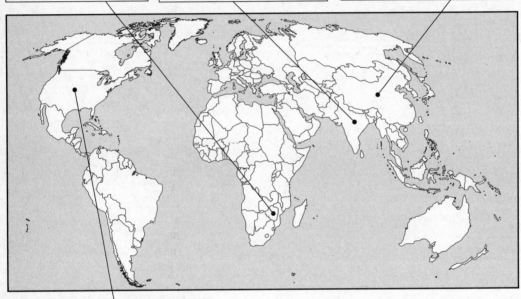

Onesimus A. Ngundu suggests that the Levitical prohibition of necromancy is relevant for Christians in Africa and elsewhere.

Surekha Nelavala discusses the challenges of reading the Levitical laws concerning women's impurity during menstruation in the context of the caste system.

Michael Shepherd proposes that the core principles of *Tao Te Ching* provide a helpful way to appreciate the contemporary relevance of the Levitical law.

Josiah U. Young III wrestles with the idea that God liberates the Israelite slaves in Exodus, but in Leviticus God is not interested in liberating other enslaved people.

READINGS

Female Purity in Leviticus and India
Surekha Nelavala

Necromancy in Africa
Onesimus A. Ngundu

Slavery in Levitical Law and Black Liberation Theology
Josiah U. Young III

The *Tao Te Ching* and the Relevance of Leviticus
Michael Shepherd

FEMALE PURITY IN LEVITICUS AND INDIA

Surekha Nelavala (India)

The concepts of purity and impurity so prevalent in the book of Leviticus are common themes in a number of ancient religions. Nowadays, most things considered impure in Leviticus are understood to be natural biological functions—for example, childbirth, sexual intercourse, bodily eliminations, and death. However, in India the notions of female impurity related to menstruation and childbirth, like the ones articulated in Leviticus 15:19–33, persist to this day. In the Hindu belief system, there is something intrinsic and inherent about female impurity: To be a woman is to be impure.Thus, women assume a lower social status, which is seen as part of the natural, divinely created order of the world. Thus the book of Leviticus presents a special challenge for the Indian-Christian woman, for the book reinforces Indian-Hindu concepts of impurity.

In Indian society, women's menstruation is viewed as impure and associated with shame and thus treated as taboo. The way in which female impurity is dealt with is based in part on the caste and culture of each individual family. In general, practicing purity and impurity varies depending on one's caste: The lower the caste, the higher the intrinsic impurity, and thus lower-caste women are less threatened by external impure forces such as menstruation. So, for example, low-caste Indian women are already seen as impure (by virtue of their low caste), so they are less affected by the impurity of menstruation. By contrast, Brahmins, the highest and supposedly purest caste, practice daily rituals to protect them against surrounding impurities. Menstruating Brahmin women observe absolute untouchability during their periods; they use different utensils, chairs, and even beds in their homes. The purity of the domestic sphere must be protected at all costs. When working Brahmin women enter public places, they do not need to practice such untouchability because they view the outside world as full of impurity anyway.

Nonetheless, regardless of class, all Hindu people consider that menstruation brings impurity. While only high-class women follow absolute untouchability during their menstruation, all Hindu women observe the status of impurity during their period. This is especially important in the religious realm. Menstruating women refrain from going to the temples, offering prayers, touching scriptures, and stepping into the holy room, a place of worship that is set aside in every Hindu house. They do not partake in celebrations or festivals, eat any of the foods that are offered to the gods, or attend weddings and other celebrations. Furthermore, anyone who comes into contact with a menstruating woman must take a ritual bath before participating in any religious ceremony.

Broadly speaking, in India, the concept of female impurity is one of the biggest reasons that women—regardless if they are menstruating or not—are treated as shameful, dangerous, unhygienic, and disgusting, Thus, women are marginalized, discriminated against, and given a lower social status than men.

The concepts of purity and impurity are significant to me as an Indian-Christian woman, for I have been thrice alienated: I am a woman; I belong to a caste community that is essentially impure by birth and therefore literally untouchable; and I am a member of a Christian community which perpetuates the notions of impurity found in Leviticus. Indeed, many Christian churches in India view women as intrinsically impure. Thus women are forbidden to serve as religious leaders or, sometimes, even to read and study Scripture or participate in certain activities.

Since the book of Leviticus is canonized Scripture, my approach is to treat it as descriptive rather than prescriptive. That is, the views expressed in Leviticus describe a particular time and place, namely ancient Israel. They reveal how that society viewed women and menstruation—how they practiced purity. The book is not to be understood or followed literally. Christian communities everywhere do not follow many of the rituals and religious practices found in Leviticus. So why should only notions of female impurity persist? For Indian-Christians, the answer, unfortunately, is that Indian-Hindu tradition has provided the context for such ideas to continue. The discrimination against women by the Indian church is largely the result of the surrounding cultural and religious values.

The Indian-Christian community has been unable to separate themselves as a holy people unto God. We have been unable to keep ourselves "pure" from the evils—the marginalization of women—of our particular location and context. The primary and overarching principle of the book of Leviticus is that God's people are to be set apart unto God. They are to practice purity in order to distinguish themselves from the people and religions around them.

Therefore, I reject any literal (prescriptive) reading of the book of Leviticus that imposes impurity on women because of menstruation, thereby marginalizing them. I deny any reading that leads to injustice against women. Such interpretations by Indian-Christians need to be changed, as unnumbered victims and sufferers cry out daily for equality and justice. We as Christians are to follow the principles of Leviticus, not its practices.

Surekha Nelavala is a Mission Developer at Global Peace Lutheran Church in Frederick, Maryland, United States.

NECROMANCY IN AFRICA

Onesimus A. Ngundu (Zimbabwe)

As I was getting ready to leave Zimbabwe for university education in the United States of America, my American missionary teachers prepared me for living and studying in a foreign culture. As I began my studies overseas, it soon became clear to me that life in Western society was indeed different from my familiar traditional African upbringing. As a Christian young man, it did not take me long to notice that there were some remarkable differences in social practices between my African cultural background and the Western culture I now found myself living in. My missionary teachers had warned me about such differences; in Christian jargon, being forewarned is being forearmed. In the same way, the Israelites, upon leaving Egypt, were warned in the book of Leviticus against some of the practices they were going to encounter in Canaan.

Today some Bible readers are tempted to skip entirely the book of Leviticus. This neglect is primarily because the book addresses matters that seem irrelevant to modern-day life. But, I suggest, we must ask not only what all these Levitical laws meant for the ancient Israelites but also what they reveal about the eternal nature and will of God. As the Apostle Paul said concerning the Law: "Whatever was written in former times was written for our learning" (Romans 15:4).

When God's people, the Israelites, departed from Egypt, God instructed them not to engage in certain pagan customs and practices (Lev. 18:1–5; 20:23). One of those forbidden practices was consulting mediums (Lev. 19:31), that is, practicing necromancy, a method of divination through communication with the dead. A necromancer (the Hebrew word *yidd'oni* literally means "knower") refers either to the knowledgeable practitioner of necromancy or the knowing spirit that the practitioner calls up for information. The Old Testament reveals that Moses and the prophets had much trouble keeping the Israelites from engaging in such heathen customs and practices (e.g., Deuteronomy 18:10–14; 2 Kings 9:22). The classic biblical example of Israel's disobedience is King Saul's visit to the necromancer (commonly referred to as a witch) at Endor (1 Samuel 28).

Consulting the dead or mediums was as pervasive in ancient Near East cultures as it is still in African society today. Like the religious ancient Israelites, some African Christians still find themselves consulting mediums from time to time in search of answers to unexplainable misfortunes, sicknesses, or untimely deaths. Because Africans live in crippling fear of being bewitched by enemies, such as envious relatives and neighbors, they like to know the "real" cause of a misfortune or death—even if the immediate cause is obvious (like a traffic accident).

Most Africans, including nominal Christians, believe that only mediums (*sangomas* or *n'angas*) from African Traditional Religion (ATR)—that is, indigenous African religions—can provide answers to unexplainable causes of sicknesses and deaths. Hence, they may secretly consult ATR mediums in fear of Church leadership reprisals. On the other hand, Christian members of African Initiated Churches (AIC)—Christian churches started by Africans, not missionaries from elsewhere—rely on their prophets to explain to them the causes of misfortune. These prophets typically perform certain religious rituals such as prophesying, exorcism, and sprinkling of "holy water" as they seek answers. AIC prophets seem to be counterfeits of mediums in the ATR because only those individuals who previously served as mediums in ATR qualify as prophets in AICs. The similarities between the *modi operandi* of mediums in the ATR and of prophets in AICs lead one to conclude that it is the same spirit that operates in both groups of men.

Both mediums through divination and prophets through prophecy always accuse only women of witchcraft, even in cases where the cause of sickness or death has been medically established (e.g., cancer). While African diviners openly claim ancestral spirits as the source of their divination, AIC prophets believe that it is God at work through them in revealing the culprits. They consider themselves to be God's prophets. However, the well-documented fact that AIC prophets, like ATR diviners, always (falsely) accuse women of witchcraft would suggest otherwise.

Consulting the dead in the form of divination is predicated on the assumption that the course of events is predictable: Its advance notices are imprinted in natural phenomena or discernible in human-made devices. In Leviticus and indeed the whole Bible, consulting the dead or the mediums is deemed ineffectual since all events are under the control of the all-powerful and all-knowing God. Mediums do not claim to depend or rely on God for their insight. Divination is also deemed heretical and abominable because of their attempts to alter the future and overrule the will and sovereignty of God. The all-sufficient, ever-present, and faithful God himself had granted the Israelites a special relationship, that of communicating directly with them. God desires and expects his people to depend on him as their only reliable source of information about their personal and national lives. Even when God seems to be silent, his people are supposed to continuously live by his true and unfailing revealed promises, instead of seeking information about the unknown from heathen diviners or mediums. God alone is the source of all wisdom and knowledge.

As it turns out, then, the specific laws in Leviticus are relevant for many African Christians: We are not to engage in any form of necromancy. For Christians who do not live in such a culture, it is the principles of Leviticus that apply: Trust God alone as the font of all knowledge.

Onesimus A. Ngundu (Ph.D., University of Cambridge; Th.D., Dallas Theological Seminary) is currently a Research Assistant at the University of Cambridge, England.

SLAVERY IN LEVITICAL LAW AND BLACK LIBERATION THEOLOGY

Josiah U. Young III (United States)

As a black theologian, I held that the Bible's God sides with the oppressed. The Exodus had been central to that claim. However, reading Exodus in its context, that is, in relation to the books that surround it, specifically Leviticus, I have had to modify the claim. This is especially the case since Leviticus is part of the Exodus saga. Together, they show clearly that YHWH is not opposed to slavery categorically. Exodus 21:1–21 reveals that YHWH permits the enslavement of His Hebrew people by Hebrew people. Leviticus 25:38–46 reveals that YHWH is against the enslavement of His chosen people and disinterested in freeing other enslaved people.

YHWH decrees in Leviticus 25 that the jubilee year will be a sacred time in which liberty is to be proclaimed "for all its inhabitants" in the Promised Land (25:10). Yet, the non-Hebrew people, the aliens living among YHWH's elect, need not be freed. The Lord decrees that those foreigners "can belong to" the Hebrews "as property." What is more, Hebrew slave-owners can hand those people down to posterity as chattel—as inheritance that they can own as permanent property (25:46).

While one cannot reduce the Hebrew Bible to the pro-slavery decree found in Leviticus 25, the decree is not insignificant. Leviticus is at the heart of the Torah. The memory of the jubilee, in addition, turns up in the Gospel, specifically in Luke 4:18–19, which alludes to the jubilee "as the year of the Lord's favor." The priestly instructions in Leviticus are YHWH's; they have the force of revelation. Yet His pro-slavery mandates irk those who cannot accept the institution of slavery. If one holds that slavery is never okay and the Lord sides with the un-free, why does YHWH sanctify *chattel* slavery?

Perhaps the answer has to do with those who wrote and edited the Torah millennia ago. Scholars indicate that the editors of Leviticus had their own agenda wed to the crises of the Babylonian exile—a time when the Israelites were captive in a foreign land. Thus, it was not their intention to make the YHWH of the Exodus the liberator of slaves from other nations. How could they know, in addition, about the enslaved Africans from whom I am descended? Still, the status of Africans as chattel slaves seems to be similar to the plight of the Leviticus aliens. Why shouldn't I identify with them? If I do, how can I assert that Exodus' YHWH has been on my side.

I am not suggesting that biblical theology and the contemporary struggle for black liberation should part company. I am suggesting that this struggle, as I understand it, makes pro-slavery theology unacceptable. I also hold that theologians should be held accountable for what they say about God and why they say the things that they do about God. Leviticus 25 is thus a stop sign for those who make assertions about YHWH's partiality to the oppressed. Leviticus blinks red, but one, having been halted, can then turn up other avenues where he or she can make a case for a liberation theology for all.

As I have mentioned, Luke 4:19 alludes to Leviticus 25; but Luke is also inseparable from Acts (not unlike how Leviticus is inseparable from Exodus). When one reads Luke-Acts, he sees that Christ has fulfilled the Law (Luke 4:21; Acts 10). As the fulfillment of the Law he has authority over it, rendering it a penultimate decree by virtue of his resurrection from the dead. This is not to say that the New Testament overcomes the problem of slavery. Consider the master–slave dialectic one finds in Luke 12, for instance. It resembles the pro-slavery dictums in Leviticus. Yet the gospel also conveys (Paul-like), that the unjust mores of this world are giving way to the mores of a righteous aeon. Why would anyone assume that slaves are to be held in bondage indefinitely there?

As a black theologian descended from chattel slaves, I read the Bible in the light of that conviction, a faith which makes Leviticus 25 more pertinent to what is passing away than to what is coming.

Josiah U. Young III is Professor of Systematic Theology at Wesley Theological Seminary, Washington, D.C., United States.

THE *TAO TE CHING* AND THE RELEVANCE OF LEVITICUS

Michael Shepherd (China)

As a collection of purity laws and tabernacle specifications, the material found in Leviticus can be easily dismissed as belonging to an ancient era which has long since past or as representing a legal theology that has been replaced by Christian faith. Although cemented in the Pentateuch, the words of Leviticus, which are foundational to the Jewish (and later Christian) perspective of God, are stale. The flattening of biblical texts has left the material in Leviticus uninteresting (due to its lack of clear narrative) or unimportant (due to its legal code of a former covenant context). To breathe new life into the teaching of Leviticus, we look to Taoism, an ancient spirituality of the East.

Taoism is not a religion, per se, but a philosophy of the spirituality of life. The Tao translates to English as The Way, which conveys the breadth of its spiritual influence upon life. This philosophy traces its roots to Ancient China, particularly the writings of a scholar-monk named Laozi. Before an expedition to the Western region of China, he (and his students) compiled the essence of his teaching for posterity. These writings have come to be known as the *Tao Te Ching* and have influenced the development of spiritual practice in China from roughly the sixth century B.C. to the present.

What keeps most people from reading Leviticus and the details of the Mosaic Law (also in portions of Exodus, Numbers, and Deuteronomy) is the sense that the specific nature of the laws is not relevant to contemporary Jewish or Christian life. They have lost their usefulness in being able to set apart a community as holy. This is where I believe the Taoist perspective can help us to see Leviticus in a new light. To find meaning in the Law is not to apply the specificity of that Law to your own life, but to understand the Law as the manner in which God established a covenant relationship with humanity. This Law becomes "The Way" in which the people understand their covenantal role and responsibilities. Faithfulness to this way becomes the standard for religious practice and identification among the developing Israelite tribes.

The core principles of Taoism are contained in the "Three Treasures." These themes are traced throughout the *Tao Te Ching* but find definition in Chapter 67: "I have Three Treasures, which I hold fast and watch over closely. The first is *Mercy*. The second is *Frugality*. The third is *Not Daring to Be First in the World*" (*Tao Te Ching*, translated by John C.H. Wu). These "Three Treasures of Taoism" serve as a template for understanding the covenant code. The different laws given to the Israelites can be read within these virtues of Taoism.

The virtue of *Mercy* in Leviticus can be seen in the prescriptions for animal and harvest sacrifice, substituting for the human responsibility of sin. The desire of sacrifice for a covenantal

God is not for retribution, but restoration. *Frugality* is evidenced in the attention paid to detail within the sacrificial system and the emphasis upon the equitable response of the people based on their economic ability. These structures also establish a means for reconciling economic debts to another party, particularly in those instances where a wronged family experienced the loss of life. Humility, or *Not Daring to Be First in the World*, is a central theme of Leviticus, as it defines the relational structure between God and the descendants of Abraham as well as the expectations for that community.

While a Taoist reading will not completely correlate with the Levitical text or the experience of the Hebrew people in the desert, by altering the framework in which we attempt to understand and synthesize the material, unique elements may speak to our circumstances in ways that familiar formulae had neutered.

The prophet Micah, reflecting upon the need for covenant faithfulness in the midst of exile, divides the Way in which the people were called to live from the rituals they were commanded to perform. According to Micah, God is not interested in the people keeping the sacrificial customs outlined in Leviticus and elsewhere; rather God expects them to "act justly, love mercy, and walk humbly before your God" (Micah 6:8). These words ring with the refrain of the Three Treasures of the *Tao Te Ching*: To "love mercy" is to live with compassion for others and respond without retribution (*mercy*); to "act justly" is the natural by-product of living with simplicity and not insisting upon my desire over another (*frugality*); and to "walk humbly before God" coincides with the final treasure, "*not daring to be first in the world*" and living within the reality that humanity has been created to be in relationship with God and community.

The Tao perspective can breathe fresh air into our understanding of Leviticus and the Law: It is as a way of life that is lived in faithfulness to the covenant code. Understood as such, the details—the specific laws—are not to be read literally, as restrictions on our freedom; but rather they invite the community into the fullness of relationship with God. When the Tao of Laozi sets forth the concept of a righteous path, the definition of that path will adapt to different seasons, situations, and generations. Likewise, the manner in which we approach the covenant Law given to the wandering Israelites is not eternal in its specificity, but is a tangible reminder to seek the Way that will lead us to greater covenant faithfulness.

Michael Shepherd is a graduate of Hope International University and Fuller Theological Seminary; he is editor of GlobalTheology.org, a collaborative online journal for world expressions of Christian theology and biblical interpretation.

QUESTIONS

1. How are the concepts of purity and impurity, as discussed by Nelavala, manifest in your cultural context? Think broadly and generally. Are there (other) ancient religious practices and beliefs that persist in your cultural context because of contemporary values?

2. How do people seek information about the future in your society? How does it compare to necromancy in Africa as described by Ngundu?

3. How does Young's identity as a "black theologian descended from chattel slaves" shape his struggle with Leviticus? What other texts in Leviticus might Young find morally problematic in light of his identity?

4. In addition to the three core principles identified by Shepherd, what other relevant and applicable "principles" might one identify in Leviticus?

CHAPTER 10

DEUTERONOMY 6, 10, 16, 24

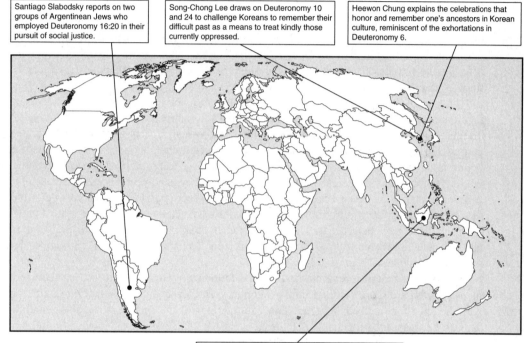

Santiago Slabodsky reports on two groups of Argentinean Jews who employed Deuteronomy 16:20 in their pursuit of social justice.

Song-Chong Lee draws on Deuteronomy 10 and 24 to challenge Koreans to remember their difficult past as a means to treat kindly those currently oppressed.

Heewon Chung explains the celebrations that honor and remember one's ancestors in Korean culture, reminiscent of the exhortations in Deuteronomy 6.

Andrea K. Iskandar suggests how Deuteronomy 10:17–19 can offer inspiration for Chinese Christians in Indonesia, who feel like aliens in their homeland.

READINGS

Korean Celebrations and Exhortations in Deuteronomy
Heewon Chung

Deuteronomy and Chinese Christians Living in Indonesia
Andrea K. Iskandar

Deuteronomy as a Lesson on How to Treat the Oppressed
Song-Chong Lee

Deuteronomy as a Blueprint for Social Justice
Santiago Slabodsky

KOREAN CELEBRATIONS AND
EXHORTATIONS IN DEUTERONOMY

Heewon Chung (South Korea)

Throughout the world, various spiritual and religious traditions hold special celebrations to honor and to remember their ancestors and heritage. We see this in both Deuteronomy 6 and in certain aspects of Korean culture. The practice of remembering generations past has been a serious concern for many centuries in Korea. Living well for Koreans has to do not only with how they live but also with how they remember their ancestors. Koreans have traditionally believed that the ancestors are actively involved in the lives of people. In this perspective, in order for one to continue to live well, one has to respect his or her ancestors and to remember what they have done in their lifetime. What characterizes this special remembrance the most is offering *che-sa* (rite of veneration) to ancestors. Such ceremonial remembering occurs several times a year, such as *Chu-suk* (Thanksgiving Day) and *Sul-nal* (New Year's Day).

On *Sul-nal*, for example, sons and daughters return home to their surviving parents, revere their parents and the late ancestors, and hold festivals of family union in the season of New Year. The festivities involve family celebrations with drinking, eating, singing, and playing communal games. They give an opportunity for people to appreciate the goodness of life and help create bonds among all family members. An integral part of these festivities includes *che-sa* to the generations before them in remembering ancestors for another good year since Koreans believe that practicing this rite insures the family's prosperity in the coming year. Therefore, in gratitude for the life they have received from their ancestors, the surviving descendents set a ritual table with food and drink, pay obeisance to the late ancestors by making bows, and invite them to the ritual table. A table fellowship follows *che-sa*. Memorizing the names of ancestors through such ritual practices is an integral part of *Sul-nal* celebration.

During the rite of veneration and table fellowship, stories about those who are being memorialized are shared among family members. However, there is something unique in the way the ancestors are remembered. The wrongdoings of the ancestors are also remembered. This is because ancestors and their descendents are understood as spiritually linked: The misdeeds of ancestors are visited on their descendents, and conversely, action taken to help the ancestors will have a beneficial effect on their descendents. Therefore, descendents must eliminate their ancestors' impurities that they had done in their lifetime. Such purifying is achieved through granting unconditional forgiveness to the ancestors, which erases their misdeeds from the family's memory. Thus, the living begins a renewed relationship with those who have passed on.

This practice of remembering, however, demands some critique. From the perspective of the person wronged by the misdeeds, the family's demand for forgiveness may be experienced as revictimization without any due recourse for justice. At the same time, it could also be understood as another way of resolving conflicts, one way of putting an end to a distorted relationship and thereby liberating the victim/survivor from the power of the abuser.

Koreans are very conscious of making devoted efforts to eliminate their present misfortune by remembering the past misdeeds of ancestors. Knowing where one comes from and how one's heritage influences current events is a basic human need for survival in any culture. Regular remembering allows descendents to realize where they come from, how they shall live, and where they will go, and it solidifies family unity. Therefore, Korean families use the ancestor veneration rite on special days of the year as an occasion to teach the succeeding generations about the importance of remembering. This practice enables descendents to learn about ancestors whom they have not met in their lifetimes and to build relationships between generations. By so doing, ancestors and their deeds are not forgotten; they are remembered by the community of the living. It also allows descendents to deal with the reality of life and death on a regular basis, and it provides opportunities for them to continue to live in a right way. People become aware of their duty to behave properly and to avoid misdeeds and abominable actions which will adversely affect subsequent generations.

This Korean practice of remembering generations past has a number of implications for understanding Deuteronomy 6:10–25. In his sermon, Moses asks the people of Israel not to forget what Yahweh promised to the first three generations of patriarchs. He urges the people to remember Yahweh and the great ancestors who have laid the foundation for their lives. Moses reminds the people of Israel that they are connected to those who have come before them and that they will influence the lives of those who follow them. He then exhorts them to remember their ancestors' misdeeds during the time of wilderness wandering. In addition, he urges all the heads of Israelite families to teach their children to remember where they came from, so that they would know the great things Yahweh had done for his people. Moses concludes with the notion that the people of Israel can solidify their intergenerational ties and establish a right relationship with Yahweh by remembering the lives of ancestors and the promises given to them.

The practice of remembering helps us appreciate life that continues on through human connections over the generations. Deuteronomy 6 and *Sul-nal* remind us that it is so important to remember those that came before us, that we must take the time to reflect back with gratitude or sorrows on what our ancestors have done. More importantly, we must take the time to reflect with gratitude on God who made the way possible. Remembering the generations before us is a wonderful opportunity to turn grief into a positive expression of our gratitude to God, who laid the foundation for our lives. By remembering ancestors, one cannot help but worship God.

Heewon Chung is Lecturer of Old Testament at the College of Liberal Arts at Keimyung University, Daegu, South Korea.

DEUTERONOMY AND CHINESE CHRISTIANS LIVING IN INDONESIA

Andrea K. Iskandar (Indonesia)

Chinese people in Indonesia are a minority ethnic, constituting approximately 3 percent of Indonesian people. Traditional Chinese belief is a blended faith, accommodating Buddhism, Confucianism, and Daoism. This faith is called *Sanjiao Heyi* (three teachings, harmonious as one) and is still held by many Chinese in Indonesia. However, there are also many Chinese in Indonesia who have converted to other religions, especially to Christianity. This happens mainly in economically more developed areas. This means that most Chinese in Indonesia are a minority both ethnically and religiously. Nonetheless, there is a widely held belief that the minority Chinese have control of 70 percent of Indonesian wealth. Despite the fact that there are many poor and homeless Chinese, it is often assumed that a Chinese person is likely to be a Christian and rich.

Now the majority of the Indonesian people are Moslems, and adult male Moslems (not women and children) attend weekly services on Friday at noon during an extended lunch time by walking from their work to mosques, which are available virtually everywhere. But Christians attend service on Sunday and they go to churches according to their own denominations, which may not be close to home. So, Christians—at least the affluent ones—drive their cars, which often creates traffic problems around uptown churches. But more than Sunday traffic jams, the general populace associates a Christian worship service with the giving of money as offering. This is not practiced by other state-sanctioned religions in Indonesia, so this gives the impression that in Christianity giving money to the church is a prominent way to show piety.

By contrast, Islam does not have offering as part of their weekly Friday service and mosques have no membership system as churches do. So when Moslems build mosques or need money for some major works, volunteers go to the streets with money containers to ask for people's charity. Of course, there are also Islamic institutions which employ more modern charity systems, such as using bank transfers and credit card payments, but still they would communicate their needs to the public and the public would respond by giving charity to these institutions, regardless of their institutional membership.

In fact, giving charity is a form of popular pietism in Indonesia. Giving money to beggars and street singers (who are easily found on overpasses, buses, and trains) is seen as a legitimate form of "social care" to the less fortunate; it is also understood as a way of giving offering to God. Many of these impoverished people are widows, invalids, and orphans living on the street without hope for education or a better future. Unfortunately, this kind of pietism is relatively unseen among Chinese Christian communities. Being more prudent with the disbursement of their money, Chinese Christians are likely to think, "They'd use the money for cigarettes anyway, so when we want to donate some money for a cause, we'd better do it through institutions which will provide, for example, scholarships." It is thus widely believed that "the rich Chinese Christian people" just don't care—they keep everything for themselves and when they do give, they give only to their own circles and causes, not to the people whom they actually meet.

Part of the problem is that the Chinese have been victimized for centuries by a series of policies imposed by Dutch colonial government and Indonesian "new order" government. This has led to serious ethnic violence, the last of which occurred in 1998 when many Chinese-owned properties were destroyed, and many Chinese men killed and women raped—an event still fresh in many people's minds. Indeed, Chinese communities were disenfranchised economically and forbidden to enter social, cultural, and political arenas. Although the condition has partially improved since the Refromasi of 1998, both the Chinese communities and those outside them continue to see the Chinese as "aliens who live among the native," despite the fact that the Chinese have been in Indonesia for many centuries prior to the segregation policies imposed upon them.

In this context, the idea presented in Deuteronomy 10:17–19—"God makes us aliens, lest we forget our calling"—offers inspiration for Chinese Christians in Indonesia today, who still feel that they are aliens in the land in which many of their families have lived for generations. This alienation has been deeply painful. However, God has blessed many people in this community so abundantly that they could be a blessing for others. They, indeed, can be a powerful tool of God's salvation, reaching out to people through big institutions and churches and, more importantly, through their personal encounters with people in need—orphans and widows and the invalids on streets, overpasses, buses, and trains. Then people outside the church will realize that the notions that "the rich Christians just care for themselves and not us" and "the church is only capable of taking care of her own" are just not true.

God, we might say, has made the Chinese Christian community aliens in our native land lest we forget who we are and where we're heading. Chinese Christians need to remember that the grand narrative of life is that we're all just pilgrims, aliens in foreign lands, heading toward our heavenly home. We can show the people around us that our God is a great God "who executes justice for the orphan and the widow, and shows love for the alien by giving food and clothing" (10:18).

Andrea K. Iskandar (M.Div., Cipanas Theological Seminary, Indonesia) is Chairman of the Board of Youth Ministry at Gereja Kristus Ketapang, Jakarta, Indonesia.

DEUTERONOMY AS A LESSON ON HOW TO TREAT THE OPPRESSED

Song-Chong Lee (South Korea)

The book of Deuteronomy contains a profound message concerning outsiders, namely *strangers* and *sojourners*. Passages such as Deuteronomy 10:19 and 24:17–18 command the Jews to do justice to foreigners and the socially disadvantaged. Its implicit motivation, however, is more than the theme of social justice demanding equal and fair treatment or human rights. The life of strangers reminded the Jews of their suffering under the oppression of Pharaoh in Egypt and provided them with an existential reference point to convert and expand the orbit of their morality into the spiritual.

Prior to the conquest of the Promised Land (Canaan), foreigners were mainly the mixed multitude who had left Egypt with the Israelites; after their settlement in Canaan, they were the remnant of the conquered people. Moses commanded his people not to oppress and vex those strangers, and also to be proactive in protecting and helping them (24:19–22); indeed, the same civil and religious laws apply to everyone equally. The motivation and basis for such action was because the Israelites themselves were strangers in foreign lands. Even Abraham, Isaac, Jacob, and Lot were all aliens (Genesis 23, 26, 37). The Israelites were asked to refresh both their past memories and their spiritual identity and duty by looking at and caring for the life of the strangers.

The message and context of the Exodus was, and is, a very useful hermeneutical tool for the *minjung* theologians. The *minjung* theology was a Korean version of liberation theology in the 1970s and the 1980s; it made a tremendous contribution to helping the nation's democratization and protecting and improving the human rights of the people. The *minjung* theologians found the harsh reality of their oppressed people (*minjung*) and hope for their salvation in the story of the Israelite Exodus from Egypt. Korean people under a series of military regimes were identified with the Jews enslaved in Egypt and the strangers in the Jewish community. Although different in historical contexts, they were similar in that people's outcry was the primary source by which the *minjungeans* believed the saving work of God was initiated, revealed, and completed.

However, contemporary Korea seems to have already settled in her own Canaan. She has obtained democracy and achieved unprecedented economic success. The Korean churches have prospered more than ever. The majority of the Korean people in the twenty-first century would not identify themselves anymore with those oppressed in the 1980s. While Korean people are currently in the position of the liberated Jews, there is a newly emerging *minjung* with whom they can identify and from whom they can find a new spiritual and moral insight and injunction.

The new *minjung* in contemporary Korea are foreign workers and immigrants from developing countries and North Korean defectors. They are the sojourners who are in the most vulnerable position. Since the late 1990s, a great number of unskilled migrant workers and foreign brides have been brought in. As of October 2009, there were 680,000 registered foreign workers. The number of marriage immigrants reached 177,000 in 2010. Including undocumented workers, the total number of foreign residents has hit almost 2 percent of the entire population. The number of North Korean defectors is also increasing. Since the Korean War, about 6,000 North Koreans have defected to South Korea. Unfortunately, they are in the position of the Korean people of the 1980s. Like Korean *minjung*, they are the people who are suffering *han* (the feeling of unresolved bitterness). According to a recent Amnesty International report ("South Korea: Disposable Labour: Rights of Migrant Workers in South Korea," October 20, 2009.), foreign workers in South Korea experience abhorrent working conditions such as delayed payment of wages, violence by employers, and exploitation associated with immigration status. Female migrant workers are often subjected to "sexual harassment and violence at work." In one survey, 42 percent of a random sample of foreign workers said that they had been beaten on the job. Another survey shows that a large proportion of South Korean elementary school children do not want to make friends with kids from *Damunhwa Gajeong* (a multicultural family).

North Korean defectors, whose number has drastically increased since the 1990s, are also experiencing hardship in settling in South Korea because of pervasive stereotypes and discrimination. One survey shows that only about 2 percent of North Korean defectors' households in Seoul have one employed family member. The most common suffering that the new *minjung* is experiencing is reportedly discrimination. They are looked down upon in social value, marginalized in politics, and thought of as incapable of upward social mobility. Without a doubt, the traditional social value inordinately emphasizing ethnic and cultural homogeneity is one of the primary reasons.

Now, I would argue, is the time for Korean people to reflect upon who they are and what they went through in the 1970s and 1980s just as the Israelites did before their new era. Looking forward to their own Promised Land, Koreans have to refresh their memories. They must take good care of the strangers because they themselves were the *minjung*, who were politically oppressed and socially alienated. They must remember that we suffered in factories with inhumane working conditions and that we cried out in torture chambers of the KCIA (the Korean Central Intelligence Agency). They must break off their Confucian attachment to the value of *soonhyul* ("pure blood"), find a way to get along with people from different cultures, and care for them for a better society. For the Israelites, who were also obsessed with the value of homogeneity, Moses allowed the strangers to participate in sacrificial rituals, Sabbath, and even Passover, if circumcised. The fair treatment was important because it not only made his community strong and stable but it also was the primary character of God.

Although most Koreans have graduated from the class of *minjung* (the oppressed people), the category of the *minjung* itself has never disappeared. There are always around us strangers, sojourners, orphans, and widows who are not as capable of defending themselves. Foreign workers and brides from developing countries and North Korean defectors are the present self-image of the Korean past and a significant reference point from which we can continue to reflect on who we want to be. Strangers are not a burden but a self-portrait that makes us humble and continues to test and stretch further our spiritual and moral potential.

Song-Chong Lee is Assistant Professor of Religious Studies and Philosophy at University of Findlay, United States.

DEUTERONOMY AS A BLUEPRINT FOR SOCIAL JUSTICE

Santiago Slabodsky (Argentina)

More than half a million Jews live in Latin America. They represent less than 5 percent of world Jewry. More than half of this population calls Argentina their home. Most Argentinean Jews immigrated to the region between the 1880s and 1940s. While the majority was escaping intense religious persecution in Christian Europe, a good number of Jews from the Muslim populated Middle East and North Africa joined them in looking for more open societies and new opportunities.

In Argentina, Jews encountered a predominantly Christian immigrant society. In more than 100 years after their arrival, Argentinean Jews were able to maintain their particularity while intensively collaborating with the construction of Argentina as a nation-state. This adaptation, however, encountered obstacles. Since the very beginning they faced discrimination. This discrimination was the result of a reproduction of European developments (that culminated in, for example, the Holocaust) and zealous nationalist schools of thought that attempted to construct a nation under the banner of religious uniformity (among them Catholic right-wing trends were predominant).

Among the Jewish groups confronting this discrimination, two of them are noteworthy. These movements, at different times, employed the Hebrew Bible in order to sustain their struggle. While there are a variety of passages in the Torah which call for justice (Exodus 23:1–9; Deuteronomy 10:17–19), in both cases Deuteronomy 16:20, "Just justice you shall pursue" was used to counter injustice toward the Jewish community and the Argentinean society at large. The first of these movements was the collective *Masorti* (my tradition), a group that fought against the genocide of a U.S.-endorsed military government between 1976 and 1983. The second was *Memoria Activa* (Collective Memory) that denounced the complicity of state powers for the collaboration and obstruction of investigations into an attack against the central Jewish institution in Argentina (AMIA) in 1994.

The first case was the collective *Masorti*. Between 1976 and 1983 a U.S.-backed military government took over power in Argentina. During this period there was a systematic plan to eradicate all opposition. At the end of this period, 30,000 young bodies and voices disappeared without leaving a trace. The *desaparecidos* (disappeared people) were kidnapped in the street or from their homes, schools, or places of employment, and, after being tortured for days, months, or years, were murdered. Most of their bodies have never been found. Of the total of disappeared people, 12 percent were Jews even though they represent less than 1 percent of the population. It is not a surprise that the perpetrators saw themselves as the fulfillers of both Catholic right-wing ideologies and local national-socialisms.

In those days a group of young, religious Jews, risking their own lives, reacted to the geno-cide. Under the banner of Deuteronomy 16:20, "Just Justice you shall pursue," they understood that they could not trust a corrupt and compromised judicial system to bring clarity concerning the disappearances. The movement started to join religious and secular resisters in underground organizations to confront the military dictatorship. The biblical call was a remembrance that only "just justice" could be contemplated, and to achieve it, sometimes, it was necessary to defy the unjust justice implemented by the status quo. The *Masorti* leader was American-born rabbi Marshall Meyer. He not only integrated the commission of notables who researched the genocide and incarcerated the perpetrators but also was honored by the democratic Argentinean government with the highest prize offered to a noncitizen, the "Order of General San Martin."

More than 10 years later, another group of Jews followed the example and took the same biblical verse as their banner. On July 18, 1994, the central community of Argentina (AMIA) was destroyed by a van-bomb attack, in which 86 were murdered, Jews and non-Jews, Argentineans and non-Argentineans alike. The institution, until then, was in charge of social welfare far beyond the Jewish community. While the Argentinean society was outraged and the government showed its solidarity with the victims, soon enough it was clear that the security forces and the government were implicated in the obstruction of justice. The official judicial channels, presum-ably independent, were politically compromised and a clear account of the events has not yet been achieved.

A group of activists, *Memoria Activa*, started to use the banner "Just justice you shall pursue" to confront the "unjust justice" they witnessed. This movement did not come about in a vacuum but retrieved the memory of the previous movement. In the 1970s several members of *Masorti* joined the mothers and grandmothers of the disappeared people in a weekly vigil, argu-ing for "just justice." For 10 years starting in 1994, the members of *Memoria Activa* gathered in a vigil the same day of the week at the same time of the attack to stand for justice. They did it in front of the palace of Justice and their closing prayer was Deuteronomy 16:20.

The cases of *Masorti* and *Memoria Activa* show the power of the Hebrew Bible to offer resources to people struggling to create a just society. Latin American Jews today still draw from the Hebrew Bible (as well as other sources of rabbinical literature) to engage in the struggle not only for the Jewish community but also for society at large.

Santiago Slabodsky is Assistant Professor in the program of Religion, Ethics, and Society at Claremont Lincoln University and in the School of Religion at Claremont Graduate University, United States.

QUESTIONS

1. What spiritual and religious traditions, if any, serve to honor ancestors and heritage in your community? How do they compare to those in Korean culture?

2. Read all of Deuteronomy 10 to see how verses 17–19, those cited by Iskandar, fit into the context. What observations do you make?

3. Analyze Lee's assertion that in Deuteronomy the fair treatment of non-Israelites was crucial because it not only strengthened the community, but it also was the primary char-acter of God.

4. In your estimation, was the biblical text foun-dational in motivating the pursuit of justice or did the text serve only as a "resource" to support a desire for justice that was already present?

CHAPTER 11

JOSHUA 1–11

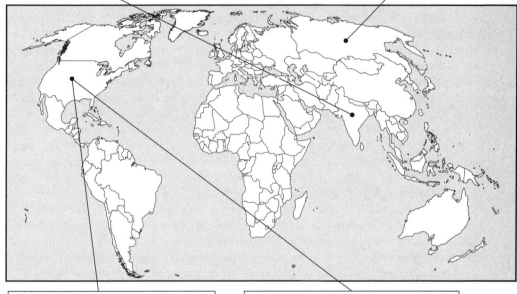

Royce M. Victor identifies two major problems with reading the book of Joshua in view of colonization and religious pluralism in India.

Maria Vlashchenko says that the God of the book of Joshua is an egotistical, power-hungry deity, who demands genocide to prove his own superiority.

Eric A. Seibert presents four strategies for reading the text "nonviolently" in hopes of neutralizing the negative effects these texts might otherwise have.

Stanley V. Udd defends God by challenging the assumptions that lay behind the question "How could God command the destruction of everyone?".

READINGS

Reading Joshua as a Canaanite
Royce M. Victor

Four Strategies for Reading Joshua Nonviolently
Eric A. Seibert

A Defense of God
Stanley V. Udd

God as an Egotistical Deity
Maria Vlashchenko

READING JOSHUA AS A CANAANITE

Royce M. Victor (India)

The first 12 chapters of the book of Joshua describe Israel's invasion of the land of Canaan by destroying the locals through a series of fierce battles under the leadership of Joshua. A closer analysis of these conquest narratives reveals that God commanded Joshua to take the "promised land" by force, which they did by destroying the "other" religions and civilizations of the land. Oddly, the God who just liberated the Israelites from bondage in Egypt now uses his power to brutally capture the land from the indigenous inhabitants. "Yahweh the deliverer" now becomes "Yahweh the conqueror." The book of Joshua shows Israel's negative attitude towards the natives who were already living in Canaan. They are clearly pictured as people who are to be displaced or destroyed. There is no room for them among the chosen people.

The book of Joshua poses two major challenges in an Indian context. First, Christianity has been regarded as a foreign religion ever since it arrived in the land. Although there has been a Christian presence here since the early centuries of the Common Era, the Church became more active during the time of colonialism, which started in 16th century C.E. From this time onwards, India witnessed the influx of European missionaries along with colonial powers. The Portuguese were the first to come, followed by the Dutch, the French, the Danes, and finally the English. All these European powers directly or indirectly encouraged Christian missionary activities. Many people were attracted to Christianity, and churches were planted all over India. However, the new churches were thoroughly Western and the new Christians were encouraged and often compelled to follow the lifestyle of the missionaries. Even today, the popular perception is that to be a Christian in India means to be an Englishman.

Since the Western missionaries came to India together with the colonial powers, Christianity has always been attached to power and authority in the land. The colonial powers initially showed their interest in trade and business, but soon they simply invaded the land and indiscriminately looted the resources. The colonialists found in the book of Joshua a justification for military strategies that annihilate the indigenous population if they did not submit to the newcomers. Indeed, Joshua 1–12, along with other similar biblical texts, has been and is still used to provide the rationale for potentially violent and programmatic ideologies. These texts, in short, have been used to legitimize and justify land grabs, racial segregation, human rights abuse, oppression and violence, in the name of God.

Secondly, religious pluralism is one of the foremost realities of India. Many great religions have emerged in this land and spread throughout various parts of the world. There are also numerous indigenous tribal religious traditions as well as new religious movements. All these traditions have their own scriptures, images, and practices. Unfortunately, the relationship between these various religions is not as peaceful as it was in times past.

Joshua 1–12 is particularly problematic in this regard because it portrays God's people imposing their religious ideology on others. In these passages, God takes sides with the powerful "chosen one" vis-à-vis the powerless, the "unelected," the indigenous people. The Christian church introduced by the Western missionaries traditionally looks at others as "heathens," "uncivilized" and "ungodly," who desperately need to be "Christianized" in order to be "saved" and "civilized." The colonizers often identified themselves with the Israelites of the book of Joshua, as God's chosen people, on the way to the promised land, and the natives correspond to the Canaanites and other indigenous people. Both the Israelites and colonial masters tend to use the name of the deity in order to achieve personal as well as national ends and ambitions.

Today's context demands a more tolerant and sympathetic approach, based on mutual sharing, learning, and dialogue. This method is important because the vast majority of Christians in these parts of the world are converts from other religious traditions, and these Christians continue to observe the cultural values and worldviews of their native land. Christianity, as a result of its encounters with other cultures and other faiths, has indeed begun to develop a new, post-colonial understanding of the Bible, world, and God. This development, which has enriched and enlivened the faith, must continue to grow as Christianity engages the global community.

The contemporary context demands that we raise our voice in objection to the use of scripture to justify violence and oppression. Presenting an exclusivist God or promoting narrow mindedness cannot solve any problem; instead, it generates segregation and tensions. The God of justice, who is the Creator of Israelites and Canaanites, of Europeans and Indians, cannot show favoritism. Therefore, these chapters need re-interpretation and new understanding in our Indian context.

Royce M. Victor is Professor of Old Testament and Hebrew language at Kerala United Theological Seminary, Kerala, India.

FOUR STRATEGIES FOR READING JOSHUA NONVIOLENTLY

Eric A. Seibert (United States)

The conquest of Canaan depicted in Joshua 6–11 is one of the most morally troubling passages in the entire Old Testament. The Israelites mercilessly massacre Canaanite men, women, and children, and they ostensibly do so in obedience to the will of God. Such indiscriminate killing not only raises serious ethical and moral questions but also casts a long shadow upon God's character. What kind of deity would issue such a morally reprehensible, genocidal decree? Of particular concern is the way this passage has been misused over the years by those wishing to acquire someone else's land. These individuals have co-opted this narrative to legitimate terrible acts of violence against indigenous people whose land they desire. The deceitful and murderous treatment of Native Americans by European settlers is but one of many examples of the way this story has been misappropriated and misapplied. Whenever sacred texts are used to encourage acts of violence, oppression, and killing, something has surely gone terribly wrong. So what can be done to avoid such destructive readings? How can the conquest narrative be read in ways that criticize rather than valorize the killing of "Canaanites," whoever they may be?

There are several strategies that can help us read this story *non*violently, in ways that do not legitimate future acts of violence. These reading strategies effectively neutralize the text's potentially lethal afterlife. One of the most rudimentary ways of reading this story nonviolently involves putting a human face on war. The battles described in the conquest narrative say very little about the human suffering that results from the experience of warfare. By and large, the participants remain nameless and faceless. The conquest narrative almost never reports the number of casualties, and very little attention is given to the actual battles themselves. For example, only two of the 27 verses devoted to the battle of Jericho actually describe the battle itself (6:20–21). Setting aside the question of whether this story actually happened for the moment, consider what is not included in these two verses. No mention is made of the raw terror the inhabitants of Jericho presumably felt the moment the walls came crashing down and the Israelites went charging in. Nor do these verses contain descriptions of pierced flesh, severed limbs, or decapitated heads. Also lacking are any tales of terrified toddlers clinging to parents or accounts of helpless babies being brutalized. But all these horrors—and many more—could be inferred from this brief battle report. Yet because these terrible deeds are never explicitly mentioned, many readers happily celebrate the Israelites' victory without ever contemplating the cruel realities of war.

Putting a human face on war means slowing down long enough to consider its devastating effects upon those who are directly—and indirectly—involved. It means recognizing that war does terrible things to individuals on both sides of the conflict; both victims *and* "victors" inevitably suffer harm. When the enormous human toll of warfare is taken into consideration, it is much more difficult to regard the violence of the conquest narrative as virtuous, much less exemplary.

A second strategy for reading this narrative nonviolently involves reading it from the perspective of the Canaanites. Most who read this story identify with the Israelites. But what happens when the story is read the other way around? What does the conquest narrative look like when read through the eyes of a Canaanite? From a Canaanite's point of view, Israel's behavior appears villainous rather than virtuous. From their perspective, the Israelites were hostile invaders intent on stealing their land. They were merciless aggressors determined to kill everyone in their path. Not even women or children were spared! Such behavior hardly seems praiseworthy. Reading this narrative with the victims rather than the victors causes us to see the story in a whole new light. We may find ourselves weeping with the Canaanites rather than celebrating with the Israelites. At the very least, reading the conquest narrative this way should keep us from simplistically appealing to such texts to justify acts of war and genocide in the world today.

A third strategy involves questioning the Old Testament's rationale for the conquest: (1) to punish Canaanite wickedness, and (2) to preserve Israel's religious purity and fidelity, since it is assumed that leaving Canaanites in the land would certainly cause Israel to go astray (see Deuteronomy 7:1–4; 9:4–5; 20:16–18). But are these compelling reasons for engaging in acts of genocide? Do they justify the slaughter of every Canaanite man, woman, and child? I think not. While the Canaanites may have been "wicked" in certain ways, it seems they were no more wicked than other people. Why would God punish Canaanite wickedness by ordering their annihilation while sparing other people who were at least as bad if not worse? Such a decree raises disturbing questions about divine justice.

The explanation that Canaanites needed to be killed in order to preserve Israel's religious purity is also quite problematic. It is hard to see how killing others can be spiritually beneficial. Moreover, while we might agree on the importance of protecting people from bad influences, we would not condone the actions of individuals who went around killing people because they thought their beliefs and practices might negatively influence others. Yet this is essentially how the Old Testament justifies Canaanite genocide. Killing Canaanites is justified as a means of preventing their religious beliefs and practices from negatively affecting Israel's. Such reasoning here, in which the ends supposedly justify the means, is morally bankrupt.

Ultimately, the Old Testament's rationale for Canaanite genocide is unsatisfying because it fails to address the most pressing and obvious problem, namely, the immorality of genocide itself. Genocide, an act which involves killing everyone—even the weakest, youngest, and most vulnerable—is never good, never moral, and never justifiable.

A final strategy for reading the conquest narrative nonviolently involves recognizing that its portrayal of God as warrior is a culturally conditioned construct, one that does not accurately reflect God's true character. In the ancient world, warfare was fraught with theological significance. Like others in antiquity, the Israelites believed that God commissioned wars and fought in them. They also shared the commonly held view that God was responsible for victory or defeat in battle. Given this context, it would seem that Israel's portrayal of God as a divine warrior says more about ancient Israel's worldview, and the cultural milieu out of which these texts arose, than it does about the true character of God. Thus, despite the way God is portrayed in the conquest narrative and related passages in Deuteronomy, there is no compelling reason to believe that God ever willed, commanded, or participated in acts of genocide.

The archaeological evidence also seems to support this conclusion. Many scholars do not believe the book of Joshua contains a reliable account of how the Israelites came into possession of the land of Canaan. This is due, in part, to evidence on the ground which suggests otherwise. Excavations at Jericho and Ai, for example, seem to indicate that these first two cities the Israelites reportedly conquered were actually uninhabited at the time. If that is the case, then it stands to reason that God did not hand over Jericho's "king and soldiers" (6:2) or Ai's king and people (8:1) as the text claims. Realizing that God never issued genocidal directives or willed the destruction of Canaanites significantly diminishes the conquest narrative's ability to do harm in the modern world.

By utilizing the reading strategies discussed here, it is possible to read the conquest narrative nonviolently. These same reading strategies can easily and profitably be applied to other problematic Old Testament texts as well. Reading nonviolently directly challenges the Old Testament's insistence that violence is sometimes necessary and that killing another person may constitute an act of obedience to God. Rather than appealing to such texts to justify acts of violence and war, ethically responsible readers will read them in ways that criticize and problematize the violence they contain, thereby neutralizing the negative effects these texts might otherwise have.

Eric A. Seibert is Associate Professor of Old Testament at Messiah College in Grantham, Pennsylvania, United States; he is the author of Disturbing Divine Behavior: Troubling Old Testament Images of God *and* The Violence of Scripture: Overcoming the Old Testament's Troubling Legacy *(from which this piece is adapted with special permission of Augsburg Fortress).*

A DEFENSE OF GOD

Stanley V. Udd (United States)

If God is purported to be good and loving, how can this be aligned with the clear commands in the Old Testament when God insisted on the slaughter of peoples including innocent children, as we see in the book of Joshua and elsewhere? There would seem to be an inconsistency here. How can a good and loving God command the destruction of infants and babies? This is understandably an oft-asked question by readers of the book of Joshua. But there are problems with the question itself, namely, there are a number of erroneous assumptions that lay behind the question.

First of all, the question assumes that the Canaanites are an innocent people and that God is simply pushing them out or killing them to make room for His people. You will recall that the ancestor of the Canaanites—Canaan—is cursed by Noah for the sexual sin that he perpetrated against his grandfather (Genesis 9:20–27). So the Canaanites are a cursed people. Their sin is an offence to God, but He is patient with them granting them time to repent. In the days of Abraham God indicates that the iniquity of the Amorites (Canaanites) is not yet complete (Genesis 15:16). So there was to be another four generations before God would bring judgment. I'm sure that God was waiting those many years hoping that some would repent of their wickedness (2 Peter 3:9). But eventually, God in His justice needed to remove these wicked people. Isn't it illustrative that at the destruction of the city of Jericho, God supernaturally destroyed the defenses to the city while at the same time preserved that portion of the city wall where the scarlet cord was hung from the window? God was simultaneously punishing the wicked and rescuing those who trusted in Him. He does not kill indiscriminately. Were not righteous Lot and two of his daughters rescued from the fiery destruction of the five cities of the plain? These people in Canaan were getting their just due—God was not killing for the thrill of the kill.

Second, the question assumes that the destruction of children condemns them to some dark destiny. The Bible, on the other hand, makes it very clear that with children there is a time before which the child knows enough to refuse the evil and choose the good (Isaiah 7:15 and 16). Children who die before they reach the age of accountability fall into the hands of a compassionate God (Jonah 4:10–11). To leave those children to grow up in such a wicked and vile setting would surely be less compassionate and virtually guarantee their condemnation. So, even the slaughter of innocent children is not the greatest possible evil. Did not Jesus say, "Let the little children come to me and do not hinder them, for to such belongs the kingdom of heaven" (Matthew 19:14)? Surely children who are truly innocent become inhabitants of heaven.

A third assumption is that the concept of "devoted to destruction" is simply the wonton murder of innocent people. The Hebrew word contains the idea that this action is a sacrifice to God—a symbolic act like a whole burnt offering. The Israelites were the weapon that God was using to appropriately discipline the Canaanites. Their death was the necessary atonement to cleanse the land for Israel. This act was a righteous act. Justice must be carried out. Indeed, Psalm 106:34–39 describes the consequences for Israel not carrying out fully God's command to destroy the Canaanites.

One final assumption is that God has no moral basis for making such bold commands. Such an assumption ignores the fact that all human beings owe their existence to God and God alone. "In Him we live and move and have our being" (Acts 17:28). He is their creator and as a result has a moral basis for expecting a certain level of morality. The Bible is very clear that no one is without excuse (Romans 1:19). On that basis alone God has the moral authority to judge people.

The righteousness of God is a verity. It is His most significant and most compelling attribute. It undergirds all that He does. It should not be questioned—even if we cannot adequately explain the ramifications or the logic of His actions. God is not capricious. He is not arbitrary. He is not cruel. But He is unquestionably just.

Stanley V. Udd (Th.D.) is retired Professor of Biblical Languages at Grace University, Omaha, Nebraska, United States.

GOD AS AN EGOTISTICAL DEITY

Maria Vlashchenko (Russia)

I've seen various Study Bibles make comments such as, "Joshua's lessons are overwhelmingly positive ones," "Here the nation of Israel meets with unprecedented success," or "The book gives a fresh breeze of hope." But to me this is a terribly one-sided view of things. Certainly the stories told in Joshua 1–12 are about death and God's unfair treatment of the native inhabitants of Canaan. As someone outside the Jewish-Christian tradition, I do not identify with the conquering Israelites. The people of Israel, following God's direct command, storm through Canaan pillaging, raping, murdering, and burning the people and towns as they carry out a massive genocide. How can there be anything "positive" or "hopeful" about such brutal destruction? And make no mistake about it. This is genocide pure and simple. The Israelites deliberately and systematically wipe out the "the Canaanites, Hittites, Hivites, Perizzites, Girgashites, Amorites, and Jebusites" simply because they were not Israelites. These people represented different national or ethnic groups; they worshipped different Gods and had different religious rituals and practices. In the name of the Lord their God, the Israelites kill them all—men, women, and children. It reminds me of the quote in the short story "Seven Feet" by Christopher Fowler: "What's the point of organized religion if you can't exclude unbelievers?"

In the book of Joshua—indeed in the Old Testament as a whole—God is the God of the Israelites only. He is a nationalistic deity who fights against other peoples and other deities (cf. the story of the Exodus). He gives land, power, wealth, livestock, prosperity, and success to only one group of people. Those who are not Israelites are treated as not human. Thus they can be exterminated and their land taken by God's chosen people. While this is remarkable enough, what is even more amazing is that some religious people in the Jewish-Christian tradition defend God's genocidal action. How is this possible in the world in which we live? How is this possible when religious people claim that God is the God of everybody?

It is important to note that the native inhabitants of Canaan do not start the battles in the book of Joshua. All they wanted to do was to defend their land, their houses, their property, and their loved ones. The Israelites are the aggressors. They not only are the ones who violently possess land that is not theirs, but they also purposefully and willfully kill all the people. They do not try to negotiate with them or convert them. They just destroy them—all of them, people and animals alike, as if they were the same thing. God is very clear that the Israelites are not to leave alive anything that breathes (e.g., 11:14–15). Everything and everyone is to be "devoted to destruction for the Lord." How can this in any way be justified or defended? Think of all the blood, gore, and carnage. Think of all the infants slaughtered by the Israelites.

Positive lessons? Unprecedented success? Fresh breeze of hope? I don't think so.

It is also important to observe God's role in the story. Not only does he command the genocide, but he himself takes an active role in the military campaign. The text reports that God "hurled large hailstones down on them from the sky, and more of them died from the hailstones than were killed by the swords of Israelites" (10:11). God, then, is not only the motive behind the destruction of the Canaanites but also the principle and primary warrior for the Israelite cause. But even the Israelites themselves are in danger if they don't follow God's commands. When Achan took some goods which were meant to be sacrificed to God, he was given a death sentence. Not only was Achan to die, but his whole family and all his animals were stoned and burned to death as well (7:24–25). Once again, innocent people were terminated to satisfy God's wishes. If you are the Canaanites, you are in mortal danger of God's wrath. If you are the

Israelites, God might be on your side, but the moment you do not follow his exact commands, God will immediately turn on you and your whole nation. (This scenario reminds me of the book of Exodus, where God destroys the Egyptians in order to save the Israelites, and then a few chapters later is ready to destroy the Israelites for their idolatry, which only Moses' intervention prevents.)

In one sense, the book of Joshua, at least ostensibly, is about the fulfillment of the promise to Abraham: God gives the people of Israel the land on which Abraham's descendents will live. But in another very real sense it seems to be much more than that. The text itself says so. Speaking of Israel's enemies, we read: "For it was the Lord himself who hardened their hearts to wage war against Israel, so that he might destroy them totally, exterminating them without mercy" (11:20). In reality, then, the bloody stories in Joshua are not about God trying to complete a promise or about God trying to take care of and provide for his own people. No. God makes this crusade for himself to satisfy his ambitions, to prove that he is the only God, that his decisions cannot be questioned. He manipulates the hearts and minds of the Canaanites precisely so that he can exterminate them without any compassion. If God wanted to give the land to the Israelites, why not devise a more peaceful plan? Why not soften the hearts of the Canaanites so that no blood would be spilled? Instead, the book of Joshua presents us with an egotistical, power-hungry God, who demands genocide to prove his own superiority.

Maria Vlashchenko is from Khabarovsk, Russia; she attended the Academy of Economics and Law in Khabarovsk before moving to the United States to study.

QUESTIONS

1. How do you imagine that the writer(s) of the book of Joshua would respond to Victor's "problems" with the book?

2. In what sense is Seibert's reading "nonviolent"? What other terms might be used to describe his approach?

3. Are the biblical references Udd uses supportive of his interpretation? What other interpretations are possible for these passages?

4. Do you personally identify with the Israelites or the Canaanites? What people or groups might naturally identify with the Canaanites?

CHAPTER 12

1 SAMUEL 16–2 SAMUEL 21

Andreas Kunz-Lübcke presents the woman of 2 Samuel 20 and Abigail as wise and active women, who intervene successfully against a male military campaign.

James N. Pohlig examines four readings of the David–Jonathan relationship: mainstream Western, gay and lesbian, West African, and Greco-Roman.

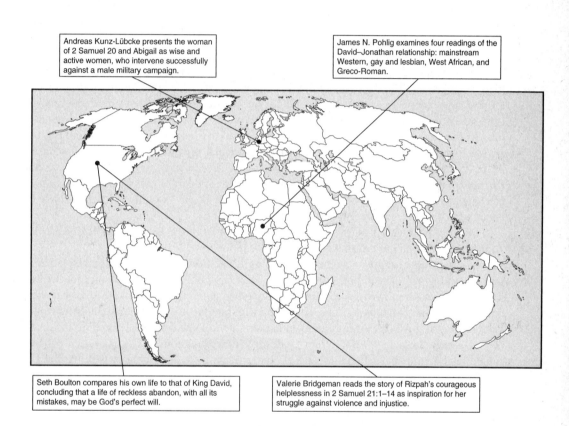

Seth Boulton compares his own life to that of King David, concluding that a life of reckless abandon, with all its mistakes, may be God's perfect will.

Valerie Bridgeman reads the story of Rizpah's courageous helplessness in 2 Samuel 21:1–14 as inspiration for her struggle against violence and injustice.

READINGS

The David Stories and a Life of Reckless Abandon
Seth Boulton

Four Interpretations of the David–Jonathan Relationship
James N. Pohlig

The Woman of 2 Samuel 20 and Abigail as Peacemakers
Andreas Kunz-Lübcke

The Inspiration of Rizpah's Courageous Helplessness
Valerie Bridgeman

The David Stories and a Life of Reckless Abandon

Seth Boulton (United States)

The truth of the matter is that even though my band never played a stadium tour or had our videos on MTV we were a huge commercial success. I lived the good life: I played the music I wanted to play every night; I had a band that consisted entirely of beautiful women who did whatever I told them to do; I partied when I wanted to party; I slept with the women that I wanted to sleep with; and when I felt like quitting, I just quit. Who wouldn't want to be that guy? I really, truly lived life with reckless abandon and if I had it to do over again, I would do it twice as hard and twice as fast.

Now I know that is not the testimony that most Christians are accustomed to hearing. I've tried and I just can't be sorry about any of it. My regrets are for the things I didn't do, things I didn't say, experiences I didn't have. Of course, this attitude has always met with opposition from many of my fellow believers, whose general philosophy is that the more you abstain from fun, the more godly you must be. I admit that moderation is an important part of life. But I have always found myself questioning whether these particular proverbial "fruits" that one bears are the best measure of one's commitment to God and the success of one's spiritual journey. In fact, I'm not even so sure that being a "Christian" is necessarily part of the equation for living a life pleasing to God. (One of my best friends is a lesbian atheist and I wouldn't change a single thing about her.) And I've got the Bible to "prove" it.

When I look at the lives of most of the great men in the Bible, specifically the life of King David, the man after God's own heart, I can identify. The life of King David is one of exquisite reckless abandon. The man sang songs, killed lions and bears and giants, led armies, became a king and danced half naked in the street (in that order), had lots and lots of wives, had lots and lots of mistresses, loved a man, Jonathan, more than he could ever love a woman, and, when he was old, took a young girl to bed with him just to keep him warm. Who wouldn't want to be that guy? But there is an even darker side to David: He sent a man to his death so he could have the man's wife, he nearly destroyed the kingdom of God's chosen people, he fought his own son and killed him, and of course there is the disturbing possibility that David raped a lot of women.

One could argue that it is recorded in Scripture that David repented for at least a few of these things. But when I look at the life of David, I don't see a man with regrets. If he truly regretted what he had done, he wouldn't have kept living the way he did right up to the end. Perhaps I am reading between the lines (but isn't that where the truth usually lies) or maybe I am focused too much on the big picture. Either way, on my reading, David did what he wanted and lived an amazing, beautiful life that really didn't necessitate an abnormal number of apologies. And if this is my example to follow, I think I've done pretty well and my Father in heaven is well pleased with me and is pleased that I have recognized the success in my accomplishments and all the other crazy things that I've done along the way and will do in the future. Indeed, I'm a lot like King David in all his imperfections. But I think we need to understand that most of what we call his imperfections was really just David living a successful life of struggle, love, frustration, ecstasy, and a vision for his own future.

Society may label our actions as acceptable or unacceptable, but the true measure of the man—whether he is hiding in a cave or sitting on a throne—is his own ability to take control of his life and live it the way he feels is right. I hope the reader doesn't construe as arrogant my comparison of myself to a great hero of the Bible. On the contrary I do not consider myself above any of the rules that govern us all. I am in fact humbled by the discovery that I bear some resemblance to the king. When the play *Death of a Salesman* was released, it was criticized by others for not being a true tragedy because its main character, Willie Lowman, was not royalty or of some aristocratic position (note his last name). If he was nothing more than a lowly salesman, how could his life have great tragedy? But, to my mind, because he was an American pursuing his dream he was in fact royalty. Any man in this country is the king of his castle and therefore has the potential for tragedy or great triumph. With this in mind, a comparison of every man and woman to King David is not only appropriate but needful in that we should understand our true potential for greatness and success. You are living the legend of you in all its archetypal grandeur. You are a great king and you may be criticized for decisions which go against the grain. But in the end, going against the grain with all of its mistakes and fumbles may be God's perfect will for all of us.

Seth Boulton was a successful full-time musician for many years; he is a born-again Christian who currently resides with his girlfriend and daughter in the United States.

Four Interpretations of the David–Jonathan Relationship

James N. Pohlig (West Africa)

Through the centuries, readers have been deeply touched by the account of David and Jonathan's friendship. It speaks of loyalty and intimacy of spirit, of Jonathan's heartbreak over his father Saul's treatment of David, and of David's heartbreak over Jonathan's tragic death in battle—themes that every age has found poignant.

However, cultures and subcultures interpret the nature of that friendship in different ways. Let us briefly look at four different interpretations, separated from each other by time and culture. First, mainstream Western culture has held up David and Jonathan as exemplars of same-gender faithfulness that has no sexual overtones. Second, the contemporary gay and lesbian movement tends to read the account as a not-so-veiled depiction of homoerotic love. Third, West Africans have their own view, which is superficially similar to the mainstream Western view but has a different cultural context. Finally, going back in time, we have a very good idea of how first-century A.D. Greco-Roman culture would have viewed that friendship.

Let us begin with mainstream Western culture. This view follows in the tradition of the ancient Greek myth of Damon and Pythias, in which each friend offers his life to the tyrant of Syracuse for the other. We take it that this model of friendship projects values that include the following: You hold each other's needs and well-being in higher priority than your own; you have similar likes and dislikes; you have similar outlooks on life; you enjoy each other's presence; you are happy to share one's own possessions with each other; and you find it safe and rewarding to share your deepest thoughts with each other. Such friendships often originate out of undergoing some extended experience or hardship together, such as schooling, military service, or common employment. In this model, David and Jonathan were strongly drawn to each other, but with no sexual overtones.

How their relative social statuses meshed is something of a riddle. David is presented as acutely aware before the king, Jonathan's father, of his humble background. If Jonathan bent over backward to befriend him, the reader is led to believe that Jonathan made nothing of it whatsoever. This point is important, because some current research on friendship emphasizes that social constraints tend to be as determinative of such relationships as personal proclivities. It is important to note that mainstream *American* culture, while affirming the nonsexual nature of this kind of friendship, at the same time does not accord it first place in the domain of the sharing of deepest thoughts and feelings. Americans assign this domain instead to marriage.

We turn now to the contemporary gay and lesbian movement, limiting our attention to the part of it that can be regarded as an outgrowth of contemporary Western culture. Perhaps the most notable early claim that David and Jonathan were homoerotic lovers came from Oscar Wilde at his trial in 1895 for sodomy, when he said in court: "The love that dare not speak its name in this century is such a great affection of an elder for a younger man as there was between David and Jonathan." Following today in Wilde's footsteps, it seems almost an article of faith among Scripture-oriented gays and lesbians to adduce in 1 and 2 Samuel indications that David and Jonathan were lovers. In this view, Jonathan concluded some kind of friendship pact with David because "Jonathan loved David as his own soul" (1 Sam. 18:3); in divesting himself of his robe and tunic in order to give them to David (1 Sam. 18:4), Jonathan is taken as offering sexual relations. David's piercing lament after his friend's death (2 Sam. 1:19–27) is often cited as well, especially verse 26: "I am distressed for you, my brother Jonathan; very pleasant have you been to me; your love to me was extraordinary, surpassing the love of women." This language is seen not only as intense but also as connoting sexual interest.

In West Africa, this friendship, however, would be instantly identified as that of two best friends. In Mbe of southeastern Nigeria, for example, the term *wuchi* is not simply "friend"; it specifically denotes the status of two men or two women who are bonded together for a long time, potentially all their lives. Developing a close affinity, each shares with the other deepest thoughts, fears, and desires to a degree that goes far, far beyond what is shared with a spouse. His wife is emphatically *not* a man's closest confidant; that role is taken by one's *wuchi*.

In the same vein, it is very common for West African cultures to completely prohibit public touching between any man and a woman, even if married. But it is very common for two men or two women to walk hand in hand. A Westerner, living in West Africa, must become accustomed to being led or accompanied by the hand of an acquaintance of the same gender. But this kind of physical touch expresses the male—or female—friendship that Africans would recognize in David and Jonathan. The statement, "Very pleasant have you been to me; your love to me was extraordinary, surpassing the love of women," would be seen as quite unremarkable among the Mbe people, for this would be expected of a man and his *wuchi*.

Finally, let us consider how the first-century A.D. Greco-Roman culture probably regarded the David and Jonathan account. Sexual activity in Greco-Roman culture did not essentially depend on personal relationships. It was instead an expression of social hierarchy. Men had relations with their wives, slaves, and prostitutes. Homosexual behavior was common, but it was never between male peers, but rather between men and boys. The Greek word *arete⁻*, although usually glossed as "virtue" or "excellence," was the essential characteristic of men and had an obligatory sexual component. A real man penetrated others, but was himself never penetrated. It was probably for this reason that male peers never had sexual relations; to do so would entail a loss of honor for one, if not for both. Since David and Jonathan appear to regard themselves as peers, Greco-Romans would probably not have considered them to be sexually involved. Furthermore, for Greco-Romans, homosexual relationships were, so far as we can tell, never considered much more than casual. Even man–boy relationships would have probably lasted only a few years. Long-term committed gay relationships were unknown. Thus, the biblical account suggesting a lengthy friendship between David and Jonathan would not have been considered sexual.

It is not known whether the Greco-Romans had any ritualistic oath or other device to establish a "covenant" of friendship such as Jonathan is depicted as setting up with David. But we do know that they had ideals of friendship, such as was expressed by the myth of Damon and Pythias. Besides this story, many relevant quotations have descended to us from the Greeks: "Be slow to fall into friendship; but when thou art in, continue firm and constant" (Socrates). "One loyal friend is worth ten thousand relatives" (Euripides). "What is a friend? A single soul in two bodies" (Aristotle). "Without friends no one would choose to live, though he had all other goods" (Aristotle). We therefore conclude that the Greco-Romans would have viewed David and Jonathan as an example of friendship worthy of that of Damon and Pythias.

We have considered four different cultural readings of David and Jonathan's friendship. Each one can be compelling to its respective cultural "insiders." The humanity that we share, however, with our transcultural "memory" of these two men makes us say to them, "Perhaps what you experienced was not exactly like what any of us today can experience, but we are sure that for you it was a powerful thing."

James N. Pohlig (D.Litt., Biblical Languages, University of Stellenbosch) has worked to analyze various West African languages, to bring literacy to them, to translate the Bible, and to author resources for Old Testament translators in general.

THE WOMAN OF 2 SAMUEL 20 AND ABIGAIL AS PEACEMAKERS

Andreas Kunz-Lübcke (Germany)

There are currently nine major conflicts taking place around the globe, each with more than 1,000 fatalities in the last year. Today, as I sat down to write this, the war in Libya broke out. In more than half of the conflicts (Afghanistan, Somalia, Iraq, Northwest Pakistan), military forces from Western democracies are or were involved. The reasons for the military engagement of the Western democracies differ and are sometime nebulous: The fight against terrorism, the overthrow of an illegitimate ruler, the establishment of democratic structures, the prevention of genocides, and others. All these conflicts have one thing in common: They are difficult to bring to an end. Here I propose that the narrators of two biblical stories in Samuel point to a successful strategy to end a conflict or to avoid it completely: send a diplomatic, peace-seeking woman into a group of violent men.

The story in 2 Samuel 20 is riveting. Under brutal general Joab, the siege becomes more heated. The ramp is headed up, the gigantic ram is assembled. Under the severe shocks of the siege-weapons a first outer wall begins to collapse. If the walls of the city are broken, every hope is lost. What will happen next is inevitable: torture and execution of leaders and defenders of the city and the deportation of the women and children. But wait. In the exact moment of the collapse of the first wall, a single woman appears on the top of a wall: "I am one of the peaceful and faithful in Israel, but you seek to destroy a city and mother in Israel! Why do you swallow the inheritance of YHWH?" (20:19). Only a few words are spoken—but they are effective words. The general stops the siege and explains the reason for his campaign. There is an insurgent behind the city walls: "Deliver this man and I will withdraw from the city!" (20:21). The wise woman negotiates "in her wisdom" with the people of the city. The insurgent is soon decapitated, his head flies over the city wall and the war is over.

2 Samuel 20 narrates an amazing story. During a siege of a city a wise woman appears on the wall and her argument is simple: Negotiations must be conducted *before* you are allowed to siege a city (cf. Deuteronomy 20: 10–12). But the woman on the wall, full of wisdom and politically eloquent, is not the only presentation of a woman within the story. After David hears of the revolt of Sheba, he takes his twenty "concubines" who were raped in public during the Absalom revolt, and detains them in a guarded house (20:3). Here they stay as "living widows." *And he never goes into them.* Twenty women enclosed by walls as living widows without the chance of motherhood on the one hand, and one woman on the wall of a besieged city (calling herself a city and mother in Israel) on the other. The story presents a very ambivalent picture of women's fate: to be a victim of male violence and power or to become a wise speaker and negotiator. To remain behind the walls of a prison-like house or to stand on the wall and rescue an entire city. The story contains extreme variations of women's fate.

The wise woman on top of the city wall who intervenes against an eruption of male-initiated violence is reminiscent of another wise woman—Abigail, who appears at the beginning of the David stories in 1 Samuel 25. David is full of wrath against Nabal, who refused to hand over a considerable quantity food. The reader is confused: Is David's demand against Nabal justified? Or does he act in a Mafia-like manner? The only thing that is clear is that he pursues a cruel strategy. "May God punish me, and even more if I let survive everybody who belongs to him *who pisses against the wall* until morning" (25: 22). These are not the words of a wise statesman; rather they are the words of a man who loses control over himself. Two men act like real men: The rich farmer refused to deliver a very small quantity of his yields. The other cannot accept the refusal. With the aid of 400 heavily armed men David leaves his camp. Four hundred armed men—the reader expects a great number of victims.

However, there is a countermovement in the story. Nabal, whose name means "fool," stands in stark contrast to Abigail, who is characterized as intelligent and attractive (25:3). When the wise beauty Abigail hears about the Fool's rejection of David's demand, she reacts instantly, approaching the disgruntled David with many gifts and a convincing theological argument: "Kill Nabal and his followers and become guilty before YHWH because you shed blood" (25:31). At her words, David relents. And what does the Lord think of Abigail and her actions? It's clear by his response: After 10 days he kills the paralyzed Nabal (25:38).

The scenario here is the same one as in 2 Samuel 20: An angry man with the aim to slaughter a great number of innocent people, a single male person who (innocent or not) is the reason for the assault, a wise woman who acts alone, the use of words to calm down the aggressive mind of the man, and the solution of the conflict by killing the single cause, thus preventing the death of many others.

These two biblical women can be contrasted to a woman in a similar situation in an Assyrian drawing of a siege on a hostile city. In this scene, there also appears a woman on the top of the wall of the besieged city. But here the woman is portrayed with a gesture of entreaty—she is a victim without hope of rescue—and the entire composition leaves no doubt that the city will soon be seized by the Assyrian troops. This highlights the uniqueness of the nameless wise woman in 2 Samuel 20 and of Abigail: They are wise and active women who interact successfully against a male war campaign.

This indeed is a hopeful end to a story of war: Lady Wisdom has beaten the General.

Andreas Kunz-Lübcke is Lecturer for Old Testament at the Missions Seminar in Hermannsburg and apl. Professor for Old Testament at the University of Leipzig, Germany.

THE INSPIRATION OF RIZPAH'S COURAGEOUS HELPLESSNESS

Valerie Bridgeman (United States)

Rizpah fascinates me. Her story in 2 Samuel 21:1–14 is horrific and inspiring at the same time. Rizpah's life was inextricably bound to David because he was a ruthless leader who "sanctified" his brutality by "seeking the face of the Lord." Rizpah was like many biblical women, a political pawn in a game of "who will be king."

I'm not sure when I first started reading and rereading this story. I just know at some point, it captivated me by its senselessness and by Rizpah's courageous helplessness. If I have to pick a time, I would say I started paying close attention to her crazy witness when my sons were teenagers in the 1990s. In Austin, Texas, where we lived at the time, gang activity had picked up and I was afraid of the streets' sway and the dangers of its allure to my middle-class sons. I was afraid of the OGs, the Original Gangstas, who were themselves kings of a certain sort. Because I was a community activist, I was keenly aware of the dangers. But like many mothers of those days, I felt helpless in the face of the pull of gangs and knew only that I would pray and stand vigilant.

Rizpah couldn't stop the violence against her sons and those of her sister-wife Merab, any more than those of us who were trying to battle gang life could stop the influence of gangsta life in our neighborhoods. Like King David, gang leaders wielded power that had impact on people caught in the crosshairs of their power grabs. Reading closely, it's easy to see that Rizpah and Merab were caught in the cross fire of David's power grab for Saul's kingdom. These seven sons were political collateral. And the pretext that their deaths were "revenge" for Saul's actions did not convince Rizpah, or me.

I like Rizpah's crazy stand for dignity for her dead sons, for her insistence that the public display of shame end. She reminds me of the worldwide movement, "Women in Black," the group that stands silently in cities throughout the world in protest against war and other forms of violence (http://www.womeninblack.org/en/vigil). Their witness, like Rizpah's, is both an acknowledgment that they have only the power of right in the face of violent regimes, militarism, and ongoing injustices. But Women in Black members believe they have the power of moral outrage and moral right on their side. Such stands are meant to shame the powers-that-be into doing right, while members also work for peace.

Another thing that strikes me about Rizpah's stance is that she looks crazy in this text. Really. She looks crazy, out on a rock protecting dead bodies from vultures by day and wild animals by night. And she does it for a long time. I often think, someone had to be with her, to relieve her while she slept. Someone *must* have stood with her, even if she started it on her own. Else, how did she survive? When did she sleep? How did she eat?

I am an African American woman who grew up in the 1960s in the United States, the height of the Civil Rights Movement. Many stories from that time feature a singular hero: Martin Luther King, Jr., speaking, Rosa Parks sitting on a bus, or Fannie Lou Hamer testifying before Congress. Though such individuals are lifted up in a singular way, the often-untold story is the cast of thousands of activists and supporters that made their action or voice possible.

Rizpah is one of those unsung heroes in the text, easily overlooked if one is reading only for David's sake. I don't want to be guilty of passing over her witness. Despite the text's insistence that the famine needed David to kill these threats to his throne, in the end we are told the famine didn't end until Rizpah's silent protest for dignity forced David to give the sons, Saul, and Jonathan proper burials.

All these years later, I continue to be intrigued by her.

Valerie Bridgeman is Associate Professor at Lancaster Theological Seminary, United States; she is an ordained preacher and published poet.

QUESTIONS

1. Evaluate Boulton's reading of the David stories. What do we learn about Boulton? About the biblical text? Do you identify with David in any way?

2. How do you understand the relationship between David and Jonathan? How, if at all, does Pohlig's discussion broaden your thinking?

3. What "successful strategy" might contemporary leaders learn from the women in Samuel about avoiding and ending war?

4. How do Bridgeman's life experiences inform her reading of Rizpah? Can you connect with Rizpah in any way in light of your experiences?

CHAPTER 13

ISAIAH 40–55

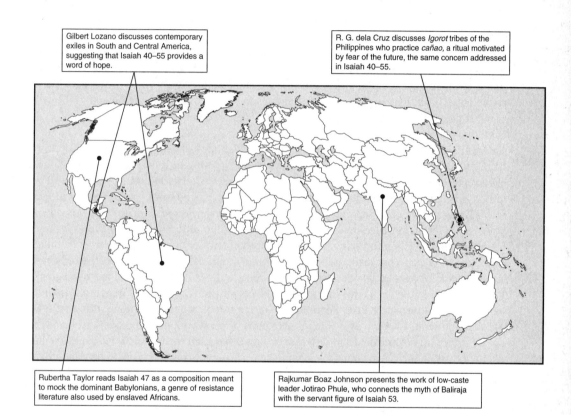

Gilbert Lozano discusses contemporary exiles in South and Central America, suggesting that Isaiah 40–55 provides a word of hope.

R. G. dela Cruz discusses *Igorot* tribes of the Philippines who practice *cañao*, a ritual motivated by fear of the future, the same concern addressed in Isaiah 40–55.

Rubertha Taylor reads Isaiah 47 as a composition meant to mock the dominant Babylonians, a genre of resistance literature also used by enslaved Africans.

Rajkumar Boaz Johnson presents the work of low-caste leader Jotirao Phule, who connects the myth of Baliraja with the servant figure of Isaiah 53.

READINGS

Words of Hope for Contemporary Exiles in South and Central America
Gilbert Lozano

Fear of the Future among *Igorot* Tribes of the Philippines
R. G. dela Cruz

Isaiah as Resistance Literature
Rubertha Taylor

The Myth of Baliraja Compared to the Servant Figure in Isaiah
Rajkumar Boaz Johnson

Words of Hope for Contemporary Exiles in South and Central America

Gilbert Lozano (Colombia)

In 586 B.C.E. the Babylonians captured Jerusalem, destroyed the Temple, and exiled many of the leaders. These events were a severe blow to the Judeans, for they marked the end of their nation. Three things resulted. First, the people's faith in their God YHWH was called into question. The Babylonian conquest meant that YHWH had been defeated by the more powerful Babylonian deities. Second, the destruction of the Jerusalem Temple meant that even if someone wanted to continue worshipping YHWH, the worshipper couldn't do that because the religious system and its structure had been dismantled. Third, the removal of the royal family to Babylon called into question God's promises to the Davidic family (2 Sam. 7:8–16). The composite effect of all these things endangered the survival of Judah as a nation and of the Judeans as a people. Isaiah 40–55 addresses a downtrodden people who had witnessed the violence committed by a powerful empire (43:1–2, 14, 17; 54:4), as can be seen from the "Do not fear" statements uttered more than 10 times throughout the book. Though we cannot underestimate the effect of those things on the Judeans, the actual splitting of a population into two groups, namely, those who were allowed to remain in the land of Judah and those who were deported to Babylon, must have been horrendous in its own way. It is on this element that I will focus.

Today people often travel hundreds of miles on business or pleasure trips. It is one thing, however, to go on a trip voluntarily. It is something quite different to be forced to leave one's homeland. And yet, the forcible removal and uprooting of entire populations is something that continues to occur. This leads us to ask, how does one define "exile"? Does it only refer to the relocation of people outside of national borders or does it also point to the relocation even within internal borders? To this day millions of people are forced to leave their homes in order to seek refuge somewhere else. People move or are forced to leave for many different reasons. Throughout Latin America, as is true in other parts of the world, people move for two main reasons. First, Latin Americans from different countries have left their hometowns and have moved internally within their own countries seeking better economic opportunities. The rapid urbanization of Latin American countries has been the result of this process. In this fashion, people from Brazil's northeast have left their impoverished states and moved to the megalopolises of São Paulo and Rio de Janeiro seeking to leave their poverty behind and to find a better life in the city. Many people have similarly left the countryside and relocated to the capital cities of La Paz, Quito, Lima, or Bogotá. Moreover, millions of people have left their homelands in order to seek a better future in other countries, especially the United States.

The second reason people have left their homes is to escape violence. Once again, there have been internal displacements of entire population groups. Due to civil strife within their countries, indigenous peoples have been forced to leave their ancestral homelands in several Central American countries, especially Guatemala and El Salvador. Then, there is the case of Colombia, which is going through one of the longer-lasting civil conflicts in the world. Since the 1960s, Marxist guerrillas have fought government forces for control of the land. In the late 1980s and early 1990s, the conflict was exacerbated by the creation of right-wing paramilitaries who fought the guerrillas. In the last decade other armed groups have been formed, leading to a veritable humanitarian crisis. These violent groups target mostly peasants (countryside inhabitants), but women (often the victims of sexual abuse), indigenous people, and Afro-Colombians are particularly vulnerable to exploitation as well. As a result, Colombia has the second-largest number of internally displaced people in the world. According to the UN Refugee Agency (UNHCR), there were close to 3.6 million people who were internally displaced in Colombia in 2010, and 115,000 refugees and asylum-seekers in neighboring countries—though it is likely that these figures are even higher. By any measure these are staggering numbers. But they are just that—numbers. They don't help us to see the unimaginable suffering of those who have been displaced, those who, like the Judeans, have been exiled from their homes.

In Colombia and elsewhere in South America, those struggles are the continuation of a long series of conflicts over resources and land that began with the arrival of the first Europeans on these shores. Control of natural resources and access to land continues to lead to the forcible removal of people everywhere on this continent. Oil companies seeking to dig often cause the migration of entire populations to new areas (e.g., Ecuador, Colombia). Even national governments set aside human rights or disregard popular sentiment in order to pursue grandiose development projects. For instance, the construction of the Belo Monte Dam in the state of Pará in central Brazil is caus-ing the flooding of hundreds of square miles of ancestral indigenous lands. The people who have lived on those lands for thousands of years are being forced to leave in order to give way to a vision of development that has no regard for indigenous rights or international appeals.

What does Isaiah 40–55 have to say to those people? What connections can be made between that sixth-century book and the people today who are exiled both internally and exter-nally? First, its message irradiates hope today, as it did in the past. To those experiencing exile, the book speaks of a God who sees their plight and encourages them (41:10, 13; 54:4). Second, the book announces judgment upon those who cause human suffering, whether individuals or empires (41:11–12; 47:1–15; 51:8–10). Lastly, throughout Isaiah 40–55 we find the witness, seen elsewhere in the Hebrew Bible, that YHWH sides with the defenseless (40:1–2; 41:17; 42:6–7; 43:1–4). This should inspire people of faith to work alongside God on behalf of suffering and dis-placed people. Indeed, although centuries separate us, Isaiah 40–55 continues to address impor-tant issues that we confront in our world and it continues to offer hope for the millions of exiles in South and Central America today.

Gilbert Lozano (Ph.D.) taught at Fidelis: the Mennonite School of Theology, Curitiba, Brazil, and is currently Associate Professor of Biblical Studies at Anderson University, United States.

FEAR OF THE FUTURE AMONG *IGOROT* TRIBES OF THE PHILIPPINES

R. G. dela Cruz (Philippines)

Among the Filipinos living in the mountain ranges of the Cordilleras are the *Igorots*. In the Province of Benguet on the northern Luzon island, there are three prominent *Igorot* tribes: the *Kankana-ey*, the *Ibaloi*, and the *Kalanguya*. Although history remembers the *Igorots* as unconquered and unin-fluenced by the Spanish colonization that brought Christianity to the Philippine Islands, many have since become Christians under the influence of American missionaries. I have been living in Baguio City since 1986, where I have developed good friendships and acquaintances with Benguet *Igorots*. Most of them are my fellow ministers of the Gospel and Christian believers.

The *Igorots* practice a ritual called *cañao*. It is a social/cultural and religious event. Although the Philippine Tourism Authority promotes *cañao* as a kind of grand cultural festival, emphasizing its sociological aspect, it is first and foremost a religious matter to common *Igorots*. Specifically, it is a ritual motivated by dread and fear of the future. The dance celebrations, the clanging sounds, and the eating festivities do not reflect the real purpose and the meaning for the person or family that sponsors the *cañao*. The *Kankana-eys*, the *Ibalois*, and the *Kalanguyas* in particular exercise their faith in the *cañao* ritual to stop a misfortune. If a person dreams about a tragedy, then a *cañao* must be done to abort the impending disaster. When a family experiences crisis and wants it to cease, a *cañao* is performed to solve the ongoing problem. These Benguet *Igorots* are willing to spend a huge amount of money and invite an elder priest shaman (*mambunong*) to lead the ritual. They will invite their family members, friends, and neighbors to join them. They butcher animals for meat to feed those who have come for the *cañao*, which makes it very expensive. It is a big community event. Even if the person or the family does not have the resources to hold a *cañao*, they will often borrow money to pay for the ritual because safety, peace, and harmony are dependent upon it.

Although many of the *Kankana-eys*, *Ibalois*, and *Kalanguyas* are Catholics or Protestants, they are still influenced by this fear of the future if *cañao* is not performed. It is indeed difficult to separate religion from culture. Many of them, however, find hope and comfort in certain passages from the Bible. One such text is Isaiah 41. Here the people of Israel are in exile—their nation has been destroyed. They have no king and no temple; the situation is bleak. They are in need of hope, of restoration; their fear of the future must be overcome. And this is precisely the word that the prophet gives. The declaration of God's oracle is plain: Those who trust in God have nothing to fear. When those who trust God are dismayed because of the enemy and forces of evil that are against them, God promises to strengthen and help them (41:10–11). God vows to eliminate their fear. The prophet proclaims that God is in control; there is no reason to live in dread. This message is deeply inspiring and encouraging for Christian *Igorots*. It encourages them, as it did ancient Israel, to be hopeful about the future; it gives them confidence that they will "thresh the mountains and crush them," that they will have the power to "make the hills like chaff," which the wind carries away (41:15–16)—and with it the crippling terror associated with *cañao*.

For many *Igorots* the question then becomes how should they approach *cañao*. Some argue that after becoming a Christian one should have nothing to do with *cañao* and other *Igorot* practices, like the rituals associated with the burial of the dead. They maintain that these are purely pagan practices which must be avoided. Many of the Protestant (Pentecostal, Baptist, Methodist, etc.) pastors and churches reason thus. On the other side, there are those (mostly Catholics and Anglicans-Episcopalians) who participate in the *cañao* because of its communal and social value. The former conservative group, for example, sees the use of gongs and the dances that are part of *cañao* as simple paganism that must be avoided. The gongs are meant to call the ancestral spirits and the dances to communicate with and appease the spirits of the dead, ideas which are contrary to the Christian faith, they would argue. On the other side, some Christian *Igorots* apply Christian content to the ritual forms. For them, the gongs and dances become a type of thanksgiving festival where the focus is now on God and his goodness.

Whether or not to continue practicing *cañao* is a hotly debated topic among *Igorot* Christians. But all can agree that passages such as Isaiah 41 offer a word of peace, hope, and security for those who are faithful.

R. G. dela Cruz is Lecturer at Asia Pacific Theological Seminary in Baguio City, Philippines; he is an ordained minister of the South Central Cordillera District Council of the Philippines General Council of the Assemblies of God.

Isaiah as Resistance Literature

Rubertha Taylor (United States)

Biblical scholars describe the literary structure of Isaiah 47 as a poetic composition of humiliation and mockery against the political structure of ancient Babylon. Various scholars classify some narratives and behaviors of enslaved Africans and their descendants under the same genre. In this project, I adopt James C. Scott's terminology to argue that Isaiah 47 and certain narratives and behaviors of captive Africans and their descendants classify as "weapons of the weak"—tools of resistance exercised behind a mask of public compliance. These parallel writings and behaviors deviate from a "norm" and provide subordinates a way to articulate a different reality. Isaiah 47 serves as an example that Israel, a subordinate nation, expressed themes that humiliated and dismissed Babylonian power.

Stories about my maternal second great-grandfather (a son of a slave woman and a white slave owner) and his descendants born into a segregated North America influence my interpretation of biblical exilic narratives. The information passed down to me from my grandparents and parents leads me to see memory, rituals, and the emergence of social leaders as tools of resistance—tools which are also present within the Israelites' exilic community. I believe this similarity demonstrates that North American captives and their descendants embodied biblical texts and that their experiences inform Isaiah 47.

Isaiah 40–55 is a compilation of thoughts that culminated into a unified, public poetic declaration of resistance against Babylon's dominancy. Isaiah 47 opens with a series of commands against the Babylonian empire. As a nation once entrusted with YHWH's people, the writer now refers to Babylon as a female disrobed of its glory with a dismal fate. At no place in Isaiah 47 is this nation given space to negotiate YHWH's vengeance. Moreover, the tone of this chapter deliberately taunts and indicts Babylon for its previous actions against Israel. Such a portrayal leads to the following question: What has led the author to make this bold declaration of Babylon's downfall?

To address this question through an African-American hermeneutic, I begin by recognizing false compliance and self-empowering messages as two covert forms of resistance operating in both social contexts. In regards to my African ancestors, public group resistance against African enslavement did not occur, for the most part anyway, after their initial arrival in North America. Those who survived the Middle Passage needed time to recover physically, emotionally, and psychologically from the horrific journey during which as many as half of the stolen Africans died. Apparently during this time of recovery, many of my ancestors began to make adjustments to living as captives in a strange new world; and yet, remembering their heritage as free people in Africa was paramount. This connection between memories and current thoughts created tension between forced compliance and an ability to think beyond physical and social restraints. As my ancestors came to know enslavement in North America, their memory produced states of mind that challenged their present social realities and made it difficult for them to perform work that misrepresented beliefs about themselves and their heritage. Consequently, covert forms of resistance began to develop and operate as means for survival.

Unlike the resistance of many Africans, public group resistance among Israelites occurred at the beginning of Babylon's invasion but faded away following the death of Gedaliah and other Judeans at Mizpah. A lack of information regarding exilic circumstances leaves many biblical scholars uncertain of social activities of the Israelites under Babylonian domination. What is certain is that many exilic passages encourage Israelites to remember their heritage as covenant people of YHWH. This indentured group considered itself servants of YHWH, not servants of the Babylonian empire. In so doing, the Israelites spoke with assurance of YHWH's redemptive powers as though there had been no hiatus in YHWH's presence or delivering acts.

The impact that memory has on autonomous forms of resistance includes individual and group ritualistic performances. To remember their heritage before living in captivity, my enslaved ancestors developed elaborate plans to practice African traditions and religious rituals in North America. They expressed themselves with music and, for those who were literate, creative writing. Their forms of expression also included images in art, stories about their homeland, and, in some cases, stories from the Bible. By combining African traditions with forms in the new world, my ancestors developed rituals that established self-identity, strengthened social bonds, and taught moral, social, and religious instructions. Still, for a number of them, this assimilation into a colonized North America did not result in absolute conformity. Instead, resistance in forms of conversations of empowerment, encouragement, contempt, and hope operated consistently beyond the purview of power holders.

Sermons, songs that promote divine deliverance, messages of contempt, and sorrow songs are all present in the exilic literature from the Hebrew Bible. A recognition of these forms is important for several reasons: First, it demonstrates that sermons encourage the Israelites to remember YHWH; second, it portrays songs of faith in YHWH as a redeemer even when YHWH is not actively involved; third, it refutes eternal slavery; and fourth, it shows that through lamentations the Israelites grieve as a collective nation. Given these four fundamental causes, the Israelite rituals serve to promote the importance of memory, faith, negation, and unity as tools for establishing modes of resistance. These tools of resistance encourage autonomous living identical to those of my African ancestors, namely self-identity, social bonding, and moral, social, and religious instructions. From this list, forms of religious instruction function as a primary cause for both groups' movement from covert to overt means of resistance.

Although my ancestors of African descent did not claim a covenant with a god as did the Israelites, religious instructions or beliefs were keys for developing an understanding of themselves in their new social context. For those captives who adopted Christianity as a major religion, some were influenced by biblical texts to lead insurrections such as the one led by Nat Turner in 1831. In a confession to his lawyer, Turner revealed that the Spirit of God told him to kill his enemies. His full confession, certain Negro spirituals, sermons, and writings all mirror Isaiah 47:3 and 6 in claiming that divine interruption into human affairs functions to initiate vengeance against social injustice and human exploitation. While this claim of divine interjection serves as a catalyst for social changes, it alone does not set in motion events necessary to transform a community; an emergence of social leader(s) and community participation are two other components.

A combination of God, social leaders, and community involvement merges religion with social issues, in which subordinate leaders emerge from the shadows of false compliance to announce God's intentions to change current social conditions and to organize people to carry out these transformations. Turner's announcement to four men of God's intention to reverse current social orders and his solicitation of them and others to carry out this divine mandate reflects Second Isaiah's announcement of a divine purpose for a new dispensation of peace and restoration to an exilic people and a call for the Israelites to declare collectively YHWH's intention to take vengeance against Babylon.

At a glance, the public declaration of Babylon's dismissal of power in Isaiah 47 appears abrupt. However, a close examination of this passage reveals YHWH's recognition of the Israelites' oppression and their faith in YHWH to deliver them. Their acknowledgment of and faith in YHWH suggests that the Israelites maintained forms of their preexilic relationship with YHWH throughout 70 years of exile.

As an African-American female biblical scholar, my reading of Isaiah 47 reveals that "weapons of the weak" such as memory, a practice of traditional rituals, and an emergence of social leaders can lead to open mockery against dominant forces. These bold proclamations clearly indicate that forms of resistance behind a mask of public compliance are *not weak*; rather, they provide subordinates a way to articulate a different normality that represents and supports beliefs about themselves and their heritage and shields them from an all-encompassing force of public humiliation and human exploitation.

Rubertha Taylor taught six years in the Bible Department at Lee University; she resides in Cleveland, Tennessee, United States.

THE MYTH OF BALIRAJA COMPARED TO THE SERVANT FIGURE IN ISAIAH

Rajkumar Boaz Johnson (India)

Isaiah 53 is the grand finale of the so-called Servant Songs in the book of Isaiah. The unnamed servant is a royal figure, yet he is portrayed as disfigured (52:14), "despised and rejected" by humanity (53:3). The servant becomes the paradigm of the depths of sorrow, pain, and rejection. Nonetheless, the final song begins and ends in a note of hope: "See, my servant shall prosper; he shall be exalted and lifted up, and shall be very high" (52:13); and "Therefore I will allot him a portion with the great" (53:12).

Who is this "servant?" In Christianity, of course, it is Jesus. The New Testament quotes this text to describe the rejection and passion of Christ (John 12:38; Acts 8:26–35; Romans 10:16). In Jewish tradition, by contrast, "the servant" is generally understood to be the corporate people of Israel—that is, not an individual but the nation as a whole. In Western biblical interpretation, therefore, one is forced to choose between one of these two. Viewing Isaiah 53 and the Servant figure in the context of Eastern traditions, namely, in conjunction with the low-caste and outcaste people of India, offers us a different—perhaps even better—approach to the text.

More than 80 percent of the population of India comes from low caste (*shudra*), outcaste (*dalit* or *ati-shudra*), and the aborigine tribes (*adivasi*). Approximately 12–15 percent of the population consider themselves as high-caste Hindus: the priests (*Brahmin*), the royalty (*Kshatriya*), and the business castes (*Vyashiya*). These high-caste Hindus are said to be descendents of the Aryans or pure-blooded people who migrated to India from Central Asia. In high-caste Hindu texts, the low caste, outcaste, and aborigines are always described in very derogatory terms. For instance, *Manu Dharma Shastra VIII, 413–414* reads, "But the Shudra, whether bought or unbought, he may compel to do the work of a slave; for he was created by the self-existent (*svyanbhu*) to be the slave of the Brahmin." Based on texts like this, the low castes, outcastes, and aborigines of India have been treated very poorly and enslaved historically by the high castes.

In the history of India, there have arisen some low-caste saints who have revolted. Here I will focus on the writings of one such low-caste leader, Jotirao Phule (1827–1890), since he makes a poignant connection with the servant figure of Isaiah 53. Born a *shudra* in the Satara district of Maharashtra, Phule develops his theories on the emancipation of *shudras* and *ati-shudras* based on the stories narrated and songs sung among the low-caste people in Maharashtra. In an important book entitled *Gulamgiri* (Slavery), published in 1873, Phule sets out the task of demythologizing Hindu myths and reinstating the *shudra* narrative. That is, for Phule, Hindu myths are political and sociological tools used to denigrate and demonize the original inhabitants of India (the low castes, outcastes, and aborigine), and his objective is to counter those by elevating the stories of low-caste people.

One such story is the myth of Baliraja, which literally means the Sacrificial King. This mythological King Bali is also found in Hindu texts. However, in the Hindu texts he is described as an Asura (a Demon). One Hindu text, for example, reads as follows:

> In the beginning the demon Bali controlled the worlds. Then Vishnu became incarnate as a dwarf, and went where Bali was performing sacrifice. He became a Brahmin and asked Bali to give him the space that he could cover in three strides. Bali was pleased to do this, thinking that the dwarf was just a dwarf. But the dwarf stepped over the heaven, the sky, and the earth in three strides, stealing the property of the demon. He sent the demons and all their sons and grandsons to hell (Patala), and gave Indra kingship over all humanity. (Vayu Purana 2.36.74–86)

By contrast, according to the *shudra* myth of Baliraja, he is not an Asura (Demon). Rather he is the King of kings. Phule notes that in the *shudra* story, the Kingdom of Bali was global. "He was famous for his just wars...He was a champion of the downtrodden. He was a lover of music...He appointed an officer to dispense justice...We can see from this account that Bali's kingdom had spread far and wide" (*Gulamgiri*, 31). Bali presided over ritual sacrifices on the banks of rivers like Narmada—an act that commemorated the *shudra* idea of creation. The Aryan gods wanted to conquer Bali, so Vishnu took the form of a dwarf. He tricked Bali into giving him the amount of land, which he covered in three strides. With two strides he covered the heavens, the earth, and the netherworld. The third step was upon the head of Bali, who was killed and pushed into the netherworld (*patal*). The *shudra* story claims that Baliraja, the Sacrificial King, became the paradigm of sacrifice. However, he will come one day to establish his just kingdom, which the *shudras* and *ati-shudras* celebrate and anticipate with several festivals and rituals.

Although Phule never became a Christian, he was exposed to Christianity in a school established by Scottish Missionaries. He called Hindu myths "despicable lies," and considered himself and his followers to be Truthseekers. In his quest for truth, he discovered the connection between the suffering Messiah image in Isaiah 52–53, the suffering image of Christ in the New Testament, and the suffering Baliraja. This image of the "fallen king who will rise in the eschaton [end-times]," according to Phule, is the low-caste and outcaste image of the servant of Isaiah 53. The servant-king or *shudra*-king is killed by the high-caste invaders of India. Yet, one day he will arise to set up his kingdom—the Bali Raj. In low-caste thought, the suffering of the individual Baliraja is a paradigm for the corporate suffering of the low-caste people at the hands of the high-caste Hindus. Their rituals enable them to reenact the death of Baliraja. Yet, this Baliraja ritually arises once a year, to express their hope that Baliraja's kingdom will come one day.

In terms of the connection with Jesus, Phule writes, "Thus the prophecy of our venerable old ladies 'May Bali's kingdom come!' seems to have materialized when the Baliraja (Jesus Christ) was crucified by a few wicked desperadoes, and a great movement of liberation was set in motion" (*Gulamgiri*, 36). When Bali's kingdom comes, there will be complete salvation, and universal peace and justice for all. This is reminiscent of the hope which is expressed in the beginning and end of the final Servant Song in Isaiah 53 and of the hope which Christians find in the crucified Jesus. In short, the servant figure, according to Phule, is both the Christ of the Bible, and the suffering *shudras, ati-shudras,* and the aborigines.

Rajkumar Boaz Johnson was reared in one of the slums of Delhi, where he witnessed many of his young friends taken into slavery by high-caste Hindus; he is Professor of Biblical and Theological Studies at North Park University, United States.

QUESTIONS

1. How does the movement of people within or across the borders of your county compare to the movement of people discussed by Lozano?

2. What would you recommend to Christian *Igorots* debating whether or not to continue practicing *cañao*?

3. Comment on a number of specific verses in Isaiah 47 which illustrate Taylor's reading of the text.

4. Can the identity of the servant legitimately be all three: Christ, the corporate people of Israel, and the suffering *shudras, ati-shudras,* and the aborigines?

CHAPTER 14

JEREMIAH

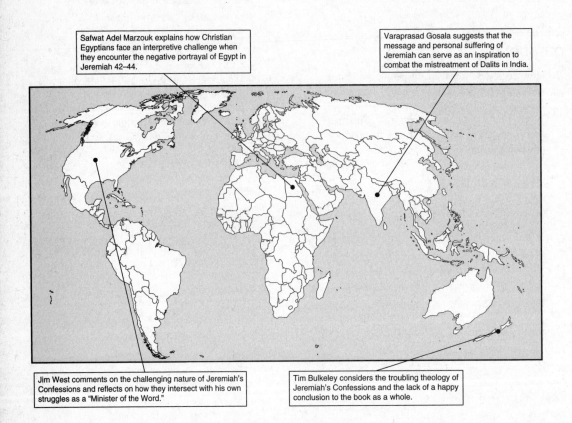

Safwat Adel Marzouk explains how Christian Egyptians face an interpretive challenge when they encounter the negative portrayal of Egypt in Jeremiah 42–44.

Varaprasad Gosala suggests that the message and personal suffering of Jeremiah can serve as an inspiration to combat the mistreatment of Dalits in India.

Jim West comments on the challenging nature of Jeremiah's Confessions and reflects on how they intersect with his own struggles as a "Minister of the Word."

Tim Bulkeley considers the troubling theology of Jeremiah's Confessions and the lack of a happy conclusion to the book as a whole.

READINGS

Reading Jeremiah as a Christian Egyptian
Safwat Adel Marzouk

Jeremiah and the Caste System
Varaprasad Gosala

The Troubling Theology of Jeremiah's Confessions
Tim Bulkeley

Jeremiah's Confessions and My Own Pilgrimage
Jim West

READING JEREMIAH AS A CHRISTIAN EGYPTIAN

Safwat Adel Marzouk (Egypt)

Christian Egyptians face an interpretive challenge when they read the Old Testament, namely, the negative portrayal of Egypt. How should a Christian Egyptian read the story of the exodus from Egypt, where the Egyptians are depicted as the enemy of God? How should one read the vilification of Egypt in the book of Ezekiel? How should we read the negative portrayal of Egypt in the book of Jeremiah? Do we read with and identify with the Israelites or with the Egyptians? The majority of Christian Egyptians read the biblical text from the perspective of the Israelites, identifying themselves with the Israelites, accepting—uncritically—the predominantly negative representation of Egypt in the Old Testament. In contrast, a minority of Christian Egyptians reject the Old Testament as Scripture because of its negative portrayal of Egypt. Can we find a middle ground?

To find such ground as Christian Egyptians, we must, on the one hand, challenge those who take the text at face value without considering how the negative portrayal of Egypt in Scripture has impacted the way they think about who they are. On the other hand, we must challenge those who reject the biblical text simply because they find it offensive to their political identity as Egyptians. Reading the Old Testament as a Christian Egyptian means living with a paradoxical identity as we are simultaneously an "Egyptian" and an "Israelite."

Here I will focus on the negative representation of Egypt in Jeremiah 42–44, a text in which Jeremiah proclaims words of judgment on the Judeans who sought Egypt as a place of refuge in the aftermath of the Babylonian destruction of Jerusalem. In the text, Jeremiah urges the people to stay in Judah, promising them that God would make them flourish (42:10). The prophet threatens that in Egypt the Judean refugees would be struck by the sword (42:16), famine, and pestilence (42:16–17). Egypt will be a large grave for the Judeans, argues Jeremiah. The prophet declares that *all* of those who will go to Egypt will die and no remnant or survivor will outlive the disaster that God is about to bring upon them there (42:16; 44:27).

Because of the disastrous and traumatic experience of the Babylonian invasion of Jerusalem (Jer. 39), and the divisions, treachery, conflict within the Judeans who survived the Babylonian invasion (Jer. 40–41), many groups among this remnant did not find the land of Judah to be secure or safe for them, thus they sought security in Egypt (41:16–18). This group of survivors claimed, "We will go to the land of Egypt, where we shall not see war, or hear the sound of the trumpet, or be hungry for bread, and there we will stay" (42:14). Despite the prophetic warnings, this group of Judeans was willing to take the risk of going down to Egypt rather than stay in the ruined Judah under Babylonian imperial power. Ironically, these Judeans forced Jeremiah and his scribe Baruch to go with them to Egypt (43:1–7). While residing in Egypt, Jeremiah pronounced words of judgment upon Egypt, its cities, and its king (37:8–13; 44:30, 46). The divine punishment focuses not only on the Judeans who are in Egypt but also on Egypt itself.

Reading with the Judeans who had to flee to Egypt, we can construct a representation of Egypt as a place of danger but also of hope. The danger resided in the reconfiguration of their identity as a people of God in a foreign land—how can they be Judeans when not living In Judah. The hope that Egypt offered is more than just a safe place—a place out of which a new expression of the Israelite faith might emerge. The paradox that characterizes Egypt in the book Jeremiah as both a place of danger and a place of refuge and hope is similar to the paradox that Christian Egyptians encounter when they read Scripture. Like the Judeans, who, despite the prophetic warning, decided to take refuge in Egypt, Christian Egyptians take refuge in a Scripture that invites them to rethink their identity as the people of God.

In order to construct a new perspective on Egypt in Jeremiah 42–44, one has to read the text employing the hermeneutic of suspicion, which demands challenging the voice of the authors and their portrayals of the characters—in our case the Judeans and Egypt. When we look closely at these chapters, we discover that assumed hierarchies are questioned in the text: prophetic authority, the Babylonians, and male figures are challenged.

The people who remained in Judah doubted Jeremiah's source of prophecy. For this group, it was not God who stood behind Jeremiah's words, but rather Baruch (43:3), who sought to hand them over to the Babylonians. Notably, Jeremiah's view that defeat by the Babylonians was God's punishment on the people is exactly what the Babylonians themselves assert (40:1–8). Understandably, then, the people of Judah were suspicious of Jeremiah's and Baruch's loyalties— were they on the side of the Babylonians. By doubting Jeremiah's words, the oppressed Judeans were attempting to oppose the Babylonian imperial authority. For them, escaping to Egypt was a form of resistance against the empire. But for this resistance to happen, a greater resistance first took place, that is, questioning Jeremiah's prophetic authority.

Furthermore, in a predominantly masculine culture, the voice of women is usually silenced. Jeremiah 44, however, narrates a dialogue, in Egypt, between the prophet and a crowd of Judean women who were accused of idolatry. For Jeremiah, idolatry is what brought the disaster of the exile (Jer. 7) and it is what will bring disasters upon the Judeans in Egypt (44:1–14). These women disagree with Jeremiah's interpretation of the events; they claim that disasters have fallen upon them only because they stopped worshipping the Queen of Heaven (probably a fertility goddess; 44:15–19). The prophet rejects their view and insists that a further judgment will come upon them in Egypt (44:20–30). The key here is that these women get to speak: they voice their perspective which differs from Jeremiah's; thus they resist and undermine a masculine and a monolithic religious perspective.

In Egypt, not only is there safety for the Judeans, but there is also the potential to experience a pluralistic culture with diverse religious expressions. By contrast, for Jeremiah, going to Egypt meant worshipping false gods, which would threaten the survival of a Jewish identity. From the women's point of view, the escape to Egypt also had the potential to produce new cultural and religious identities for the Israelite community. And indeed that is exactly what happened: the Jewish community in Egypt did flourish and it made great contributions to religious thought beginning in antiquity and continuing all the way down to the modern period. And for me, as a Christian Egyptian, who lives in a complex, pluralistic society, that is a compelling and comforting thought.

Similar to the Judeans who decided to take the risk by going to Egypt, Christian Egyptians are invited to take the risk of reading the Old Testament despite its negative portrayal of Egypt. Learning from the Judeans who challenged the prophetic authority, the male voice, and the imperial discourse, Christian Egyptians are encouraged to wrestle with any monolithic hierarchy that pushes them to either accept uncritically how Egypt is portrayed in the Old Testament or reject the Old Testament as Scripture just because it is offensive. Wrestling with Scripture is risky, but also has the potential of creating new and profound expressions of faith.

Safwat Adel Marzouk, a Christian Egyptian, is Assistant Professor of Old Testament at the Anabaptist Mennonite Biblical Seminary, United States.

JEREMIAH AND THE CASTE SYSTEM

Varaprasad Gosala (India)

Dalits in India are the most oppressed and vulnerable people victimized by the exploitative nature of the caste system. Astoundingly, even in the twenty-first century untouchability, discrimination, oppression, exclusivity, and humiliation continue to be employed in cruel proportions. No magical spell can combat the hegemonic caste system; rather serious action-oriented strategies need to be explored, mobilized, and utilized.

This article is an attempt to enlighten and sensitize diverse readers to the realities of the inherent manipulative mechanisms of the caste structures, and to counter it through collaborative strategies and solutions that are truly effective and liberative. The life and message of Jeremiah can assist in this regard.

Though the practice of the caste system has supposedly been abolished, it no doubt continues in today's postmodern India. For example, in Karnataka (South India), the practice of *Made Snana* (rolling bath) is a contemporary ritual. As part of festival activities, the Brahmins (one of the members of the four castes who occupy the top cadre of the caste structure) are served food on plantain leaves, and upon completion of their meal, the Dalits roll on the leftovers of the high-caste Brahmins. The dominant belief behind this is that when the Dalits come into contact with the *yengili* (food defiled by touching the mouth or saliva) on the leftovers of the Brahmins, it will help to cure the diseases of the Dalits. Recently, the Dalits protested against this as a humiliating and inhuman ritual.

Furthermore, the day-to-day lives of Dalits can be difficult. To give but one of many possible examples, on February 16, 2012, in Saniyan village of Haryana (North India), Rajesh Kumar, a Dalit, was travelling on a tractor-trolley along with 14 others to a neighboring village. When they made a stop on the way, Kumar looked around for a drink and found an earthen pot full of water in a nearby field. It happened to be the pot and field of a man named Pappu, a high-caste farmer. When Pappu saw Kumar drinking from the pot, he attacked him with a sharp weapon, almost severing his hand and inflicting serious injuries on him: Pappu was angry because the earthen pot and the water within had been polluted by the touch of a Dalit.

The book of Jeremiah portrays Jeremiah as both a true prophet and a true human. Not only did his message show concern toward the sufferings of lower-strata people, but Jeremiah too became a victim of severe abuse (e.g., Jer. 36–39). His message emphasized the plight of the marginalized by chastising the leaders for neglecting the less-fortunate (7:1–15; 21:1–10; 22:1–5; 23:1–4).Jeremiah observed that the judiciary system had become corrupted and failed to uphold the law of the land and that monarchical authority resorted to oppression and robbery, causing violence to the downtrodden. He reminded the leaders to observe the law, which says not to oppress the alien, orphan, and widow. He also reminded the king that it was his job to see that justice be implemented for every member of the society (22:3–5). In 23:1–4, Jeremiah portrays the king as the shepherd; but instead of leading the flock in the right direction toward the green and safe pastures, the kings have destroyed their flocks, the people. Instead of feeding them, they are greedily filling themselves. Instead of unifying the flock, the kings scatter them. Thus God himself will gather the people whom the bad shepherd-kings have scattered among different lands (23:1–4).

Because of his confrontational message, Jeremiah was imprisoned (26:11–18; 37) and treated cruelly. He was thrown into a cistern and left to die (Jer. 38). His words were burned (Jer. 36). He was, in short, treated like a Dalit for standing up for the Dalits of his day. Sometimes, it seems, Jeremiah had to confront God about his own mistreatment (e.g., 20:7–18). Regardless of the obstacles he faced, Jeremiah pressed on, as one with fire in his bones. His uncompromising prophetic zeal is essential to reconstruct a classless, casteless society that will offer equal and ample opportunities for a new creation here on earth—forever and ever.

Varaprasad Gosala is an ordained minister of the Andhra Evangelical Lutheran Church (AELC); he is currently pursuing his doctoral studies in Old Testament at the United Theological College, Bangalore, South India.

THE TROUBLING THEOLOGY OF JEREMIAH'S CONFESSIONS

Tim Bulkeley (New Zealand)

Once upon a time, when I was young and impressionable, I thought that Jeremiah was one of the finest and most inspiring books in Scripture. I had not then actually read Jeremiah, just selected passages that had been mentioned and sounded interesting. There was powerful language, vivid pictures, and, above all, a theology which presented an all-powerful creator God truly engaged with the world, and sharing the suffering and pain inherent in human life. I attributed all this to Jeremiah the prophet, who must, I thought, have been one of the great theologians.

Then I became a theology student. I learned that the book was the product of a history of redaction. I practiced spotting the handiwork of Deuteronomists and other editors tampering with the pristine words of Jeremiah. Some years later, I was asked to teach Jeremiah. I like to have a good feel for material I teach, so I recorded the book and played it back during my commute for a couple of weeks. The result was shocking.

This book, and Bible character, I had loved appeared self-centered, salacious, and vindictive. Successive listening only made the problem worse. The tone and contents of the book of Jeremiah are (with the possible exception of the parts we read most often in church) horrid.

Many scholars move beyond the romantic notion of the book as a memoir recording the prophet's teaching and recognize that the only "Jeremiah" to whom we have clear access is the character who serves as the book's main subject (and often its narrator). This just shifts the blame from a sixth-century prophet to an unidentified number of "editors." The book remains just nasty.

The passages known as the "Confessions of Jeremiah" (which are not "confessions" in any usual sense, but poetic pieces cast as intimate conversations between "Jeremiah" and his God) serve as examples (Jer. 11:18–20; 12:1–6; 15:10–21; 17:14–18; 18:18–23; 20:7–13).

In the first passage in 11:19 we are encouraged to sympathize with the speaker, who casts himself as victim: "like a gentle lamb led to the slaughter" who was, until God revealed them, ignorant of his opponents' schemes. He appropriately commits his problem to the Almighty: "But you, O Lord of hosts, who judge righteously, who try the heart and the mind, let me see your retribution upon them, for to you I have committed my cause" (11:20). Yahweh informs him of the villains' identity and aims, before promising violent retribution: they will die by the sword, their sons and their daughters will die of starvation, and not even a remnant will survive (11:22–23).

This announcement is shocking. These are not unknown and unidentified random victims of warfare, but the speaker's neighbors' children, who will die by famine till none are left. The reason for this atrocity is not large-scale, systematic evil in their society, but rather it is precisely because of their threat to the prophet himself. Yahweh's retribution does not fit the restrictions of the LexTalionis (Leviticus 24:20), for he promises to take not one life for the threat of murder but the lives of all the children of those who threatened.

Something strange is going on here. The response seems disproportionate. Is this because the text is "primitive" and we can from our advanced ethical standpoint ignore it? Such chronological snobbery reflects a myth of human perfectibility that twentieth-century wars, genocides, and other atrocities have surely exposed as untrue.

Abhorrent features of the book of Jeremiah, like this disproportion, can perhaps be at least somewhat softened when one recognizes that in the book "the story of Jeremiah" is used to explore the story of Yahweh and the fall of Judah. Jeremiah's Confessions (with their dialogue form) engage with Yahweh around themes of the "word" of God (warning, exhorting, and finally threatening), what it means to be faithful to a God who, unlike other gods, stands beyond the demands of human ideologies, but who stands in covenant solidarity with human creatures.

The last "Confession" begins by accusing Yahweh of seducing Jeremiah (20:7). The word is usually translated as "entice," "coerce," or "deceive," which suggests its negative overtones but fails to capture its sexual connotation. Indeed the conjunction of seduction with "overpowering" here is often interpreted as presenting an image of the divine rape of the prophet. However, the compulsion comes from within the prophet: "If I say, 'I will not mention him, or speak any more in his name,' then within me there is something like a burning fire shut up in my bones; I am weary with holding it in, and I cannot" (20:9). This suggests the image of a girl seduced by her lover and ridiculed by the villagers (20:7), rather than rape.

Given the intimate tone of the Confessions, this charge of seduction speaks of the powerful and personal issues the book explores. Like Job, Jeremiah considers questions of theodicy and theology by recasting the discussion as the "story" of an individual. Unlike Job, Jeremiah resists any neat packaging of an answer, even that of trusting the creator God to know what is best for creation (cf. Job 42:1ff. in context).

After accusing Yahweh of seduction (20:7), Jeremiah explains that this message of violence and destruction makes him a laughingstock (20:8). So that in verse 10 his neighbors seek in their turn to "seduce" him (the same verb as in 20:7) and thus take vengeance. Despite all this, Jeremiah expresses confidence in God's power (20:11) and justice (20:12) before singing his praises in thanksgiving for delivering him from his enemies (20:13).

If we stopped reading here, this might seem a happy ending for the story (told in the "Confessions") of the troubled prophet. However, regardless of where the supposed "original" lament ended, the text of the book continues with no apparent break into 20:14–18. There Jeremiah curses the day of his birth.

Here again, a contrast with the book of Job is instructive. Job's final words are a confession, of faith if not of guilt, leaving the reader, if not untroubled, at least content (Job 42:5–6). Quite differently, neither the "Confessions" nor the book of Jeremiah as a whole has a happy ending. The "Confessions" leave the prophet cursing his birth, and the book closes with a grim account of the fall of Jerusalem to Babylonian forces. Readers should therefore not expect to close this book satisfied, but rather troubled and still searching. It supplies no neat answers but rather poses deep questions about the nature of the divine and of any human relationship with God.

Tim Bulkeley has taught at Université protestante du Congo, Carey Baptist College, and University of Auckland; he now teaches in the Laidlaw Graduate School, Auckland, New Zealand.

JEREMIAH'S CONFESSIONS AND MY OWN PILGRIMAGE

Jim West (United States)

The prophet Jeremiah's astonishing message (or better, messages, since he preached a number of themes) assaults the people of Judah in an unremitting barrage of condemnation for their wickedness. From his assertion that there were no righteous people in Jerusalem to his scathing rebuke of their trust in the temple of the Lord, Jeremiah was called to "be an iron wall" and he surely must have been. He was isolated, he was scorned, and he was even plotted against by members of his own family. He was tossed into a cistern and left to die and he was accused of being a traitor to his people and his land. Tradition asserts that at the end of his life, he was taken to Egypt and planted neck deep in a road where chariots and horses were driven, running him over and killing him.

Nevertheless, in spite of all that, the most intriguing segments of the book are the texts which scholars have for many decades now called the "Confessions." In those texts Jeremiah accuses God of being deceitful, unfaithful, overpowering, vindictive, cruel, and, yes, even of committing rape! The language of the Confessions is rife with the imagery of power and power-lessness. Jeremiah is forced, he insists, into the prophetic office where, he believed, God would, according to his calling promise, protect him. Yet Jeremiah saw his task as virtually without merit; the people wouldn't believe and they showed absolutely no signs of repentance. And he was right. There was never any sort of "revival" in the days of Jeremiah, and the people of Judah were carted off into exile not once, but twice (in 597 B.C.E. when the leaders were taken and a puppet king installed, and in 586 when the city was finally destroyed and those who remained alive were taken to Babylon).

Since the mid-twentieth century, the "Confessions" have been widely discussed. And while some see the Confessions as the authentic "confessions" of the prophet himself, others see them as Jeremiah's "Confessions" on behalf of the righteous people of Judah as a whole. While the latter is certainly possible, I take the Confessions as Jeremiah's own, very profound, struggle with his calling. My reading of Jeremiah is from the perspective of a middle-aged, middle-class, white male. I serve the community of faith as both a Pastor and an Adjunct Professor of Biblical Studies. My residence is in the Southern United States (Tennessee to be specific) though my place of origin is California. Theologically I am both conservative (concerning social issues) and thoroughly middle-of-the-road (concerning my rejection of Fundamentalism in its right-wing political garb).

Even a cursory reading of the Confessions opens for the reader a window on the life of the prophet which simply cannot be, and is not, found in any of the other prophetic books. Jeremiah's rhetoric seems to escalate with each successive outcry. In 11:18–20 Jeremiah begs God for his protective care, having heard that his own family has plotted against him and intends to kill him if they can. As might be expected, Jeremiah is none too pleased with his family and turns from them to seek God alone as defender.

In 12:1–6 things become a bit worse and Jeremiah enquires of God how it is that the righteous seem to be worse off than the wicked. Why doesn't God intervene and punish the perverse, Jeremiah wonders. God replies in a not-to-comforting tone, "If you have run with men and been worn out, what will you do when you have to race with horse." Or, in other words, "If you think it has been hard till now, what will you do when it really becomes difficult?"

That would have been as satisfying an answer to Jeremiah as it would be to us. By 15:10–21 Jeremiah is about to snap. He asks God why he hasn't carried out his word and then he accuses God of deception and rape! "You overpowered me, and forced me" to this prophetic task and then you left me high and dry, he asserts. God's response to this outburst is, "Repent! Or you'll be removed from your prophetic office. Stop speaking such rubbish!"

Jeremiah17:14–18 seems a bit more mild and here Jeremiah simply calls on God to destroy the nation (!). But by 18:18–23 and 20:7–13, Jeremiah has had all he can take and so has God, of Jeremiah. Aside from wishing the entire population exterminated, and yet hearing from God that he will allow a remnant to remain even after the punishment of exile, Jeremiah, it seems, breaks down. God is more powerful than the lowly Jeremiah and there's nothing the prophet can do to find relief from his misery. His message has been rejected and God, he believes, has turned a deaf ear to him. He even mocks God saying, "Sing praise to God…" while simultaneously saying, with Job, "Curse the day I was born!" Or, more plainly and in a language forceful enough to carry the sense of the underlying Hebrew, "Damn my life! I wish I were dead!"

To this there is no reply from God. No appearance in a whirlwind as Job was privileged to experience; only the cold dreary silence of a closed heaven and a God who has turned his back on his faithful (albeit dissatisfied) prophet.

There isn't, in the entire span of Scripture, anything like this elsewhere. It is powerful and it is human and it is the way that many have felt but few have had the courage to utter even to themselves in the quietness of their own homes or the stillness of their own battered, bruised, beaten spirits.

Indeed, my own pilgrimage as a "minister of the Word" has been pockmarked with "confession" moments. There have been trials and disputes, and dismay and disgust aplenty at the apathy of many for and toward the will and work of God. Asking "why" is a nearly daily question and complaints concerning the indifference of the people of God nearly an hourly event. God's reply, as to Jeremiah, is usually along the lines of, "Stop speaking worthless words and I will remain with you and make you an iron wall and bronze gates." So, in the spirit of Jeremiah, I trudge forward—awaiting the day when some angry mob tosses me in a cistern and leaves me to die. Or worse, takes me to Egypt and plants me in the street to be run over by horses and chariots. Thankfully, however, since I lack his courage, I doubtless will perish quite quietly.

Jim West is Adjunct Professor of Biblical Studies at the Quartz Hill School of Theology and Pastor of Petros Baptist Church, Petros, Tennessee, United States; he has written a number of books and articles.

QUESTIONS

1. What are the implications of challenging the prophetic word, as Marzouk says, of those who remained in Judah? If Jeremiah's threatened disasters on the Jews in Egypt did not come to pass, what does that say about him as a prophet?

2. Based on your reading of Jeremiah, in what sense is he like a Dalit? Are there elements of Jeremiah and his preaching which make Gosala's comparison of Jeremiah and the Dalits difficult?

3. Are complex characters like Jeremiah and books without happy conclusions preferable to simple characters and books with neat endings? How would Bulkeley answer that question?

4. How does your reading and interaction with Jeremiah's Confessions compare to West's?

CHAPTER 15

EZEKIEL 1–24

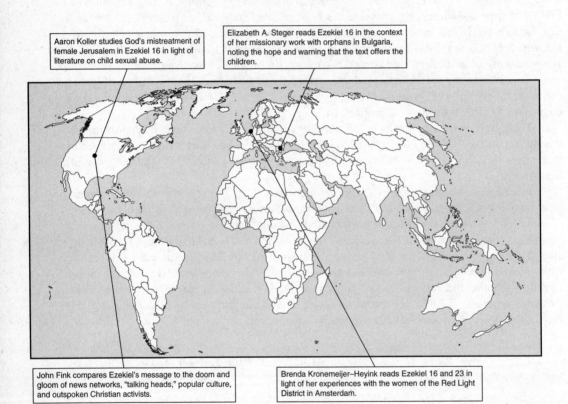

Aaron Koller studies God's mistreatment of female Jerusalem in Ezekiel 16 in light of literature on child sexual abuse.

Elizabeth A. Steger reads Ezekiel 16 in the context of her missionary work with orphans in Bulgaria, noting the hope and warning that the text offers the children.

John Fink compares Ezekiel's message to the doom and gloom of news networks, "talking heads," popular culture, and outspoken Christian activists.

Brenda Kronemeijer–Heyink reads Ezekiel 16 and 23 in light of her experiences with the women of the Red Light District in Amsterdam.

READINGS

"Doom and Gloom" in Ezekiel and Today's News Networks
John Fink

God's Mistreatment of Female Jerusalem in Ezekiel 16
Aaron Koller

Ezekiel 16 as Hope and Warning for Orphans in Bulgaria
Elizabeth A. Steger

Reading Ezekiel 16 and 23 in the Red Light District
Brenda Kronemeijer-Heyink

"DOOM AND GLOOM" IN EZEKIEL AND TODAY'S NEWS NETWORKS

John Fink (United States)

At first glance, from a historical perspective, Ezekiel's place in history may seem very similar to our own. Finding himself in a time of conflict and upheaval, when the "status quo" had changed, Ezekiel identifies himself as an "exile" (1:1), claiming to see visions from God while amongst the insurgent forces of King Jehoiachin. The majority of his writings describe his encounter with "the glory of the Lord" (1:28) and how he was directed to serve as a prophet (a "watchman") of God's displeasure and harbinger of doom (2:3), with the caveat of "whether they listen or fail to listen—for they are a rebellious house—they will know that a prophet has been among them" (2:5). He describes the destruction of Jerusalem and the Temple as God's continued punishment of the Israelites (Ezek. 4–24), before closing with the prophesied restoration of a Jewish state and the construction of a new Temple (Ezek. 33–48).

We ourselves are surrounded by similar tidings of doom, gloom, and impending disaster, although we may not think of 24-hour cable news, "talking heads," popular culture, or outspoken Christian activists as modern-day Ezekiels. The news carries tales of horrors—past, current, and future—with self-proclaimed "watchmen" seeking to sculpt popular opinion as they feed on the fears and uncertainty of the times to gain viewership. Popular culture, such as the "History Channel," have embraced the so-called Mayan calendar "2012 Disaster" phenomenon, when the ancient long count calendar ends, marking the end of the current "age" and the transition to a new one. Fringe elements of Christianity, such as Westboro Baptist Church of Kansas, claim that the United States has angered God in various ways, including the legalization of abortion and same-sex marriage, going so far as to picket certain events with signs claiming that "God hates fags" and other divisive messages.

It is my belief that we find ourselves in a position much like Ezekiel. While our nation has not been crushed by outsiders and oppressed, with our citizens scattered to the winds, we do live in a time of warfare and strife, having deployed our military to engage enemies in other lands for nearly a decade now. Our economy is struggling, with millions of people having lost their jobs. Crime and other social hardships continue to run rampant. People in our time wax poetic for the past, remembering it much more fondly than the present, and hope for the future, sincerely wishing it to be better than today, while secretly dreading that it will only be worse. We are afraid, and because of that fear, we turn to whoever will provide reasons and answers for that fear.

Compare those thoughts to what the Israelites of Ezekiel's time must have felt, having been dominated by the Assyrians, the Egyptians, and the Babylonians, rebelling several times before finally being crushed by Nebuchadnezzar in 586 B.C., with both Jerusalem and the Temple being pillaged and burned and their people scattered into exile. They too were afraid of the present and future, either believing themselves unfortunate or having angered God and therefore suffering His punishment. Their present was unpleasant, their collective past, when they had a home and a cultural identity, was believed better, and the future was uncertain at best. They too were looking for answers and reasons for their punishment/misfortune wherever they could find them, whether those answers came from a rebellious leader who had grand hopes for the future or a priest who moved among them spreading the Word of God. Who amongst us, after all, enjoys being told we are or have done wrong?

Regardless of their message, we find ourselves surrounded by those who would be modern-day Ezekiels. The message of impending doom and destruction, either because we have displeased God or because of secular, scientific, or hypothetical reasons, are everywhere. Ezekiel's words could easily have been written today, and would quite possibly rocket to the top of various best-seller lists. This is not to say that I am declaring Ezekiel to be antiquity's equivalent of Glen Beck, Rush Limbaugh, Keith Olbermann, or Pat Robertson. I am merely attempting to draw a comparison between the tone of Ezekiel's writings and the messages and sources we are confronted with today. Perhaps some of these activists believe they are twenty-first-century "watchmen," reaching out with strident voices as they seek to make their understanding of God's Word understood, much as Ezekiel was charged. Perhaps they find us as equally stubborn and rebellious as God warned Ezekiel the Israelites would be (2:4). There is, on the surface, very little difference between a sign declaring "God hates fags" and Ezekiel declaring in the name of God that "he who eats at mountain shrines, defiles his neighbor's wife, oppresses the poor and needy, commits robbery, does not return what he took in pledge, looks at idols, does detestable things, and lends as usury and takes excessive interest" will not live (18:10–13).

John Fink has worked as a middle and high school band director, a special education teacher, and a police dispatcher.

GOD'S MISTREATMENT OF FEMALE JERUSALEM IN EZEKIEL 16

Aaron Koller (United States)

In Ezekiel 16 Jerusalem is personified as a girl: abandoned as a baby, saved by God as a foundling, and later taken by him in marriage. The bride takes her newfound possessions and newfound confidence and seeks many extramarital sexual partners, including the legendarily virile Egyptians and the Mesopotamians, but she is not yet satisfied. She is the antiprostitute, paying others for sex. Her husband undertakes to punish her, handing her over to her many lovers, who strip her naked, stone her, and cut her up with their swords.

Despite what some modern exegetes have written, it is clear that God does not care for the girl in even the most basic ways until she has reached sexual maturity. Rather than direct nurturance, he used some sort of magic formula to ensure Jerusalem's survival (16:6); he even left her unclothed and unwashed in the field. When God finally cleanses her (16:9), there are probably three bloods mingled: the hymeneal blood of her first sexual encounter, the menstrual blood showing her new maturity, and the birth blood in which she has been wallowing for more than a decade.

The deeply troubling images used in this chapter have provoked impassioned and thoughtful critiques by a generation of feminist scholars, and they have done well to identify the objectionable imagery used here. The failing of this scholarship is that it has not gone far enough in interrogating the text: It has often portrayed the offending imagery as a problem for *us* rather than for Ezekiel and his original audience, as if *they* would have seen nothing objectionable about humiliation and sexualization. The assumption, sometimes made explicit, has been that males will sympathize with the male in the story, and thus that the narrative spun by Ezekiel glorifies God's behavior and castigates everything done by female Jerusalem.

Two facts about myself prevent me from adopting this approach. First, I am male, but am repulsed by the behavior attributed to God in this chapter. Thus it seems to me that the sharp gender divide posited by some scholars, insisting that males and females will inevitably read the text differently, is an ironic misstep, which overessentializes the male–female dichotomy.

Second, as someone who grew up as a religious Jew, and who teaches Bible in a Jewish university, I am not prepared to accept the view that "we" ought to reject the text's portrayal of God, which was acceptable to "them." I instinctively feel myself to be part of the community addressed by the prophet. My "we" cannot insist on difference between "us" and the text's audience, because we *are* that audience. (I should add that I am a devout feminist, as well, but do not believe that to be relevant to the interpretation of this text, which is offensive to all humans.) One need not be part of the Jewish community to hold this view; some have argued that no listener would have sympathized with God as portrayed in this text. Indeed, the Talmudic Rabbis, who lived in a far more male-dominated society than ours, were apparently deeply troubled by this text: Some forbade its public reading in the synagogue (Bavli Megillah 25a–b). Most importantly, within the rhetoric of the text, the people of Jerusalem—the audience—is identified as the *female* Jerusalem, *against* the male God.

In certain contemporary societies this marriage would be considered statutory rape. Indeed, it would be child sexual abuse (CSA). The literature on CSA and its effects is huge. Many of the documented effects of CSA closely resemble the descriptions of Jerusalem in our text. One of the important points that emerges from this literature is that effects are not culturally specific. Psychologists have come up with a number of good hypotheses to explain this phenomenon, but the phenomenon itself is quite clear and has to do with psychological realities rather than cultural expectations. Even 2,500 years ago in Iraq, therefore, the same reality should have applied.

CSA is statistically associated with different types of risky sexual behavior, including multiple partners. In many cases, when CSA victims reach adulthood, their sense of betrayal resulting from the abuse may lead to a series of shallow, unfulfilling short-lasting sexual relationships, as part of a desperate search for a meaningful relationship. It must be emphasized: In our text, the girl had her first sentient encounter with another human being at around age 12, when an all-powerful male figure appeared, had sex with her, and entered into an eternal marital bond with her. Her later life was certainly unsatisfying, as she took all she had and gave it to potential lovers, enjoying the trysts but never feeling satisfied. Is this not clearly an example of a CSA victim in a desperate search for a redeeming relationship?

Ezekiel is psychologically perceptive, and depicts his characters with pathos and verisimilitude. Scholars have observed that later in the chapter, God is described as an abusive husband: He beats his wife because he suspects her of infidelity, and blames the abuse on the battered wife; he claims that these actions will bring his wife in line, and expresses satisfaction when she is cowed into submission. Jerusalem, in turn, is depicted as a battered woman, in a state of learned helplessness, hoping against hope that if she does not raise her husband's ire, he will not beat her again.

The question, then, must be this: Why would Ezekiel portray God in such an unflattering, even damning, light? It should be observed that Ezekiel is nothing if not consistent. In Ezekiel 23, he again describes Jerusalem's early life as one filled with uninvited sexual experiences. Referring to Jerusalem's childhood in Egypt, Ezekiel says, "there their breasts were squeezed, and there they pressed their virgin nipples" (23:3); that is, in their youth they were sexually abused, and the rest of the chapter essentially blames the victims. If Ezekiel's goal is to chastise Israel, why would he tell a story in which it is difficult not to pity her? If his goal is to explain God's actions, why would he tell a tale in which it is difficult to sympathize with God?

An answer must be sought in the literary-theological realm, since Ezekiel is fundamentally a book of literary theology. Perhaps Ezekiel chooses descriptions which undermine the character of God in order to make the point that the past does not matter in judging the present. That the present is independent of the past is, of course, a major theme of Ezekiel's theological platform (cf. Ezek. 14 and 18). Might it be that in his retellings of history, he specifically paints the origins of the relationship as one-sided and portrays God in a negative light, in order to avoid getting into an argument over whether in fact Israel owes God anything at all?

Hosea and Jeremiah claim that since God was beneficent to Israel, Israel's turn to others is betrayal. Ezekiel does not think that defining his generation's behavior as betrayal is dependent on what God has done for them. This leads Ezekiel to a radical conclusion: Jerusalem is bound by loyalty to God *even if God did nothing for them*. It may well be that God was not justified in initiating the bond; it may well be that Jerusalem's chafing at the bond is understandable and almost predictable. But a bond is a bond, and, Ezekiel says, there is no escape from it.

The suggestion is, then, that the use of the offensive images in Ezekiel is meant to force a theological reevaluation of claims Israel may make against God. Some of Ezekiel's contemporaries may have argued that God has lost their trust, since he is no longer acting toward them with love, beneficence, or kindness. By denying that God was ever good to Israel, Ezekiel undercuts any defense based on the claim that he has stopped.

Aaron Koller is Assistant Professor of Near Eastern and Jewish Studies at Yeshiva University, New York, United States.

EZEKIEL 16 AS HOPE AND WARNING FOR ORPHANS IN BULGARIA

Elizabeth A. Steger (Bulgaria)

As a nurse desiring to provide medical and spiritual care in Bulgaria, I have toured through a number of government-sponsored facilities for children of all ages. One houses beautiful infants that could easily be loved and cared for by any family, as well as babies with deformities that make them look more monster-like than childlike. These little ones live with conditions that could have been prevented or would never be left untreated in the United States.

Another is filled with children who are injured from hitting their heads against the wall, who cower in the corner, or who simply rock back and forth resisting touch. These same children sleep on vinyl flooring on their beds rather than a mattress covered with a sheet for the ease of the employees hired to provide care to the children. One orphanage is filled with happy toddlers who sing and play, seemingly unaware that there is any other type of life.

Then, there are the facilities that house older children, wild with energy, unsupervised, and craving attention. These older children are perfect targets for predators and perverts who lurk outside their doors. One of these cement homes shelters disabled young adults who would likely be unable to establish a life on their own because of their mental or physical challenges.

All of these children have something in common, the stigma of being outcasts. They are abused, abandoned, or unwanted. While some families cannot afford to provide for a child and consider it a kindness to relinquish their parental duties to the state, there are many terror-filled stories that seem to belong more in a horror movie than in the life of a child. One such story is that of two sisters I've developed a relationship with over the years. Both girls have mental impairments and were removed from an abusive household; one of them had been hit in the head with an axe by her mother.

Many of the boys in this same orphanage have begun cross-dressing and experimenting with homosexuality and many of the girls are overly sensual in their interactions with men, likely as a result of exposure to sexual abuse and the evil and darkness that surrounds them. They, too, are striving to fill a void.

Where can they find hope?

In Ezekiel 16, a story is told of a nation that was without the care and compassion of a loving parent. Israel had not always been solely Jewish, but God rescued her. He adopted her as His own. She would have perished without Him. He not only nurtured her as a child but, as she matured, he served as her Bridegroom and loved her fully and passionately. He clothed her in the finest garments and accessories as a queen.

God gave Israel every orphan's dream: love, acceptance, security, and provision as if they were royalty. He was worthy of complete trust and faith. After observing the plight of the orphans in Bulgaria, and the response that these children exhibit from the smallest gestures of kindness, I would anticipate that Israel would wholeheartedly follow God's instructions for her. I could imagine that much like Nadia, Vasilka, Tiho, and Greta freely express love, adoration, and affection in response to a piece of fruit, a soda, or a small gift, the Israelites would show an outpouring of heartfelt gratitude for the new life that God gave them. They were given a new identity that allowed them to leave a life filled with shame and isolation for a life full of promise.

However, Israel did not respond in this way to the Almighty. Instead, she rejected God and sought other lovers. Israel engaged in countless acts of idolatry and immorality without remembering her covenant with God. She rejected the One who had saved her from certain death. She took the gifts she was given and heartlessly offered them to another. Just as an undisciplined child becomes unruly and despised, Israel had turned into a self-centered, entitled, and depraved nation.

A response was needed. God allowed the Israelites to fall to neighboring countries and to experience the consequences of their sin. Suffering through the difficulties and challenges of living without the diplomatic immunity to which she had become accustomed got Israel's attention. Eventually, God did provide atonement for Israel's unfaithfulness and the covenant was restored, but Israel would endure shame for her actions and pain when she remembered the way she had so easily discarded her Redeemer.

God desires to adopt the discarded and rejected in society. This message is truly transformational and life changing to those who have lived in isolation and seclusion from the mainstream, with little to call their own. For them, a "forgotten" life is reality, but the opportunity to be adopted by God changes their identity completely. Like a newborn who is unaware of the dangers that await him as he is not cleansed and swaddled at birth, those orphans who do not know God are pursued by a compassionate Savior. God desires that none perish outside the atonement He offers.

The acceptance these children can find in a Savior who unconditionally loves them and communes with them is unlike any parental relationship they have ever had. Their past and present are encumbered by adults who, at best, are overwhelmed with hardships and impossibilities and, at worst, who exploit them. They are accustomed to having their dreams, desires, and individuality removed, rather than promoted. Few people offer them anything without expectations.

They see other children at school who go home to families who provide warm meals and hugs. In those families, if the children's hearts are broken, they have someone to reassure them that they will love again. If they are afraid at night, they have a bed they can jump into for security. If they are admitted to the hospital, there is a family member to stay with them. The orphans have none of this. Inclusion in the family of God may be the first time these "outcasts" have been included in anything of worth in their lives.

Understandably, the orphans may embrace the opportunity to become a child of God fairly readily. But once they have called upon God for salvation and rescue, it is tempting to quickly forget God, their first love. The worldly and base environment of the orphanage does not foster purity. The mentors in the Christian faith are few in this part of the world. If the converts fall away, Ezekiel 16 offers both warning and hope. God fully adopts a child, which includes discipline to align believers with Him. Consequences and shame result from rebellion and disobedience. However, God never forsakes His child.

The rejection God experienced in this passage and ultimately that Jesus faced on the cross was more pronounced than that of my friends in Bulgaria. He truly knows agony and feelings of abandonment. He has the remedy for ailments. He can heal hurts. He can bring peace beyond understanding, quell that nagging feeling of unworthiness to receive authentic love, which includes discipline.

While Ezekiel 16 offers answers and life for the orphan, the ability to enact principles of Christian living and instruction into the environment of the orphanage is challenging. It is difficult to overcome the many social concerns, language barriers, and personal demons that these children face. When a conversion to Christianity occurs, discipleship is extremely limited and may result in a faith that is easily set aside. My prayer for these lovely orphans is that they would be drawn to grace and that there would be a continual Christian influence available to foster an ever-deepening relationship with the One who calls them His children.

Elizabeth A. Steger (MSN, RN, NEA, FACHE) is Vice-President of Patient Care Services at Presbyterian Hospital in Charlotte, North Carolina, United States; she is involved in medical missions in Eastern Europe, especially with the orphanages of Bulgaria.

Reading Ezekiel 16 and 23 in the Red Light District

Brenda Kronemeijer-Heyink (The Netherlands)

Calling someone a prostitute is generally considered a great insult. In Ezekiel 16 and 23, however, Jerusalem is called more than a whore: she is considered to be worse than a prostitute as she scorns payments and bribes her lovers to come to her. Furthermore, the descriptions of her prostituting would make many readers blush. The prostitution of Jerusalem is clearly shown in the text to be a metaphor for Jerusalem's chasing after other gods, but that hardly abates the prostitution motif. The question asked here is whether a fuller understanding of prostitution as a social phenomenon affects how the reader understands these texts.

When I moved to the Red Light District in Amsterdam a number of years ago, I was immediately confronted with women behind the windows who were selling sex. Wanting to know and understand these new neighbors of mine, I read studies on prostitution, read prostitutes' own stories, and even had short conversations with the women as I helped bring coffee with the Salvation Army. I also tried to see my neighbors: from the skinny young blond model type to the Eastern European with limited Dutch knowledge to the grandmotherly types who seemed like they'd be more at home entertaining in the kitchen. It soon became clear to me that prostitution is complicated, just like the text of Ezekiel.

Based on its use in Ezekiel 16 and 23 it would appear that to act as a prostitute is unambiguously wrong and deserving of punishment, even death (cf. also Deuteronomy 22:21). However, the stories of prostitutes named in the Bible paint a different picture: Tamar was declared righteous (Genesis 38), Rahab was the only one rescued from Jericho (Joshua 6), and Gomer was bought back as Hosea's wife (Hosea 2:5). Prostitution in the Bible, then, like the phenomenon of prostitution in society, is not simply seen as all bad.

Those working behind the windows in Amsterdam perceive their prostituting themselves in various ways: a necessary evil, an interesting and even enjoyable job, or one's worst nightmare come true. For some, prostitution is seen as the only option (whether by force or general circumstances) and for others, prostitution is hardly their only option but the one they still choose because of the opportunities it presents. The description of Jerusalem and Samaria in Ezekiel 16 and 23 falls into this latter category, what is sometimes referred to as the "happy hooker." In such an understanding of prostitution, the person is so infatuated with sex that prostitution would be considered the "ideal" and he/she could not imagine doing or wanting anything else. Jerusalem fits this category through her longing after foreign men, bribing them to come to her. Yet, describing Jerusalem as happy in her prostitution is going too far: she is constantly thirsting for more and despises the men after she has been defiled by them. The judgment depicted in the text—that of being stripped bare and stoned—further clarifies that, irrelevant of any claims made about Jerusalem's willful intention in prostituting herself, she experiences too many "bad tricks" for her to be described as a happy hooker.

The other extreme is to see the prostitute as being inherently a victim—no one could willingly choose to have one's body used by so many different men. Human trafficking, pimps, and loverboys have most likely forced and sometimes brainwashed the women into selling their bodies. Abuse, lack of self-worth, political unrest, addictions, and/or a love of money push women into prostitution. Seen in this way, Jerusalem and Samaria would be understood as having been brainwashed by these other gods; these are loverboys who had promised her their love, but ultimately just abused her and pushed her into turning to even more gods. This understanding clearly shows Jerusalem's need to be rescued by God; yet, it seems difficult not to hold Jerusalem responsible, since her blatant guilt is one of the main points of these chapters.

Very few prostitutes fall into either extreme: For many, prostitution is seen as a means to an end. While few of them would consider prostitution an ideal job, they have made some choice in either becoming or staying prostitutes, even if leaving is exceptionally difficult. Few would argue that prostitution is healthy or good for them; it is harmful for their body, it messes with one's emotions, and it is often demeaning. Yet, few are rushing to leave the life; the money is too good, the other options are lousy, and this is the life they know. It is in this context—the complicated reality of prostitution—that one can better understand Ezekiel 16 and 23. As despicable as the description of her actions is, Jerusalem cannot be simply despised and dismissed as a deviant woman. Rather, she is a complex character in a messy and complicated world, much like each of us and much like the women in the Red Light District. To some degree, Jerusalem was lured into prostituting herself by the other gods, unaware of the dire consequences, and she became a victim of her own bad choices. The text depicting her story is intended to shock the reader; the shock is even greater when we realize that we are being asked to identify ourselves as the prostitute in the story, as people who also whore after other gods. This identification allows us to turn away from condemnation and toward hope for restoration for both Jerusalem and ourselves. Jerusalem and Samaria have been promised that their fortunes will be restored in order that they, and those who identify with them, might remember and be ashamed.

In the years that I have lived in the Red Light District, one specific topic of conversation stands out. Visiting the women with a cup of coffee often leads to simple conversations about the weather, business being bad, children, and house pets—fascinating conversations, but it is not always easy to sense that the regular visits serve any kind of pastoral function. Yet, when a person decides to leave the work, then no matter how short or mundane the conversations previously were, there is no holding back in sharing this good news. There is a great joy in finally leaving—not only having survived the physical and emotional dangers of the work, but also anticipating the start of a new and different life. It is that joy and wonder that is missing from these chapters in Ezekiel; that part of the restoration comes only later in the biblical narrative.

Brenda Kronemeijer-Heyink is currently completing her Ph.D. at the VU University, Amsterdam; she lives in an intentional Christian community in the middle of the Red Light District.

QUESTIONS

1. In what ways does the comparison between Ezekiel and modern day "watchmen" shed new light on the prophet's message? Does Fink's last sentence sum up the matter perfectly or does it go too far?

2. How might one further extend the insights that Koller makes as a result of reading through the lens of contemporary psychology? How would a victim of child sex abuse (CSA) react to this text? Should such a person be discouraged from even reading it?

3. Assess Steger's comparison of orphans in Bulgaria to Israel in Ezekiel 16. Does it help "put a face" on Israel?

4. Comment on the way in which Kronemeijer-Heyink interacts with the women in the Red Light District. Would you recommend that she take a different approach?

CHAPTER 16

JONAH

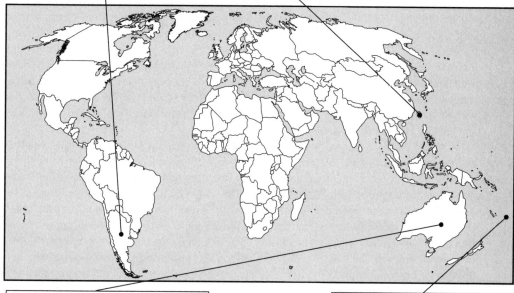

Mariel Pons compares the challenges and contradictions of her city, Buenos Aires, to Jonah's life context and work.

Jonathan Seitz reads Jonah as a missionary, comparing the biblical prophet to the cross-cultural challenges he faces ministering and living in Taiwan.

Jione Havea observes that the book of Jonah is full of surprises and reversals, the most notable of which is that Yhwh repents and decides to spare Nineveh.

Nāsili Vaka'uta, as an islander from Tonga, offers a reading of Jonah that is oriented toward the ocean (*moana*), rather than away from it.

READINGS

Jonah as Missionary
Jonathan Seitz

Jonah and the Ocean
Nāsili Vaka'uta

Jonah and the Challenges and Contradictions of Buenos Aires
Mariel Pons

Jonah as a Book of Surprises and Reversals
Jione Havea

JONAH AS MISSIONARY

Jonathan Seitz (Taiwan)

I did not expect to be "Jonah," but the name suits me. When I came to Taiwan to teach mission and religion, the president of my school gave me the Chinese name for Jonah. Where Jonathan abbreviates as "Jon" in English, it becomes "Jonah" in Taiwanese or Mandarin. Soon I took to joking that Jonah was the worst missionary in the Bible, but also the most successful, and I was not sure yet what type of Jonah I would be. However, as I have worn the name longer, I've come to see Jonah as an unflattering but often accurate portrait of mission and as a challenging foil for my work here. It has not been common to read Jonah as a missionary, but such a reading gives us new insights into Jonah the prophet and the challenges of mission today.

Theologians have almost always treated the story of Jonah allegorically, since it's so hard to take literally. We have to contort biology to keep Jonah stewing in stomach acids for days, and it's difficult to explain how such a vast conversion of Nineveh occurred without leaving any historical trace. Moreover, the story lends itself to allegorical interpretation, teeming with theological images of vengeance, disaster, repentance, resurrection, salvation, and rebirth. There's no dominant interpretation of Jonah, but he has sometimes been an image of the unrepentant Jew or a sign of warning and an example of what not to be. He's a figure starkly lacking in redemption, without a denouement that resolves the conflict, as in, for instance, Job. At the end he is sitting and cursing God's salvation of Nineveh.

As a missionary, Jonah's message is even more jarring. I like to think of Jonah as the archetype of bad mission, the patron saint of displaced preachers. He's not "missional," to use the new, faddish term recently created to describe the church's sending; at best he's "dismissional" or "remissional." He hates the people to whom he is sent. He goes only when forced, indeed only through the supernatural mechanism of the fish. He doesn't learn the language. He stays three days, during which he walks the length of Nineveh, denouncing all the while. He preaches judgment, and judgment only. His sermon is apparently a single line: "Forty days more, and Nineveh shall be overthrown!" When the people repent and God relents, Jonah's response is bitter anger and self-hatred for the role he has played in God's forced redemption of Nineveh. Jonah wishes that he had died instead of seeing his enemy saved. He reflects the worst tendencies of mission. The book of Jonah portrays the prophet-missionary as angry at God and Nineveh; he is moody and peevish and resentful of divine goodness given to others.

At the same time, Jonah shows God's great grace, which is also portrayed with comical hyperbole. Even animals are covered in sackcloth and every Ninevite turns to God. The God of the Israelites redeems their enemy, and God speaks clearly about God's love for all people: "And should I not be concerned about Nineveh, that great city, in which there are more than a hundred and twenty thousand persons who do not know their right hand from their left, and also many animals?" (4:11).

As a missionary, Jonah reflects a key duality: the recognition of human chauvinism and ethnic hatred and the affirmation of God's concern and grace. This duality is also reflected in our own cross-cultural work, where the missionary's primary task is to share God's grace, even though in daily life missionaries are inevitably stammering and confused. We are ordinary people who often take offense at the grace shown to others. In Taiwan, I'm keenly aware of the frailty of the missionary task, even as I admire its capacity to bridge cultures and provide new insights. Challenges are legion:

INCOMPETENCE   A challenge of cross-cultural work is that we are constantly confronted with our difference. Language, custom, food, and celebration all change in a new context. Chinese is a famously difficult language for Westerners, with four tones and tens of thousands of characters. Taiwanese is in some ways even harder, with eight tones and many local oral traditions. Where the biblical Jonah shows no interest in the culture, language, or religion of daily life, most cross-cultural workers are deeply interested in these areas but limited by background and training.

OBSOLESCENCE   I am a missionary serving at the Presbyterian seminary in Taipei. In the early twenty-first century, denominational mission has largely waned. The classical missionary apparatus has evaporated, and the few of us still related to the Presbyterian Church, the major Protestant church here, stay as guests. Where 2,000 Presbyterian missionaries served a generation ago, now there are 200 of us, mostly working in Presbyterian schools, churches, and hospitals. At my school, I am the youngest member of our faculty, and the least experienced. The church here does not *need* me.

ALIENATION   I sometimes feel Jonah's sense of isolation and alienation, even though in truth we have a lot of support and many friends we can rely on here. One of the ironies of Christian expansion is that most Christians prefer to worship with those like themselves. Social scientists have noticed that while diversity may allow for pluralism and mutual respect, it often reinforces the sense of difference and may harden ethnic hatreds. Those living in multicultural contexts, ironically, are often more likely to distrust their neighbors. While we wish that living together automatically led to friendship, in reality it's never so simple.

NAIVETY AND DISILLUSIONMENT   Mission faces many temptations. It is common to fetishize the place we live, to put a golden halo over it, but to largely ignore the differences. This may take the form of idealizing and simplifying local people, of becoming an uncritical advocate. The opposite side of such naivety is disillusionment or hatred. The honeymoon of early weeks of cross-cultural life may give way to an aggrieved or besieged mentality. Like Jonah, it's also possible to feel estranged and bitter. A not small number of missionaries leave after a short time, feeling defeated or abused, confounded by cultural difference. Many of us also aspire to "go native," to learn the language and culture and blend in. However, it's never that easy. Most of us struggle to become hybrid beings, ambivalent about our two cultures.

Jonah concludes with the prophet unconsoled. God, meanwhile, contrasts Jonah's anger with God's concern for humanity. God, seeing from all directions, replaces human anger with divine compassion. We find ourselves living and writing from one—or perhaps two or three— contexts that we know deeply, and yet most of the world remains off-limits to us. We may encounter this world superficially as consumers, readers, or travelers, but we rarely have a great depth of knowledge of any culture but our own. We may react with anger, as does Jonah, or sadness, fear, or even joy. Nonetheless, the book of Jonah concludes by reminding us that God's purview is greater than ours, and that while our human capacity often precludes forgiveness, much less compassion or love, God's grace extends even to the despised neighbor. For me, a wayward Jonah in a foreign land, the tale of the angry prophet, and a God who saves whole cities—even the animals—is good news.

Jonathan Seitz (Ph.D., Princeton Seminary) teaches at Taiwan Theological Seminary in Taipei as a Presbyterian Church (USA) mission coworker.

JONAH AND THE OCEAN

Nāsili Vaka'uta (Tonga)

Paddling across and around Jonah, I found myself caught up in two conflicting currents. One flows toward Nineveh, the other toward Tarshish. The "Nineveh orientation" calls for commitment and "obedience to the will of God, the same God who sent Jonah on his mission to Nineveh." This orientation resides in the claims of domination by one party and the need for submission by another. It involves imposition of one's interest and values upon others; it requires the suppression of other interests and values. It demands total "turning back" (conversion) from one's belief system and worldview. The current of the "Nineveh orientation" originates from either a divine command or action that directs toward an individual or a group. The "Tarshish orientation" stands in opposition to the "Nineveh orientation." It is one of resistance, confrontation, and departure. Its current originates from an attempt by an individual or a group to resist and depart from a dominant force, be it human or divine. Both currents, however, are oriented toward dry lands.

As an islander from Tonga, I am not interested in such orientations, because I am from a region (Oceania) that has more ocean space than land space. We perceive and value the ocean (the *moana*) differently from its portrayal in Jonah 1 and a large part of the Hebrew Bible. The *moana* in Jonah 1 is constructed as a destructive force, an instrument of God's wrath. It respects no one. It is there at the service of Yhwh, even if it means compromising the lives of innocent people (e.g., sailors), who do not deserve to suffer. The trouble at sea in Jonah 1 happens for one reason: to drive Jonah toward dry land, Nineveh. For that reason, I would like to offer an alternative reading; one that is oriented toward the *moana*, rather than away from it. I will attempt herein to give Jonah 1 a *moana* reading.

This *moana* reading is based on the following island insights. First, the *moana* (ocean), the huge watery space we call Oceania, is a shared home for islanders. It is a home that none of us owned; we all belong to it. Second, the *moana* largely defines our identity. Besides referring to ourselves as islanders, we are also proud to call ourselves at times "peoples of/from the ocean" (Tongan, *matu'a mei tahi*). Third, the *moana* is a source of food; it is our "oceanic garden." Fourth, the *moana* links islands together. It is not a boundary that divides, but one that connects islands and islanders. Fifth, the *moana* is an accommodating space, a place of difference. Oceania is home to different island cultures, yet they share a common watery heritage. Sixth, the *moana* is vast and deep. The vastness of the *moana* counters the continental (or land-based) view of islands as small, peripheral, and insignificant. The *moana*, the home to our islands, is immeasurable. The depth of the *moana* resists the common misunderstanding that anything is fathomable. One's view is *ipso facto* defined by one's limitations. To claim otherwise is an illusion.

This *moana* reading of Jonah 1 begins by acknowledging its limitations. First, the focus is strictly on the ocean space (the sea) as presented in the story, and all the events that happened therein. Second, I enter the story through that watery space; the space Jonah chose as his escape route away from Yhwh; the space Yhwh used to exhibit his might; the space where Jonah encounters the "people of the sea," the sailors. It is in that space that I sneak into the story, to listen to the conversations and to witness the unfolding of events. Third, I read as an Oceanic islander, but I do not speak for all Oceanians. As the *moana* is a space of difference, so is *moana* reading. It is always plural, multidimensional, and diverse. My reading is but one amongst many, and I can only read Jonah 1 through the limits of my eye/I as a Tongan.

What new insights, if any, can this *moana* reading bring out of Jonah 1? First, the ocean offers a different space of encounter. Boarding the Tarshish-destined ship, Jonah has the company of people who were different from him in terms of faith, and perhaps culture. The sea serves as a multireligious (and multicultural) space. Whereas in-land Yhwh demands conformity and conversion, everyone at sea worships his own god. The well-being of the whole group comes before promoting one's value and belief. In the midst of crisis, each person works for the common good. Second, we know very little about the identity of those at sea except that they are referred to as captain and sailors; they are "peoples of the ocean." Like islanders, the ocean is part of their lives. The ocean defines who they are.

Third, the ocean links and connects. Whereas in the story the ocean is seen as an instrument of Yhwh's wrath, a *moana* reading focuses on the connections and links that the ocean allows. Geographically, the ocean connects different places such as Israel and Tarshish (despite the obscurity of its location). Socially, it connects people together such as it does to those on the ship. Religiously, it brings different faiths together; even the sailors respect Jonah's deity. The ocean, despite the trouble Yhwh caused, accommodates the difference amongst the sailors themselves, and between them and Jonah. On dry land, however, that sense of belonging and accommodation is blurred by a demand to repent.

Fourth, the ocean serves as a space of freedom. If freedom means having the opportunity to make decisions for oneself, the ocean offers Jonah that opportunity. Instead of praying for help, he opts to sleep. Why would one ask for help from a deity who comes after him with terrifying force and aggression? Jonah's decision brings out two different perceptions of the divine. To the captain and sailors of the ship, the divine is a source of help, whereas in Jonah's case the divine is controlling, demanding, and requires conformity and unreserved respect for his sovereignty.

Fifth, and finally, the ocean, the *moana*, the watery space, offers Jonah a home away from dry land. When the crew suspected Jonah to be responsible for the situation at sea, they did not force him out of the ship. Nor did Jonah ask that he be saved. Instead, he made an odd request: "cast me into the sea." Two points are worth noting: (i) At sea, Jonah puts the well-being of others before his own, and (ii) like an islander, he prefers to make the ocean, the *moana*, his home, rather than going with the flow of the current toward Nineveh.

The story continues with the narrator's attempt to take Jonah on to dry land, out of the *moana*, toward Nineveh. However, as an islander, I would rather remain in the ocean—the place where difference is accommodated, and freedom is not compromised.

Nāsili Vaka'uta, a Tongan, is Lecturer in Biblical Studies and Oceanic Hermeneutics in the School of Theology at University of Auckland and Trinity Methodist Theological College, Auckland, New Zealand.

JONAH AND THE CHALLENGES AND CONTRADICTIONS OF BUENOS AIRES

Mariel Pons (Argentina)

Buenos Aires, La Boca, southern quarter in the great city, suburbs, harbor, sailors, immigrants, poverty, exclusion...church. We can apply this description to many of the cities in the world. Although the book of Jonah does not specifically describe the wickedness of the city of Nineveh, perhaps it was much like my city, Buenos Aires. We suffer from a large gap between the rich and the poor, which is especially difficult on the many poor children; increasing individualism without any authentic social relationships; abuse of the environment—both water and land; increased violence, especially against women; and a failure to love each other and God.

These contexts, like Jonah's, have their own contradictions. In light of these challenging circumstances, many times we choose the comfortable belly of the great fish. We hide in those safe places where we are surrounded by like-minded people. We think that we bring light to these dark spaces with our thoughts and our many words, all the while praying and recognizing and claiming a merciful, kind God—just like Jonah. But, like Jonah, we find it difficult to get out of our comfort zones, difficult to see the world in new and unexpected ways, difficult to truly share the love and mercy of God when it appears in surprising places and unanticipated ways. How many times do we fight the temptation of thinking that nothing can change; and then if something does change, we get annoyed, as if some great injustice has occurred? How many times without moving from our own quarter, our own world, are we in fact escaping to Tarshish?

One aspect in Jonah's story that draws our attention is the literal and metaphorical use of the number "three." Focusing on that number helps us to rethink our faith and the way to share it, but mainly the way to live it.

Jonah's actions occur in three scenarios: The first one is in the ship in his attempt to flee. Here, despite his resistance to heed the Lord's call, we see that Jonah is courageous enough to tell the truth when confronted by the sailors. He knows that he is the cause of the storm (1:9–10) and he knows what must be done in order for the storm to cease (1:12). He then finds himself inside the great fish for three days, where he recognizes the loving care of God. Jonah, it seems, has a conversion experience, as he now goes to Nineveh.

Second, Jonah arrives in Nineveh—a large city that takes three days to walk across. Interestingly, the text reports that Jonah went only one day's walk into the city before stating, rather tersely, that Nineveh will be destroyed. Surprisingly, the people of the great city, from king to animal, repent of their evil ways. In response, God too changes his thinking and decides not to destroy the city (3:10). So far, everyone has changed their thinking: Jonah, the Ninevites, and God.

But the third scenario provides yet another change. Under the pumpkin plant or *ricino*—a plant in which each leaf has three seeds—Jonah is unable to accept the fact that God has chosen to save Nineveh. He cannot deal with God's change of mind and the love and compassion that God shows to all of his creation—even the enemies of Israel. Jonah had proclaimed God's mercy in his prayer in the belly of the fish. But now he is not able to live what he had proclaimed. Instead, he is upset with God for showing love and mercy on the people of Nineveh; he even claims that he knew that God would save the city, which is why he fled in the first place (4:2). Jonah is so distraught that he wants to die (4:3); but he apparently still holds out "hope" that God will destroy Nineveh, as he sits down on a hill outside the city to see what will happen. He then becomes even more despondent when the plant that was shading him withers and dies. And he defends his right to be upset about the plant. In response, God asks Jonah a question, comparing Jonah's concern for the plant with God's concern of Nineveh. The book ends here. We do not know Jonah's answer. Does Jonah turn to the God who is able to be moved by his creatures or does he continue to be annoyed because he gives Nineveh the possibility of a new existence?

By ending in this fashion, the book of Jonah calls each of us to answer that question for ourselves and our communities of faith. Like Jonah, my context in Buenos Aires is complex and fraught with contradictions and challenges. As we wrestle with the ambiguities of life, we must actively listen to God's word and, at the same time, truly see the world around us and be moved by it.

The name Jonah means "dove." This recalls the dove that Noah sent out from the ark, a dove which announced a new earth, a fresh, clean start. It also anticipates the dove that descended on Jesus at his baptism, signaling that God was about to do something new in the world, that God's kingdom was breaking in on the messiness of life. The book of Jonah, concluding as it does with a question, calls us to given an answer. Will we live out the love of God in our own contexts of contradiction—even if that love does not always seem fair? In each of our realities we are asked for an answer. The decision is open.

Mariel Pons (B.S., Theological Studies) is a Pastor in the Evangelical Methodist Church, Argentina.

JONAH AS A BOOK OF SURPRISES AND REVERSALS

Jione Havea (Australia)

Before Jonah arrives at Nineveh, the narrator expects readers to trust the judgment of Yhwh and so to believe that the Ninevites were a bad people who deserved to be crushed (1:1). Any half-decent reader, Jewish or otherwise, who is aware of the doings of the ancient Assyrian empire, whose capital was Nineveh, would concur. No one in her or his right mind dare speak up on behalf of Nineveh—just as today no one dare defend Nazi Germany. The bad guys, the enemies, deserve to be destroyed. But the book of Jonah is full of surprises and reversals.

The story indeed contains several incredible turns: a prophet does not follow orders, a sea rises and calms abruptly, a big fish swallows a man whole, a man survives in the belly of the fish for three days and three nights, a crew of believing sailors, and swiftly repentant city folks. Oh, so incredible! If those are incredible, difficult to accept as true, why should one accept Yhwh's perception of Nineveh? Why should one accept the narrator's portrayal of non-Hebrew sailors and Ninevites as if they were unthinking seaweed who drift to wherever the waves take them? If (literary) context matters, the incredible turns of events in the story problematize the very mission of Yhwh. In other words, Yhwh's perception of Nineveh is just as "too good to be true" as the story of Jonah is.

Surely, Yhwh can't be wrong! The story of Jonah has duped many readers on this very issue. Readers' allegiance to Yhwh, carried by thick theological clouds, veils their eyes from the one critical characterization of Yhwh in the story: Yhwh repents (Jon. 3:10). Divine repentance is not an unusual characterization of Yhwh in the Hebrew Bible. Before the great flood, Yhwh repents of having created humanity (Genesis 6:5–8) and the upshot was destruction. Later on in the wilderness, to the contrary, Yhwh repents of wanting to destroy the chosen people, deciding to spare them instead (Exodus 32:11–14). This time, Yhwh spares the Israelites. Similarly, but benefitting a different group of people, Yhwh repents and decides to spare Nineveh in the story of Jonah. If repentance is acknowledgment that one has made a mistake, in action and/or in perception, the same is true of Yhwh also. Indeed, Yhwh can be wrong!

Remarkably, Jonah claims that he knew from the outset that Yhwh was "ready to relent from punishing" (4:2). Thus, to follow Yhwh's command and go to Nineveh was an utter waste of his time, so Jonah set off for Tarshish instead. I consequently sympathize with Jonah because Yhwh permits the survival of the Assyrian empire—the wicked oppressors.

The story ends with Yhwh asking a question that could also be understood as a declaration: "And should I not be concerned about Nineveh, that great city, in which there are more than a hundred and twenty thousand persons who do not know their right hand from their left, and also many animals?" The final scene, then, is of an inconsolable and discomforted or, more appropriately, un-comfort-able Jonah. And rightly so, for Yhwh's repentance spares the capital of one of the empires that oppressed Jonah's people. Yhwh's compassion for Nineveh is good for Nineveh but problematic for Jonah and the Israelites. Readers are thus torn between looking out for the interests of Nineveh and identifying with the cause of Israel. The story of Jonah is fascinating in this regard, for readers are discomforted no matter with whom in the story they identify.

Jione Havea is Senior Lecturer at United Theological College and School of Theology at Charles Sturt University, Parramatta, NSW, Australia.

QUESTIONS

1. Seitz sees Jonah as a bad missionary. How could one rehabilitate Jonah's image?
2. What is the most compelling insight of Vaka'uta's *moana* reading? On what point(s) might it be challenged?
3. Evaluate Pons's connection between the wickedness of Nineveh and Buenos Aires.
4. Based on your particular social, cultural, and religious location, who are some of the people or groups for whom no one "in her or his right mind dare speak up"?

CHAPTER 17

MICAH 3, 6

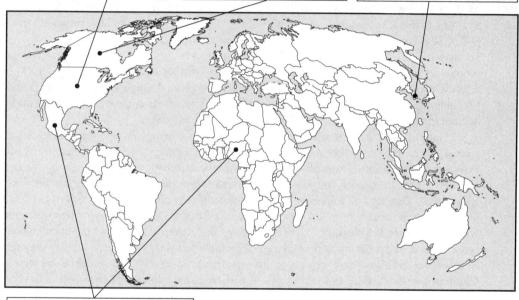

Rebecca T. Alpert inverts the order of Micah 6:8's three commands in light of her identity as a Jewish lesbian: love God/yourself, love others, seek justice.

Shannon E. Baines details the plight of the poor living in downtown Toronto and presents Micah 6 as a text of hope for them.

Hyung Won Lee reads God's accusation and punishment against the leaders of Israel in Micah 3:5–12 as a word of warning to greedy preachers in Korea.

James N. Pohlig explains the values and views of "The Image of Limited Good" societies and offers an interpretation of Micah 6 through that lens.

READINGS

Micah 3 as a Warning to Greedy Preachers in Korea
Hyung Won Lee

A Jewish Lesbian Interpretation of Micah 6:8
Rebecca T. Alpert

Micah and Hope for Toronto's Poor
Shannon E. Baines

"The Image of Limited Good" and Micah
James N. Pohlig

MICAH 3 AS A WARNING TO GREEDY PREACHERS IN KOREA

Hyung Won Lee (South Korea)

Micah 3:5–12 is a part of God's accusation and punishment against the leaders of Israel and Judah in the eighth century B.C. It shows that the religious leaders, that is, the prophets and the priests, were just as responsible as the political and social leaders in keeping their countries just and holy. Their false leadership and sins result in the total devastation of the country and the agony of the people (3:12). Verses 5–6 describe the false prophets' twisted motives of greed or economic expediency. In order to achieve personal gain and materialistic abundance, their sole theme in preaching became that of peace "when there was no peace" (Jeremiah 6:14). The images of proclaiming "peace" to the congregation who give them delicious and nutritious foods "to bite with their teeth," while preparing to wage war against the ones who do not give anything to them, become vivid examples of the twisted motive of the false prophets. In verses 6–7, God announces harsh punishment against them: total darkness, no vision, no divination, no answer from God, and total shame and disgrace. Micah's own "vision statement" for his prophetic ministry in verse 8 indicates some of the essentials of being a true prophet: (1) being filled with divine power, justice, and might which are given through the Spirit of the Lord, and (2) declaring transgression and sin to the people. "Might" in this context refers to the courage to declare transgression and sin of the people without compromise.

Unfortunately, the image of the false prophets' proclaiming peace to some and waging war against others transcends time and space. In the context of the churches in Korea, many similar cases can be introduced as examples: Some ministers become highly sensitive every November and December when the Church budget (including the raising of the minister's salary) for the next year is discussed. They tend to emphasize the importance of providing for the servants of God, and the blessings which are sure to follow for those who do. They sometimes compare their own ministry with that of their friends in order to complain about their comparatively poor treatment in housing, car, insurance, and pensions. Some of the greedy ministers eagerly wait for the holiday season when many church members bring presents or gift certificates. Some revivalists expect to be served in a luxurious hotel with delicious foods as well as with brand new shirts and pants—which has become a custom. Reservation at a golf course during or after the revival makes them happy. Some of them are boastful of the expensive gifts they receive from the revival meetings at which they preached.

If they are treated well, they proclaim peace and divine blessings to the congregation. On the contrary, if their expectation is not met, they express their dissatisfaction in their sermons by proclaiming the themes of divine judgment and curse. In order to gain more offerings, the emphasis of the sermon is put on the materialistic blessings given to the one who offers to God wholeheartedly. In addition, some false preachers prophesy during the revival meeting that the Lord designated some rich elders or deacons to give a certain amount of money (usually a large sum) to the church or even a brand new car for the pastor. While this is not true of every minister, of course, it is a problem nonetheless.

The negative impact of greedy false preachers is enormous. Their preaching as well as greedy lifestyle becomes a bad witness of the true stewardship of Korean Christians in general. Church members have to bear severe financial burdens in order to satisfy the crooked desires of their leaders. In addition, the misuse of offerings results in the reduction of funds available to help the needy, evangelize nonbelievers, and perform overseas mission work.

Churches in Korea have been growing rapidly over the last 125 years since missionaries from the United States started churches, hospitals, and schools here. Currently, over 10 million people, one-fourth of the entire Korean population, are protestant Christians. There are around 50,000 protestant churches in Korea. Over 20,000 missionaries are sent out to other countries around the world. There are presumably many theological, sociological, and ecumenical reasons behind this rapid and steady growth. But one thing is for sure: The growth is the result of the faithfulness of Christian ministers who have served the people of Korea with a sincere motive like one the prophet Micah expressed: "I am filled with power, with the spirit of the Lord, and with justice and might, to declare to Jacob his transgression, to Israel his sin." While preparing and leading early-morning prayer meetings throughout the year, Christian ministers in Korea ask for the fullness of the Holy Spirit every day and its accompanying gifts of power, justice, and might. They also remind themselves of the "vision statement" as Micah expressed in 3:8.

There is a saying among Christian ministers in Korea handed down from their ministerial predecessors: "Be prepared to be hungry; be prepared to be moved to another church; be prepared to be martyred." This saying helps them to be alert when greed darkens their spiritual insight and personal gain interferes with their motives for ministry. It helps them to treat their congregation with justice and equality and to be cautious of the prejudices which hinder their just and righteous service to the people. It also helps them to be the contemporary "true" prophets of God not only by declaring transgressions and sins of the congregation but also by providing true repentance for them.

Micah 3:5–8 is a crucial passage for contemporary ministers around the world. It teaches Christian leaders what to avoid (greed), what to expect when they become false preachers (total spiritual darkness, no vision, no divination, no answer from God, and full of shame and disgrace), and what to remember in their daily ministries (the necessity of the fullness of the Lord and its gifts and the solemn calling of preaching the Word of God without compromise).

Hyung Won Lee is Professor of Old Testament at Korea Baptist Theological University/Seminary, Dae Jeon, Korea.

A JEWISH LESBIAN INTERPRETATION OF MICAH 6:8

Rebecca T. Alpert (United States)

Micah 6:8 offers an ideal framework for examining Jewish lesbian concerns. Here the prophet summarizes his understanding of "what is good" as follows: "Do justice, love well, and walk modestly with God." Micah's threefold precept suggests three areas of particular concern: how to live with and present oneself in the world (how to walk modestly with God), how to establish social relationships (how to love well), and how to make the world a better place (how to do justice). My interpretation inverts the order of Micah's precept. Micah culminates with the individual's relationship with God in keeping with his theocentric (God-centered) worldview. From my human-centered perspective, I begin with the individual's relationship with God, expressed through her relationship with herself. It is this relationship that enables her to love others, and then to translate that love into acts of justice for all humanity, which is for me the ultimate goal.

The process begins where Micah ends, with the enigmatic phrase, "walk humbly with God." I interpret this statement to be about the way an individual understands her own place in the world. I assume that the way in which a person approaches her own life will determine her ability to behave ethically toward others. A central Jewish precept demands that we love our neighbors as ourselves. Commentators have understood this to mean that we can only learn to love our neighbors if we learn to love ourselves.

Walking with God is a metaphor for the way each person approaches her own life. It is a way to conceptualize one's innermost feelings and thoughts. It is not necessary to hold a traditional concept of God, or to imagine God in human form, to appreciate this metaphor. To see oneself walking with God requires a vision of God as the most important value in life, which is with us always and everywhere. God may be in the image of a human being, but God could also be a power, force, feeling, idea, or anything that helps one perceive holiness in the world.

As Jewish lesbians, we begin with the assumption that we can only walk with God if we know and accept ourselves for who we are. Walking with God requires self-knowledge. Those who walk with God know their way and consciously claim a path in the world. They are guided by the understanding that all human beings are holy, having been created in God's image. They respect the mysterious process, whether it derives from nature or society that makes them women who are erotically attracted to other women and who prefer to build their lives with each other. This is not an easy task to accomplish. I share my own coming out story as an example.

I grew up knowing that I was strongly attracted to members of my own sex. But everything I saw in society—movies, popular songs, my parents' relationship, Bible stories—pointed to heterosexuality as the norm. I often had crushes on girls and women teachers and had sexual relationships with girlfriends in high school. Yet as an adolescent I would never have called myself a lesbian; I assumed I was going through a stage. When I was growing up, lesbians were found in bars, underground magazines, and pulp novels. They were assumed to be poorly adjusted women who wanted to be men, not courageous women who dared to be different. I did not want to be one of them.

For me, focusing on my Jewish identity provided a perfect alternative to exploring my sexual identity. I married, became a rabbi, and had two children. Despite my wishes to the contrary, the strong erotic attraction I felt toward women never left me. At some point it became clear to me that I needed to make a choice. It was then that I left my marriage and developed a primary relationship with a woman.

Coming out to myself, calling myself a lesbian, was not an easy thing to do. I had achieved status and visibility in the Jewish world as a rabbi, and I was afraid that if I came out I would be forced to give that up. I was concerned that people I had worked with would be uncomfortable around me or that they would no longer respect my ideas and judgments.

But at a certain point I developed a strong conviction that it would be better if people knew, and that I couldn't worry if they did or not. I came out because I got tired of hiding and lying; it had a corrosive effect on my soul. In coming out I experienced a sense of pride in being a lesbian. I gained peace of mind and a sense of freedom unattainable in the closet.

The second part of Micah's precept is about loving well. Loving is the connection we make to others, whether in intimate or social relationships. Loving well in social relationships means respect for the other person; loving those with whom we are intimate involves passionate feelings and intense closeness in addition to respect. Loving well forms the link between individual self-acceptance (walking modestly with God) and universal justice. We cannot love others unless we accept ourselves. And we cannot bring justice to a world where people do not know how to treat others with whom they are in relationships.

While loving well is applicable to heterosexuals and lesbians alike, the concept raises issues that are particular to lesbian lives. There are differences in the ways that lesbians create loving networks with people around us. Lesbians also have a different perspective on coupled relationships and on the bearing and raising of children. Looking at the subject of loving through a lesbian lens contributes a new perspective to the ongoing Jewish conversation about human relationships.

Typically, Jewish families are created through biological ties, institutionally sanctioned marriage, adoption, and conversion. Jews inherit or claim a place in the Jewish community. We may choose to belong to a different religious or secular community from our family of origin, but for most of us, our primary connections to Judaism are set in our early lives.

Lesbian connections are not based on biological ties. Like converts to Judaism, most lesbians are not raised by parents who share our orientation. Unlike converts, the children we raise are mostly not like us either. Our lesbian family is a loosely defined network that incorporates our parents, children, and other family members who are willing to support us along with friends, former lovers, and members of their families.

It is imperative that the Jewish community comprehend and support the new concept of family that is derived from the context of Jewish lesbian existence. Changing the concept of family also demonstrates the need for new forms and rituals to celebrate our lives.

I now end where Micah began, with "doing justice." The commitment to do justice requires us to go beyond our own lives and to look at larger issues in the world around us. In the conception of Micah's precept that I describe here, these efforts are intrinsically interconnected. We cannot make a choice between accepting ourselves, caring for our circle of loved ones, and doing justice in the world. These efforts must be woven into one framework.

What, then, is the justice that we seek? Our goal is to live in a world where every person has what it takes to satisfy basic human needs: food, clothing, and shelter. Where every person has the opportunity for health care, safety, education, and work. Where all people have the opportunity to participate in decisions that affect their lives. Where nations do not make war against one another. And where the planet itself, and all that lives on it, is treated with dignity and respect. These are the goals of a just society.

When we work for justice, we do it as Jewish lesbians. It is important that we maintain our cultural heritage and identity, and bring the wisdom that this heritage provides into our work in the world. Guided by Micah's precept we have a set of goals to work toward: Begin with self-acceptance, continue with love within our close communities, and reach beyond ourselves to demand and create a world within which there is justice for everyone. These goals are not for lesbian Jews only. This is a model for the transformation of Judaism from a lesbian perspective that derives from our interpretation of the biblical text.

Rebecca T. Alpert (Rabbi) is Associate Professor of Religion at Temple University, Philadelphia, Pennsylvania, United States.

MICAH AND HOPE FOR TORONTO'S POOR

Shannon E. Baines (Canada)

I will provide a reading of Micah 6 from the perspective of the poor living in a densely populated neighborhood in downtown Toronto where alcoholism, drugs, prostitution, violence, and poverty are visible to the naked eye. This will be based on my firsthand experience as a frontline resource worker at an inner-city Christian mission which helps people to participate more fully in society.

The poor come in many shapes, colors, and sizes in this tightly knit community. Whether children in households have one parent/guardian or both parents present, these families work hard to try to make ends meet. Many people, including senior citizens and those with physical and mental disabilities, depend on government assistance for survival. While people who are fortunate enough to attain subsidized housing tend to reside there over the long term, others wait patiently for affordable housing units to become available. In the meantime, they live with friends or family, in rooming houses, or small, cramped apartments, sometimes in substandard conditions. As an alternative, there are a few homeless shelters in the area, which are usually quite full on any given night.

The area has a high population of immigrants who have come to Canada seeking a better future for their families, only to find themselves working long hours in jobs that do not necessarily utilize skills acquired in their home countries. For those immigrant families that are fortunate enough to establish themselves financially, they leave this area and move to safer neighborhoods in the city or even further out into the suburbs. One can hardly blame parents for wanting a better standard of living and a better environment to raise their children. The lure of drugs, gangs, prostitution, criminal activity, and violence looms in the streets, alleyways, schoolyards, parks, and lobbies of apartment buildings day and night.

Some officials impose suffering on the poor living in this inner-city neighborhood. It could be the social assistance worker who treats the single mother poorly, without dignity and respect, and either fails to inform her of the full range of benefits that she and her child are entitled to under the government program or delays receipt of these benefits. Some employers discriminate against people living in the neighborhood by passing over their employment applications. Police enforcement in the area is rather severe and unfair especially in dealing with the youth. Municipal authorities and developers are working to improve the inner-city neighborhood through regentrification, but their plans displace some of the poor either temporarily or permanently to other parts of the city where services are more limited.

The poor not only experience suffering by institutions and authorities but also by members of their own community. Whether it is the local crack-addicted prostitute who is trapped by her addiction and the controlling, violent pimp who won't let her go free or the senior citizen who is rightly afraid to venture out after dark for fear of being attacked. Landlords provide a slow or nonexistent response to urgent repair requests for basic water and heat. Tenants who cannot afford to move into better accommodations are forced to live in these circumstances.

The poor have suffered much more than has been briefly mentioned here. But today they have entered into a local courthouse to hear a case that is of utmost importance to their lives. Ironically, they are not there in support of a friend or family member, as is often the case, but have come to witness an almost inexplicable historical event. The small courtroom where this case is being held is packed beyond capacity.

What is so special about this particular case that has attracted so much attention in this community? People who have treated the poor unfairly in any way are on trial and are being called to give an account of their actions before the almighty God. Apparently, these defendants should have known to seek justice, enact mercy, and walk humbly with God (Mic. 6:8), but they did nothing that was required of them. Witnesses have been called to provide testimony to the injustices that they have inflicted on the poor. These are no ordinary witnesses. They are absolutely impeccable in their credibility and have been in existence for a long time, watching and listening to every word and deed of these defendants. Countless stories of abuse, oppression, and injustice of every kind imaginable are being vividly retold. The evidence is overwhelming. God cannot and will not let any of these perpetrators go unpunished, for they have been judged guilty in all respects. Though the exact nature of the sentence has yet to be determined, the reaction of the poor as they witness the trial is overwhelming: joy, exuberance, and shouts of celebration pour out into the hallways of the courthouse. The windows and doors cannot contain their excitement.

Finally, after many years of either silent suffering or voiced frustration, justice has prevailed. This is real justice stemming from God which convicts the perpetrators and puts an end to the suffering of the poor. There is renewed hope of real restoration in the lives of thousands of poor people in this community. The native Canadian or the disabled person on social assistance will now soon be diagnosed and treated adequately with the utmost dignity and respect. The single father working multiple jobs to make ends meet will soon be able to spend time with his children instead of leaving them alone, susceptible to the lure of gangs. Many young people who have been stereotyped by authority figures will soon be treated fairly with all false accusations being dropped. Whether it is the fear and shame of being teased and bullied or other forms of violence, locals will soon be able to go about living their lives in a safe environment. The prostitute who has been struggling for years to break away from her pimp is finally free to seek a better quality of life. The countless families who have struggled to attain adequate work and pay will be able to provide for themselves and even help their neighbors. The coveted subsidized daycare spaces which have been so limited for poor-income families will become abundantly available, thus freeing up time for parents to attain meaningful employment or pursue educational dreams during the day.

In sum, Micah 6 can provide hope for the poor who experience injustice, suffering, and oppression—hope that one day their situation will improve. In the midst of daily suffering, the poor who have committed their lives to God know that God is close at hand, hears their prayers, and will give them strength and courage to persevere. At the same time, Micah 6 can inspire us not only to act justly towards the poor but also to become an advocate on their behalf. We are called to intervene and help the poor because they often do not have the knowledge, resources, power, influence, or voice to defend themselves. A reading from this perspective sensitizes us to the reality of suffering and God's justice, and provides a glimpse into how peoples' lives and communities may be restored.

Shannon E. Baines is a Ph.D. candidate at McMaster Divinity College, Hamilton, Ontario, Canada.

"THE IMAGE OF LIMITED GOOD" AND MICAH

James N. Pohlig (Nigeria, Mexico)

Micah 6 is part of a metaphorical legal charge that YHWH brings upon Israel, his covenant community. He had brought the nation up from Egypt, releasing them from slavery. He had given them leaders to explain his pact with the new nation: that he would be their God and that they would worship and follow him. One part of the agreement with the nation was that Israel would act as a just society by following YHWH's covenantal laws.

What is the American notion of justice? Surely there is a heavy individualistic bias to our version of justice. It is for this reason that, when Micah 6:8–15 calls for justice among God's covenant people, we see this call as an emphasis on the individual's rights vis-à-vis the rest of society, especially the organized, influential, and powerful parts of society. Democracy, after all, seems to depend on the sincere belief of the vast majority in society that everyone has the same rights before the law as the next person. On the economic level, Americans are not willing to see fellow citizens starve or suffer unnecessarily in other ways. But we still do not tend to condemn vast differences in personal wealth. Bill Gates is admired, not generally condemned.

However, American anthropologist George M. Foster presented in 1965 a theory that he named "The Image of Limited Good" (ILG), which he applied to so-called "peasant societies"— societies that are for the most part closed to economic growth from outside themselves. Foster and others had observed that in various regions of the world, many such societies seemed to view things of value—and not only material goods!—as existing in limited quantities, and never enough to satisfy everyone's wants, at least for very long. This proposed cultural view is seen as producing significant effects, as shown in the following examples.

In southeastern Nigeria in the 1950s, an American church established a seminary at which eventually a local Nigerian became the first national professor. Because of his salary, he became the first in his village to have electric lights at home and to own an automobile. But one day he was put on trial as a witch by his village. Fortunately, he survived the experience; not all accused witches do. Moral: A sudden increase in wealth is often viewed with suspicion in ILG societies, on the assumption that the culprit has acquired more than his fair share of goods. If one's economic position significantly improves because of employment or relationships *outside* the community, this event tends to be regarded in a better light; it is evident, after all, that the villager has not taken more than his share of *local* wealth. In this situation with the professor, however, such was not the case.

In Huautla, in southwestern Mexico, Mazatec women are (or should be) known for the exquisite embroidery on their clothes. When American linguist Eunice Pike asked one of the women, "Who taught you how to do this?" the answer came back, "I just know how." Again, when she asked a village baker how he had learned to bake bread, she was told, "I just know." Pike could find no Mazatec who would acknowledge to have learned anything from another villager. Moreover, Pike once taught a Mazatec woman to read her newly written down language. At the woman's request, Pike then taught her eldest daughter. When she desired to teach the next daughter as well, Pike suggested that the mother teach her, but she shied away from doing so. Several children learned to read from Pike, but they themselves steadfastly refused to teach others. Pike eventually deduced that within ILG societies, one cannot appropriate another's know-how without being considered as stealing it (from Eunice V. Pike, 2008, "The Concept of Limited Good and the Spread of the Gospel." Forum of Bible Agencies International. Available online).

In addition, Foster ("Peasant Society and the Image of Limited Good," in *American Anthropologist*, 1965 [67:2]: 293–315) offers the following examples.

1. In Tzintzuntzan, Michoacán, Mexico, land is increasingly limited because of population growth. No villager has enough land to become wealthy by farming, only enough to hopefully eat throughout the year. Even the best of human interrelationships—friendship, affection, and love—seem to be jealously guarded. On one occasion, Foster brought a villager to his own home in California. Near the end of his stay, his guest told him that his brother was working nearby, but that he did not want to give him any of his own joy in being in Foster's home.

2. Among the Buganda, the largest ethnic group in Uganda, a woman does not want to become pregnant if she has not yet weaned her previous child. There is a risk of the unborn baby being jealous of its elder sibling and poisoning the mother's milk in revenge.

3. In rural Mexico, it seems common for men to feel their masculine nature to be threatened if their wives want a share of their authority at home. Every wife should be beaten once in a while, to reinforce the point that the male is in charge.

Peasant societies said to possess the ILG tend to have coping mechanisms in common. For example, an unexpected financial windfall is liable to be spent in throwing a huge feast for the village. In the ILG view, this villager is preempting accusations of undue greed by "giving" the money back to the community. Again, leadership roles tend not to be willingly accepted, because one's increase in prominence might have an unsettling effect on local harmony: After all, there is only so much prestige to go around.

What would a reasonable ILG interpretation, therefore, of our Micah 6 passage look like?

- "To act justly" (6:8): Justice amounts to not wanting more than your fair share of what is good, whether it is tangible or not. Humbleness is simply knowing your proper place and sticking to it.
- "your ill-gotten treasures" (6:10): How is gain dishonest? When it is made at the expense of the others in the community, leading to a breakdown in community harmony.
- "dishonest scales [and] a bag of false weights" (6:11): Dishonest scales and weights are bad, not primarily because they violate the truth, but because they enable unequal accumulation of wealth at others' expense, thereby endangering community peace.
- "her rich men are violent" (6:12): The rich men are violent because ILG assumes that *it is through violence that they became rich*. Westerners would likely regard this "violence," as do some commentators, to be a disregard for the law, which may show up as the seizure of another person's property, as giving false witness in court, or as bribing judges, other civic leaders, or priests. But ILG communities will regard violence here as first and foremost the undue appropriation of more than one's equitable share of a good.
- "Therefore, I have begun to destroy you, to ruin you because of your sins" (6:13–15): God's judgment will fall on a society like this in the most characteristic form imaginable—there will be even a greater shortage of the limited good than ever.

James N. Pohlig (D.Litt., Biblical Languages, University of Stellenbosch) has worked to analyze various West African languages, to bring literacy to them, to translate the Bible, and to author resources for Old Testament translators in general.

QUESTIONS

1. How does Lee determine true from false prophets/pastors? How might his criteria be assessed?

2. Explain why Alpert inverts the order of Micah 6:8. Which one is "better"—Alpert's version or the biblical version?

3. If you were in charge of improving the conditions described by Baines in Toronto, how would you go about it? Would religion or religious ideas factor into your equation?

4. How does the notion of an ILG society help to analyze the dynamics of your own culture? Are there instances in your context where people think and act as if goods and resources are unlimited?

CHAPTER 18

PSALM 22, 23, 42, 148

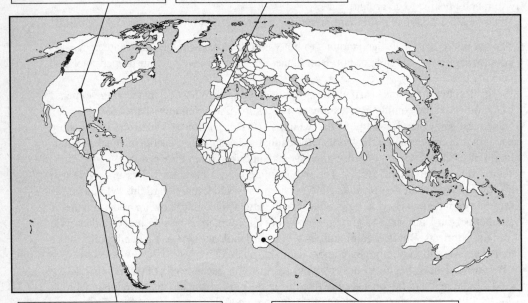

Amy Lambert comments on the opening verses of Psalm 42 from the perspective of those who struggle with the eating disorder anorexia.

Danielle Smith reads the shepherd metaphor of Psalm 23 in light of her knowledge of West African shepherds and through a Christian lens.

David Aftandilian reads Psalm 148 in light of the Native American idea of other animals as people like us, capable of sensing and relating to the divine.

Zacharias Kotzé shows how Psalm 22 is naturally understood in Africa as a spell against the attacks of a witch who is responsible for physical illness.

READINGS

Psalm 22 as an African Spell
Zacharias Kotzé

Psalm 23 and West African Shepherds
Danielle Smith

Psalm 42 and Anorexia
Amy Lambert

Psalm 148 and the Native American View of Animals
David Aftandilian

PSALM 22 AS AN AFRICAN SPELL

Zacharias Kotzé (South Africa)

Psalm 22 is one of many prayers of lament in the book of Psalms. It became famous in the Christian tradition because Jesus quotes its opening lines on the cross: "My God, my God, why have you forsaken me?" Much of its content constitutes complaints against an obscure enemy, and is therefore also called an enemy psalm. Interestingly, the enemy is described by means of animal imagery in verses 13–17, which has intrigued European and Western scholars. Although I am of European descent, I would like to attempt an interpretation of the enemy in Psalm 22 from a traditional African perspective.

Although many Africans have become Westernized, the majority still make use of traditional methods in dealing with illness, misfortune, and death. Like the peoples of the ancient Near East, Africans traditionally ascribe hardship and trouble to evil forces. More specifically, it is believed that certain people have the ability to cause harm through the practice of witchcraft. As a result, most Africans have a perceived enemy who is held responsible for all evil that befalls them. Even feared illnesses, such as HIV/AIDS, are commonly ascribed to powerful witches. In order to protect themselves against magical attacks, Africans go to a traditional healer who furnishes them with spells and herbal remedies for their protection. In addition to traditional African spells, some Africans also use the Psalms as incantations in an attempt to secure health, wealth, and good fortune. Viewed from an African perspective, Psalm 22 may be interpreted as a spell against the witch who is held responsible for a severe physical illness in the supplicant, particularly one that involves loss of bodily fluid.

Viewed from a European perspective, the psalmist's description of his infirmities is obscure: "I am poured out like water, and all my bones are out of joint; my heart is like wax; it is melted within me. My strength is dried up like a potsherd, and my tongue cleaves to my jaws; and you lay me in the dust of death" (vv. 14–15). In verse 17 the supplicant further says that one can count all his bones. No doctor would be able to make a diagnosis from the above description of suffering, but it is clear that the psalmist emphasizes the motif of dryness. This is evident from the images of water pouring out, the melting of the heart and intestines, and the dryness of a potsherd and dust. In the ancient Israelite worldview, dryness is associated with weakness. Similarly, the Sothos living on the hot, arid plateau of the South African Highveld, for example, would use images of dryness to describe discomfort. In short, dry is bad.

Interestingly, the psalmist seems to ascribe his illness/discomfort to the attack of his enemies. The above description is enclosed by references to animals attacking the supplicant in verses 12–13, and then again in verse 16: "Many bulls have surrounded me; strong bulls of Bashan have encircled me. They gaped open wide their mouths, as a ravening and roaring lion…For dogs have surrounded me; a band of evildoers has encompassed me; they pierced my hands and my feet." In their interpretation of these verses, some scholars have pointed to the numerous depictions of dangerous deities and demons as animals in the iconography of the ancient Near East. On a cylinder seal from Uruk in ancient Mesopotamia, for example, the "bulls of the pit" are depicted with the bodies of bulls, snake-like necks, and the gaping mouths of ravenous lions, much like the description of the "bulls of Bashan" in verse 13. Incidentally, "Bashan" is sometimes used as a synonym for "Yam," or "Rahab"—the ophidian sea-monster as Yahweh's enemy—in the Psalms. However, in view of the fact that the enemy is described in both human and animal terms, the majority of interpreters view the references to animals as metaphors for the strength and ferocity of the psalmist's human enemies.

From an African perspective, however, the mixture of animal and human elements is commonly associated with the witch. For example, in South Africa, it is believed that the Pedi night-witches transform into animals at night and go around scavenging. In the South African Lowveld, witches are thought to have the ability to combine elements of various animals, as well as humans, to take on the form of monsters with superhuman strength. Witches are suspected of meeting up with other witches at night, not only to go around stealing but also to cause illness by feeding on humans. It may be significant that the Zulus call HIV/AIDS *isidliso*, a word that is derived from the Zulu word for "to eat." In Nigeria, too, witches claim that they drink human blood day and night. From a traditional African perspective, therefore, the enemy in Psalm 22 may be viewed as a monster-like witch familiar in spiritual form who eats away on the flesh of the supplicant.

Some scholars have suggested that the Psalms contain magical formulas that were used as protection in ancient Israel. In this view, the psalms originally constituted incantations against demonic forces and witchcraft before they were reinterpreted by later editors who tried to rid them of their superstitious nature and dress them in a Yahwistic cloak. Still, traces of magical formulas can be detected. Psalm 22 is addressed to the "hind of the dawn" (v. 1). The Hebrew word for "hind" also refers to an ancient Canaanite moon-goddess type who was commonly invoked in spells. Also, the word for "dawn" is the Hebrew equivalent of the Ugaritic name of a well-known protector god associated with the dawn in the Ugaritic texts of Ras-Shamra. Not surprisingly, the word is associated with protective magic in the Old Testament. Similar to the peoples of the ancient Near East, Africans believe in the power of words and names. Many of their spells include various names of deities that are to be repeated several times. From an African perspective, the prayer in verses 19–20 may be regarded as an invocation to the deity who is called "my Strength."

Psalm 22 constitutes a remarkable text with a long history of development and interpretation. The words that Jesus quoted from the cross and the motif of enemies dividing the psalmist's clothes have captured the attention of Christians from a Western background. For those Africans who seek in the Psalms magical elements for everyday use, however, the psalm is most naturally used as a spell against the attacks of the witch who is believed to be responsible for some physical illness involving dehydration.

Zacharias Kotzé (Ph.D.), an Afrikaans-speaking South African, is a postdoctoral research fellow in Old Testament and Ancient Near Eastern Studies at the University of Northwest, South Africa.

PSALM 23 AND WEST AFRICAN SHEPHERDS

Danielle Smith (Senegal)

My first memories as a child are of my life in West Africa. Although I was born in the United States, at 10 months of age my family moved to Sierra-Leone as missionaries. In 1997 we moved to Senegal and I spent the majority of my formative years in the northern part of that country where nomadic lifestyles were the norm. This setting has deeply impacted how I now view the Bible.

A theme of shepherding is woven throughout the Psalms, including the well-known Psalm 23, in which David compares God, the shepherd-king, to an earthly shepherd watching over his flock. In Western Africa there is a nomadic people called the Peul, who are known for their Bedouin lifestyle as keepers of cattle, sheep, and goats. Their livestock is the measure of wealth and social status. For them, shepherding is more than work or tradition; it is a way of life that offers meaning and purpose. Shepherding consumes them to the point that, when grass becomes sparse, they move their entire clan and all their belongings to the next location in hopes of better fields. In comparing God to a shepherd, we recognize that God is with His people and that He is always looking out for them, even when such care creates an inconvenience for God Himself. To be a shepherd is a sacrifice, a sacrifice not only of time and effort but of safety.

A well-known African proverb says, "That which does not kill a shepherd never kills the whole herd." The caretaker is the first line of defense and he is trained to let absolutely nothing get past him. As long as he is alive, he will fight the predator in order to save his sheep. To me, this shows that in the same way, God does not give up on His children; He fights for them and even gave His own son's life to save them. A shepherd would never knowingly or intentionally lead his flocks into danger (v. 3). Like the Peul, God plans everything around His flock; He leads His sheep down the safest paths to protect them from eternal death and suffering.

In sub-Saharan Africa, water and greenery tend to be sparse and sand is found in an overabundance. To remain healthy, shepherds have to find food and water for their livestock even during the dry seasons when rivers and lakes dry up. To not be in want (v. 1) does not imply comfort, but necessity; we are not promised the best or easiest life, but rather to be provided for if we follow our Shepherd. As sheep we are vulnerable, weak, and do not know how to take care of ourselves. Sheep blindly follow their shepherd and they obey all his commands without questions or hesitation. Occasionally, while driving in the rural areas of West Africa, you may find flocks of sheep unattended, roaming around. They know their way home, but during the day they may wander about wherever they please. Because of this, many sheep are killed by oncoming traffic while crossing the road. This is a picture of the sheep that have walked astray, who know where they should be but, without their shepherd's guidance, fall into traps. How often in the Old Testament is Israel presented as electing to follow false shepherds instead of Yahweh? Their lives, like those of the wandering sheep in Africa, become casualties of injustice, violence, and depravation and they represent the stark consequences of living outside the care of the Good Shepherd.

There is hope for us, however, when we walk through these difficult and dark times because God is still with those who follow Him. In verse 4 we read, "Even though I walk through the valley of the shadow of death, I will fear no evil, for You are with me." A shepherd is with his sheep not in a theoretical way, but in a tangible, real way and there is no greater proof of this real love than the coming of Jesus into this world. He was dedicated to his cause— suffered rejection, ridicule, and mocking from humans, yet still risked his life to save us. He was the Good Shepherd (John 10:11) who, unlike the hirelings, laid down His life in the face of danger. Shepherds cannot be cowards, running at the first sign of distress. They must be brave and, above all, ready, vigilant at all times to defend their sheep; they must be willing to suffer pain in order to save just one little lamb. In the final verse of this Psalm, David reveals the overarching theme of the chapter about the need for us as God's sheep to wholeheartedly follow the true Shepherd in trusting obedience. Unlike those exposed to danger by blindly wandering through life, David reminds us that the life of the faithful will be marked by goodness and love.

If we trust, He will guide. He will not abandon us in the face of death because His paths are safe. He will not deliver us to our enemies; rather He will anoint our heads with oil. He comforts and guides. He provides and it overflows. Most of all, He welcomes us one day to live forever in the Great Shepherd's house.

Danielle Smith spent her early life in Senegal and is currently studying cultural anthropology in the United States.

PSALM 42 AND ANOREXIA

Amy Lambert (United States)

In recent American culture, there is a perpetual focus upon food: the good and bad foods, the diet plans around food, how to prepare food, how to eat this food versus that food, and how to eat the foods you want and still lose weight. And the list continues on. In the midst of this societal craving, a group of people stay hidden behind this socially acceptable mask: those who struggle with an eating disorder called anorexia. It is through this lens that I wish to comment on Psalm 42.

Anorexia nervosa is an eating disorder in which an individual becomes obsessed with her weight and the intake and output of food. A person who struggles can be severely underweight and still restrict her nutritional intake in order to lose more weight. As the disease progresses, the mind is literally consumed with thoughts on food. However, the current environment of diet mentality in America creates a space for such individuals to hide within plain sight.

Throughout the starvation process, an anorexic learns ways to dim the body's hunger cues. Though an anorexic may feel hungry, over time, those cues are dulled and the ability to recognize hunger and the body's needs are also undone. As the stomach shrinks and the body's processes slow down, an anorexic can honestly say, "I am not hungry" despite the fact that she may not have eaten for days. A young anorexic woman once wrote in her journal to God:

> To eat again, after fasting for days and weeks leaves me feeling nauseous and sick. It is so disgusting that food is put in front of me and I recoil. The mere whiff of food turns my stomach. It seems at this point that starving would be easier than the painful reintroduction of food. I even spat out my communion wafer last week because it caused me to gag to have a foreign object in my mouth. People keep asking in complete shock—aren't I hungry? It takes everything not to laugh at their foolish ignorance.

Whereas hunger can dim over a time of starvation, thirst only becomes more intense as the body has no water. It is medically known that a body can go weeks without food, but fatal dehydration can occur in three days if the body has no water. An anorexic is well aware of her thirst, and she also knows that with enough liquid, she can temporarily drown her hunger and maintain her life. It is here that liquids become lifesaving. For an anorexic, because there is such a lack in proper amount of nutrition, the body becomes dehydrated more quickly than under normal circumstances. The young woman again pens to God:

My body…my weakened heart and kidneys…my bones…my mind…my very soul thirsts though. My thirst is never satisfied. It is barely quenched these days. The less I eat and the longer I drink diet sodas in order to create a deceitful semblance of energy—the stronger the intensity becomes. Even when I drink water incessantly, it vanishes instantly as though I have not even put the glass to my lips. I wish this pain would go away—the way my emotions are numbed because of no food. And yet…it persists.

She is writing about a desperate thirst caused from dehydration intensified by starvation. As time wears on, thirst moves from a nagging feeling to an intense burn. From the intense burn and desire, thirst becomes a raging need that causes the mind to hallucinate and the skin to dry and crack. Extreme thirst moves into severe pain that a simple glass of water is unable to tame.

It is here that the opening verses of Psalm 42 ring out with new meaning. When the soul thirsts for God, the "living God," the suffering or recovered anorexic becomes vividly aware of the extremity of such words. How much does the soul ache and groan when its very life source is pushed away? The human soul (brought to life by the very "breath" of God as explained in Genesis) yearns, desires, and needs the living God in order to be quenched. A few months later, this same young woman once again writes to God:

I saw a deer today lapping up water from a stream. Psalm 42 came rushing back to me—so suddenly I stopped what I was doing to reread the passage. My own body will always be in need of water. Just as that deer innately knows that it must have water to function and exist—my body will always need water and my soul will always need you. Those days, months and years that I fed and watered my being with my eating disorder withered my soul. How amazing it is to know that my soul will never be fully quenched. God, just as a deer escapes a dangerous situation and like the psalmist who experienced exile, may I always remember that in the good and the bad times, I am always in need of you, the Living God.

Amy Lambert (M.Div., Duke Divinity) is currently working as an Intern Pastor for ordination in the Universal Fellowship of Metropolitan Community Churches.

PSALM 148 AND THE NATIVE AMERICAN VIEW OF ANIMALS

David Aftandilian (United States)

In Psalm 148, we find all of creation united in praise of God. Not just people but also the sun, moon, and stars, the depths of the ocean, fire, frost, and wind. Among this vast chorus of voices raised in grateful worship of the Creator are those of animals from all the cosmological realms: sea monsters, wild animals, cattle, creeping things, flying birds, and humans.

Although differences between the animals are noted in this passage, especially in terms of what part of creation they inhabit, we do not see a hierarchy among them. This contrasts with other biblical texts, such as Genesis 1:26, which have been interpreted to mean God has subjugated other animals to humans. Instead, Psalm 148 directs our attention to the commonalities we share with other animals, rather than our differences from them. Specifically, all animals, including humans, are described as having the capability to recognize the divine and to honor God through worship.

Many stories of animals and saints in the Catholic tradition also describe animals as capable of recognizing the divine, praising God, even asking for and receiving the sacraments. Nor are Judaism and Christianity the only world religions to see animals in this way; similar visions exist within Buddhism, Hinduism, Islam, and, most prominently, indigenous spiritual traditions, including those of Native North Americans.

Among the Muscogee Creek and Cherokee, for example, animals are viewed as very much like people (both of these native nations used to make their homes in the Southeast, and today live both there and in Oklahoma). The animals can talk, think, create social and political organizations, pray and perform ceremonies, and have souls. For example, Creeks describe the other animals as meeting in council to decide whether and how to create the lands on the flooded earth (Frank Speck, "The Creek Indians of Taskigi Town," *American Anthropological Society Memoirs* 2(2):1907, 145–146), and the Cherokee speak of bears doing dances of thanksgiving and panthers performing the Green Corn ceremony, one of the most important annual ceremonies known to the Southeastern tribes. The Cherokee even say that certain animals, such as bears and rattlesnakes, were once humans; therefore, the Cherokee feel they have a direct kinship relationship to the other animals (James Mooney, *Myths of the Cherokee* [New York: Dover Publications, 1900], 324, 327–329).

The animals are also seen as different from humans in Native American conceptions. But unlike some Judeo-Christian interpretations of Genesis 1:26, which ascribe superiority to humans because we are the only beings created in God's image, Native American sacred stories of creation often refer to humans as having been created last and *least*. For example, in Creek, Cherokee, and other native creation stories, birds and water animals existed in the world before humans were created; this means that these other animals have more practical and spiritual knowledge than we do. They are therefore referred to as our elder brothers and sisters, worthy of respect because of their seniority. Furthermore, other animals also have greater spiritual power than we do, which they can choose to use to help or harm us. Owls, for instance, can share their power to see beyond this world with Creek medicine people, helping them with divination (John R. Swanton, *Creek Religion and Medicine* [Lincoln and London: University of Nebraska Press, 2000], 621). But when humans started killing too many animals, both Creek and Cherokee traditions say the animals retaliated by creating diseases that could cripple or even kill disrespectful hunters (Mooney, 250–252; Speck, 148–149).

Among the Creek and Cherokee, these ideas of other animals as people, like us, but also peoples with greater practical knowledge and spiritual power, have inspired a series of natural laws or ethical norms that regulate human relations with other animals. First, humans should treat other animals with the respect that is due to elder relatives. Ways to demonstrate this respect include thanking hunted animals for the gift of their lives, only hunting as many animals as we need to survive, and not wasting any of their bodies. Contemporary Cherokee storyteller Edna Chekelelee, for example, explains that when you hunt a deer, you should only kill one, and you should not waste any of the meat (Barbara Duncan, *Living Stories of the Cherokee* [Chapel Hill and London: University of North Carolina Press, 1998], 129–130).

Second, humans should give something back in return for what the animals give to us; this principle is known as *reciprocity,* and it is one of the most important ethical norms among Native Americans. Respect and thanks are two things we can give back to animals. But perhaps more importantly, we also have a responsibility to care for the other animals in at least two senses—to protect their habitats and numbers, and to perform stories, dances, and ceremonies of world renewal on their behalf. In Native American traditions, every being has its proper role to play in the world; that of humanity is primarily to perform these world renewal ceremonies which involve our sacrifice for the good of all creation. We might compare this concept to contemporary reinterpretations of Genesis 1:26 by religious environmentalists, who read this passage as speaking of our stewardship responsibility to take care of all creation—"to till and tend" the Garden we know as Earth (Genesis 2:15).

How, then, might we read Psalm 148 in the light of Native American conceptions of other animals as people like us, capable of sensing and relating to the divine, and worthy of our respect and care? If animals are capable of worshipping God, as Psalm 148 clearly says they are, this shows that Judeo-Christian traditions, too, often describe the other animals as similar to us. Just as the gift of animals' lives to hunters necessitates a reciprocal relationship between animals and humans among Native American peoples, so too does the shared ability of other animals and humans to praise God suggest that Jews and Christians also ought to recognize a reciprocal relationship between themselves and animals. Furthermore, the similarity between animals and humans in Psalm 148 might also lead us to rethink our theologies of animals, to shift them from focusing on what makes humans different to what makes us similar to other animals.

David Aftandilian is Assistant Professor of Anthropology at Texas Christian University; he is the editor of What Are the Animals to Us? Approaches from Science, Religion, Folklore, Literature and Art.

QUESTIONS

1. Reread all of Psalm 22 carefully, assuming that it is a "spell against the attacks of the witch." What new questions and insights emerge?

2. Does one need Smith's knowledge of shepherds in Africa to fully understand the meaning of Psalm 23?

3. Read carefully the rest of Psalm 42 through the eyes of someone who has suffered from anorexia. What insights can be gleaned? What questions arise?

4. What significance might one draw from the fact that in Psalm 148 not only animals but also "sun, moon, and stars, the depths of the ocean, fire, frost, and wind" praise God?

CHAPTER 19

PSALM 137

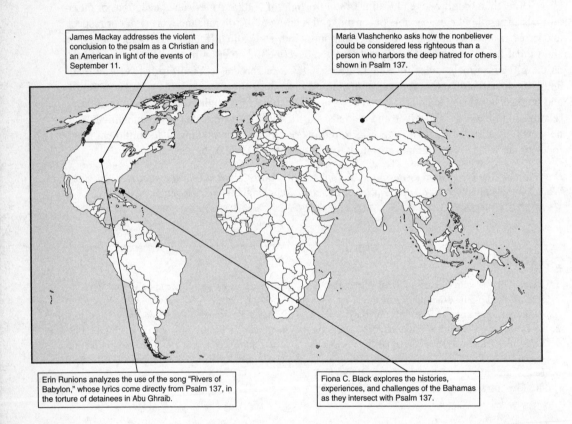

James Mackay addresses the violent conclusion to the psalm as a Christian and an American in light of the events of September 11.

Maria Vlashchenko asks how the nonbeliever could be considered less righteous than a person who harbors the deep hatred for others shown in Psalm 137.

Erin Runions analyzes the use of the song "Rivers of Babylon," whose lyrics come directly from Psalm 137, in the torture of detainees in Abu Ghraib.

Fiona C. Black explores the histories, experiences, and challenges of the Bahamas as they intersect with Psalm 137.

READINGS

Psalm 137 and the Bahamas
Fiona C. Black

"Rivers of Babylon" and the Torture of Detainees in Abu Ghraib
Erin Runions

The Violence of Psalm 137 and 9/11
James Mackay

Righteousness and Hatred in Psalm 137
Maria Vlashchenko

Psalm 137 and the Bahamas

Fiona C. Black (Bahamas)

Christopher Columbus came to the Caribbean, observes Samuel Murrell, with a sword in one hand and a Bible in the other. Subsequently, the Bible was used there to form and dominate colonized peoples. Over the last few centuries, however, through Christianization, the Bible has become central and highly valued in the spiritual lives of many Caribbean peoples. Here I will consider the applicability of Psalm 137 to the Caribbean context. This is a significant text, since it voices the pain of exile; provocatively considers migration, loss, and belonging; and has interpretive/cultural connections to African diasporas. Herein, I explore some of the histories, experiences, and challenges of one Caribbean context (the Bahamas), along with the issues of migration, diaspora, and memory. These come into sharp focus in the Psalm, which offers a complicated message to ancient and modern audiences alike.

I operate out of a specific interpretive environment, which I bring to my reading of the biblical text. I write as a Caribbean (Bahamian) immigrant to a multicultural country, Canada. I read as one who is thinking about the Bible in connection with a web of colonial relationships, past and present, and to a host of traumatic, migratory, historical events. I also consider these matters in connection with poetics, since I am convinced that texts such as Psalm 137 are able to focus matters concerning identity and subjectivity in ways that are distinct from narrative texts.

Geographic, linguistic and historico-cultural variety abounds in the Caribbean. Aboriginal peoples first occupied the Caribbean; once largely exterminated, these were followed by a rapid influx of millions of diverse African peoples. Moreover, Dutch, Spanish, French, British, and South Asian colonial roots are all present here, which include the diversity one would expect from disparate African and European religions and cultures. Added to these historical resonances are the dynamics of contemporary immigration to the region.

In the Bahamas specifically, the picture is just as varied: The current population includes descendants of slaves or transplanted slaves, of loyalists expelled from America, of British colonialists, and so on, as well as a large, changing population through the influx of Haitian migrant workers and illegals, tourists and off-shore buyers. Like many other Caribbean nations, the Bahamas' socioeconomic and cultural situation is complex, suffering from extremes of wealth and poverty, with attendant problems around social issues, health care, education, and housing. The country also appears to be consolidating its energies into tourism and development, arguably beneficial for the economy but troubling for nationals, since it causes displacement and limitation of industry. Proudly independent since 1973, the predominantly Christian Bahamas finds itself between two colonial powers: a historical but still influential British past, and an economically and culturally impactful American present. Consideration of the Bible's problematic past and its potential to heal is both beneficial and necessary. To the Bahamian context, therefore, which is growing, changing, increasingly disconnected from its cultural roots, and troubled in many ways, it is plausible that the Bible has something to contribute in a positive way.

Highly applicable for the Caribbean context in general, Psalm 137 laments the calamity of exile and the desolation of displacement and lost generations; it also emboldens the desire for retribution. In this way, as a type of memorialization of the Middle Passage—the forced migration of Africans across the Atlantic—the psalm addresses the historical memory of Bahamian and other Caribbean peoples. Indeed, the psalm profoundly articulates loss of all causes—the loss of land, the desire to remember what is gone, the recognition that return is not possible. For the present day, this text might also address the failure of Bahamians to hold on to the land that is now theirs, to work it, to live off it, to own it, since they are being edged out by ongoing development and off-shore ownership. As they negotiate their past and their present, the psalm speaks to the myriad cultural and spiritual concessions that must be made. Thus, for the collective history or memory of Caribbean peoples, the psalm "fits" in many ways. And yet, it is not just the subject matter of the psalm that makes it work for the Bahamian context; it is also its mechanisms of memory and affect. Like other laments, the psalm carries the concept of memory in its interpretive cache—it works as a vocabulary for grief and loss, because it has worked this way originally, and for others over time throughout its interpretive life (e.g., in the Rastafari community through music). Memory, therefore, is both linked to specific events and transcends them. The psalm also, however, problematizes memory. It is there, at the speaker's insistence (indeed, he stakes his health on it); he also, however, struggles to let go, to end what ails him. Do not forget, but do forget, he seems to be saying. This multifaceted aspect of memory constitutes the very essence of the speaker: It defines his experience, but equally seems essential to allow him to have a voice, to continue his life.

To explain this another way, we might say that the lamenting language of Psalm 137 (and others) is affective—that which, though specific and descriptive, can also modulate its speakers. In other words, it helps actually to constitute the subject in lament, since people are formed by their experiences and by the descriptive language they use. Thus, lamenting language has longevity and variability. Since it is able to shift in these ways, describing past and present events, and in essence describing subjects in a state of loss (which one could argue all Caribbean peoples are—though we need to be cautious of creating a nostalgia for an imagined past), it is an excellent model for describing the subject "on the move," or in a state of flux.

This seems an apt way of understanding Bahamian life and culture—as in a state of flux. That model takes into account the Bahamas' historical past, its current disjuncture from the land, and the perceived loss of culture and society through cultural and geographical proximity to America, tourism, disenfranchisement of its peoples, and social problems, such as rape, incest, legalized homophobia, immigration, economic enslavement, and so on. This idea of shifting or fluctuating subjectivity—which is mirrored by repetitions and inversions in the language of the psalm itself—reflects the hybrid identities of Caribbean peoples, in all the ways they are constituted. It pushes them not to identify wholly with land lost *or* new, but to negotiate their existence somewhere in between.

One aspect of the psalm remains for comment: the troubling, violent ending. Violence forms the immediate memory of the speaker, but it also speaks to his past (colonial power) and future (revenge to be exacted). So visible is it, in fact, that the speaker makes it excessive: It is inflicted upon children; it is aimed at destroying generation; it is the vile taste in the mouth that comes after grief. Here, the contours of the psalm engage the contemporary Caribbean listener to think hard about violence, both as it operates excessively in our midst and as it frames the experience of the displaced. In the psalm, violence indicates that the rivers of Babylon are in places turgid and muddied, offering no clear reasons for, or solutions to, displacement. Through remembrance, community and resettlement appear possible in the psalm, but anger and violence are never far behind. The psalm, in other words, crosses from here to there, from lament to violence, from desolation to contempt, in ways that ought to leave us uneasy.

Perhaps the violence here suggests that Bahamians look more closely at the neocolonization at work in their midst. They might look to the violence of their own peoples by government or by society, where these turn a blind eye to failures of education and protection of the weak, and to the cultural losses of stories and traditions. At the same time, Bahamians might also look at the ways that the practices and structures of violence are reinscribed, as, for instance, through the quasi-enslavement and displacement of Haitians, who are brought in (or whose illegal entry is allowed) to service the tourist industry, but who are denied citizenship and other benefits of society.

Perhaps, though, it is possible to learn from contradictory texts and the painful realities of migration that might be represented there. Psalm 137 signals that "to belong" means we must not attempt to fix identity and claim those factors that come with it (voice, power, privilege), but be comfortable in their failure to contain us. In other words, contradictory texts and migrations teach us how better to understand ourselves, and potentially to create diasporas and communities that embrace migration and change in better ways. It might be that such work is what is needed for the Bahamas as it looks to its past and attempts to articulate its present.

Fiona C. Black is Associate Professor and Head of the Department of Religious Studies at Mount Allison University, Sackville, NB, Canada.

"RIVERS OF BABYLON" AND THE TORTURE OF DETAINEES IN ABU GHRAIB

Erin Runions (United States)

Psalm 137 is a powerful and disturbing text. Equally powerful and disturbing is the fact that it was used in the attempt to break detainees in Abu Ghraib, the U.S.-operated prison in Iraq, where Iraqi prisoners were subjected to physical, psychological, and sexual abuse and torture. Boney M's song, "Rivers of Babylon," whose lyrics come directly from Psalm 137, was one of the songs played at ear-splitting volumes to wear down the prisoners. Haj Ali Shalal—the man whose experiences match the now-iconic photo of the hooded man on a box—reported being subjected to high-volume repetitions of the song. The inclusion of "Rivers of Babylon" in the "torture playlist" at Abu Ghraib reveals much about the belief system that enabled other atrocities.

Chosen no doubt for its reference to captivity in Babylon, and perhaps also for its quickly maddening disco beat and repetitive tune, we might wonder to what degree Shalal's interrogators thought through the song's cultural, mythical, and allegorical reverberations. The song repeats and slightly modifies the first four verses of Psalm 137, a text that expresses agony over the Babylonian exile of the Judean elite in 597 and 586 B.C.E. A refrain is included from Psalm 19, asking that the song be acceptable to God.

Did U.S. soldiers think through the implications of playing this particular incarnation of this biblical text as a form of psychological stress? In what theological world might they have thought their actions acceptable in God's sight? Even if the most minimal planning was operative, the thick strata of irony and ambiguity surrounding this musical selection beg for exploration.

At the very least, the decision to play "Rivers of Babylon" at Abu Ghraib indicates that an allegorical-mythical figure of Babylon was grafted onto Iraq in some way. Aided by a long apocalyptic interpretive tradition, the story of Babylon conquering ancient Israel (Judah), destroying the temple, and exiling God's people is read as one moment within an ancient mythical and spiritual struggle that continues into the present. In the apocalyptic tradition, Babylon becomes a transhistorical symbol of tyranny, evil, and godlessness, most clearly embodied by the figure of the Whore of Babylon in Revelation 17. Such evil must be fought, by any means necessary, or so the logic goes. In this case, Babylon seems to stand in for Iraq, since Iraq is where ancient Babylon was actually located, while ancient Israel becomes the United States.

Yet the allegory is somewhat ambiguous. For instance, to whom do the song's captives refer—weeping by the rivers of Babylon and refusing to sing in a foreign land? U.S. servicemen in Iraq? The detained Iraqis? In neither instance does an allegory to the situation in Iraq work as expected. The first possibility would suggest that U.S. forces occupying Iraq were somehow captive, which they were not. The second interpretation would somehow put U.S. soldiers in the position of the ancient Babylonian captors, which, given the usual associations with Babylon, they might reject. Moreover, what does it mean when a country like the United States, which likes to think of itself as beyond slavery and other civil rights injustices, plays a song about freedom to people they are torturing? An ambivalence about Babylon emerges. The use of the song at Abu Ghraib perhaps suggests that the United States is more like Babylon than it would like to think. The ambiguity of the allegory shows how the United States can think of itself as victimized (weeping by the rivers of Babylon), and at the same time, be oppressors (emulating Babylon).

Though the song quotes only the first few verses of Psalm 137, we must also consider the troubling final lines of the psalm: "O Daughter of Babylon, doomed to destruction, happy is he who repays you for what you have done to us—he who seizes your infants and dashes them against the rocks." The psalmist dreams of a violent role reversal, in a way that might telegraph a repeating pattern of cross-identification through the ages, so that U.S. soldiers can feel like captives and captors at the same time (Israel *and* Babylon). Did this biblical text in any way, even unconsciously, justify the heinous, often sexualized, abuse of men, women, and teenagers at Abu Ghraib? Revenge has the unfortunate trait of making seem righteous what would otherwise be considered woefully wrong.

A number of biblical scholars have tried to understand the violent ending of Psalm 137 as an understandable response to acute oppression, often citing the Holocaust as a scenario through which one could possibly understand the psalmist's rage. These biblical scholars are acting in the best of faith, honestly trying to make sense of a difficult passage. But the problem is that when Babylon (and subsequently Iraq) is identified with Nazi Germany, the ancient empire is further mythologized as somehow spiritually associated with one of the terrible evils of the modern era. Once put into uncritical hands, these associations and connotations justify military strategies that would not otherwise be permitted. Imitation of the ending of Psalm 137 becomes thinkable.

These, indeed, are the dangerous pitfalls of biblical interpretation. It is easy for contradictory truths to materialize when ancient texts are used to represent cosmic truths of good and evil, which are then applied to shifting contemporary geopolitical ambitions. Even if the soldiers were not biblically literate or thinking through all the implications of their choice of songs, these verses are part of the fabric that has formed a cultural attitude toward Babylon, which, as their particular musical choice of interrogation technique shows, has been vaguely particularized to Iraq, the U.S. occupation, and the war on terror.

But why make so much of this one incident now, so many years after Abu Ghraib has closed? Because torture is still under discussion, and the way we think about the Bible can influence national consciousness and attitudes toward what happens in war. We should reflect carefully on how the Bible comes to be used as torture, and what responsibility we have in that scenario. We might worry about the way we allegorize good and evil, the portability of allegories, the harm they do when literalized, and the way that they can subtly reflect actual power relations.

Erin Runions is Associate Professor of Religious Studies at Pomona College, United States.

THE VIOLENCE OF PSALM 137 AND 9/11

James Mackay (United States)

The book of Psalms is filled with songs of praise to God, expression of hope, trust, and confidence that God will be with us. Psalm 137, however, is different. The writer of this text is being held captive by his enemy—he is a modern-day prisoner of war (POW). He has been forced from his homeland into slavery in another land. He and his people have gone from having freedom and liberty to facing exile and possible death. They find themselves in Babylon, which is modern-day Iraq, having given up on all motivation and praise (v. 2). Their Babylonian captors torment them by mockingly demanding a song about their now-destroyed homeland, Zion (v. 3). The writer asks rhetorically how he could possibly sing such a song in light of his awful circumstances. Indeed, the first four verses are sad and depressing. The writer is exhausted.

But he is also resilient—and angry. In verses 5–6 he vows to keep the songs of Zion in his heart. He refuses to forget his home, his country, his family, and his life. He not only takes joy in thoughts of Jerusalem, but also, in verses 7–9, he takes delight in imaging the destruction of the enemy. He calls for revenge on the Babylonians and their children, not just as enemies of Israel but as enemies of God. And he does not hold back his venom, expressing the desire to see the heads of the Babylonian children dashed against the rocks.

This can be a very confusing text for Christians today. Aren't we supposed to love our enemies as Jesus commanded in the Gospels? Shouldn't we pray for those who persecute us? So what do we do with the rage expressed here in Psalm 137 (and a few other places in the Psalms)?

Sometimes we face great obstacles and life-changing moments. For most Americans our country changed on September 11, 2001, when Muslim extremists attacked our way of life and killed thousands of innocent people simply because we are different from them. Now we find our nation's military spread across the globe fighting and deterring terrorists like this. Stateside citizens have lost some of their freedoms as they are subject to more scrutiny at public events, embarrassing pat downs at airports, and other intrusions into our daily life that did not exist prior to 9/11. In essence, then, the scenario is this: We have an enemy that has killed our people with no cause, has enslaved us to a life of heightened and invasive security concerns, and has made us live with the constant fear of another attack upon our people.

So do we simply forgive the terrorists and forget everything that they did? Absolutely not. To do so would be irresponsible and not biblical, as we learn from Psalm 137. This is an enemy that is clearly against human rights and has declared war upon the United States, the rest of the world, and God. We must respond; we must retaliate in order to defend ourselves, our nation, and our way of life. This is precisely the sentiment that is voiced by the writer of Psalm 137. This is not to say that we should kill or smash terrorist babies' heads against the rocks, but we should rise against our enemy and destroy them. There is a big difference between an adversary that is out to rob you of your coat and one that is out to do nothing short of kill you and your loved ones. As is evidenced by 9/11, we are dealing with the latter. As the writer of this psalm recognizes, the only way to protect your family against such foes is to do your best to remember your nation, your people, and your heritage, and to trust God through the pain, suffering, and loss of the life that we once knew. With God's help we can overcome the enemy.

James Mackay served nine years in the army and is currently a Sergeant in the Indiana National Guard.

Righteousness and Hatred in Psalm 137

Maria Vlashchenko (Russia)

For religious people, the book of Psalms contains songs, poems, and hymns that proclaim the glory of God and his power. The psalms show not only the Lord's supremacy over people, nations, and indeed the entire world but also his love toward humanity. But for a nonreligious reader, such as myself, the book of Psalms represents something else. Namely, the book is filled with psalms of hate and loathing toward those who do not believe in God. Nonbelievers are associated with all forms of wickedness and evil. All kinds of aspersions are cast at them. But why?

The book of Psalms divides people into two groups—righteous and wicked—from the very beginning: "Blessed is the man who does not walk in the counsel of the wicked or stand in the way of sinners or sit in the seat of mocker" (Ps. 1). This black-and-white way of viewing the world continues through the remaining psalms. There is no gray. There is no third option. One is either faithful and righteous and on God's side or a nonbeliever and wicked and opposed to God. But what about the person who simply chooses by his or her own will to have beliefs about God which are not in line with the Judeo-Christian tradition. What if one is a member of another religious tradition? What if one simply believes in a "higher power" without believing in the existence of the God of the book of Psalms? Or what if one believes in no God at all? Does that automatically make them wicked and evil?

The book of Psalms pulls no punches. It represents "wicked" people as "sinners," "mockers," who have a "heart filled with destruction," have a "deceitful tongue," are "bloodthirsty," and "love delusions and seek false gods" (Pss. 1:1; 4:2; 5:6, 9, 10). And that is just to name a few aspersions in the first couple of chapters. But is that right? Making a choice to believe or not to believe doesn't make one person good and right and another evil and wrong. Not every person who does not believe in God is evil, bloodthirsty, and full of lies. Yes, there are undoubtedly some people who do fit this description. But certainly a belief in the Judeo-Christian God is not the primary determining factor between who is righteous and who is wicked.

Moreover there is a real and remarkable paradox here. When we read through the psalms we find plenty of places where the psalmist, the righteous believer in God, is the one who is "bloodthirsty" and has "a heart full of destruction." The writer calls on God to destroy his enemies—using graphic and offensive language to do so. To take just a few examples, Psalm 58 says concerning the wicked, "Break the teeth in their mouths, O Lord…Let them vanish like water that flows away…like a stillborn child, may they not see the sun." Then "the righteous will be glad when they are avenged, when they bathe their feet in the blood of the wicked." This is disturbing rhetoric and language. How can a "righteous" person ask a supposedly "holy" God to kill their enemy so that it dies like an aborted fetus? Is this a religious tradition that a nonbeliever should be drawn toward? Surely this blurs the simple black-and-white world that the book of Psalms envisions?

While many other Psalms could be quoted, I will mention only one more. In Psalm 137, the writer again uses explicit imagery to express loathing and hate toward the enemy, in this case the Babylonians who have defeated Israel. Here the "righteous" psalmist proclaims, "Happy is he who repays you for what you have done to us—happy is he who seizes your infants and dashes their heads against the rock" (v. 9). While we can perhaps sympathize with the psalmist's suffering, still, how can these be the words of a good, religious person? How can any decent human being take joy in seeing an infant smashed to death? Belief in God—any God—does not give one license to say such things. How can the nonbeliever feel that they are less righteous than a person who harbors such deep hatred for others? Who, really, is the wicked person here?

Blaming "the wicked" for all one's misfortunes and calling on God to utterly destroy them is not only offensive to us nonbelievers, but it is also an example of religious hypocrisy. How can someone ask God to "Banish [the wicked] for their many sins, for they have rebelled against you," while also pleading with God to "Remember not the sins of my youth and my rebellious ways" (Pss. 5:10; 25:7). If the psalmists recognize that they themselves have been sinful and rebellious, it seems deeply misguided for them to call down curses on the wicked. Don't they see themselves under such curses? Don't they see the irony in all this?

Maria Vlashchenko is from Khabarovsk, Russia; she attended the Academy of Economics and Law in Khabarovsk before moving to the United States to study.

QUESTIONS

1. Explain and evaluate how Black connects Psalm 137 to life in the Bahamas. In her view, how can Psalm 137 "contribute in a positive way" to the Bahamian context?

2. Find a version of Boney M's song "Rivers of Babylon" on the Internet and reflect on its use in torture tactics. Try to imagine it played at high volumes as Runions mentions.

3. How do Mackay's experiences as a soldier shape his interpretation? How does Mackay's belief in God play into his thinking?

4. Evaluate Vlashchenko's critique of Psalm 137 and other biblical texts. How would a believer in the Judeo-Christian God respond? Could a believer "side" with Vlashchenko?

CHAPTER 20

PROVERBS 31

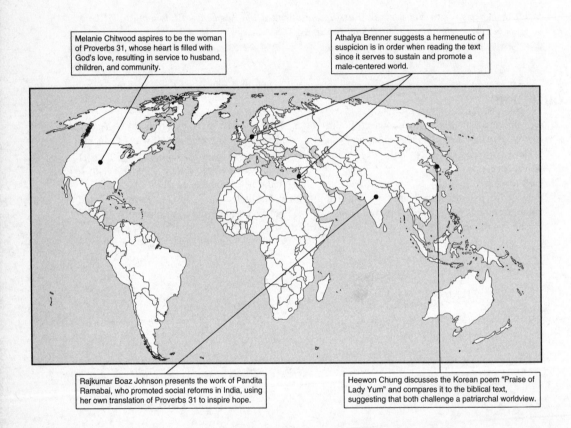

Melanie Chitwood aspires to be the woman of Proverbs 31, whose heart is filled with God's love, resulting in service to husband, children, and community.

Athalya Brenner suggests a hermeneutic of suspicion is in order when reading the text since it serves to sustain and promote a male-centered world.

Rajkumar Boaz Johnson presents the work of Pandita Ramabai, who promoted social reforms in India, using her own translation of Proverbs 31 to inspire hope.

Heewon Chung discusses the Korean poem "Praise of Lady Yum" and compares it to the biblical text, suggesting that both challenge a patriarchal worldview.

READINGS

Aspiring to Be the Woman of Proverbs 31
Melanie Chitwood

Reading Proverbs 31 Suspiciously
Athalya Brenner

Pandita Ramabai's Translation and Use of Proverbs 31
Rajkumar Boaz Johnson

"Praise of Lady Yum," Proverbs 31, and a Challenge to Patriarchy
Heewon Chung

ASPIRING TO BE THE WOMAN OF PROVERBS 31

Melanie Chitwood (United States)

When I first read the description of the woman found in Proverbs 31:10–31, I thought, "She's not just an excellent wife, as described in verse 10. She's Superwoman and Betty Crocker combined, and I am quite sure I cannot be her." Knowing, however, God had a reason for including in Scripture the example of this godly woman, I decided to dig deeper.

Scholars tell us this passage describing the qualities of a godly wife was birthed from a mother's lessons to her son, a young prince. Since her son would one day be king, this wise mother knew how important his future wife would be. With the 22 letters of the Hebrew alphabet in sequential order as her guide, the mother creates an acrostic poem, with each verse describing an essential trait of an excellent wife. This poem would have been repeated often in the home, even memorized so it would be buried in the prince's heart and mind.

Although retold by the male writer of this passage, I appreciate how this description of a godly woman stems from the life of a woman who has "been there—done that." As a wife and mother herself, she is still doing that, turning her heart to God and seeking to obey Him in all she does. This real-life advice from another woman encourages me, helping me to believe that being like the Proverbs 31 woman is not an unattainable ideal but a worthy goal.

Along with providing a profile of a desirable wife, this poem also provides us with an example of the kind of godly woman, single or married, God wants us to be. We see the woman described in the New Living Translation as "virtuous and capable." Other versions of Scripture use the word "noble" (NIV) or "excellent" (NAS). For each, the Hebrew root word *hayil* can be translated as strength, capability, or valor. So the question beginning this passage could be worded as, *Who can find a strong woman? Or who can find a capable woman?*

No doubt about it, the Proverbs 31 woman "is energetic and strong, a hard worker" (v. 17). She works diligently around her home, serving her children and husband, and reaching out to the community. She plans and prepares meals, attends to clothing needs, and invests in business ventures to profit her household, to name a few of her many tasks. And all without the modern conveniences of a dishwasher or washing machine!

She's a woman not only with physical strength but also with strength of character. She is trustworthy and her husband is assured that she will "greatly enrich his life" (v. 11). She's generous to those in her community. She's at peace, "without fear of the future" (v. 25). She is wise and kind.

Because Proverbs 31 describes so many of the woman's strengths, it's easy to be intimidated by her and mistakenly to think I couldn't possibly be like her. Surely she must be gifted with superpowers or have an unusual bent toward homemaking. However, to truly understand this woman and to see her as the real woman she is, we need to take a look at what's behind her "to do" list.

Tucked in a verse at the end of the passage is the key to explain the source of this exemplary woman's strength: "Charm is deceptive, and beauty does not last; but a woman who fears the Lord will be greatly praised" (v. 30). Her excellence overflows from a heart which respects, trusts, and obeys God. One commentator sums her up perfectly: "Her heart is full of another world, even when her hands are most busy about this world."

She's not a picture of what a woman can do or become overnight. Rather she's a portrait of a woman who has spent a lifetime choosing moment by moment, day by day to be the woman God wants her to be. As I make daily choices to seek God, I find that just like the Proverbs 31 woman, I too will be a woman whose heart spills over with God's love, resulting in love and service to my husband, children, and community. I will be a rare and beautiful treasure, a woman whose heart and life belong to God.

Melanie Chitwood serves with Proverbs 31 Ministries (proverbs31.org), a Christian organization for women; she is the author of What a Husband Needs from His Wife *and* What a Wife Needs from Her Husband.

READING PROVERBS 31 SUSPICIOUSLY

Athalya Brenner (The Netherlands, Israel)

Proverbs is considered a "wisdom" book, a teaching for life, but I wonder whether this collection, including the poem in Proverbs 31, indeed contains "wisdom" that is universally applicable and useful for past as well as contemporary readers.

I am a woman scholar, Jewish, a native Hebrew speaker, a first-generation Israeli born to immigrant Ostjuden parents, a-religious, a mother to a son, divorced, living in Amsterdam and Haifa, teaching Bible and Jewish studies in Amsterdam and Israel, of working-class origins, a feminist with left-oriented political opinions. The world in which I live and with which I identify myself cannot be defined, simply and straightforwardly, as "Western." Rather, I see myself as both Orientalized and Westernized. And, importantly, I belong to a secular world, even though my business is to study and teach texts that are, by Western and non-Western cultural consent, religious texts. Thus, my attention to matters of faith lags far behind my interests in literary structure, forms, and content; issues of gender and class; epistemological questions; and the biblical text's influence on early twenty-first-century life, mine and that of others. It is no hardship or sorrow for me to concede that, in Proverbs, "religion" functions as a general background for sustaining societal stability and the politico-economic status quo. The advice dispensed in Proverbs is largely conventional and conformist—it promotes continuation rather than change. Obedience and authority are valued above independence and original thought. Agism (in the sense of age superiority) is the order of the day. In short, the status quo that Proverbs wants to promote and sustain is one which privileges elite-class, urban, educated males. Thus, I have many good reasons for not accepting Proverbs' counsel as universally applicable. A hermeneutic of suspicion when reading Proverbs 31 is indeed in order.

To appreciate the dynamics of Proverbs 31, we must begin in Proverbs 1–9. Here advice is dispensed from a parent to a "son," or from an "elder" or "elders" who are "wise," while the target audience is imaged implicitly or explicitly as male, young, "foolish," "ignorant," "insensitive," and in need of instruction and teaching. Whether this implies an actual family teaching praxis or rather a teaching situation at schools where elder persons prepared younger males for the privileged life of public office, scribal activity, or economic viability remains uncertain. What can be deduced, though, is the class situation in which such counsel could be formulated and transmitted: urban elite class males that had the leisure, money, and inclination to invest in the continuance of their ways through the training of whoever needed prompting in the right direction. That the producers as well as the consumers of this training were males seems to be borne out by the texts themselves, as well as by the preoccupation with female figures, personifications, and metaphors.

Throughout Proverbs 1–9 there is an interchange of father/mother's "instructions" to presumably a young son(s). It is filled with propaganda for the attractions of a feminized and eroticized Wisdom figure, and descriptions of a fatal Other woman (Loose or Strange Woman), whose assessment is obviously negative. The parents try to persuade the son—and ignorant male customers/readers in general—to follow Woman Wisdom with promises of health, wealth, and the good life, rather than sex. Her direct opposite, Woman Folly, also goes out into the street to attract customers but, as the Other woman, her attempts to promote hidden pleasures are inexplicably deadly, although her powers of persuasion are considerable.

The last section of Proverbs, once again, displays a deep concern with women and femaleness/femininity. Proverbs 31:10–31 is an acrostic poem that draws a portrait of a virtuous wife who works round the clock, keeps her family, and is commercially active, in addition to doing all traditional female crafts and tasks. She carries out economic transactions and is Yhwh-fearing, charitable, wise, and a source of praise and comfort for her sons and husband.

Proverbs' opening and closing units, then, foreground some points that are endemic to the collection as a whole and meaningful for understanding it. To start with, these units serve as the book's frame and its framework: All the other units are enveloped by or embedded in the frame. The frame contains much discourse that is concerned with femaleness and femininity—more specifically, it elaborates the roles of a legitimate wife/lover and mother over against illicit sexual ties of a man with Other women. This is in keeping with Proverbs' general interest in safeguarding the family as an ongoing, [re]productive social institution. This impulse makes sense for social continuation and self-perpetuation. At the same time, it betrays a male anxiety about the social project it promotes.

The curious persona or metaphor of woman as Wisdom, an erotically portrayed wife/lover and female teacher of commonsense, is deeply meaningful for identifying the underlying wishes and anxieties about the promoted social order of Proverbs. It would make no sense to advance and sustain a female Wisdom figure at the beginning of the book (Proverbs 1–9) and to attribute a teaching function to the virtuous wife at the book's ending (v. 26), if such a function was unimaginable for regular wives and mothers. The prominence of Woman Wisdom suggests an appreciation of womanhood—more specifically endogamous wifehood and motherhood—that is overtly absent from the androcentric (male-centered) world order advocated. Thus, a mixed and at least dual-layered message to and about women is implicit in the book of Proverbs.

The virtuous wife who closes Proverbs is a paragon of virtue: no wonder that Jewish husbands still recite the poem to their wives today, either at their wedding or on Shabbat eve. Incidentally, as I have learned recently, in some Orthodox Jewish communities the poem is recited also at the graveside during a deceased woman's funeral service (in Haifa); I have no idea whether an unmarried woman receives the same ritual treatment. At any rate, during her lifetime, such a wife is convenient to have, since she has everything, apart from beauty (v. 30). Like Wisdom, she is "far more precious than rubies" (v. 10). In fact, she is the personification of the metaphorical/metaphorized or personified Woman Wisdom of Proverbs 1–9. The essence of feminine/female achievement is a woman who has totally adapted to her required role. This is the ultimate male victory: a useful woman, the complete antithesis to the woman Other. Presumably, the final goal was for this exaggerated blueprint for wifely behavior to be taught by mother to daughter—after all, the virtuous woman does have the capacity to instruct wisely!

Athalya Brenner is Professor of Bible at the University of Amsterdam, The Netherlands; and Tel Aviv University, Israel.

PANDITA RAMABAI'S TRANSLATION AND USE OF PROVERBS 31

Rajkumar Boaz Johnson (India)

English translations of the Bible usually describe the woman of Proverbs 31:10–31 as a "capable wife" or "wife of noble character" or as a "virtuous wife." But these translations miss the main meaning of the Hebrew words *eshet chayil*: strong woman. By contrast, Pandita Ramabai translated it correctly and lived it.

Pandita Ramabai was a woman from India who intensely grappled with the question of the place and meaning of womanhood in late nineteenth-century and early twentieth-century India. She was also the first woman to have translated the whole Bible into a low-caste Indian language, Marathi. Indeed, she was the first woman to have translated the whole Bible into another language anywhere in the world. Research in the thought and writings of Ramabai make it clear that two things were paramount in her mind: injustices in India against women and injustices against low-caste/outcaste people. Ramabai's impact on India was so great that in 1989, a hundred years after the founding of Ramabai Mukti Mission (the House of Salvation), the government of India acknowledged her legacy with a commemorative stamp. The official brochure with the stamp reads as follows:

> Pandita Ramabai (1858–1920): Pandita Ramabai was a social reformer, a champion for the emancipation of women, and a pioneer in education. Left totally alone by the time she was 23, Ramabai acquired a great reputation as a Sanskrit scholar. Deeply impressed by her prowess, the Sanskrit scholars of Calcutta University conferred on her the titles of "Saraswati" and "Pandita." She rebelled against the caste system and married a shudra advocate, but was widowed at 23, having a baby girl. In 1882, she established the Arya Mahila Samaj for the cause of women's education in Pune and different parts of Western India. This led to the formation of the Sharda Sadan in 1889, a school which blossomed into an umbrella organization called Pandita Ramabai Mukti Mission, 40 miles outside Pune. In 1896, during a severe famine Ramabai visited villages of Maharashtra with a caravan of bullock carts and rescued thousands of outcaste children, child widows, orphans and other destitute women and brought them to the shelter of Mukti and Sharada Sadan. A learned woman knowing seven languages, she translated the Bible into her mother tongue—Marathi—from the original Hebrew and Greek. Her work continues today, a memorial to her life and path.

Ramabai wrote quite widely describing the state of the Indian woman. She wrote in her work *A Testimony of our Inexhaustible Treasure*:

> There were two things on which all those books, the Dharma Shastras, the sacred epics, the Puranas…were agreed: women of high and low caste, as a class, were bad, very bad, worse than demons, and that they could not get Moksha (salvation) as men. The only hope of their getting this much-desired liberation from Karma and its results, that is, countless millions of births and deaths and untold suffering, was the worship of their husbands. The husband is said to be the woman's god; there is no other god for her.

In the same token, commenting on injustices against low-caste and outcaste people in society, she wrote (*A Testimony*, 7):

> The same rules are applicable to the Shudras, the untouchables. The Shudras must not study the Veda and must not perform the same religious acts which a Brahman has a right to perform. The Shudra who hears the Veda repeated must be punished by having his ears filled with liquefied lead.... His only hope of getting liberation is in serving the three high castes as their lifelong slave.

Ramabai's life's work was dedicated to setting right these two injustices. She spent the last 18 years of her life translating the whole Bible into Marathi, the local language of Maharashtra, a state in India. Her translation makes it clear that the issue of injustice was topmost on her mind. For instance, she did not use the word *Parameshvar* for "God," as do other vernacular translations. *Parameshvar* is the God who introduced and propagates injustices against low-caste/outcaste people and women in Hindu mythology. Instead, Ramabai used the word *Deva*, which is the term used by low-caste/outcaste people to refer to God. This God frees the downtrodden masses and women from the oppression of high-caste people and gods. Further, Ramabai taught the languages of the Bible to the low-caste girls she rescued from prostitution, child widowhood, and poverty. In a sad—but perhaps fitting—note, the Bible Society of India, which was dominated by high-caste men, did not accept her Bible translation.

Ramabai describes the woman of Proverbs 31 as a Saduni Bai, that is, "mentally, emotionally, physically, and spiritually strong woman." This is distinct from other Marathi and Hindi translations, which describe this woman as a Bhali Patni, that is, an "innocent, dutiful, devoted wife." In Indian culture, this is obviously the model of a woman, even in today's society. The English translations we mentioned above (virtuous, capable, noble) are not as misguided as the Indian vernacular translations, but they nonetheless are inferior renderings. Indeed, Ramabai's translation is closer to the meaning of the Hebrew words, *eshet chayil*, the strong woman. The choice of these words makes it clear that Ramabai was very keen on setting right the place and meaning of womanhood in Indian society.

We further note that Proverbs 31 concludes with the words, "Many women have done excellently, but you surpass them all." The Hindi and the Marathi renders the word "women" as *stree*. In Hindu mythology *stree* are women who serve high-caste men, and in the Hindu concept of heaven, they serve men there as well. Ramabai avoids the word *stree* and renders instead, "Many daughters have done mentally, emotionally, physically and spiritually strong deeds." Without a doubt, Ramabai's translation sought to give the women of India, and especially the girls she rescued from terrible conditions, an emancipatory model of womanhood.

In sum, the "strong woman" of Proverbs 31 becomes the model for Ramabai and all the young women who found their home at Ramabai Mukti Mission, women who endured injustice in the Indian context of that time, as so many do even today.

Rajkumar Boaz Johnson was reared in one of the slums of Delhi, where he witnessed many of his young friends taken into slavery by high-caste Hindus; he is Professor of Biblical and Theological Studies at North Park University, United States.

"PRAISE OF LADY YUM," PROVERBS 31, AND A CHALLENGE TO PATRIARCHY

Heewon Chung (South Korea)

Ancient Korea was a patriarchal society, in which women were regarded and depicted as unskilled, dependent, and unwise in many aspects. Yet, a few songs and stories in honor of the "wise woman" were recorded in certain genres of literature in ancient Korea. One such example is a poem entitled "Praise of Lady Yum," which describes the virtuous deeds of a wife. Its author is Nubaek Choi (?–1205), a high-ranking official of the *Korye* dynasty. After the death of his wife, Kyognae Yum (1100–1146), he composed the poem to commemorate her virtue, and later inscribed it on a massive monument as a tribute to her and to instruct his descendents. The following is the abbreviated translation of the poem:

> As a person, my wife was pure and modest. She was very literate and well understood moral obligations. In speech, appearance, skill, and conduct, she was superior to others. Before marriage she ably served her parents; after marriage she was extremely diligent in wifely ways. She was the first to perceive and carry out the wishes of the elders, and with filial piety she nourished my now deceased mother. In good and bad fortune, in congratulations and condolences, she could share the feelings of immediate family members, in-laws, and neighbors. There was no one who did not praise her.
>
> When I was involved in military matters, she endured hardship in our poor home and often made and sent military uniforms. And when I was a palace attendant, she used every means possible to supply delicacies to present to the king. How she followed me through all of these difficulties for twenty-three years I cannot entirely record.
>
> One day she said to me, "You are a man of letters. Mundane matters should not be important to you. I consider providing clothes and food for the family to be my task." When I was promoted to a drafter of royal edicts and proclamations, my wife, showing her happiness in her face, said, "It seems we have almost seen the end of our poverty." I responded to her, "Being a policy critic is not a position to earn a rich stipend." My wife said, "If suddenly one day you are standing in the palace court with the king arguing over an issue, even if I am forced to wear a thorny wooden barrette and poor cotton skirts and carry heavy burdens in making our life, I will accept willingly." These were not the words of an ordinary woman.
>
> I continued to be promoted many times and successively received higher stipends. In looking at my family's present situation, however, it is not as good as in the days when my wife struggled to make ends meet. How could anyone say my wife did not have wisdom? When my wife was about to die, in leaving her last instructions to me and our children, all her words were wise and worth listening to.
>
> When she died, her age was forty-seven. Her epitaph reads: "I, your husband, pledge not to forget you. That I am not yet buried together with you gives me great pain. Because of you, the children will live in harmony and expect to be prosperous forever."

This poem praises a woman who followed the four basic obligations of the traditional Confucian teaching for women: moral conduct, proper speech, proper appearance, and womanly tasks. She was filial to parents-in-law, harmonious with neighbors, and obedient to husband.

Notably, however, the wife is acclaimed as a wise woman for her individuality: She was literate, intelligent, and wise enough to instruct her husband although women in the period were excluded from formal education. In fact, the male-oriented society of ancient Korea believed that women should not be educated because they might discharge the duties appropriate to their role. Given this ethos, she went beyond cultural and societal views of stereotypical gender roles; she elevated herself to becoming an integral member of a multigenerational family unit and a paragon of virtue for the public. Lady Yum, therefore, significantly changed the status and image of wife from that of submissive spouse and caregiver to that of an advisor and helpmate.

As one can easily notice, "Praise of Lady Yum" demonstrates a number of striking lexical parallels and thematic correspondences with Proverbs 31:10–31. The biblical poem also praises the active good works of a woman in the ordinary affairs of family and society. She is depicted as having wisdom, diligence, modesty, compassion to the poor, administrative skill, liberality to neighbors, prudent speech, and judicious instruction. For these reasons, she was praised by her husband, children, and neighbors. Overall, the wise woman in Proverbs 31 represents more than simply a model for performing everyday tasks of marital life—she is more than simply a woman whom the young males dream of. Her astonishing capacities and wisdom overturns an ancient sociocultural ethos that a woman's role was to bear children and equip them for survival in a male chauvinist society.

In this framework, "Praise of Lady Yum" and Proverbs 31 offer a moment for reflection on the matters of gender role and gender equality in our society. Particularly, it is critical for Korean immigrant communities and other contemporary immigrant groups in the United States, mostly from non-European, Third World countries. For example, while only a small proportion of married women participate in the labor force in South Korea, the vast majority of Korean immigrant wives work outside the home. Their increased economic role and the persistence of their husbands' traditional patriarchal attitude and ideology cause marital conflicts and tensions in many immigrant families. Indeed, most Korean husbands have not modified their rigid form of patriarchal ideology brought from Korea because they are socially segregated from mainstream U.S. society. Furthermore, men's role as provider and their social status have significantly weakened with immigration.

What do Proverbs 31 and "Praise of Lady Yum" say to those who cherish a patriarchal ideology or a male chauvinism? As indicated above, the poems picture the wise wives as indispensable helpmates and advisers, and as the foundation for the peace and stability of the family. They also depict the female as a person-in-community and indicate the capabilities of women in cultivating and maintaining a web of social relations. Even though the poems still retain some aspects of reality for women in patriarchal society as "the way it is," the wives represented in the biblical poem and "Praise of Lady Yum" set themselves as examples in male-oriented societies to show that women can take active and authoritative roles in communities. Therefore, these two poems provide worthy interpretive and cultural rationales to dismiss a male-dominated mind-set and a patriarchal worldview.

Heewon Chung is Lecturer of Old Testament at the College of Liberal Arts, Keimyung University, Daegu, South Korea.

QUESTIONS

1. Assess Chitwood's reading of the biblical text. Is it accurate to describe the woman of Proverbs 31 as Superwoman and Betty Crocker combined?

2. Why is Woman Wisdom an important part of Brenner's reading? Explain what Brenner means when she says that a "mixed and at least dual-layered message to and about women is implicit in the book of Proverbs."

3. Compare and contrast the social and cultural context of Ramabai and the writers of Proverbs 31.

4. Imagine a conversation between Lady Yum and the woman of the biblical poem. How might they sympathize with and critique each other?

CHAPTER 21

JOB

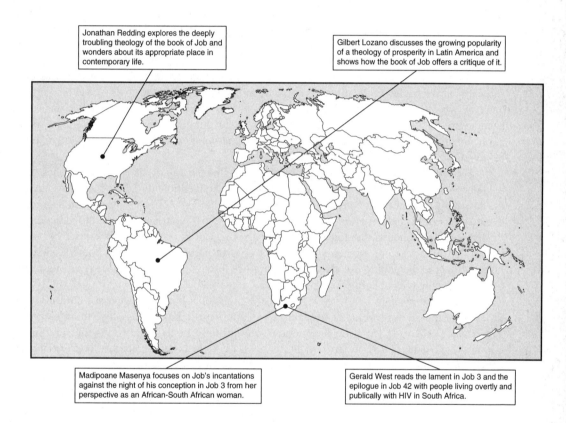

Jonathan Redding explores the deeply troubling theology of the book of Job and wonders about its appropriate place in contemporary life.

Gilbert Lozano discusses the growing popularity of a theology of prosperity in Latin America and shows how the book of Job offers a critique of it.

Madipoane Masenya focuses on Job's incantations against the night of his conception in Job 3 from her perspective as an African-South African woman.

Gerald West reads the lament in Job 3 and the epilogue in Job 42 with people living overtly and publically with HIV in South Africa.

READINGS

An African-South African Woman's Perspective on Job 3
Madipoane Masenya

Reading Job 3 and 42 with People Living with HIV
Gerald West

Job's Critique of a Theology of Prosperity in Latin America
Gilbert Lozano

The Troubling Theology of Job and Its Place in Contemporary Life
Jonathan Redding

An African-South African Woman's Perspective on Job 3

Madipoane Masenya (South Africa)

An African Proverb says, *bošego ga bo rone nta*. When translated it means: A night cannot remove lice from the seams of clothes. Its underlying tenor is that it is difficult to work efficiently in the night because dangerous experiences are usually linked with the night. The night thus cannot be safe; it cannot be trusted. Perhaps it is no wonder that acts of witchcraft in African cultures were and are still basically linked with the night. In Job 3, Job is not only scared of the night but also of the night's darkness and all the images which were conjured by the ancients when they thought about the night. He has a great distaste for the night, believing that nothing good could come from the night, that *bošego ga bo rone nta*.

Several observations are in order. First, in the incantations against the day he was born, Job calls on the negative, the night, to come upon his day and mess it up (3:4). He also reflects a narrow view of God and even a distaste for God. It is assumed that as the day becomes darkened, deprived of light and thus blackened, Job's God would not seek it! Has Job's view of creation suddenly changed? Was the night and its darkness not created by the same God who was believed to have been responsible for all of creation?

Second, as for the night of his conception, just like the day of his birth, Job wishes that it would come into oblivion (3:3). Even though Job 3 is conventionally labeled as Job's curse of the day of his birth, there is considerably more focus on the night of Job's conception than on the eventual day of his delivery on Mother earth. That the two are intricately bound together cannot be disputed. Nonetheless, the foregrounding of the night of his conception is crucial because it shows the importance of women's bodies, not only in providing a suitable home/security for human life at its beginning but also in nurturing life through the very early stages of its formation, influencing it even before its arrival on Mother earth.

Third, the incantations leveled against the night of Job's conception are not only three times more than those leveled against the day of Job's birth, but they are also more elaborate. The images emerging from the incantations on the night include the following: (1) intense darkness, (2) sadness, (3) no fertility/ barrenness, (4) light-less/dark stars, and (5) permanent darkness. In Job's view, that night must not only be darkened, but it should never have been fertile! The night's provision of suitable space for the fruitful sexual relationship between Job's parents is viewed with distaste by their offspring. Job particularly shuns the fact that his mother's womb became fertile ground for the beginning of his existence. For Job, the night cannot and should not be trusted, *bošego ga bo rone nta!*

Contrary to Job, from my perspective as an African-South African woman, the night does in fact have the capacity to remove lice from the seams of clothes, *bošego bo rona nta*! Why? First, it is on that night that a woman played a critical role in the process of cocreation. Second, had it not been for that night, where would Bible readers have gotten the story of a devout man whose relationship to God could apparently not be tampered with by what he perceived to be God's unjust dealings with him? Third, Job's character affords readers with a rare model of a male human being who faces the pain caused by grief with both frankness and humanness. Fourth, through Job's lament, the reader is also provided with a positive view of death and the place of the dead. A Bible reader coming from the Two-Thirds World is naturally empowered by Job's observation that in and through death, the ground is level: both the great and the small, royalty and those with no royal blood, the rich and the poor, those designated wicked and those designated righteous. All these will be and are united in death. Yes, that night which gave birth to the beginning of Job's life *e rona nta*! It can remove lice from the seams of clothes. It can thus be trusted.

An important issue here is Job's attack on his mother's reproductive organs. He curses the cervix of his mother's womb (3:7–10) and attacks his mother's thighs and breasts (3:12). Job's attack on his mother's body and reproductive organs does not resonate with the sociocultural reality of an African woman in South Africa. In African cultures, one who wants his or her rival to feel the real pinch will swear at them by swearing at their mother's private parts. Job's misogyny is revealed not only in his distaste for women (women's anatomy) but also in his lack of respect for women as human beings in their own right. Job does not have any appreciation for the importance of the human womb—a symbol of life for all human beings, irrespective of their gender and age. Life was precarious in Job's day, given the risks entailed in pregnancy and the birthing processes, especially without modern medicine. How could Job trivialize such crucial processes?

Job, who probably played a lesser or no role in communal mothering and never tasted what it means to carry a human being in the womb, has the luxury to speak about the female body as he so deemed fit. In his anger, he can simply say, "Why did I not die at birth, come forth from the womb and expire?" (3:11). It is indeed disturbing to note Job's lack of sympathy for someone (and their anatomy) who had treasured a human being and nurtured life in her womb for nine months. Only outsiders to female anatomy can in their moments of distress wish that their mothers' wombs were their tombs!

What about the life of a woman in such circumstances? Distressed men, such as Job whose misery has also inspired him to long for the tomb, apparently do not want to die alone. No! Their mothers, these women who should have possessed failed wombs, were then expected to serve as their son's graves. In essence, these mothers have a responsibility to accompany their sons to their own tombs!

In this vein, one wonders whether Job's assault on female anatomy is an indication of the control which men as property-owners (then and today) had/have on the bodies of those who are powerless. One thinks of powerless women today whose bodies are controlled by men: sex slaves, prostitutes, and girls and women from the Two-Thirds World who are used for sex trafficking by the rich—not to mention the many married women, widows, and daughters who fall into the same category. Job's assault of female anatomy follows the same line of thinking: Men control the bodies of women.

Job's lament reveals his problematic view of reproductive female anatomy, which is not helpful for (African) women, especially those who must struggle with the loss of a child. Such women are likely to be more pained after reading Job 3 than they were before they began. Another African proverb states thus: *Tswala ga e gane ka teng fela, le ka gare e a gana,* which is translated as: Birth (it) does not only fail inwardly, even on the outside it does fail. This proverb is usually cited by parents who had raised deviant children, children who dared to swear at their mothers. If Job had an African mother, not only would she have cited the preceding proverb, Job's African mother would have out of frustration leveled the following incantation at him for all that he said against female anatomy: *bakgekolo nke ba go dule godimo!* This means "Would that the old midwives would have sat on you immediately after your delivery onto Mother earth!"

Madipoane Masenya (ngwan'a Mphahlele) (Ph.D.) teaches in the Department of Old Testament and Ancient Near Eastern Studies at the University of South Africa.

READING JOB 3 AND 42 WITH PEOPLE LIVING WITH HIV

Gerald West (South Africa)

Since the 1950s the haunting sounds of the following lament have been heard in South Africa, at funerals, mostly, but also in political marches and in church. *"Senzeni na?* What have we done?/ *Sono sethu, ubumyama?* Our sin is that we are black?/ *Sono sethu yinyaniso?* Our sin is the truth?/ *Sibulawayo!* They are killing us!/ *Mayibuye iAfrica!* Let Africa return!" In the 1980s this song could be heard almost daily, and definitely on Saturdays, when the communities gathered to bury those murdered by the apartheid regime.

Unfortunately, a decade and a half after liberation we still sing this song. The terrain of struggle has shifted from political liberation to economic liberation, and the related struggle for deliverance from HIV and AIDS. Funerals are still the primary social location of this song. *"Senzeni na?* What have we done?"

In our work with people living overtly and publically with HIV, the Ujamaa Centre for Community Development and Research has turned to the book of Job. With the poet Mzwakhe Mbuli we have wondered, "Why are there so many more funerals than weddings?/ Do you [God] know that our graves are overcrowded?" Trusting in the solidarity of God, we have had the courage to ask hard questions. Experiencing in our bodies the life-giving effects of antiretroviral treatment, we have had the luxury of time to lament. Like Job we have turned to interrogate God.

Here at the Ujamaa Centre we have undertaken Contextual Bible Study, where we read parts of the Bible with a group of people living overtly and publically with HIV. As we explored Job 3 together with this group, a young man, one of the few men at that time to participate, voiced his despair, declaring that he knew exactly how Job felt, fantasizing about his death. Trembling with emotion, he told us how he had had to fight the desire to take his own life after he was diagnosed as HIV-positive. He had managed, he continued, to live "positively," drawing deeply on the support of the group. But, he declared, turning directly to me as one of the facilitators, our reading of Job 3 had reignited the smoldering desire for death. Why should he not, he asked me, take his own life?

It was a moment of utter terror for me. I realized I had made a terrible mistake in offering this text to the group. In that moment of complete panic I looked to my cofacilitator and colleague, Bongi Zengele, hoping desperately that her wisdom would offer a word of guidance and hope. Instead, she embraced and calmed me with her wonderful smile, silently encouraging me to trust the Contextual Bible Study process. So, doing what facilitators do, I turned to the group and asked them if they had anything to offer our brother. But he interrupted this attempt to draw on the resources of the group, stood and pointed at me, and said, "No, why do *you* say I should not leave this place and take my life?" He was insistent that I respond. Again, I looked in alarm at Bongi, and again she smiled. So I turned to the text, saying that though Job, like him, had fantasized about his own death, using an array of images, he had not contemplated taking his own life. He had directed, instead, his desire for death toward God, imagining the many ways in which God might have brought about his death at birth (3:3–19) or before he had experienced his current troubles (3:20–26). Though Job continued to lament his life, I said, he seemed to accept that his life was in God's hands.

Remarkably, my turn to the logic and flow of the text seemed to satisfy him, and he nodded and sat amongst us again. But I now felt the need to respond to his outburst, fearing that he might feel he had done "the wrong thing" by so openly lamenting his life. So I carried on, following the poetic narrative through to the end, summarizing briefly how Job refused to restrain his lament in the face of his friends' arguments, how Job even refused to retract his lament when finally he came face-to-face with God (38–42:6), and how in the prose epilogue God commended Job for "having spoken of/to God what is right" (42:7). It seemed to me, I concluded, that both what and how Job had spoken to/of God was appropriate, given Job's reality.

Others now rejoined the discussion, sharing their own doubt, fear, and despair. After nearly three hours together, Bongi brought our time together to a conclusion, inviting us to breathe deeply in unison and to pray for one another. We were exhausted but strangely at peace. It was then that we were asked whether we would be willing to do this same study of Job with their families.

Returning the notion of lament to the lives of those whose churches insist on the retributive theological trajectory of Job's friends (that all suffering is deserved) was clearly a liberating experience for the group members. But what was it that they wanted their families to know? Was it that lament was a "biblical" and therefore legitimate aspect of their (and the Christian) faith? Was it that Job refused to accept the dominant theological tradition of his (and our) time? Was it that Job persisted in his integrity (2:9) before his friends and even God? Was it that God affirmed Job's mode of engaging with God?

Each aspect of the poetic Job may have resonated with the group's members. But I suspect that it is probably the last mentioned element that resonated most clearly: By drawing their attention to how God responds in 42:7, I was offering them a potential line of connection with a God who takes a clear stand with the stigmatized Job over against Job's friends.

Job 42:7 seems to be pivotal point for those who are HIV-positive. The shift from verse 6 to 7 is massive, for we now leave the "private" domain of a dialogue between Job and God and enter the public domain. First, God, in front of Job's friends, takes sides with Job. Second, God then involves the whole community, by calling upon the friends to perform a public ritual, for which they are required to obtain resources—cattle, sheep, fire, knives—from Job's local community. Having in this manner drawn Job's community into the discourse, God then has Job praying, publically, for his friends, who in their folly have not, God repeats, spoken of/to God what is right (42:8). We are to imagine, I suggest, an audience of those who have stigmatized and withdrawn from Job listening and watching as God takes sides with Job. They then become participants, contributing to and so becoming implicated in the ritual that redeems the friends and reintegrates Job into his community. This, I think, is why the Bible study group wanted us to do the same study with their families.

And what might be the result of such a public affirmation? The answer can be found in 42:11, where the restoration of Job is not magical, but involves the acceptance and support of the whole community: All his brothers and sisters and those who had known him before came and consoled him and comforted him and ate with him.

The fundamental restoration is the restoration of a stigmatized Job to his community. "A person is a person because of other people" is the core value of African society, and yet the stigma associated with HIV has eaten away at us, devouring our communities. But if God is for us, who can be against us? If it is clear to the families of those who are HIV-positive that God stands with the infected, how can the family cast them out?

Gerald West teaches at the Ujamaa Centre in the School of Religion and Theology at University of KwaZulu-Natal, South Africa.

JOB'S CRITIQUE OF A THEOLOGY OF PROSPERITY IN LATIN AMERICA

Gilbert Lozano (Brazil)

The so-called theology of prosperity, or Prosperity Gospel, is spreading like wildfire through-out Latin America. Preachers from several theological strands have realized that this is a good marketing tool and that the masses are attracted to a message that speaks of earthly rewards instead of heavenly ones, and the gifts that God can bestow on the faithful. One watches with amazement as the masses are led to believe that the central message of the Bible is their own prosperity and enrichment.

A few years ago this message was restricted to Pentecostal churches, and then it was picked up by the neo-Pentecostal movement, a loose conglomerate of churches that attracts large crowds due to their emphasis on miracles and on the belief that the individual is the proper locus for God's actions in the world. In other words, the concerns of individuals have taken center stage. Religious services have little teaching, and biblical readings are selected mostly from those parts of the Bible that talk about blessings and promises. The neo-Pentecostal movement revolves around charismatic leaders who guide their flocks with hardheaded tactics. Religion has entered the realm of entrepre-neurship. The leaders and their followers stand in a symbiosis in which the leader is able to lead because of his (for it's mostly, if not exclusively, a male-directed movement) capacity to innovate in religious matters. Likewise, the followers' entrepreneurship is tested in their ability to respond positively to the message by way of acting out the promises, for example, by starting new businesses and by making increased financial contributions to the churches. Entrepreneurship is also seen in the innovative theological concepts and practices that are being developed. In this sense, every church meeting is supposed to need a new practice, a new anointment, new ecstasies—for instance, bless-ings in which the believer is endowed with the strength of animals, and so forth.

It can be argued that a self-serving attitude motivates many who attend those services. It's a reciprocal *quid pro quo*, an exchange of commercial proportions whereby the believer gives something to God expecting to receive something in return. This new brand of faith is eminently a pragmatic one—people do such and such because it works and it is the best course of action for success.

The messengers of prosperity promise their audiences rich rewards based on texts largely taken from what scholars call the wisdom tradition. They use an assortment of proof texts without any other connection if not the common assurance of blessings. Texts such as Proverbs 12:2, "The good obtain favor from the LORD," and Proverbs 22:4, "The reward for humility and fear of the LORD is riches and honor and life" are commonly recited as proof texts of what awaits the faithful who follow these churches' doctrinal line and who contribute generously. I have heard this text from Deuteronomy used in those churches: "The Lord will make you the head, and not the tail; you shall be only at the top, and not at the bottom—if you obey the com-mandments of the Lord your God, which I am commanding you today, by diligently observing them" (28:13). Unfortunately, these messages lack ethical appeal, or an other-oriented ethical direction. The only ethical option or line pursued at those services is that of adhering strictly to the church's rules and giving tithes and other financial contributions. The prevailing ethics seems to be one of self-interest that puts individuals and their happiness in the center stage with promises of long life (Proverbs 3:1–2; 9:11), safety (Proverbs 12:21), and above all, wealth and prosperity (Proverbs 8:18–21; 22:4; Psalm 1:3).

This theology of prosperity has enormous appeal. However, it only takes a little empirical evi-dence to know that life is just not always easy or rosy colored. In fact, life for most people around the world is hard. Countless millions still suffer from the lack of the most basic of things, such as food and sanitation. In Latin America many people go to bed at night without having had a single decent meal during the day. Poverty in this continent is endemic, and this is true from the countryside to the great urban areas. Moreover, religiosity doesn't seem to help. Latin Americans are amongst the most religious and fervent of people on the planet, and yet their misery continues at alarming rates. In fact, the neo-Pentecostal message of earthly rewards is just a variation of the Catholic teaching that the impoverished people of these lands would be rewarded by God in heaven. The neo-Pentecostals have simply anticipated the time of the rewards, bringing them to this life. It's questionable, however, what world-changing orientation this message may cause among followers.

The message of God-given prosperity was questioned already in antiquity. The book of Job contains a sophisticated rebuttal to it. The book consists of three rounds of speeches between Job's friends—initially Eliphaz, Bildad, and Zophar, and lastly Elihu, who are defenders of the traditional classical wisdom. The theory behind the wisdom theology is simple. It proposes that if a person behaves a certain way, then she will receive rewards. Conversely, bad things (curses) will derive from not following the teachings of the sages. It's all very mechanical because the world is supposed to function almost like a machine.

The book of Job opens with a wager between Yahweh and Satan whereby Job is a mere pawn in a cosmic plot. Job begins by lamenting his birth and wishes to have been stillborn (3:1–16). Job's friend Eliphaz responds that righteous people don't suffer and that it's good to be punished by God. Today we would say that he defends the view that suffering holds lessons for people. Job, however, insists on his innocence (6:25–26), and refuses to accept his suffering (7:11). Bildad, the second friend, points out that God makes no mistakes (8:3)—Job's suffering must be justified. Job again points out that his trial is unfair since nobody can win a case against God. Job wishes for a fair trial based on justice. At this point the third friend, Zophar, emerges. He appeals to the mystery of God. Job accepts that, but he retorts that his friends have defended God, assuming Job's culpability. Elihu, the last friend to appear, argues that God does not pervert justice (34:12).

Job's friends accuse Job of obstinacy for his reluctance to confess the sins that undoubtedly were the cause of his misfortunes. The "friends" defended that system of rewards for good behavior and curses for wrongdoing. Moreover, their intent was to persuade Job to recognize the folly of his ways and to confess his sins. Job, however, defended his innocence and argued vigorously for his right to speak even before God. Furthermore, he pointed out that the wisdom system doesn't really work: There are evil people who enjoy long and prosperous lives and pious or just people who have died prematurely. Job complains bitterly against God in 10:1–22. He asks to be left alone. In fact, he accuses God of scheming to destroy him (21:27), while the wicked seem to do quite well (21:7–16).

God finally shows up in Job 38–41. God's speech stresses his power and knowledge, which contrast with humanity's insignificance (38:4–39:30). Job apparently admits that because he interrupts his defense (40:3–5). At the end, ironically God sides with Job, and not with those who had defended God. The book of Job, in short, gives a severe blow to a simplistic understanding of wisdom in a mechanistic fashion. Life is more complicated than that.

The book of Job corrects many of the distortions seen today in Latin America in the preaching of a theology of prosperity. This magnificent book stands as a witness that it's just not possible to manipulate the divine—that is, to reduce faith simply to a transaction that guarantees prosperity and happiness, and where the believers can expect to have it all here on earth.

Gilbert Lozano (Ph.D.) taught at Fidelis: the Mennonite School of Theology, Curitiba, Brazil and is currently Associate Professor of Biblical Studies at Anderson University, United States.

THE TROUBLING THEOLOGY OF JOB
AND ITS PLACE IN CONTEMPORARY LIFE

Jonathan Redding (United States)

The perplexing and discomforting God in the book of Job makes few pastors and ministers enjoy preaching and teaching the text. A quick reading of the first two chapters may make the reader believe that God turns a blind eye as "the Accuser" ("Satan") orchestrates a plan that destroys Job's livestock, kills his sons and daughters, and covers Job's body in sores. Closer reading only worsens the portrayal of God's character because the text explicitly states that pious Job suffers as the result of a capricious wager between God and the Accuser. God's eventual reappearance and the content of God's response to Job (in Job 38–42) further denigrates the deity and troubles the reader. Job's heavenly bully seems fallacious compared to modern liberal religious idealisms, and my attempts to interpret this God from my progressive Christian perspective only obfuscates my understanding of God's actions.

My life has been easy and simple; I have never gone to war, nor have I ever experienced great physical anguish or trauma. America has no mass genocide or violent totalitarian leader in its brief history. Thus, I speak of suffering as I see and experience it occurring around the world. Unimaginable evil happens daily and Job's presentation of God makes this evil even more irreconcilable and horrifying. Nothing within the book provides idyllic resolutions.

Many children's sermons and countless childhood Vacation Bible School themes have a common message: God is loving and would never willingly harm anyone; therefore, being afraid of God is unfounded and misguided. Job's God shatters these youthful romanticized notions and makes one rethink the supposed benevolence of God. If Job's presentation of God is true, then God is responsible for the world's suffering and God is culpable for horrific events like the Holocaust or the genocides in Rwanda. Banal phrases such as "it is all part of God's plan" arise in the aftermath of catastrophic tragedies, and though the words are trite and arguably inappropriate, they do hold out hope that everything, even disasters, has a purpose. But the problem is that what befalls Job because of God's actions is trivial and purposeless, as God admits in 2:3. It was a perverted, pointless bet. There is no divine plan.

Job laments his life and mourns inconsolably. He cries to God seeking answers and God remains silent for over 30 chapters. When God does ultimately respond, the Accuser is gone and God alone speaks with Job. God's retort is just as appalling as the initial bet because God reminds Job of his lowly humanity and states that God is the one who created and upholds the universe. In summary, God asks Job, "What place do you or any human have in questioning me?" All humans, even the virtuous like Job, are to remain subservient as God's subjects. God is unapologetic and never shows remorse or regret; God essentially reprimands for Job questioning God's judgment. God's speech is akin to a schoolyard bully spitting and rubbing dirt on the child he or she has just beaten. Job's apparent acceptance (42:6) of his place as a mere pawn within God's cosmos is disheartening because God makes Job's life dispensable, which in turn questions the value of human existence. In the end, God restores and doubles what Job had previously, which Job enjoys with reverence and humility until his natural death.

To speak frankly, God is unjust in Job. The deity authorizes the Accuser to make sport of torturing and killing innocent people. God remains silent as Job mourns his unjustified circumstances. God's response is pompous, arrogant, and downright frightening. God's restoration of Job's belongings and family is belittling because God seems to believe that replacing what Job lost atones for God's behavior. Ask a mother and father who lost a son to a drunken-driving accident or a widower who lost a young wife to cancer: Would a new son or spouse compensate for the initial loss? Surely the answer would be a resounding "no." God's act of replacing dead children—ten of them no less!—severely diminishes the importance of human life: God seems to equate life with something that could be acquired from the local department store.

My reflections on God's character in the book of Job settles on a simple question: What place does the book have in contemporary life? Should people console mourning loved ones and friends by reading Job? Or should the entire book be in an editor's trash can? Job raises more questions than it answers, which may be intentional. Perhaps the author compiled this story as a personal therapeutic act as he or she attempted to reconcile recent catastrophes. Maybe the writer wanted to challenge traditional notions of divine omniscience and justice by writing something so outlandish that readers had no choice but to reconsider their assumptions and conclusions regarding God, suffering, and evil. It is also conceivable that the author genuinely felt this was how the world worked and composed this narrative as a reminder of humanity's insignificant place within creation. The text leaves the reader seeking answers.

What we can assert, however, is that the book's presentation of God contributes to the Bible's theological cacophony. The Bible's disharmony is an intrinsic and inflexible product of human effort, which gives readers the right to question, dispute, speculate, and deny its claims. The book of Job shows one individual's (or individuals') view of God and the world. Thus, the book must be placed within a broader understanding of scripture that encompasses humanity's limited understanding of the past and its idealized perception of the present. Making Job's theology doctrinal—elevating it to the status of truth—degrades the value of lived experience and discredits the simple hope that inspires humanity into daily living. If we take nothing else away from the book, we can find solidarity with long deceased humans as they struggle and live amidst chaotic evil.

Jonathan Redding is a student at Wake Forest School of Divinity and a parttime Minister with Youth and Families at Peace Haven Baptist Church in Winston-Salem, North Carolina, United States.

QUESTIONS

1. Assess Masenya's suggestion that Job's words are an indication of a social context in which women's bodies are seen as the property of men. Imagine how Job might respond to Masenya on this point.

2. Evaluate West's response to the young man contemplating suicide. Does West accurately interpret the text of Job 3? Does it matter?

3. How might a Prosperity Gospel preacher respond to Lozano?

4. Evaluate Redding's notion that God and Satan make a "wager" in Job 1 and 2 and his argument that God's speech in Job 38–41 is arrogant and frightening. How might one compose a counter-reading on these two points?

CHAPTER 22

SONG OF SONGS

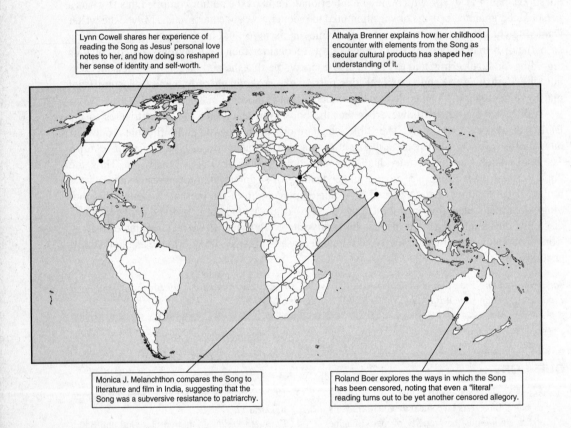

Lynn Cowell shares her experience of reading the Song as Jesus' personal love notes to her, and how doing so reshaped her sense of identity and self-worth.

Athalya Brenner explains how her childhood encounter with elements from the Song as secular cultural products has shaped her understanding of it.

Monica J. Melanchthon compares the Song to literature and film in India, suggesting that the Song was a subversive resistance to patriarchy.

Roland Boer explores the ways in which the Song has been censored, noting that even a "literal" reading turns out to be yet another censored allegory.

READINGS

Comparing the Song to Literature and Film in India
Monica J. Melanchthon

Hearing the Song as a Secular Cultural Product
Athalya Brenner

The Song as Jesus' Personal Love Notes
Lynn Cowell

The Song as a Censored Allegory
Roland Boer

COMPARING THE SONG TO LITERATURE AND FILM IN INDIA

Monica J. Melanchthon (India)

Discussions of sexuality in India invariably begin with attention to a time in India's "ancient" past when public expressions of sexuality were not considered taboo. The extant Kama Sutra and the narrative surrounding it perhaps contributed to this impression, a product of colonial history, nationalist aspirations, and European theorizing that sought to present a free and sexually liberal Orient (East) that was in variance with a prudish and repressed Occident (West). But any discussions of Indian sexuality need to go beyond the Kama Sutra since that text restricts our understanding of modern manifestations of sexuality in India. India is diverse and so also its sexual cultures. Today, one sees small-town magazines and women's magazines which are part of a semi-illicit circuit of debate and discussion on sexuality, drawing participants that are not part of official or dominant discourses on sexuality and sex-education. These magazines have created a forum for nonmoralizing discussions on desires, fantasies, anxieties, and intimacies. These in my estimation are peripheral and marginal discussions on and constructions of sexuality. They are perhaps radical and liberating but considered perverse and not welcomed; they are policed by the State and the dominant culture that seeks to protect India from bad influences.

I see the Song of Songs as a similar text that perhaps arose as a peripheral and marginal text in the contesting and disorienting context of postexilic Israel. It was a time when, in the interests of the community and its identity, restrictions and proscriptions were inscribed on the bodies of women, considered to be the conduits of tradition and culture, objects of regulation and control. It is within such a context that the Song explores the subject of love and sexuality with a sense of candor and freedom of expression. At times, love is all passion, blazing and fierce. At times it is all compassion, gentle and reserved. The theme of love seems to act as a prism resolving a variety of attitudes toward women and the subject of desire. The Song can best be described as a reaction to the male essentialist description of feminine character, the female body, and female sexuality, longing, and desire. It resists patriarchy and articulates an unapologetic subjective female worldview on these issues in a traditionally restrictive patriarchal culture, and presents a female sexual self that will not be silenced or belittled by the normative injustices of the status quo. The author presses for the worth of a woman's being as body, affirms it as a form of feminine empowerment, and celebrates it, and the varied dimensions of her being as woman positioned in a patriarchal frame of reference.

The Song is part of our scriptural tradition. Could the Song have been included in the canon in an effort to integrate sexuality and spirituality? Was sexuality regarded as an integral part of life, a gift to be honored and enjoyed? Is this why this Song of Love was made part of the canon? The history of interpretation of the Song does not seem to point to this possibility. The subversive nature of the book and its potential to disturb a male-dictated society has been to a large extent domesticated and suppressed by rendering the Song as an allegory for the yearning of the devotee for God. Seen in this way, the inclusion of the Song was a way of co-opting it to diminish its revolutionary potential, its social and political dimensions, and to undermine its constructions of sexuality, particularly that of women.

In the Indian context, it is this allegorized reading that is emphasized. When one is led to see it primarily as a metaphor for love between the divine and the human being, one misses the subversive and the resistant nature of the Song. Read from the perspective of the Indian woman who, by and large, lives a life of unwilling compromises within given/imposed circumstances, the Song is preeminently a protest against the male control of the female body and the silence into which it has been coerced. The author mines the boarded up space that is the woman's body, loosens the fetters that have bound and shrunk the woman's body, and offers them to the world. As a means of protesting the silence into which it has been coerced, the female body keeps imprinting on itself all the seasonal changes as being wrought continuously by nature. A discerning reader and an engaged interpreter in tune with women's experience of subjugation and discrimination, of violation and pain would be able to recognize the Song's capability of engendering subjective epiphanies, of perhaps producing inner tremors resulting in the inner renewal and transformation of the woman in relation to her body, her relationship to her lover, and her perception of the self.

The fact that the book is presented as a song is of exceptional significance for the Indian reader, for there is a strong Indian tradition of narrating mythology, history, tales, and the like through song and dance, but particularly expressions of love. The form comes from Indian theater. Songs are considered a natural mode of articulation, to express emotions, advance the narrative, provide catharses, and entertain. Anyone who is familiar with Indian films would recognize that a majority of the songs are about love and sung by people in love. The backdrop for these love songs in Indian cinema is often the outdoors, in beautiful natural surroundings, lush green meadows, snowy mountain tops, flower-filled gardens, or architecturally grand settings in India, but more often in foreign locales. The viewer is transported to a different world. Devised as visual pageants, these songs are often contrived as "dream sequences," permitting change of costume and location, thus, expressing the inexpressible, and inviting the viewers to indulge in the pleasure of looking, while actors display their physical beauty and exhibit themselves as pure objects of desire to be visually feasted upon by their fans. If the camera makes strategic moves offscreen to shots of birds and trees, this is quite enough to suggest activities that the censors might not approve of. Filmmakers go through great lengths to showcase emotions through rain, and wind, from delicate sensuality to aggressive. Indian filmmakers make no attempt to conceal the fact that what is shown on the screen is a creation, an illusion, a fiction heightening the fantasy. Anything can happen that would not normally happen in the real world. For the majority poor in India, the film and the song provide temporary escape from daily troubles.

I cannot help but question if the Song of Songs is part of a dream. Was a woman in a traditional Israelite society able to exercise such sexual liberty in real life? What might the repercussions be? Even more noteworthy are the Song's appreciation of the verdure and variegation of nature and its description of the settings/locales of the meeting of the two lovers, its metaphors drawn from nature, to showcase their love, desire, and sexuality. For example, in Song of Songs 2, the woman can hear the leaping and the bounding of her lover across the mountains and hills, even from afar. The natural setting helps enhance the beauty of love. It stresses the notion that love cannot be confined to time and place. It helps the couple see beyond their mundane environments and their immediate problems. It transfigures the most ordinary of circumstances and transforms their immediate surrounding into a place of beauty and wonder. This interweaving of metaphors drawn from nature with the human experience of love and desire is significant and appealing, and strengthens the solacing camaraderie between nature and the human being. The Song seems to be saying that love and desire are natural, innate, and cannot be legislated, curtailed, or controlled.

The Song of Songs is first and foremost the cry of the female body in its essential yearning for love and the delight that can be found when in union with the body of a lover. The Song therefore may be part of a dream, a fanciful depiction, or even reality. Either way, it is purposeful and provides opportunity for academic and textual activism for the sake of the woman. To a liberated reader, the Song connotes the joy of freedom. To a reader still suffering from oppression and fear, the Song may be perceived as a fantasy, a dream, an escape into a space that she yearns for—something to hope for, to look forward to, to fight for. In either case, the Song has the potential to enter the beings of women; it provides women the opportunity to shake its quiescent images into wakefulness for the purposes of emancipation.

Monica J. Melanchthon is a Professor in the Department of Old Testament Studies at Gurukul Lutheran Theological College, Chennai, India.

Hearing the Song as a Secular Cultural Product

Athalya Brenner (Israel)

Imagine living with the Song of Songs (henceforth, SoS) in Hebrew, as a secular cultural product, without and before knowing it's a biblical text. "I am dark and/but comely." That is not SoS 1:6 but a popular song on the radio, in Radio Times Israel of pretelevision days (i.e., pre 1967). It is sung by a well-known female singer of Yemenite descent. Her Hebrew diction is Sephardi (Oriental), perhaps exaggerated. The tune is certainly Oriental.

"My beloved is mine and I am his" (2:16; 6:3) is another song, once again performed by a female voice. It is also a formula uttered by many brides under the *chuppah* (bridal canopy), a modern addition to the male-biased orthodox ceremony that is the law of the land for Jewish marriages.

"Many waters cannot quench love" (8:7). A piece of folk wisdom, isn't it? "I went down to the nut orchard..." is a song and a folk dance. "Folk" in both cases since most people who quote the former and dance the latter don't know or remember who was the inventing source or the choreographer; both are quoted, sung, or danced by many. The dance is easy to learn and danced by couples, normally heterosexual.

There are more lines to be cited. Kisses sweeter than wine. I am the lily of Sharon. My beloved is... All seem to be public property, known by all, sung by all, danced by many, part of the cultural milieu, and needing no explanation, or an inquiry into their origin.

And then, one day, I think I was in my mid-teens, it was Pesach (Passover), and we were all tired after reading part of the *Haggadah* and doing the *Seder* (the Pesach family ritual, according to its text) and eating the traditional Ashkenazi heavy meal, when my father—who managed the proceedings, as befits a paterfamilias-for-a-day—started intoning some text; and from within my state of being depleted with good but too plentiful food, I started hearing, not songs set to music, but a recitation of lines I knew full well outside this annual occasion. The lines quoted above. And looking at the *Haggadah* text, and the explanations thereof, I made a discovery: Those songs, sayings, dances I grew up on, practiced in earlier then teenage life, were part of a biblical book—the SoS. For, in Jewish tradition, the SoS is read on Passover: in some communities, such as my source community, on the *Seder* night and at home; in others, at the synagogue, on Passover weekend. It is one of the Five Scrolls (together with Ruth, Lamentations, Qoheleth, and Esther) that are ritually recited, annually, in Jewish Holy days.

The fact that I had met and practiced—so to speak—the SoS before I knew it was "biblical" undoubtedly shaped my understanding of this biblical text; or, at the very least, this is how I see it in hindsight. Also, the way I met those texts has been influential, consciously or otherwise, in my scholarly but far from "objective" interpretation: It takes but little self-awareness to realize this. And, I believe, this has also given me an edge for understanding the "original" settings, or a little of them—and by so writing, I don't wish to sound superior or arrogant. This is what may happen when the cart precedes the horses. So here is how I view the SoS.

- The SoS is just that: songs. Not poems or lyrics to be read, recited, but texts performed to music. That the music is lost to us is a great pity; but that the Hebrew words, *shir ha-shirim*, mean "song of songs" and not "recitation of lyrics" is made abundantly clear by my cultural experiences.
- Most of the SoS songs, as set to music, that I heard in my life prior to discovering that they were biblical, were performed by female singers. Hence, it is natural for me to acknowledge not just an equal, but in fact a superior, presence of females in the SoS. Women in these poems seek their lovers actively, more so than their male lovers seek them. Women's voices comprise more than 60 percent of SoS lyrics, once we count the lines of lover women as well as the "Daughters of Jerusalem" chorus lines. Women lovers move more, act more, say more, are more articulate, and are more prominent. When we watch a play, a TV program, don't we assume that the actor who has the most lines, who performs the most actions, and who is seen the most is the chief actor? There you go then. Moreover, a female voice starts the proceedings (1:2–4) as well as ends them (most of SoS 8 to its very end). The love credo, the definition of love as strong as death or stronger than death, is uttered in a female voice (8:6–7).
- There is no "Father's House" in the SoS, just a "Mother's House" and brothers who seem ineffective as guardians of female sexual modesty (1:6; 8:8–10). Again, no problem. With so many female voices trilling, female power—even within the "Mother's House" and not outside it, where the City Guards may restore patriarchal order (3:3; 5:7)—is obvious. In love, if not necessarily in the world.
- In my childhood and youth I heard many singers, more females than males, singing SoS lines, at times as they appear in the Bible, at times fragmented or joined. These were not always the same singers, not even when the same lyrics were used. It is therefore no hardship for me to view the SoS as a *collection* of love lyrics. I don't need to speculate about a plot, or other unifying elements, or one single heterosexual couple, or a single romantic triangle (Solomon–shepherd–damsel). For me the variety of singing voices represents a variety in the SoS itself. This variety is eventually harnessed by editorial skill into a structure that climaxes in the middle of the book (4:8–5:1), then unfolds similarly in a chiastic manner on both sides of the climax.
- Is the SoS a wedding collection? Some scholars, from Origen on, would have it so. My early experiences of it undoubtedly make it easier to understand that, although a wedding for King Solomon is mentioned in SoS 3, the book is not a wedding collection; it doesn't celebrate an official union, and it certainly doesn't celebrate the otherwise foremost reason for marriage in the Bible—giving birth to offspring.
- The life contexts in which I first "met" SoS texts—secular, nonallegorical, young, completely unattached to matrimonial or theological situations—make it easier for me to view this biblical book as a collection of love songs, nothing more or less, so popular that its existence could not be suppressed; a solution would and did entail allegorical interpretations, but this is a different story altogether.

In sum, I grew up as a native Israeli, Hebrew speaker, daughter of immigrants from Eastern Europe. Most of the SoS for me was music, dance, geography, romance, life, before it became a biblical text. It took decades before I understood how my life context influenced my scholarly, definitely feminist reading.

Athalya Brenner is Professor of Bible at the University of Amsterdam, The Netherlands; and Tel Aviv University, Israel.

THE SONG AS JESUS' PERSONAL LOVE NOTES

Lynn Cowell (United States)

Are you like me? Do you tend to gravitate toward certain books of the Bible, while avoiding other parts of God's Word? This is exactly what I did until I discovered something. I was missing out. I was missing some of the best parts about knowing God, because sometimes His love notes to us are hidden.

Unsure about its content, the Song of Solomon was one of the books I avoided. I knew that to some it is a picture of the passionate love that occurs between a groom and his bride, and to others a poetic metaphor of the love of Christ for his bride, the church. But what really was in the book?

A friend encouraged me to delve right in. She helped me realize I could personalize it to find hidden love notes from God. I began to look at the Song of Solomon from a different perspective; rather than see it as a book about God and all those "other people," I began to put myself into the verses. I was amazed at what I saw.

When I put my name into a passage in Song of Solomon 6, it felt like God was whispering directly to me: "I think you are so beautiful, Lynn...Let me start at your feet and go all the way to your head. Your toes are so pretty...they each should have a ring on them and then be slipped into soft and lovely slippers fit for a princess. Your hands are so soft, with fingers that are slender and feminine...a diamond placed on each one. Your arms are strong and defined, but perfect for a lady...they each deserve silk gloves to your delicate elbows. Your cheeks are smooth and rosy, surrounding a smile that is captivating. Just looking at your hair makes me want to run my fingers through it and never stop!"

Read that passage again. Listen to the powerful words. They are very emotional! I was shocked when I found words like these in the Bible. I had never known that God could have these feelings—that Jesus could feel *this* way about me. I had grown up following Him, knowing Him as my shepherd, savior, and friend, but I had never seen this side of Him before!

As we read Song of Solomon, it can bring perspective to our lives. This book can help us see another side of our multifaceted God. Genesis 1 tells us that we are made in His image; part of that image is an emotional being. While our walk with Him should not be based on emotions, emotions are a part of it. Love is a huge part of it. He doesn't just want to be the God that I serve; He wants to be the God I love. This book lends itself to helping us love our God.

I started reading His "love notes" over and over and over again. Exploring these treasure-filled verses changed me. I began to understand God felt a strong love for me. I also began to change. As I filled my mind and heart with these words of love from Jesus, loneliness, low self-esteem, and fear left me—there was no room for them! I began to see myself differently. The desperate need to be perfect inside and out began to fade.

Listen to *these* powerful words: "All beautiful you are, my darling; there is no flaw in you" (4:7). The word "flaw" in Hebrew means defect, blemish, shame, or defilement. I began to see that when He looks at me, He is not disappointed in me. He doesn't see the things I see. He sees what He created and He says that it is good. He sees the one He came to die to forgive: His own.

God says it again in 5:2, "Open for me, my sister, my love, my dove, my perfect one." Sounds strange? How can He say, "my perfect one"? He calls you perfect because when He sees you, when you have accepted Jesus as your Savior, He doesn't see your sin—He sees His forgiveness. He's cleansed us; that's what He sees. His word reassures us that we belong; we are loved. "My lover is mine and I am his…" (2:16) settles feelings of rejection and loneliness. This is what we were created for: to love and to be loved.

Lynn Cowell (www.LynnCowell.com) is author of His Revolutionary Love: Jesus' Radical Pursuit of You.

The Song as a Censored Allegory

Roland Boer (Australia)

Censorship is the context in which I wish to read the Song of Songs, since the Song has always had to deal with censorship of some form or another. Censorship seems undesirable when someone else is doing it to you, but necessary when you are imposing it on someone else. In theory, most of us would prefer to see no censorship at all (in the name of freedom of expression); in practice, we will come down in favor of some form of censorship: denial of the Holocaust in World War II, inciting hate crimes against people due to their gender, religion, or ethnic identity—these acts and others are forbidden in many countries. Undesirable but unavoidable—that sums up the dilemma of censorship.

As I write, in Australia the furor over censorship hinges on the Internet. It may be easy to rant and rave about censorship in China or to decry the closing down of the Internet during the 2011 revolutions in Egypt, Tunisia, or Libya, but when it comes closer to home, the question becomes touchier. The Australian government is in the process of imposing a series of Internet filters in order to block "undesirable" content. Much of that filtering applies to extreme political views, especially to what now goes under the name of "terrorism," but mostly it applies to graphic sexual material (violence, animals, and so on). And that is where this legislation has a direct bearing on my reading of the Song of Songs.

The Song with its acknowledged sensual and sexual tone has always attracted the censor's black tape. To begin with, it was one of the last texts to be included in the canon of the Hebrew Bible. Why? As a collection of poems that is all about the fecundity of nature, and the blend of human lust and love, it does not mention God at all, let alone offer any religious teaching. With its references to breasts, night sprinkles, hands in "latches" or on "bolts" (4:5; 5:2, 4, 5; 7:3), so much so that one can almost hear the slapping, squelching, and groaning of sex, more than one question was raised about the Song's status as authoritative and canonical, especially in the first and second century C.E.

So that the Song might become acceptable, three factors played a role. The claim of Solomonic authorship was one (it is, on this level, a product of his virile and lusty youth), and the use of the Song in rituals, especially the Day of Atonement, was another. These two are already subtle acts of censorship and theological appropriation. But the third factor is the most interesting of all—interpretation itself. The Song was read allegorically; that is, it really speaks about Israel's relationship with God, or later for Christians about the Church's and God's love for one another. So we find Rabbi Aqiba's famous and oft-quoted statement, at least as it appears in the Mishnah:

> Heaven forbid! – No Israelite man ever disputed concerning Song of Songs that it imparts uncleanness to hands. For the entire age is not so worthy as the day on which the Song of Songs was given to Israel. For all the scriptures are holy, but the Song of Songs is holiest of all.

You really are one of us, Aqiba is saying, but you just didn't know it. This is not merely a classic case of subtle interpretive censorship, shifting the troubled status of the Song and making it central, but it actually protests too much, going overboard to make the Song fit in: Not just holy, not a latecomer to the party who stands alone at the edges, the Song is in fact the "holiest of all." So much so that, as far as Aqiba is concerned, there was no dispute over the Song—but only if the Song is read allegorically.

This issue came back to haunt interpretation of the Song when this allegorical reading was discarded and a more "literal" sense gained ground. Tied in very closely with the Renaissance and Reformation, and appearing at about the same time as pornography was invented in the early sixteenth-century, the Song now becomes a collection of poems about human lust and love. Yet even here censorship is crucial: It must, it was argued, be lust between a heterosexual couple, preferably "betrothed" to one another. It cannot be a homosexual couple, for instance, or the expression of lust between multiple partners (such readings are perfectly possible with the Song and do no violence to the text). Once again, the Song has had to deal with the heavy hand of the biblical interpreter's censorship.

Yet all of this has a final and unexpected twist: Any reader of the Song finds precious little explicit and graphic sex described or celebrated. Instead, the Song is full of animals cavorting, of plants budding, flowers popping, of pollens and smells in the air. Indeed, a close reading reveals a text full of fluids, liquids, juices, running over and around the lines of the text. If it is about sex, then it is sex well beyond human engagement, for the sex we find in the Song is of a much wider realm that includes endless flora and fauna.

What are the implications for the so-called "literal" interpretation in which the Song is about human lust? That reading turns out to be yet another allegory, for the "literal," sexual meaning must be read at another level from the text itself. In that respect, interpreting the text as an expression of heterosexual lust is not different, at a formal level, from seeing it as an expression of God's love for Israel and/or the Church. It is hardly "literal" at all. The implication is clear: Both interpretations are forms of theological and scholarly censorship. So what would an entirely uncensored reading look like? Is it possible?

Roland Boer is a cyclist, ship-voyager, and research professor at the University of Newcastle, Australia.

QUESTIONS

1. Explain and evaluate Melanchthon's claim that the Song is subversive. What parts of the Song might counter this claim—that is, what part(s) might not "resist patriarchy"?

2. How does its place within Scripture influence one's interpretation of the Song? If it were not part of a religious text, how would the Song be read differently?

3. Assess Cowell's approach—identifying its potential problems and benefits. Does she appear to perceive a sexual element to the Song?

4. If Boer is right that both literal and allegorical readings are forms of censorship, then indeed what would an uncensored reading look like?

CHAPTER 23

RUTH

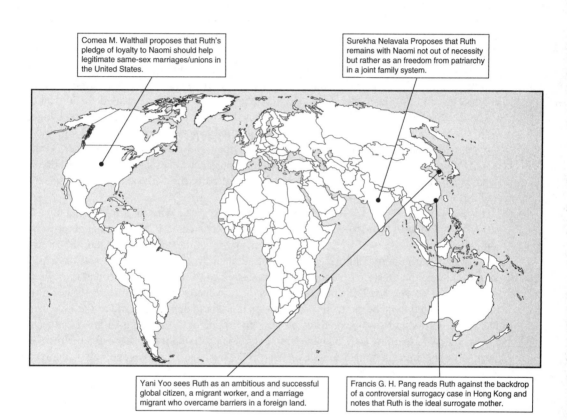

Comea M. Walthall proposes that Ruth's pledge of loyalty to Naomi should help legitimate same-sex marriages/unions in the United States.

Surekha Nelavala Proposes that Ruth remains with Naomi not out of necessity but rather as an freedom from patriarchy in a joint family system.

Yani Yoo sees Ruth as an ambitious and successful global citizen, a migrant worker, and a marriage migrant who overcame barriers in a foreign land.

Francis G. H. Pang reads Ruth against the backdrop of a controversial surrogacy case in Hong Kong and notes that Ruth is the ideal surrogate mother.

READINGS

Ruth and Naomi in a Joint Family System
Surekha Nelavala

Ruth as a Marriage Migrant
Yani Yoo

Ruth's Relevance to the Same-Sex Marriage Debate
Comea M. Walthall

Ruth as Ideal Surrogate Mother
Francis G. H. Pang

RUTH AND NAOMI IN A JOINT FAMILY SYSTEM

Surekha Nelavala (India)

Contrary to most mother- and daughters-in-law in a joint family system, Ruth and Naomi share an extraordinary—unusually affectionate—relationship, which is unlike the situation in many families in which a polite and cordial relationship is as deep as the feelings become. The joint family is still the prevailing system in India at two different levels: (1) the physical joint family, where several individual family units live together with one person at the head and all other members taking their place in the social hierarchy; and (2) the conceptual joint family, where individual family units live in their own houses, but there are expectations and obligations between the closely-related family units, especially pertaining to major decisions. In these circumstances, one of the most challenging relationships is the one between the mother and daughter-in-law. Similar to the Indian context, larger households prevailed in biblical times where several family units, headed by a male member, lived and shared resources together. Ruth, for example, belonged to the household of Elimelech, where his wife, Naomi, and their two sons, Mahlon and Chilion, and their wives, Orpah and Ruth, resided together. From my Indian feminist perspective, I do not join the traditional interpretations of Ruth which praise her as an excellent, ideal daughter-in-law who is committed to the well-being of the household. I read differently based on my own lived experiences.

As it is famously said in India, in a marriage, a man gets a wife for himself, and the woman gets his whole family. To live up to that saying, it is considered ideal for a daughter-in-law to completely immerse herself in the household of marriage, thus dislocating and alienating herself from her birth family and place. It is expected that a woman disorient herself from her own people, culture, and lifestyle in order to reorient herself to the people, culture, and lifestyle of the new marriage household. The same is not, however, expected of the man in marriage. At most, a man is expected to incorporate his wife into his household generously and to facilitate her role and status until she is accustomed to the new environment. A daughter-in-law is expected to adjust quickly to her new environment, and it is not appreciated if she expresses feelings of dislocation or alienation, whether or not everyone in the husband's family genuinely welcomes her. Indeed, a daughter-in-law is often received into a household with a pinch of suspicion, as she is seen as a stranger and potential threat to that household. A new daughter-in-law, then, experiences alienation—a Diaspora of sorts—on both sides: she is dislocated from and no longer a part of her native family and she is an outsider to her husband's household. It is a difficult transition for new wives to make.

In the book of Ruth, Naomi wants to go back to her family and people once her husband has died. She finds that her native land is better off, as the Lord as brought prosperity to it. Perhaps Naomi has been building an argument to return home, and she justifies her decision by pointing to the Lord's intervention on behalf of her people. Similarly, Orpah, the other daughter-in-law, goes back to her own hometown and people, as her husband has died and thus there is no household for her anymore. However, Ruth—quite unlike the typical daughter-in-law—expresses her wish to go with Naomi, rather than go back to her people. Why does Ruth do this? Many commentators propose that it was because she was an ideal daughter-in-law. For me, in light of my own context and experiences, this is not the case. Rather Ruth's actions reflect her new freedom and her desire to forge a new relationship with Naomi.

To explain my reading further: Orpah demonstrates obedience to and respect for Naomi by returning to her family, as she does not want to become a burden on her widowed mother-in-law.

However, when Naomi asks Ruth to go back to her people, she resists and expresses instead her determination to follow Naomi until death separates them (1:16-17). In doing so, Ruth does not fulfill the role of a good daughter-in-law; instead she transcends the daughter-in-law role and establishes a new relationship between the two women, not one based on the hierarchal power structure that would have existed within their former patriarchal/kyriarchal household (presumably under Elimelech), but one of equality, a woman-to-woman relationship of sisterhood that gave both of them liberation to act differently from their expected social roles. Because of the deaths of their husbands, Naomi, Orpah, and Ruth have been liberated from the rules, expectations, and boundaries of a patriarchal household. This leads Ruth to stand by Naomi out of freedom, not out of desperation or compulsion that resulted from vulnerability, loneliness, and powerlessness. Thus the relationship that these women share with each other is no longer of a mother-in-law and daughter-in-law, where hierarchal power is the central focus, but that of a woman-to-woman—of mother-to-daughter, or even true sisterhood—where the focus is on empathy, care, and support for one another

In short, given my Indian context and understanding of the mother and daughter-in law relationship in a joint family system—which is typically a cordial one at best, not a true, heartfelt one—I see Ruth's insistence on joining Naomi as a reflection of a deep, meaningful relationship that has developed between them. The natural thing would have been for Ruth to follow Orpah's course of action—go back to her family and her people. There, perhaps, she would have resumed her subservient role in her father's household. Like other readers of the book, I admire Ruth for staying with Naomi, but I do so for different reasons. Ruth was a true feminist, exercising her freedom from patriarchy. She was not a weak or dependent woman who had no other option.

Surekha Nelavala is a Mission Developer at Global Peace Lutheran Church in Frederick, Maryland, United States.

RUTH AS A MARRIAGE MIGRANT

Yani Yoo (South Korea)

This essay sees Ruth the Moabite as an ambitious and successful global citizen, a migrant worker, and a marriage migrant who overcame human and customary barriers in a foreign land, Israel. The background of this reading is the recent global phenomenon of migration. With globalization, more people are becoming migrant workers, including women from the so-called developing countries who marry men in the so-called developed countries. They are called marriage migrants. Some countries receive migrants and others send them.

My country, Korea, is one of the receiving countries. Although in general Koreans have good intentions toward migrants and there are many nongovernmental organizations (NGOs) working for them, it is correct to say that the Korean government does not treat migrants fairly; severe forms of sexual, cultural, racial, economic, and other discriminations are committed against migrants. Koreans have lived as a monoethnic group for hundreds of years and have only recently begun to learn to live with people from other ethnic backgrounds. From this backdrop I read the story of Ruth both from the perspective of a citizen of a receiving country and from my own experience of having had been a temporary illegal alien while studying in a Western country.

I call Ruth a global citizen because of her crossing national borders, being a migrant worker in a foreign country, and being a marriage migrant because of her marriage to a national of the receiving country based on an economic reason. Although Ruth is a foreigner, a widow living with her mother-in-law, young, and poor, she is determined not to just survive, but to succeed in a new land. She has two major hurdles to overcome to fulfill her goal: local people and customs.

Ruth faces the cold responses of people. To begin with, her mother-in-law Naomi is an immediate stumbling block for her to build a new life. Naomi knows many locals but would not connect Ruth to them. This unwilling ally seems to be depressed, unable, and unkind. Naomi tries to expel her daughters-in-law out of her life. While Orpah says goodbye, Ruth stubbornly remains. In Bethlehem, Naomi does not look for ways to make a living although she had patrimony to claim and knew what to do about it. She knows of dangers in the field which may befall a foreign young woman but does not give Ruth any advice about it when the latter leaves for gleaning for the first time. It is only after Ruth's gleaning and her mention of the field owner Boaz that Naomi offers information about him as their possible supporter (2:20) and comes up with a honey trap using Ruth as the bait (3:3–4). We doubt that the honey trap is Naomi's only option. It is at the expense of not just Boaz's honor, but also Ruth's.

If Naomi is not so considerate of Ruth, the Bethlehemite women are even more so. At the beginning and end of the story, they converse with Naomi but never with Ruth. There is no report that Ruth was welcomed by women in the field, whereas there is an exchange of greetings between Boaz and his workers (2:4). Being a woman does not guarantee solidarity among women.

Men in the field can be sexually or otherwise violent to women as they may "meet" (2:9) and "touch" (2:22) the latter. No male relative steps out to offer any long-term social security to Ruth and Naomi. The *goel,* the nearest male relative who has the right to redeem Naomi's land, denies the right (4:6, 8). The male elders are portrayed as those who mix up practices of two customs of the levirate (taking off the shoes; cf. Deuteronomy 25:5–10) and the *goel* (Leviticus 25:24ff.). Although Boaz said and did nice things to Ruth in the field, he has not offered any fundamental solution to Ruth and Naomi. He seems reluctant to follow the progress of events after spending a night with Ruth at the threshing floor. Women chose and entrapped him. No wonder that there is no further interaction described between the couple other than the typical patriarchal report, "Boaz took Ruth and she became his wife. And he went to her and the Lord gave her pregnancy" (4:13).

Ruth as a foreigner takes advantage of not knowing the local laws and customs or she pretends not to know them. First, Ruth challenges the regulation of gleaning in the empty field. For her, it only makes the poor continue to remain poor. So she boldly asks to glean among the sheaves, demanding more than the custom in quality and quantity. Boaz concedes, saying to his workers, "You must also pull out some handfuls for her from the bundles and leave them for her to glean" (2:16). Ruth finds in this nice owner of the land a good target for her new future.

In her report to Naomi after the night at the threshing floor, Ruth twists Boaz's words about barley. He gave her the barley, simply saying, "Bring the cloak and hold it out" (3:15). But Ruth lies to Naomi by reporting that he said, "Do not go back to your mother-in-law empty-handed" (3:17) and thus nudges her mother-in-law in the ribs so that she can plan for the young woman's future.

Second, Ruth demands Boaz to carry out the levirate and the *goel* duties although he is not the immediate male to have the right to do it. It is understandable that she as a foreigner mixes up the two customs, but Boaz and the men in town mimic her in combining the two. Perhaps the text is mocking Boaz and the elders, pointing out that they cannot handle their own customs correctly, let alone use them to control a foreigner: Institutions and cultures born long ago do not work even for locals, not to mention for newcomers.

The genealogy at the end sums up Ruth's final victory. Only three generations after this first migrant worker, a king is born to her family. When viewed from the perspective of the locals, this is a radical proclamation. This bold genealogy can be read as a challenge to any people who deny the rights of migrants. Here we remember that the book of Ruth is the only book in the Bible which is named after a foreigner.

In sum, originally Naomi and her family had migrated to Moab to avoid famine. We do not know whether the Moabites were nice to them. Now a Moabite migrated to Bethlehem and the natives must decide whether or not they will be good to the foreigner. But regardless of their actions, the new migrant finds ways to survive and thrive. In our globalized world, people with new faces in foreign lands can read Ruth as a global citizen's success story, even if it is bittersweet. Although Ruth initially faces a number of barriers, she eventually becomes the great grandmother of Israel's greatest king. The book of Ruth points us to a place that does not have classes among people, where migrant workers are not paid much less than the locals. Our reading of Ruth can empower global citizens and nomads who must start new lives in new lands. It can also challenge the locals who think they lose opportunities because of migrant workers. Indeed, Ruth destroys national borders and demands that we have broader worldviews.

Yani Yoo is Lecturer in Old Testament at Methodist Theological University, Seoul, South Korea.

RUTH'S RELEVANCE TO THE SAME-SEX MARRIAGE DEBATE

Comea M. Walthall (United States)

Ruth 1:16–17 is a powerful testament of undying affection between two people: "Entreat me not to leave thee, or to return from following after thee; for whither thou goest, I will go, and where thou lodgest, I will lodge. Thy people shall be my people, and thy God my God. Where thou diest will I die, and there will I be buried; the LORD do so to me, and more also, if aught but death part thee and me." These words are often read at wedding ceremonies and used in sermons to illustrate the ideal love and passion that spouses should have for one another. What is most interesting about the verses, however, is that they are not words spoken between a man and a woman, but they are the words of a woman, Ruth, spoken to the mother of her deceased husband, Naomi, who is also a widow; both women are without sons.

To understand the full impact of Ruth's decision to "cleave" to Naomi, we need to put ourselves in the mind-set of the time. When Ruth was written, women had only two acceptable places in society: They could be a daughter in their father's household or a wife in their husband's household. A woman without a man had no social standing. There are several stories in the Old Testament about widows who almost starved to death because they had no man to take care of them. The context makes Ruth's decision to stay with Naomi almost unbelievable in light of the social vulnerability of a widow, let alone, two widows together.

The book of Ruth may be a brief four chapters, but for a woman, it is very powerful. Out of 66 books in the Bible, Ruth is one of only two books named for a woman (the other is Esther;

also Judith and Susanna if including apocryphal texts). Ruth is also the only book in the Bible dedicated to the history of a woman. For a queer woman, understanding the context of Ruth and Naomi's precarious social position and Ruth's decision to stay makes the relationship between the two women even more powerful.

I had heard Ruth 1:16–18 twice, as part of wedding ceremonies, without knowing the context, but still appreciating the significance and power of such words between two people pledging to be together until death do them part. It was not until 1994, when I saw the film *Fried Green Tomatoes* that I decided to *really* read the book of Ruth for myself and to try to understand the context of those words. In the film, the characters Idgie and (appropriately) Ruth display subtle undertones of a lesbian relationship. For a budding lesbian on the cusp of understanding her own sexuality, reveling in the subtle relationship of the film's characters and the biblical reference (used in the film to convey a message from Ruth to Idgie) left me curious.

Ruth, indeed, was an epic discovery for me, when in 1994 I was unsure and somewhat at odds with what to believe about my feelings and my religion (especially in conjunction with one another). The book of Ruth has been a study for me throughout my life. In college I used it as a reference for papers in both women's studies and religious studies. Further inquiry led me to discover the connection between Genesis 2:24, "Therefore shall a man leave his father and his mother, and shall cleave unto his wife; and they shall be one flesh," and Ruth 1:14, "And they lifted up their voice and wept again; and Orpah kissed her mother-in-law, but Ruth cleaved unto her." The Hebrew word "cleave" that is used in Genesis 2:24 to describe how Adam felt about Eve (and how spouses are supposed to feel toward each other) is the exact same word that is used in Ruth 1:14 to describe how Ruth felt about Naomi.

Ruth's vow to Naomi has been used to illustrate the nature of the marriage covenant. The irony lies in the fact that across the United States, thousands of years after the story of Ruth and Naomi was scribed, it remains illegal for same-sex couples to make the same covenant. Often opponents of same-sex marriage or unions reference the Bible to support claims that two people in love can only get married if they are of opposite sex. It is interesting that those opponents seem to skip over Ruth 1:16–18. These words were originally spoken by one woman to another, their tale important enough to survive years and a multitude of biblical edits. The power of Ruth's vow to Naomi has played a significant role in the covenant for many new husbands to their wives. One day, Ruth's vow will (legally) bind me to my "wife" of almost nine years, defeating the scorn of those who skipped the Bible's eighth book.

Comea M. Walthall has Bachelor's degrees in Psychology, Biology, Religious Studies, and Sociology; she is currently working in retail sales and is a GLBTQ Youth Outreach Advocate.

RUTH AS IDEAL SURROGATE MOTHER

Francis G. H. Pang (Hong Kong)

In late 2010, the eldest son of a Hong Kong (HK) real estate tycoon announced that he became a new father of triplets. Since he did not disclose any information about the identity of the mother of these babies, rumor has it that he hired a surrogate mother in the United States to give birth to his three sons. Since having male offspring is a big concern for the traditional Chinese and his father was very vocal in expressing his desire for a grandson to carry the family name, the public had little problem accepting the rumor. When his younger brother's wife failed to produce sons, it was not very difficult for the public to connect the dots and see the attempt of the elder son to father sons as a competition among the two of brothers to gain favor in the eyes of their old father. Unfortunately, this has come at a time when popular sentiment toward the rich is vastly negative due primarily to the alarming level of income disparity in HK. Therefore, when the picture of the proud grandfather holding his three newborn "grandsons" hit the newswire, it sparked a heated discussion regarding the morality of such an endeavor.

Although surrogacy is nothing new in the West, it has always been a rare and controversial matter in HK because of religious beliefs and traditional Chinese morals. After the story of the triplets came to light, the press criticized the family for disrespecting human dignity and ignoring the children's rights. The church in HK also sternly condemned the family, contending that getting male offspring for self-interest through surrogacy is immoral and ignores the children's right of growing up in a healthy family. Furthermore, there is also a legal issue here. A decade ago the government of HK passed a bill on the use of human reproductive technology, restricting it to a strictly noncommercial basis and only under special circumstances (e.g., a legally married but infertile couple). Technically, a surrogate license will only be issued to someone who is willing to bear a child for a family without any monetary arrangement and who will subsequently give up the custody right of the newborn baby in order for the donor to adopt the child. Under such stringent rules, there has not been a single successful application for surrogacy since this legislation, presumably because it requires a high degree of sacrifice on the part of the surrogate. Since pregnancy involves considerable amount of mental stress and physical risk, it is rather difficult, if not impossible, to measure the value of such endeavor in monetary terms. The subtle yet inevitable conflict of interest between the donor (biological parents) and the surrogate mother in a commercial surrogacy arrangement is inevitable. Thus, in essence, the aim of this law in HK is to discourage any commercial surrogacy arrangement to safeguard children's rights and avoid endless courtroom drama on custodianship.

Reading the book of Ruth under this cultural context and particularly using this incident as a backdrop, several things stand out to the reader regarding the role of Ruth. First, throughout the narrative Ruth has been referred to as a Moabite (2:2, 6, 10, 21; 4:5, 10). This seemingly unnecessary title helps the reader to connect this story of the origin of the Moabites (Genesis 19:30–38). The episode of Lot and his daughters is in fact a story that involves metaphorical surrogacy. These two stories share some similar plot elements. Both narratives involve an old man sleeping with a young girl(s). Although it is not stated explicitly in Ruth, the reader can easily infer from conversations that Boaz is an old man (3:10). In both stories the male protagonist becomes intoxicated and unable to recognize the woman lying/sleeping with him. These features in Ruth allude to the Lot narratives to remind the reader of the Moabite origin of Ruth, the descendent of a gestational surrogacy.

Second, the fact that the child Ruth gives birth to is called Naomi's son (4:17) and is nursed by her also resembles the circumstance of the present-day surrogacy arrangement. The threefold blessing of Boaz by the legal assembly (4:11–12) supports this reading. Three names (Rachel, Leah, and Tamar) that were mentioned in the blessing link the story of Ruth and Naomi to two narratives in Genesis. Both narratives involve a woman bearing a child for another woman/family. It is also stressed in these narratives that the status of a woman in ancient times is anchored in childbearing, thus when a woman cannot bear a child for her husband, it sets a perfect stage for surrogacy arrangement. For example, in the Jacob narrative both Rachel and Leah ask their handmaid to sleep with Jacob (Genesis 30).

As noted by scholars, the similarities between the Tamar narrative (Genesis 38:1–30) and the story of Ruth are overwhelming. The narrative explicitly compares Tamar to Ruth by the statements of the elders (4:11–12). Both stories involve a family moving to foreign soil, mixed-marriage with a Gentile woman, and the deaths of a spouse and two sons. In both stories, the reader witnesses the female protagonist removing her widow's garments, which changes her social status and breaks the social and physical boundaries, to try to obtain a child for the levirate rights owed to her deceased husband. Finally, both narratives contain an element of surprise. Judah (the donor) does not know Tamar's (the surrogate mother) intention and her identity when he sleeps with her. Similarly, when Ruth follows Naomi's plan and uncovers Boaz's feet (lower body), he does not know Ruth was lying with him until the middle of the night (3:7–8).

The story of Ruth and Naomi can be viewed as the biblical surrogacy arrangement *par excellence*. Neither the donor nor the surrogate mother uses the child to gain an upper hand in the family (contra Rachel and Leah). Ruth as the surrogate mother also demonstrates excellent moral character (contra Tamar)—she does not fight for her own interest but rather considers the interest of her donors (Naomi and to a lesser extent, Boaz). The donors also demonstrated genuine concern for the surrogate. In fact, if we plot the story in modern-day HK, Ruth might even pass the stringent requirement by the government of HK and be granted a surrogate license. The narrative clearly demonstrates that the custody right ended up belonging to Naomi. Ruth does not use the baby to gain any benefit from the donor's family, neither financially nor in terms of social status. Although one can argue that she finally finds a patron for herself, Ruth is definitely as good a metaphorical surrogate mother as one can find in the Old Testament.

Francis G. H. Pang, originally from Hong Kong, is a Ph.D. candidate at McMaster Divinity College, Canada.

QUESTIONS

1. How does the joint family system, as described by Nelavala, compare to the family system(s) in your culture. How is the mother- and daughter-in-law relationship viewed in your context?

2. How does the experience of migrants and/or marriage migrants in your culture compare to Korea as described by Yoo?

3. Assess Walthall's reading of Ruth. Is she justified in using Ruth 1:16-17 as support for gay marriage?

4. Evaluate Pang's intertextual approach (drawing on other biblical stories). What particular insights does it bring to a reading of Ruth? Are there other biblical or non-biblical texts to which Ruth could be linked?

CHAPTER 24

LAMENTATIONS

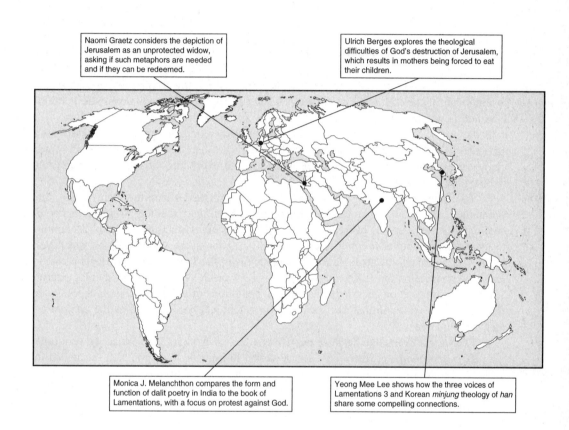

Naomi Graetz considers the depiction of Jerusalem as an unprotected widow, asking if such metaphors are needed and if they can be redeemed.

Ulrich Berges explores the theological difficulties of God's destruction of Jerusalem, which results in mothers being forced to eat their children.

Monica J. Melanchthon compares the form and function of dalit poetry in India to the book of Lamentations, with a focus on protest against God.

Yeong Mee Lee shows how the three voices of Lamentations 3 and Korean *minjung* theology of *han* share some compelling connections.

READINGS

Lamentations and *Minjung* Theology of *Han*
Yeong Mee Lee

Lamentations and the Form and Function of Dalit Poetry
Monica J. Melanchthon

The Theological Difficulties of God's Destruction of Jerusalem
Ulrich Berges

The Depiction of Jerusalem as an Unprotected Widow
Naomi Graetz

LAMENTATIONS AND *MINJUNG* THEOLOGY OF *HAN*

Yeong Mee Lee (South Korea)

Life is full of joys and sorrows. The book of Lamentations deals with the agony experienced during a time of extreme suffering. It was a time when a mother was forced to eat the flesh of her own child. Nothing captures the degree of the suffering more vividly than this graphic image. In facing such extreme suffering, the human reaction can be quite diverse. The biblical reaction to the suffering found in Lamentations 3 provides a good analogy to Korean *minjung* theology of *han*.

Lamentation 3 introduces three voices of "I," "He," and "We," each of which show their reaction to the suffering. "I" reminded people of the disaster (vv. 1–24) and explains the special suffering of "He" who suffers because of the sin of the community (vv. 25–39). "He" is a member of the community. But He is separated from others as the one who is faithful to God and is waiting for salvation. He bears the agony of the community upon him. "I" then calls the people to return to God immediately. "We" responds to him with confession of their sin (vv. 40–47). The responses of these three bodies illustrate the importance of communal confession of sin and the collective responsibility to overcome the suffering and eventually to bring forth salvation.

The term *minjung* refers to those who are marginalized from the main society through economic, cultural, social, and gender discrimination. *Minjung* theology is a Korean contextual theology that was derived from the communal confession of sin and the church's commitment to share the suffering of *minjung* under the Park's regime in the 1960–1970s. It was developed in the 1980s through the struggle for democracy under the Jeon regime which suppressed *minjung*'s demonstration for democracy in the city of Kwang Ju. While *minjung* theology during the 1960–1970s focused on economic and cultural conditions of *minjung*, *minjung* theology during the 1980s dealt with political and social concerns that had been evoked by the *minjung* movement for democracy.

During the 1970s, the death of two Korean factory workers highlighted the seriousness of the suffering of *minjung*. Mr. Jeon Taeil, a worker in a textile trade company, struggled for the basic legal rights of labor and burned himself as a sacrificial action for the request of legal compensation. He asked for keeping the labor standard of working eight hours a day. Ms. Kyeong Sook Kim, a worker and the leader of the union of a wig trade company, was killed during a forced dispersal of the workers by a large and strong police force. Several theologians and ministers who worked in the Protestant Urban Industrial Mission had joined them in their struggle. They also called upon society and the religious community to participate in communal confession and advocacy for change.

Minjung theologians further developed the collective experience of suffering through the concept of *han*. *Han* is a Korean term for an underlying feeling of the oppressed people. It is an accumulation of suppressed and condensed experiences of oppression. Many Korean folk songs express *minjung*'s *han*. *Han* is very deeply rooted in Korean history and culture. The country's entire way of life has been profoundly shaped by it. It is a culturally complex entity. Koreans have suffered numerous invasions by powerful surrounding nations to the point that the very existence of the Korean nation has come to be understood as *han*. Also, under Confucianism's strict imposition of laws and customs discriminating against women, the existence of women was *han* itself.

Han is moral evil originating and promulgated by imperialistic, feudalistic, and ideological power, in addition to gender discrimination.

Lamentations 3 and Korean *minjung* theology of *han* share some compelling connections. First, *minjung* theologians represent the "I" of the biblical text. The "I" explores the situation of the suffering and the agony of "He," namely, people like Jeon Taeil and Kyeong Sook Kim. The "I" plays a role in bringing the community's attention to the suffering and helps them to realize its social dimension; eventually it evokes the participation of the community into the struggle for resolving the agony.

Second, just as the biblical text explains "S/He" bears the sufferings because of the sin of the community, so too *minjung* theology perceives that the suffering of *minjung* is not an individual matter but is the reality of oppressive and miserable social existence. The lament of "S/He" and the *han* of *minjung* is not just the sound of weeping, but is also a prophetic voice that motivates the action of the community.

Third, as "We" confessed their responsibility for the suffering of "He" in Lamentations 3, so too Korean churches shared the responsibility of *minjung*'s suffering. In the stage of *han*, of hopelessness and despair, the Christian faith community must not be silent but share the suffering of *minjung* and be "a priest of *han*." The community participates in the process of comforting and healing of *minjung's han* and breaking the vicious circle of violence. With the evoking voice of "I" and solidarity of "We," the *han* of *minjung* (S/He) will transform into a prophetic voice for change.

Yeong Mee Lee (Ph.D.) is Associate Professor of Old Testament Studies at Hanshin University, Seoul, South Korea.

Lamentations and the Form and Function of Dalit Poetry

Monica J. Melanchthon (India)

One of the more significant, concrete, and palpable achievements of the dalit struggle and movement in India is dalit literature. Dalits were traditionally denied any access to learning and all fields of intellectual activity were barred. Their cultural and creative activity was either denied or considered debased and vulgar. The situation today is almost totally changed, as even mainstream critics recognize dalit literature as a valid, robust, and progressive genre. It has challenged assumptions of prevalent theories of literary critics and aesthetics. It exposes the atrocities of higher societies with burning anger and hatred and calls for ruthless vengeance against the society and people who have created inequality—indeed, it is rejection of the all-embracing conventional Hindu world vision. The literature aims at total revolution and uplift of the entire lower classes. It has become propagandist and collective, rather than individualistic in nature; it express the aspirations and frustrations, convictions and courage of the community.

Dalit poetry to some extent bears many parallels to the Hebraic tradition of lament, both individual and communal, through which are expressed alienation, suffering, grief, anger, and the questioning of God. Dalit poetry's ultimately positive purpose of life affirmation, emotional release, remembering, and communal healing allow this form of poetic metalanguage to resonate with the lament traditions of the Hebrew Bible, for it has become a literature of extreme situations, a literature of survival.

The occasion for the poems in the book of Lamentations was the watershed event of 587 B.C.E.—the destruction of Jerusalem which greatly influenced developments in Israel's religious thought and practice. The five poems, authored perhaps by different poets during or soon after this event, give us a glimpse of the horror and grief of the survivors and their expression of primal outrage through the medium of language. As survival literature, Lamentations stresses the need for survivors of any calamity or oppression to give verbal or written expression to the experience of pain. The poems are a deliberate opportunity to give vent to the full horror, distress, and agony that has been experienced, providing an invaluable vehicle to remember and recount the diverse aspects of the assault. By giving expression, the community is enabled to face the calamity and to come to terms with the many dimensions of the suffering inflicted on the community.

Furthermore, a major theme is protest, but more specifically it is a protest against God who inflicts pain and suffering and sanctions destruction of God's own people (1:1–10; 2:1–10; 4:11–16). While there is an acknowledgment of sin on the part of the people, God is also placed alongside the "enemy" as being responsible for the acute suffering. God as betrayer is perhaps one of the most disturbing features of the book, as the deity is approached with anger and reproach (2:20).

Unlike the Hebrew laments, many dalit poems do not mention the divine, perhaps because of the atheist/Buddhist leanings of the poets. Neither is their cry addressed to a deity nor is the deity blamed. There is hard questioning of the caste system and its proponents. Hence, the resolution of crises, the annihilation of caste, and the attaining of freedom are only possible by means of resistance and revolt against the oppressor and the unjust social system. Hope is articulated in secular terms. Where the divine is mentioned, as in the Hebrew laments, there is no fear of offending God, nor are there any religious qualms from being acrimonious with God.

In another stream of dalit poetry, God is not seen as the source of suffering, but as a cosufferer. Dalit gods are spirits of ancestors and deified heroes and leaders. These gods are also stigmatized and discriminated and hence suffer along with the community. The divine is therefore constructed from the perspective of dalit limitations rather than from the vantage point of the "power" of the dominant-caste groups. The shrines, temples, and abodes of dalit gods are polluted places and their Gods, muted and disfigured, are as helpless as the people. Such conceptions of dalit gods therefore seem to aid in the process of catharsis and coping with the crisis.

Inherent in such dalit poems and the Hebrew laments is a rejection of religious optimism that shies away from examining suffering in its multiple dimensions or an optimism that sanitizes God by removing God from the ugliness of suffering and pain. This is made possible by the fact that the Hebrew conception of God as the one who identifies with the poor and suffering, the one who suffers "along with," is rooted and derived from the experience of the oppressed and marginalized. If God is responsible and has to be blamed, so are the people.

I would like to believe that embedded within the accusation against God, in the anger, the questioning, and the reproach against God in Lamentations is also a poetic critique of the Israelite community for its silence in the face of oppression, its passivity, its complicity. If it is a reminder to God that the human situation is not as it should be, it is also a reminder to the community that all is not as it should be. God and the community as covenanted partners are called to act and must act. The cause of the Lamenter is God's cause and vice versa. They raise their voice in pain, do not flinch from naming the sorrow of the circumstances, and insist that they be transformed. By articulating such pain, by naming their own volition in the suffering and calling on God to act, the book of Lamentations rouses the community into action. Through description of the situation, the grief and the sorrow, and the questioning of it, the community, and perhaps God as well, finds the answers and the directions for a better future.

Monica J. Melanchthon is a Professor in the Department of Old Testament Studies at Gurukul Lutheran Theological College, Chennai, India.

THE THEOLOGICAL DIFFICULTIES OF GOD'S DESTRUCTION OF JERUSALEM

Ulrich Berges (Germany)

There is no doubt that YHWH, the God of Israel has an impressive record of violent depictions in the Hebrew Bible. There are more than 600 entries in the OT where nations, kings, or individuals are depicted acting violently against each other. But nearly 1,000 times it is affirmed that YHWH smashes, destroys, and kills peoples, nations, or individuals. Approximately 100 times it is stated that the God of Israel ordered the death of persons. What are we to say and think about passages in which even innocent children are the object of God's wrath and anger? Can we still consider God's actions against children as part of his legitimate rule and dominion? Are they simply paying the price for the sins of their fathers and mothers (cf. Exodus 34:7; Numbers 14:18)? Are there theological reasonings to justify that kind of violence against children—or ought we to call it what it really is: pure violence!

There is no other book in the Hebrew Bible in which the wrath and violence of YHWH are depicted in such gloomy colors as in the book of Lamentations. In 1:12–16 he behaves like a terrible enemy against Jerusalem and Zion. The personified city as mother of her inhabitants plays here (as elsewhere in Ancient Near East) the role of the female goddess who speaks and acts on behalf of the victims of divine wrath and anger. God's fierce anger went as fire into her bones, he spread a net for her feet, turned her back like a hunted animal. He bound her transgressions into a yoke and handed her over to those she could not withstand. These images depict the destruction of Jerusalem by the hands of the Babylonians. The cruel fate of the population is highlighted in 2:11–13 when the poet looses control of his emotions when seeing children dying in the arms of their mothers: "My eyes are spent with weeping; my stomach churns; my bile is poured out on the ground because of the destruction of my people, because infants and babes faint in the streets of the city" (v. 11). That's not enough: Like a news-reporter on the battlefield he directs his camera and microphone on the fainting and starving children. Thus he witnesses their last words: "They cry to their mothers, 'Where is bread and wine?' as they faint like the wounded in the streets of the city, as their life is poured out on their mothers' bosom" (v. 12). This is a very touching scene: Not often does the Old Testament show the last moments in the life of the victims of violence and war. Here it does: The bosoms of the mothers become the graves of their children!

These are very dangerous pictures and politicians in our days try to be sure that such scenes are not shown in the news on TV. The so-called *imbedded reporters* in modern wars are not allowed to report scenes like these! Where does that reluctance come from? Why censor the *real reality* of war? Because the images of dying children tell the real truth—not the truth of the powerful, but of the innocent victims!

At those places where rational justifications become insufficient to explain God's wrath and violence, critical voices are heard. The culpability of Jerusalem and her prophets is strongly affirmed (2:14, 17) and there can be no doubt about the right of YHWH to punish the evil city and her leading class, but the violence he employed or did allow to be employed against her was totally out of proportion. Even in his anger, YHWH is bound to his own standard of justice and ethical behavior. In very dramatic words, mother Zion holds YHWH himself responsible for all her grief (2:20–22). She addresses him as the real cause of her suffering and that of her children: "Look, YHWH, and consider! To whom have you done this? Should women eat their offspring, the children they have borne? Should priest and prophet be killed in the sanctuary of the Lord?" (v. 20). The situation is very much that of a female victim confronting her male aggressor who should acknowledge the enormous pain he caused. God himself should see and consider *to whom* he did all this, namely, to her beloved children (2:19–20; cf. 2:11).

In contrast to YHWH who apparently lost control of his passion in his fierce anger, mother Zion does not loose her composure, because there is no hair tearing, skin gouging, or loud hysterics, which are the normal elements in Ancient Near Eastern depictions of mourning women and goddesses. Zion's lament is voiced in critical terms against the one who slaughtered infants in the streets and priests and prophets in the sanctuary (2:20). At first glance, the death of the temple officials seems to be an anticlimax but the parallelism with the dying children has to be taken seriously. Like mothers who lost their children, YHWH looses his religious personnel. The perversion of mothers eating their children stands parallel to God not preventing his priests and prophets from being killed in the sanctuary. As the motherly bosom symbolizes warmth and nutrition, the sanctuary stands for prosperity and life. Thus the center of life has become a deadly trap.

In 2:21 Zion underlines three times YHWH's violence: "*you* have killed…*you* have slaughtered…*you* didn't pity." Interesting enough, no objects are named, but it is absolutely clear that Zion's children are meant. That YHWH acts *without showing mercy* is never stated in the Psalms or in other prayers in the Hebrew Bible, but it is well known from the prophets, especially from Ezekiel.

Can one imagine something of more cruelty? YHWH killed and slaughtered without pity those children mother Zion had given birth to and had raised up. Thus God is no less cannibalistic than the mothers eating their own children (cf. 4:10). In none of the Assyrian texts are mothers the ones who eat their children: Thus the poets of the book of Lamentations intensified the borrowed language from the Ancient Near Eastern environment.

The perversion of the mother–child relation is stressed by the characterization of the mothers as "compassionate" using the Hebrew word which relates to the "motherly womb." Like the mothers in Zion boil their offspring, YHWH consumes the foundations of his beloved city. But there is a fundamental difference between the mothers in Zion and YHWH: The former were forced to do what they did because the latter did not restrain his wrath. Should YHWH not have been obliged to restrain his anger in the face of dying children and the forced cannibalism of their mothers? Why didn't he act according to what he himself had urged from the aggressors of Israel (cf. Jeremiah 25:8–14)? Do ethical standards apply to every one else but not to YHWH? The voice of mother Zion is the voice of all the innocent victims: There is no human reality so dark that it can't be brought before YHWH.

There is no philosophical solution to the question of God's justice (theodicy) but only the practical solution of keeping the hope alive. Zion doesn't get an answer from God, as her children didn't get an answer to their plea for bread and wine (2:12)! The answer is given in the middle of the third poem (3:31–33). There the suffering person who experienced God as "antishepherd" who afflicted him with the rod of his wrath, driving him into darkness without light, comes to the conclusion: "The Lord will not reject forever. Although he causes grief, he will have compassion according to the abundance of his steadfast love; for he does not afflict out of his heart." This practical solution of steadfast hope does not stand as the great finale at the end of the book of Lamentations but rather in its very center surrounded by lament and protest. Therefore, hopeful faith in YHWH and fierce protest against him are not antagonistic attitudes but "brothers in arms."

Ulrich Berges is Professor of Old Testament Exegesis at the Catholic-Theological Faculty at the University of Bonn, Germany.

THE DEPICTION OF JERUSALEM AS AN UNPROTECTED WIDOW

Naomi Graetz (Israel)

On the ninth day of the month of Av, the Jewish people commemorate the destruction of the first temple by the Babylonians (586 B.C.E.) and the destruction of the second temple by the Romans (70 C.E.) by fasting, reading the book of Lamentations, and special prayers of lament. In commemorating these destructions, some of us also remember the Holocaust and other tragedies that have befallen the Jewish people. Some observant Jews remember this date, and the three weeks preceding it, by abstaining from eating meat, not listening to music, and by not participating in any joyous event.

In Lamentations 1:1–2 Jerusalem is described as a widow after the destruction of the Temple. The theological intent of Lamentations 1 is to justify God's destruction of the Temple in Jerusalem as punishment for sin. The disaster that befell the community is because of the sin and infidelity of the people, not God's failure. The widow accepts the blame and says, "The Lord is in the right, for I rebelled against His word" (1:18). Indeed, Jewish theology tends to be self-blaming for what has happened: "On account of our sins, we have been exiled from our land [Israel]" goes the refrain in prayers Jews recite on certain Sabbaths. But is a "widow" guilty of sin? Should we be blaming ourselves for being the subject of God's aggression? Our modern sensibility suggests that perhaps we should be blaming the Angry God who has caused the destruction. For a believing Jew, this is not a blasphemous stance, for in our tradition there is a heritage of doubt and protest.

The depiction of Jerusalem as an unprotected widow (usually lumped together with the stranger and the orphan), abandoned by her husband/God, destroyed by her supposed protector can be seen as a metaphorical justification of abuse of women by men. Israel is not only abandoned by God, but she is also considered responsible for her own downfall—and therefore deserving of punishment. However, widowhood could be constructed positively; it could mean freedom from an abusive marriage. Today more women are single by choice and widowhood has become a normative, not a deviant, status. Yet there are many who still think they (or others) are missing something when they are not married. Widowhood, therefore, is naturally constructed as loss (of more than just the husband) and not gain.

The rabbis sense that it is unjust to blame the widow as a sinner, so they say she is not a real widow. She is in the situation of a woman whose husband has gone off for a while—leaving her as a "grass widow." It could not be that Jerusalem, or the people of Israel, can be likened to a real widow. Were that to be the case it would imply that God is dead! She is not a real widow, just like one whose father or husband has gone abroad and who intends to return to her, for it is said that Israel and Judah are not widowed from their God (Jeremiah 51:5).

The use of negative feminine metaphors to depict God's relationship with Jerusalem is both dangerous and powerful. There is a midrash in which God is likened to a heroic figure with great strength. He hits another man and the man immediately dies from the blow. This hero then goes into his house and hits his wife and she withstands the blow. Her neighbors say to her, "All the great athletes have been killed from one of the hero's blows—but you are able to survive more than one blow." She answers them that "he hits *them* with all his might, out of anger, but to *me*, he gives what I am able to take" (presumably out of love). In a continuation of this same midrash, the rabbis ask, why it is that the people of Israel can stand up to God's anger? The answer is this: It is because God hits us and then returns immediately and re-creates us. This is the comfort that Israel can take in their unique relationship to God.

But why do the prophets and rabbis need such myths and metaphors to depict their relationships with God? What, if any, are the redeeming possibilities of studying such texts? Here I will mention three other suggestions, before referring to my own.

David Blumenthal suggests a theology of protest in response to the possibility that abusiveness is an attribute of God. He writes that the definition of abuse is when the punishment is out of proportion to the sin. In his mind, God is sometimes abusive, and in wrestling with this truth, one must acknowledge and react to it. Blumenthal raises the question of how God does *teshuva* (repentance). The acknowledgment of abuse by the abuser is not enough. There must be a commitment never to abuse again. Obviously the abused person has to accept the commitment and accept reconciliation; but even with it, it is difficult to maintain a relationship of mutual trust with the abusing God. This is part of a theology of protest and sustained suspicions which are a proper response to God's abuse. The book of Lamentations is clearly understood as a possible response and reaction to God's specific abuse of the Jewish people.

Walter Brueggemann perceives lament as a "genuine covenant interaction" between us and God. He points out that when lament is absent, a cover-up and a practice of denial and pretense characterizes our relationship with God. When lament is allowed we can criticize God for not functioning properly. Lament happens when God's dysfunction reaches an unacceptable level, when the injustice is intolerable and change is needed. In lamenting, we are recognizing the abusiveness of God, and we are also rejecting that aspect of Him or Her.

J. Cheryl Exum proposes a three-fold way of dealing with gender-biased prophetic rhetoric. One strategy is to pay attention to the differing claims these texts make on their male and female readers. The second is to recognize the violent representations of God's sexual abuse of a nation personified as a woman and to expose this "prophetic pornography" for what it is. Finally, she suggests looking for competing discourse to uncover evidence of the woman's suppressed point of view in biblical texts.

Picking up on Exum's final point, I try to re-create a world in which women had a place. I find this a legitimate and necessary enterprise. It is a way of contributing new insights and/or perspectives to our Bible. Modern feminist midrash attempts to redress the misogynist tendencies of traditional mainstream midrash. The consequences of a patriarchal worldview for us are clear. Conventional attitudes toward women are still being transmitted to us as part of our heritage and too often we respond unquestioningly to these views as if they were absolute truths. Women should not have to identify against ourselves. On the one hand, we must seek out old texts where women appear and bring them to the surface; on the other hand, as part of our theology of protest against previous and present abuse, we must be revisers and revisionists. With new vision we bring new perspectives to the old text, and in doing so, we contribute to the ongoing work of revelation.

Naomi Graetz taught English for 35 years at Ben Gurion University of the Negev, Israel; she is the author of a number of books on women in the Bible and Midrash.

QUESTIONS

1. Lee focuses on Korean *minjung* theology of *han* as it connects to Lamentations 3. How might it connect to other elements of the book? In what ways might it not fit particularly well?

2. In addition to the one mentioned by Melanchthon, what other differences exist between dalit poetry and the book of Lamentations?

3. Reflect on your experiences of news reports of wars. Analyze Berges' claim that the reality of war is censored to promote the agenda of the powerful. Is the book of Lamentations also somewhat censored in this regard?

4. Elaborate on the "dangerous and powerful" nature of "negative feminine metaphors" in Lamentations. In this vein, explain what Graetz means when she writes, "Women should not have to identify against ourselves."

CHAPTER 25

ECCLESIASTES

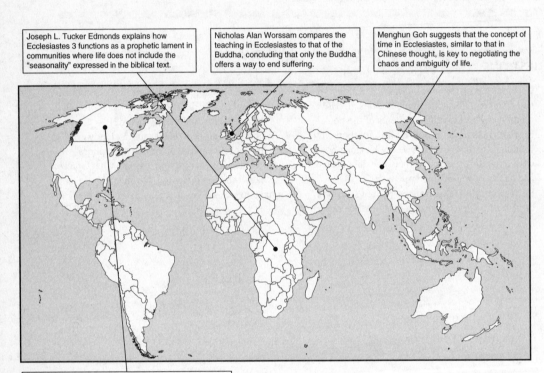

Joseph L. Tucker Edmonds explains how Ecclesiastes 3 functions as a prophetic lament in communities where life does not include the "seasonality" expressed in the biblical text.

Nicholas Alan Worssam compares the teaching in Ecclesiastes to that of the Buddha, concluding that only the Buddha offers a way to end suffering.

Menghun Goh suggests that the concept of time in Ecclesiastes, similar to that in Chinese thought, is key to negotiating the chaos and ambiguity of life.

Barbara Mei Leung Lai seeks to appropriate the Preacher's lived experience to the "Grand Narrative" of all humanity and to the crafting of her own "Text-of-Life."

READINGS

The Concept of Time in Ecclesiastes and Chinese Literature
Menghun Goh

Ecclesiastes 3 in Africana Communities
Joseph L. Tucker Edmonds

Qoheleth and the Buddha
Nicholas Alan Worssam

The Preacher and One's Own "Text-of-Life"
Barbara Mei Leung Lai

THE CONCEPT OF TIME IN ECCLESIASTES
AND CHINESE LITERATURE

Menghun Goh (China)

Focusing on Ecclesiastes 3:1–15, I propose that the contradictions in Ecclesiastes (e.g., 3:14 vs. 8:17; 2:2–3 vs. 3:13; 7:1 vs. 9:5; etc.) aim to highlight the chaos, ambiguities, and ambivalences in life. For Qoheleth, the writer of Ecclesiastes, if all is "vanity" (*hăbēl*), that is, absurd and incomprehensible (1:2, 14; 2:11; etc.), then one cannot systematize the ambiguity and ambivalence in life. Indeed, contrary to wisdom tradition that asserts a cause-and-effect notion of distributive justice (e.g., the reward–punishment schema according to one's actions in Proverbs), Qoheleth finds that both the wise and the fool (2:16) and the just and the wicked (9:2) end up the same, dead. In fact, the just person even receives what the wicked deserves and the wicked receives what the just deserves (7:15; 8:14)! The contradictions become more pronounced when God has made everything beautiful in its time (3:11; cf. 11:5). And, if Qoheleth has a positive portrayal of God, then the attention to absurdities can make his audience aware of social injustice and empower them to approach and perceive their world anew. Thus, even if life is burdened with toil and irony (1:3; 3:9; cf. 2:21; 4:4), Qoheleth maintains that we should be *ṭôb* (good, beneficial, efficacious, virtuous, fortunate, etc.) on the *ṭôb* day and on the evil day, as God has made both (7:14). Qoheleth even declares that it is *ṭôb* to be happy, do *ṭôb*, and consider *ṭôb* in toil (3:12–13).

This theme of doing and being *ṭôb* according to time is prominent in Chinese classical literature and culture. Here, the notion of time (*tian-shi*) comprises two main aspects. One is the phenomenon of time (*tian-zhi-shi*) and the other the "original" time (*yuan-fa tian-shi*). The former refers to human's observation and categorization of the passage of time into seasons and hours, and so forth. The latter refers to human's recognition *and* decision about the critical time. As Chinese view the material and immaterial worlds as a continuum in which everything is made of *Qi* (breath or energy) and is correlated and interchangeable, there is no dichotomy between these two aspects of time. If we can use the imagery of *yin-yang* in *tai-ji* (or popularly known as *tai-chi*)—*yin* refers to the moon or the shady side of the mountain and *yang* the sun or the sunny side of the mountain—then *yuan-fa tian-shi* is neither linear nor simply circular. The past, present, and future are existentially interdependent and reach their critical moment at a certain point or duration, when everything is at its optimal timing. Humans not only need to recognize *yuan-fa tian-shi* but also need to respond to it. Hence, in Chinese history and culture, we read about the importance of making use of the pattern of *yuan-fa tian-shi* in war, politics, ritual and art, agriculture, medicine, and so on. In the language of Qoheleth, as there is a season and a time for every matter under heaven (3:1; cf. 3:17, 8:6), we should recognize and take responsible action in relation to the pattern in time-event (3:2–8).

Whether or not Qoheleth was responding to the turmoil and oppression, this attention to time is noteworthy. In Qoheleth's terminology for time, *zəmān* (or *chronos* in the Septuagint), meaning "chronological time," only appears once, whereas *ēt* (or *kairos* in the Septuagint), meaning "critical time," appears forty times, with 31 occurrences in Ecclesiastes 3. The significance of *ēt* is further highlighted in the pairs of opposition in 3:2–8. In the face of a predetermined time (*zəmān*) and the framework of time—that is, a time to be born and a time to die, a time to plant and a time to uproot (3:2), and so forth—Qoheleth seems to advocate a tactical and responsible lifestyle. That is, how one lives in *ēt* or *kairos* between birth and death or between planting and uprooting hinges upon one's choice. The constraints may delimit one's options, but one can still meander through them. For instance, when Qoheleth posits that "what has been is what will be, and what has been done is what will be done; and there is nothing new under the sun" (1:9; cf. 3:15), the boundary that marks the past, present, and future is blurred. Not only is the future what is yet to come, the past is not a mere bygone either. The aspect of time in *ēt* becomes much more discursive. The past can haunt the future and replace the present and the future. What is crucial is the current moment, as it is the link where the past and the future converge into one another (3:15). In the face of one's past or heritage, one needs to decide what to do with it. If one is stuck in the past, then one's future is stuck too. But if one is too anxious about the future (cf. 7:14; 9:12; 10:14), one forgets the present, which can set the condition for the future (11:4–5). So if the present can redeem the past and prepare for the future, then this in-betweenness of the present is what empowers one to live through the ambiguities and ambivalences of life. In the midst of the past and future, one cannot be too timid or calculative; one needs to take risk and take heart from the fact that God has made everything beautiful in its time (3:11). Indeed, if there is a time for every event, and if there is a time for construction and destruction (cf. 3:2–8), then there is also a time for de/con-struction, a time of in-betweenness that is characterized by neither construction nor destruction.

This time of de/con-struction way reminds one not to get caught up in the either/or of construction or destruction, in particular if God seeks out what has gone by (3:15; cf. 11:9ff)! As an '*ēt* that is dynamic, the framework of past-present-future does not follow the logic of totality or mere recurrence; after all, if no one can grasp what goes on under the sun (8:17; cf. 1:14, 17; etc.), then the past-present-future is always open to new possibilities. So while the events of birth and death, planting and uprooting, and so on (3:2–8) may be relative to one another, each event should be treated as singular, lest we normalize it into a fixed pattern. This notice of singularity because of the inscrutability of time-event is also an important reminder to Chinese culture, lest we overlook the conditions, roles, and (responsible) decisions of human beings in the Chinese conception of time-event.

Menghun Goh is writing his dissertation in the Department of New Testament & Early Christianity at Vanderbilt University, United States; he lived in Kuala Lumpur, Malaysia for 18 years.

ECCLESIASTES 3 IN AFRICANA COMMUNITIES

Joseph L. Tucker Edmonds (Democratic Republic of the Congo)

In many parts of the world, technology and medical advances are extending life expectancies, reducing untimely deaths and infant mortalities, and providing quick and easy ways for people to gain access to life-sustaining treatments and medications. However, economic and political theorists have argued that we are entering into an age, created by neoliberal global economic realities, that results in a deep chasm between the global elite and those who are dispossessed. In this radically divided world, there is a growing group of people who do not have access to the life-sustaining technologies and treatments, and, in these communities, death and dying are not reserved for the old, but death comes early and often. These communities look to the Bible not as a supplementary text to support capitalist growth and expansion but to answer the long-held questions that reverberate throughout the Hebrew Bible: why does a good God cause suffering and what is the proper response in the face of death? These populations seek meaning in the biblical texts that highlight the fallow years of the wilderness (Exodus), the pleas and cries of Job, the prophetic utterings of Amos, and the reflective musings of Ecclesiastes. Specifically, the book of Ecclesiastes stands out in the Hebrew Bible as there seems to be little, if any, resolution to the problem of death and dying in this text. If anything Ecclesiastes proclaims that death, suffering, and pain are inevitable in the course of life, but the book does not just function as a funeral dirge that accepts death and dying. Rather, Ecclesiastes emerges as a lament, a sorrowfulness not simply over death but a critique of the context and conditions that create certain types of pain, suffering, and untimely deaths.

This essay will address the ways in which this early literature functions as a reordering and rethinking of unjust economic situations and provides a model for dealing with the problem of death and dying. Specifically, this essay will engage how marginalized Africana communities use Ecclesiastes to respond to the turbulence and instability of the postmodern world while not foreclosing against God's intervention in the contemporary moment. I will particularly highlight Africana communities' response to AIDS/HIV on the continent of Africa as an example of Ecclesiastes' function as both an acceptance of death and also a call to transform systems that create premature death and suffering in certain communities.

The oft-quoted third chapter of Ecclesiastes exposes the existential malaise the writer of this text faces. He is engaging the arbitrary contours of life and death within the frame of the divine creator's ultimate sovereignty, and the goal of this chapter and entirety of Ecclesiastes is to impart wisdom to the faithful in the midst of the uncertain terrain of human life. Ecclesiastes 3 has often been read as a descriptive elegy, simply outlining the shape and trajectory of the human experience in the physical world. In the Western world, this text is often used in conjunction with rituals of death and dying. In this normative reading, it is assumed that the vast majority of people experience all the seasons of life. However, this text is read quite differently in Africana communities, where the experience of life does not include the "seasonality" expressed in the Ecclesiastes text, but rather is constituted by a state of perpetual suffering. Here the text is read not so much as an account of the average human life, but as a reformulated prophetic utterance. It is a lament against the systems of oppression, violence, and selfishness that the writers of Ecclesiastes identify in other moments in the text, and a call for human community and formation that would offer all people access to seasonality and the quality of life espoused in the beginning verses of Ecclesiastes 3. This prophetic reading of Ecclesiastes is especially important in marginalized communities for whom perpetual states of war, poverty, death, and refugee status stand in contrast to the divine plan. Thus, while the logic of Ecclesiastes seems to accept the frivolousness of life and defeat in a chaotic world system, these other readings of Ecclesiastes suggest that it can function as a source of protest and a resource for community and healing in the midst of "meaninglessness."

Meaninglessness, in this regard, is not a critique of all life, but it is associated with lives and practices dominated by a desire for power and acquisition. However, a "meaningful life" is one that privileges community (4:9), prioritizes the end of oppression and dehumanization (8:12), and maintains a divine covenant (12:13). In this regard, the language of Ecclesiastes is not simply complaint or divestment from the current age or lived conditions, but it is a call to participation and a reordering of an unjust society. While the normative Christian church has often dismissed the wisdom literature and the prophetic musings of Ecclesiastes, those who are looking for models of protest and resistance available in the Hebrew Bible have embraced it. More specifically, Ecclesiastes has provided a space to simultaneously deal with the inevitability of death and dying while working to challenge the radical imbalance that impacts certain populations.

In communities that face death and suffering in alarming rates and where there seems to be no seasonality to life, Ecclesiastes is used as a model to support their emphasis on healing and healing rituals. In these postcolonial Africana communities, healing functions as a way to challenge the perpetual states of dehumanization, alienation, and subjugation that have become consonant with postmodern life. Healing in these movements are not simply spirit-based rituals practiced to minimize, if not erase, the impact of diseases like HIV/AIDS and other chronic maladies, but they also function as a symbolic response to the misery and suffering of the postmodern era.

Healing rituals in the Kimbanguist movement, a twentieth-century Christian movement founded in what was then Belgian Congo (now Democratic Republic of the Congo), function to highlight the radical humanity and subjectivity of Africana groups. The ritual situates the Africana body as a body worthy of all the seasons of life rather than one dominated by disease, death, and dehumanization. The healing ritual is also practiced among a community and requires communal participation for its efficacy. Therefore, healing responds to the physical and existential crises of Africana subjects and articulates a response to the suffering that includes the physical body of the person as well as the body politic. Moreover, healing functions to restore the social covenant and in the case of the Kimbanguist movement there is re-privileging of the village and the values of the village against the values of the urban lifestyle. In the prioritization of the village, there is a critique of aggressive acquisitiveness and the profit-centered ideology of capitalism, and in the place of capitalism and the "meaninglessness" of its project there is a renewed interest in social well-being and justice-seeking institutions.

Overall, the recovery of Ecclesiastes as prophetic lament and its use in marginalized Africana communities provide us resources for a renewed engagement with the postmodern condition and reveals the efficacy of biblical texts for those who experience unprecedented levels of death and suffering in this age.

Joseph L. Tucker Edmonds is Assistant Professor of Africana Studies and Religious Studies at Indiana University-Purdue University, Indianapolis, United States.

QOHELETH AND THE BUDDHA

Nicholas Alan Worssam (United Kingdom)

Which teacher of wisdom is the surest guide to enduring happiness, Qoheleth, that is, the Teacher in Ecclesiastes (c. Third Century B.C.E) or Siddhartha Gautama, the Buddha (c. Fifth Century B.C.E)? Both seem to assess the problem of life—suffering—in remarkably similar terms, but do they have the same prescription to cure the disease?

In the *Dhamma-cakka-pavattana Sutta* (*Setting in motion the wheel of the Teaching*), the Buddha delivers his first extended sermon after his enlightenment. He says, "Birth is suffering, ageing is suffering, illness is suffering, death is suffering; union with what is displeasing is suffering; separation from what is pleasing is suffering; not to get what one wants is suffering; in brief the five aggregates subject to clinging [body and mind] are suffering" (*The Connected Discourses of the Buddha: A New Translation of the Samyutta Nikaya*, translated by Bhikkhu Bodhi [Wisdom Publications, Boston: 2000, vol. 2], 1843f.).

This is not unfamiliar territory to Qoheleth. The Hebrew *hebel*, often translated "vanity," means something like "futile, absurd, useless," ineffectual as a fleeting breath. Qoheleth subtitles it as "a chasing after wind." This, in tone, is rather more elegiac than the visceral pain/dis-ease of the Buddha's Pali word *dukkha* (suffering). Still, following the basic meaning of "unsatisfactory," there is a definite point of contact between the two. Qoheleth says of mortals that "all their days are full of pain, and their work is a vexation; even at night their minds do not rest" (2:23). The problem is not just physical pain (the burden of toil he so often refers to) but also mental disquiet. Ageing is a particular fear of Qoheleth, for example, in the lyrical poem of Ecclesiastes 12. Association with the displeasing (chiefly fools) and loss of the pleasing (such as the rewards of labor) are bitterly lamented by Qoheleth, and all is finally abandoned to futility in the oblivion of death.

And what is the cause of this suffering? The Buddha says, "It is craving which leads to renewed existence, accompanied by delight and desire, seeking delight here and there; that is craving for sensual pleasures, craving for existence, craving for extermination." Qoheleth recognizes this too: "All things are wearisome; more than one can express; the eye is not satisfied with seeing, or the ear filled with hearing" (1:8). He goes on to give what sounds like a classic definition of *samsara*, the endless round of rebirth from which the Buddha taught the escape: "What has been is what will be, and what has been done is what will be done; there is nothing new under the sun" (1:8). Everything is characterized by impermanence (*anicca* to the Buddhists): "A generation goes, and a generation comes… The sun rises and the sun goes down…" (1:4–6). The experience of craving, or thirst (*tanha*), pointed out by the Buddha, is well known to Qoheleth: "The lover of money will not be satisfied with money; nor the lover of wealth, with gain… All human toil is for the mouth, yet the appetite is not satisfied" (5:10; 6:7). There is even a hint in Ecclesiastes of the Buddha's teaching of "not-self" (*anatta*): "The dead know nothing… Their love and their hate and their envy have already perished; never again will they have any share in all that happens under the sun" (9:5f). (But would the Buddha lament the loss of love, hate, and envy?)

Already here we begin to see the paths diverge. Although the Buddha teaches that there is no enduring individual entity, still there is a reward for good and bad action that carries on over the divide of death. All beings are "heirs of their actions": action (*kamma*) always has its result (*vipaka*), whether experienced in this life or in a future rebirth. Qoheleth says, "I perceived that the same fate befalls all of them [wise and foolish], since all alike die" (2:14). True, the Buddha would say, everything dies, but beyond death a world of difference separates the wise and the foolish. In a summary of the "graduated discourse," a kind of model sermon often preached by the Buddha before getting to the Four Noble Truths, he teaches the merits of almsgiving, the duties of morality, the reality of heaven, and the evils of desire coupled with the blessings of the abandonment of desire. Qoheleth does not recommend such things. He hates the thought of sharing the blessings of his life's work with others (2:20), rarely mentions the commandments (12:13 probably being an editor's dismayed epilogue), has no conviction of the rewards of heaven or the punishment of hell (3:16–22), and, albeit with some irony, actually recommends sensual pleasures, "for there is nothing better for people under the sun than to eat, drink, and enjoy themselves" (8:15).

For the Buddha, the first two Noble Truths, suffering and its cause, are only half the story. He then goes on to proclaim, "Now this, monks, is the noble truth of the cessation of suffering: it is the complete fading away and cessation of that same craving, the giving up and relinquishing of it, freedom from it, non-reliance on it." The only cessation Qoheleth knows is the shadowy gloom of Sheol where people are no better off than animals, and even the memory of them perishes. There really seems to be no hope in Qoheleth, except for the enjoyment of a fleeting youth while you still have the chance.

And the Buddha is very practical about how this cessation of suffering can be found: "It is this Noble Eightfold Path; that is, right view, right intention, right speech, right action, right livelihood, right effort, right mindfulness, right concentration." At times Qoheleth seems to counsel right action: for example in 8:12, expressing faith that the wicked will eventually experience the judgment of God, while "it will be well with those who fear God." Yet, in the next verses, he complains that actually he sees the opposite happening, and so commends enjoyment instead. Perhaps more than anything there is no systematic mental culture or meditation (Pali: *samadhi*) in Ecclesiastes, and from a Buddhist perspective this all but removes any possibility of coming to an end of suffering.

So if you want an amiable, eloquent, witty, and slightly acerbic drinking companion to while away the afternoon, Qoheleth is certainly your man. But if you really want an end to suffering, try an optimist: ask the Buddha.

Nicholas Alan Worssam is a member of the Anglican (Episcopalian) religious community, the Society of Saint Francis; he is based at Glasshampton Monastery in Worcestershire, England.

The Preacher and One's Own "Text-of-Life"

Barbara Mei Leung Lai (Canada)

Self-introduction to one's contextual background may take different paths. In light of the nature of Ecclesiastes as an "I"-discourse, and the expected level of my self-involvement in engaging the text, I have chosen to begin with a precise "I"-statement that can best indicate my ethnicity, bicultural shaping, immigrant status, reading location, and place of origin. I am a first-generation Chinese-Canadian, born and raised in the (then) British Colony of Hong Kong. I have spent my last 40 plus years in North America, first as a foreign student in the United States and then as an academic, teaching in Canada. As a late bloomer now at the prime of my academic life, I survived many years of hardship being a minority scholar in the academy. Navigating often deeply political waters has become normality in the broader context of my work life. This subtle demand has had profound impact on my self-hood—alternately feeling driven, defeated, and lost.

In my immediate life-context, I am a "prime-timer" (or "babyboomer" for this generation). My peers are all well-educated professionals, middle-class empty nesters who have a plurality of options in life (e.g., early retirement, career change, relocation, putting money into whatever is deemed meaningful). Among the social and economic privileges that we enjoy, there is still one thing that persistently disturbs the community of babyboomers. We are all shaken by the sheer reality of the cruelty of wars, and the magnitude and intensity of suffering and misery in the collective lived experience of humanity under the sun. Our collective Canadian/Chinese-Canadian culture, our professions, and our social and economic status cannot adequately provide directives to our inquiry. All attempts to make some sense out of this totally chaotic world are futile. Moreover, the burden of caring for our aging and dying parents tends to overwhelm the goodness in this season of our lives. Embracing life together with its uncertainties seems to be a thin but heavy slice of truth. The search for the "order-of-things" has been, and will continue to be, a driving force in shaping our lives—both corporately and individually.

The above is a self-articulation of my contextual background as an individual reader as well as the collective "we" (the community of readers). This is not a sophisticated description, but one that is rooted in our collective "flesh and blood" lived experience under the sun. It resonates with the rational mind-set and the emotive realm of the preacher in the book of Ecclesiastes.

As one of the characteristic I-texts of the Old Testament, the book of Ecclesiastes was written in the form of an "I"-discourse. As a window into the preacher's inner life, the "I"-voice in the text carries a transitive affect upon all readers. In this sense, the preacher's self-expressed sentiments have the potential of becoming our own felt emotions. The "I"-voice of the preacher invites all readers to identify with him the kind of vanity and senselessness that he has witnessed under the sun, and the emotive impact that these "commonalities" bear on him—"Everything is utter meaningless" (1:2, 12–14; 2:1, etc.)! The magnitude of absurdity in life (2:7; 3:16–17; 7:15; 8:12–14, etc.) drives the preacher to a weighty summary appraisal—seeking to make some sense out of the nonsensicality in life is like "a chasing after the wind"—doomed to fail! Simply going by the logic of "cause and effect" will disappoint us. What he shares with readers are not merely deep, self reflective statements. The weight of his outcries is found in the burdensome commonalities that he embraces (in all "flesh") and his address to slices of the reality of the "Grand Narrative" in which we all share and contribute to crafting—again, with our flesh and blood.

Intriguingly, not only does the book lay raw the preacher's intimate inner feelings, but it also provides a step-by-step guidebook in formulating the significant episodes in one's "Text-of-Life." In doing so, these steps are not merely life's important milestones but layers of cumulative wisdom. I have identified numerous textual indications pointing to a dynamic process of inscribing collective and cumulative lived experience to one's "life-text" and have appropriated it to the crafting of my own. This inscribing occurs through the cycle of seeing-reflecting-perceiving-concluding (1:14–18; 2:1–26; 3:16–22; 4:1–12, 15–16; 5:13–20; 6:1–12; 7:15–18, 25–29; 8:10–12, 14–17; 9:1—18; 10:5–15). The seemingly pessimistic outlook of the book is balanced by the preacher's "active initiation" in search for understanding ("Then I looked and saw") "Seeing" is transcending to "perceiving" ("Then I saw and perceived"); and the "conclusion" (cumulative wisdom) is the outcome of cycles of self-engaged reflection (e.g., 3:16–18, 22; 6:1, 12, 18).The uplifting moments in the preacher's self-narrated "life-text" are found mostly in his concluding statements as a result of self-engaged reflections (sometimes it can be a "pain-embracing" process, 8:16).

Some readers may think the "I"-voice in the book represents the voice of the sceptics, challenging and shaking the core of their faith in God. However, as I bring my "world "in front of the "world of the Text" self-engagingly, I echo each of the outpoured cries of the preacher and the deep-rooted, burdensome (though occasionally uplifting) concluding statements he utters. The thrust of the book is an engagement with slices of real life with which all humanity can resonate. Without the Book of Ecclesiastes, I, Barbara Leung Lai, simply don't know *how* to live. The shared ideological reflections of the preacher are not constructed sophistically or after a rigid frame of reference (i.e., the "order of things" after the two-way doctrine —"blessings and cursing"). Rather, it is rooted in the flesh-and-blood collective lived experience of all humanity. It is further substantiated by the preacher's intentional and persistent cycle of "turning-seeing-reflecting-perceiving-concluding," as an exemplary dynamics in life. The results of such life-engagement are reflected in the several summary appraisals (e.g., 2:7; 3:16–17; 7:15; 8:12–14).

As I seek to chart the next chapters of my own "Text-of-Life," collectively, they become a set of examined and realized blueprints for coping strategies in my life. As in the concluding

statements of the book, amidst the harshness of life, there are still glimpses of uplifting momen-
tum (e.g., 7:29; 8:12b; 11:7–9; 12:9–12)—aspiring to acquire cumulative wisdom in crafting
one's own "Text-of-Life." As the DJ on Toronto's classical music channel (FM 96.3) remarks
after each episode, "listening to beautiful music in a chaotic world"—there is still lovely music
resounding in the air (cf. 9:7–10)! There is indeed always a coexisting, healthy "tension." This
short essay exemplifies a "Leung Lai-version" of appropriated *re-expression* of Ecclesiastes out
of my own life-context—another chapter in my "Text-of-Life."

*Barbara Mei Leung Lai is Professor of Old Testament at Tyndale University College and Seminary
(Canada), one of the most culturally diverse institutions in North America.*

QUESTIONS

1. How do the concepts of time in Chinese culture, as Goh explains, compare to those in your
cultural context? How does your own personal
view of time shape your life?

2. How would Ecclesiastes 3 be read in your
context in comparison to the communities
described by Edmonds? Is there "seasonality"
to life in your community?

3. Do you agree with Worssam's conclusion?
How might Qoheleth reply to Worssam?

4. How does your own personal "I-statement"
compare to the one with which Leung Lai
begins? Do the words of the Teacher/Preacher
relate to your own "Text-of-Life"?

CHAPTER 26

ESTHER

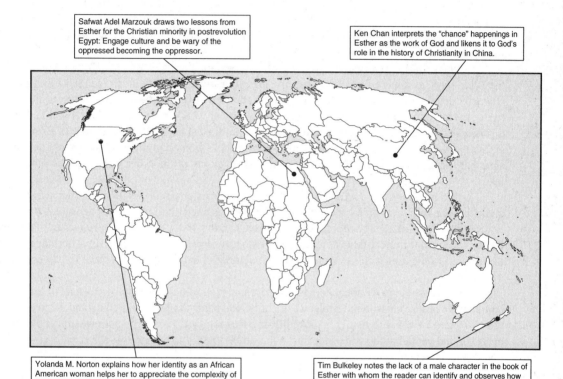

Safwat Adel Marzouk draws two lessons from Esther for the Christian minority in postrevolution Egypt: Engage culture and be wary of the oppressed becoming the oppressor.

Ken Chan interprets the "chance" happenings in Esther as the work of God and likens it to God's role in the history of Christianity in China.

Yolanda M. Norton explains how her identity as an African American woman helps her to appreciate the complexity of Esther's character and her struggle in a "foreign" land.

Tim Bulkeley notes the lack of a male character in the book of Esther with whom the reader can identify and observes how later retellings conform the book to conventional gender roles.

READINGS

Reading Esther as an African American Woman
Yolanda M. Norton

A Masculine Reading of the Book of Esther
Tim Bulkeley

Lessons from Esther for Christians in Egypt
Safwat Adel Marzouk

The God of Esther and Christianity in China
Ken Chan

READING ESTHER AS AN AFRICAN AMERICAN WOMAN

Yolanda M. Norton (United States)

The Hebrew Bible is not a safe space for women. In the text, violence is perpetrated against women in multiple ways; if not explicitly, women are wounded in the text through the interrogation and malformation of their identities. Violence against women occurs in the form of physical abuse, sexual assault, emotional torture, manipulation, isolation, and exploitation, among other things. Further, women's power and authority is depicted as rooted in their sexuality and ability to be manipulative, with little exception. Women seldom demonstrate ingenuity and agency outside of a sexualized context. As such, female independence is rarely framed as fully positive.

In that vein, I am intrigued by the character development of Esther. Most often women in the Bible serve as a mere function in moving the plot forward. Rarely do women have dynamic character development. Scholars have long debated whether this biblical phenomenon is indicative of the larger role that women inhabited in antiquity or whether the biblical writer was largely disinterested in the role of women in religious and political spheres. While the story of Esther is definitely more intricate than other narratives that involve women in the Hebrew Bible, I am not sure that she serves a different function in this plot than any of the other women of the biblical text.

Esther is a victim to all of the aforementioned intrusions and violations. Esther was first given into the king's harem by Mordecai, her cousin. It is difficult to judge such action, as we are unsure of the level of agency Mordecai would have had to prevent such action. However, once in the king's court, it is clear that Mordecai uses Esther to serve his political needs. After angering the officials of the king's court, Mordecai manipulates Esther, using her as a pawn to prevent his own demise.

Throughout the story, the reader is given little insight into the psychological state of Esther. Unlike male protagonists in the Bible, we are not given painstaking detail to the mental and emotional insights of women. Esther is moved from place to place. Extraordinary pressure is placed upon her and yet the author does not find it important to tell the reader how she feels in light of this. Women are supposed to do—not feel or think. Even while Esther's actions arelauded, her motives are less than pure. She is not able to be above reproach.

So how do we deal with this complex woman and her role in Israel's history? My own experiences as an African American, educated, young woman allow me the ability to appreciate the multivalence of Esther's character and her struggle. I grew up in a middle-class household but come from a working-class family. My grandparents were sharecroppers and farmers. My parents were in college from the time that I was in elementary school until I was in college. I grew up in an upper-middle class, white neighborhood. Why? Not because my family was upper-middle class but because it was a reasonable sacrifice that my parents were willing to make in order to ensure that their children received a good education. As a result, I understand what it means to attempt to survive in "foreign" territory, in the proverbial "enemy's camp." In addition, my own complicated existence has forced me to struggle not only with what it means to be truly Black/African American but also what it means to speak with and for Black/African American people.

America has a torrid history with Black and Brown people. From the institutionalized chattel slavery of Africana people, to segregation and lynching of the Blacks in the Jim Crow era, to the contemporary economic oppression and segregation and what some might call the modern-day lynching of Trayvon Martin and Troy Davis the United States of America is far from being racially united. Consequently, from my perspective as one who lives in the razor sharp abyss between Blackness and American, my perspective on the book of Esther is both religious and political. This tension is heightened by the lack of religiosity in the book of Esther. One must wonder how it is that this book of the Bible, which makes no mention of God, and is about a woman, was able to secure its place in the biblical canon.

The narrative of Esther begins not with the story's protagonist but instead with another queen on the throne—Queen Vashti. Vashti was summoned before the king and for some reason, unknown to the reader, she refuses to come. Vashti's refusal upsets the power dynamics of that time and sends King Ahasuerus into a fit of rage and his court into an uproar. King Ahasuerus' request to parade his wife around the court is not uncommon based on our understanding of male–female dynamics in the patriarchal ancient world. Modern convention would afford us the privilege of applauding Vashti's bold defiance, especially in light of her husband's intoxicated state. However, the narrative is not so kind to Vashti. She is dismissed from the king's presence, and the decree goes forth proclaiming that "every man should be master in his own house" (1:21).

Esther is an orphan girl under the care of her cousin, Mordecai (2:7). Upon hearing of the king's decree for a new wife, Mordecai places Esther in the harem of the king. The narrator gives no attention to the detail of how Esther, an innocent Jewish girl, ends up as a part of the harem of a Persian king. What is first problematic here is that there is no mention of God; there is no language that suggests that Esther and/or Mordecai acknowledge God's providence in their situation. The tone of the narrative suggests that once there Esther actively pursues a privileged position among the other women. That is, she ascends to power at the expense of other women. Esther rises because Vashti falls. Then, Esther must pit herself against the other women in the harem in order to be successful and distinguish herself from among them. In order to save her people, she had to compete against other women. This tension mirrors that of African American women, who are often caught in a web of competition with one another. We have been made to believe that resources are so limited for us that we must take them from one another. Further, we have been sold the myth that such competition is necessary to the survival of "minority" populations.

Second, the author is careful to tell the reader that Esther "wins" favor with the king, rather than the normal language of "finding" favor. Esther's rise to power is attributed to her own exploitation of her physical beauty and sexual prowess. Such language further robs Esther of her agency; she does not gain merit based on any of her inherent or intrinsic qualities. Likewise, for African American women there are always explanations to account for their success. Such explanations assume that it is only the exceptional that are capable of achieving and such merit is not acquired without significant assistance and guidance from external forces. Such forces are rarely divine, as in the book of Esther, where God is completely absent.

Yolanda M. Norton is a licensed Baptist minister who has served as a Children's Pastor and Campus Minister; she is currently a PhD student in Hebrew Bible and Ancient Israel at Vanderbilt University, United States.

A MASCULINE READING OF THE BOOK OF ESTHER

Tim Bulkeley (New Zealand)

When we "read" narrative, we discover our world in fresh ways, in large part by identifying with characters and perceiving the story "world" through their "eyes." Often we do this through a process of more or less realistic empathy as we identify with aspects of a character whose life, personality, and experiences make them similar to us. Greater similarity between us and our chosen character means such empathy is more realistic. Such realistic empathy is likely to produce more incisive and informative readings.

Gender is a near-ubiquitous and powerful component of human life and all texts are gendered in both subtle and obvious ways. Bible texts are written (almost exclusively) from male perspectives. Skillful, humorous, and passionate Feminist readers have regularly highlighted ways in which this makes Bible Stories problematic for women readers. The biblical texts that have the best claim to being woman-centered, or at least from a less strongly masculine perspective, are not similarly problematic for male readers. One of these, the book of Ruth, is a straightforward narrative that both focuses on its female characters and presents events from their point of view. Another, the love poetry of the Song of Songs, while not a straightforward narrative, nevertheless has storylines implied in its poetry. The poems speak with several voices but overall readers often feel that the woman's voice has at least an equal weight to the man's, and some readers suggest it is the controlling voice of the book. There are also strong arguments that it really is a woman's voice, unlike most biblical women who are given "voice" by male authors. These books do not pose particular issues for male readers perhaps in part because there are strong male characters with whom we can identify. The "bridegroom" in the Song may not be the "dominant" voice but his is a clear and strong one. In Ruth, Boaz is clearly not the central character, but he is one who offers a positive and attractive role model for men reading the book.

The book of Esther, however, is interestingly different. Despite the claim (made by most Feminist readers) that the story is clearly told from a masculine perspective, it has no man with whom a reader is strongly invited to identify. Ahasuerus is a bumbling nonentity, even though 127 provinces from India to Ethiopia must obey his every command (1:1), his counselors and his wife successively and easily bend him to their opinions (1:21; 2:4; 3:10; 5:3). Haman is an evident fool, as well as being a melodramatic villain. While he makes a desirable character for Jewish children to play in Purim reenactments of the story, such a caricature of the blind idiocy of evil is hardly an appropriate role model for a reader's life.

Mordecai is the most promising candidate. Being a Jew, and so ideologically and ethnically aligned with the narrator, in some ways he seems to be the hero of the story. He is introduced before Esther (Mordecai is introduced at 2:5 and Esther herself at 2:7 as his dependent orphan cousin and ward), and at the end of the book he is elevated to second position after king Ahasuerus (10:3) while Esther is not mentioned in Chapter 10.

At the start of the story, as might be expected, Esther follows Mordecai's advice (2:10), and he watches over her (2:11). But one must question whether he offers the male reader a potential male character through whom to experience the story. The more the tension mounts the less significant his role. In Chapter 2 of the book of Esther, he is uncovering conspiracies, and using Esther as a channel to communicate the intelligence to the king. In Chapter 3, he staunchly refuses to offer undue homage to the evil Haman. But in Chapter 4, as the genocidal decree is promulgated far and wide, he is reduced to mourning in sackcloth until Esther sends the king's eunuch Hathach to prod him into action, and at the close of the chapter he goes and does "everything as Esther had ordered him" (4:17). He is extravagantly honored in Chapter 6, but this pantomime honoring of Mordecai serves more to humiliate the villain, Haman, than to present Mordecai himself as a role model. After Haman's hanging, Mordecai is honored because he is Queen Esther's relative; roles are reversed and she is now his protector and sponsor.

With whom, then, are male readers invited to identify and through whom should we experience this narrative world? When reading Jane Austen's *Pride and Prejudice* most readers will likely experience events through Elizabeth Bennet, coming perhaps to share and understand her frustration and sense of being stifled by expected social roles. Similarly in the book of Esther the character most easily available to identify with, and therefore through whom to experience the narrative world, is Esther herself.

Like Elizabeth Bennet, Esther is constrained and used by social expectations. The "winner" of a beauty contest that she does not seem to have chosen to enter, she is cast as the (assumed to be) acquiescent subject of men's gazes, and so the opponent of Queen Vashti's resistance to this hegemonic gaze (1:11–12, 17). The biblical book of Esther, therefore, offers a potential for the education of male readers as they are encouraged to bend their assumed gender and perceive the world of the Persian Imperial court through the life of Esther, the Jewish orphan who becomes queen.

Naturally such a challenging work has been tamed, for seeing the world as others see it is never easy. Already the two ancient Greek versions of the story conformed it to the cultural and religious expectations of the dominant readers. In the Greek versions, Vashti's insubordination is downplayed and she is made responsible for her own death. In these texts Esther speaks less and the men speak more. Among numerous other changes, these versions increase Mordecai's role and diminish Esther's. Compared to the Hebrew text, the ancient Greek versions make the religious message clear and overt, give the men more dominant parts to play, and reduce ambiguity.

A tendency to conform the book to conventional gender roles is also evident in retellings aimed at children. The 14th *Veggie Tales* episode "Esther… The Girl Who Became Queen" adapts the story to make the religious elements more explicit even more strongly than the Greek versions did. At first sight, it does not increase Mordecai's role at the expense of Esther's as significantly. However, on a closer examination a series of cumulative changes become noticeable. At the start we see Mordecai instructing Esther about life and morals, while in the Hebrew version this is hinted at but not featured, thus Mordecai's authority as guardian is highlighted, preparing for the later changes.

The biblical book highlights issues of gender relationships near the start, with Vashti's refusal to obey her husband and the men's fear of such "rebellion" (1:18). In the video the reason Ahasuerus needs a new queen is obscured, thus removing this issue from the story. When Esther is in the palace, the *Veggie Tales* version does not highlight her common sense and initiative, which gain her favor; rather her rise seems to occur just because she sings well. Furthermore, Mordecai's advisory role is much increased in the animated version. Once Haman's plot is revealed Mordecai takes initiative to inform Esther of this; by contrast, in the Bible, he sits in mourning and Esther must actively send messengers to find out what is happening. Likewise, in the video Mordecai offers to call for prayer on her behalf; in the biblical version Esther herself orders prayer and fasting from the Jewish community. Thus in the video, Esther obeys Mordecai (as traditional roles might suggest), instead of the reverse. Overall Haman and Mordecai speak as much or more than Esther, while in the biblical account Esther speaks more than any male character. In short, in subtle ways throughout the telling, this modern adaptation of the story renders Esther's role as more submissive and allows her to show less initiative.

The book of Esther has had its opposition, from the debates of the Rabbis who mistrusted its failure to speak of God to Luther who distrusted its partisan Jewish character. Perhaps in part such opposition has come from the book's gentle highlighting of Esther's initiative and authority following Vashti's overt challenge to male dominance. While the bowdlerizing of retellings ancient and modern may make the book more acceptable to male readers, it diminishes its power by diminishing its challenge. A more true masculine reading of Esther will be more supple in its gender stereotypes and expectations, allowing these to be bent, and in the process learning to see the world more clearly.

Tim Bulkeley has taught at Université protestante du Congo, Carey Baptist College, and University of Auckland; he now teaches in the Laidlaw Graduate School, Auckland, New Zealand.

LESSONS FROM ESTHER FOR CHRISTIANS IN EGYPT

Safwat Adel Marzouk (Egypt)

In contemporary Egypt, religion is an important component of one's identity. Whether or not one actually practices one's faith, one is labeled a Muslim (ca. 89 percent of the population), a Christian (ca. 10 percent), a Jew, or other. One inherits one's religious association from his or her parents. Birth certificates and official IDs specify one's religion. Egyptians are thus classified based on their religious traditions. While for the most part, relationships between Muslims and Christians are fairly peaceful, various incidents take place here and there in which violence disturbs and fractures the Egyptian society. In a predominantly religious context such as Egypt, a conflict over an ordinary matter, for example, a business-related issue, could turn quickly into an extended fight if the ones involved in the conflict are of different religious affiliations.

Challenging and changing this tribal way of thinking about religion has become a serious need, especially after the events of the Arab Spring. During those 18 days of revolution in January of 2011, the people of Egypt—both Christians and Muslims—were united in El-Tahrir Square against the oppressive regime of Mubarak, whose 30 years of governing deepened the division between Christians and Muslims. Now in the postrevolution era in Egypt, Christians and Muslims must formulate new paradigms for their relationships as equal citizens. The challenge that the Muslim majority and the Christian minority face is how to nourish a peaceful relationship that allows for those of different faiths to live together in harmony.

Christian Egyptians can look to the Bible for guidance on difficult questions, one of which is how to survive as a minority. Here the book of Esther is instructive. When read in the context of contemporary Egypt, the book of Esther offers at least two lessons.

First, the book inspires the Christian Egyptian minority not to isolate itself from its surrounding culture. The way to overcome any potentially abusive power is not to withdraw from the public sphere, but rather to engage it wisely and faithfully. When a minority falls prey to fear of the power of the majority, it is only natural for the initial tactic to be withdrawal and isolation. The book of Esther, however, offers an alternative approach. The book urges the minority to be open to the surrounding culture, to use wisdom, faith, and courage to step out into the public social and political arenas. Both Esther and Mordecai do just this. For example, Esther is willing to marry a non-Jewish king. She then shows courage by risking her life by coming uninvited before the king; this underscores her willingness to push against the limits that are set for her as a woman (4:11; 7:1–10). Esther also conceals her Jewish identity at the beginning, but then reveals it at just the right time in order to bring salvation to her people (2:10; 3:2–3; 7:1–10). Wisdom, in this case, is knowing the right time and the right way to reveal who you are. Furthermore, Mordecai showed faithfulness to the foreign king by uncovering the plot to kill the king, which leads subsequently to his being honored and to the demise of Haman (6:1–11). Finally, some interpreters, though the text avoids mentioning God, try to read divine providence into the text. The absence of God from the text, however, invites us as humans to take full responsibility and to acquire the appropriate skills to survive.

The second lesson that comes from the book of Esther is a cautionary warning. It is crucial to reflect on how the book ends, namely with the Jews killing their enemies. The book should not be read as an invitation to destroy one's foes. In a subtle way the book shows that the Jews, who were saved from annihilation, became similar to their enemies when they massacred those who hated them. In this vein, the book of Esther invites the Muslim majority and the Christian minority in Egypt to learn that abusive power is fragile and is not as stable as it looks on the outside. Though at the outset Haman seemed to possess a lot of power, his deep-seated insecurity is seen in his reaction to Mordecai's rebellious behavior: He plans genocide against all the Jews that live in the kingdom simply because Mordecai refused to bow down to him. His disproportionate wrath against Mordecai unveils Haman's insecurity. The fragility of Haman's power is humorously evident a second time when he falls on the couch of Queen Esther pleading with her to forgive him for scheming against the Jews (7:6–8). The king is enraged because he thinks Haman is attempting to seduce Esther, and so the king orders that Haman be hung on the same gallows that he had prepared for Mordecai (7:9–10). This ironic reversal is heightened because Haman had originally demanded that Mordecai the Jew bow down to him, and now his "bowing down" to Esther the Jew results in his own death.

Once the Jews possessed power, however, they acted in a way that is not very much different from what Haman sought to do (8:9–12). This point is enhanced when we notice the similarity between Haman's issued decree aimed at the destruction of the Jews and Mordecai's decree aimed at the destruction of the enemies of the Jews (3:12–15; 8:9–14). In addition, Haman's attempt to massacre all of the Jews just because one Jew did not bow to him can be readily compared with Esther and Mordecai's excessive decree to kill the enemies of the Jews in other provinces, not only Haman. The book of Esther, then, confronts us as humans with the complex relation between possessing power and enacting violence. Why does a community that once was powerless and was near destruction turn into violent victimizers once they possess power? Does the community's security depend solely on the annihilation of the other?

Safwat Adel Marzouk, a Christian Egyptian, is Assistant Professor of Old Testament at the Anabaptist Mennonite Biblical Seminary, United States.

THE GOD OF ESTHER AND CHRISTIANITY IN CHINA

Ken Chan (China)

It was the 14th and the 15th of the month of Adar, and the Jews throughout the Persian empire were jubilant. They were celebrating the festival of Purim because they had been scheduled to be slaughtered—and the tide turned the other way (Esther 9:1–2).

This was truly amazing because the king, by the instigation of his right-hand man, Haman, had decreed the 13th day to be the time of death for all the Jews under his imperial rule (3:7–11). The Jews did not know what to do at first except to mourn (4:3). They thought they were dead-meat. Their despair was only a symptom of a much deeper sense of hopelessness, which began with the destruction of the first temple in Jerusalem by Nebuchadnezzar of Babylon. Not only did they lose their religious center, but they were also incredulous that their God would "abandon" them. Since then, the Jews lived as second-class citizens in other people's land. The geopolitics was volatile back then (as it has been throughout much of history). Power changed hands. By the time of Esther and Mordecai, the Persians ruled the land. The Jews kept their heads low and tried to get along. When the king was choosing a new queen, Esther joined the other beauties in the harem (2:8).

This was the Jews' situation when God began to deliver them from genocide. This is history recorded to teach the readers that history is in God's hand. A series of ironies shows the contrast between what happens in human affairs and what can happen when God steers it in another direction: (1) Queen Vashti who was chosen for her beauty somehow refused to display her beauty (1:11). (2) Esther, who did not ask for more than her share of the beauty treatment program (2:15), somehow attracted the king more than all the other beautiful girls in the harem. (3) The fact that Mordecai saved the king's life from assassination (2:21–23) did not elevate him to a post in the civil service, until the king somehow could not fall asleep (6:1) and heard about the account as it was read from the chronicles of the empire. (4) Haman's desperate plea for his life in front of Esther was somehow interpreted by the king as molestation (7:8).

And of course, the "somehow" was the work of God.

Going to the other end of the spectrum of time, we see God's fingerprints throughout the history of the growth of Christianity in China in the last 1,400 years. The Nestorian Christians arrived in China in the seventh century. By the beginning of the ninth century, there were over a hundred Nestorian churches (or "temples") throughout the land. Unfortunately, an emperor in the middle of the ninth century banned the Nestorians, who then moved to Mongolia. There, they worked among the Mongols until the second half of the fourteenth century, when plagues and religious intolerance decimated their population. The official records of the next Imperial dynasty contained zero trace of them. But, a breakthrough was to begin with the arrival of the Catholics. Matteo Ricci gained access to the court by introducing the European sciences to the emperor in the early seventeenth century. The successors of Ricci—Schall, just to name one—continued this policy and were successful. But all was not well. In the middle of the seventeenth century, some jealous officials planned to have Schall (and six others) executed. But "somehow" there was an earthquake and a fire in Beijing on the day of the sentence. The mother of the emperor, who was a friend of Schall, managed to reverse the sentence. So Schall was released unharmed, whereas five of the officials who were against him were executed instead. Moreover, an emperor at the end of the seventeenth century unexplainably ended the ban on Christianity. In short, when Ricci first arrived in China, there were virtually no Chinese believers; a century later, there were 257 churches and 300,000 believers.

At the beginning of the eighteenth century, a religious controversy led to a ban on Christianity again. This was unchanged until a century later, when Protestant missionaries were "somehow" able to reenter China. And they had great success. One agency alone started 700 churches, which led to an increase in the number of believers to 19,000 by the early twentieth century.

The next tide opposing the spread of Christianity was the rise of the Boxers, an anticolonial movement in the beginning of the twentieth century that confused Christianity with colonialism.

They killed 241 missionaries as retaliation against the capture of Beijing by the colonial forces. Remarkably, Christian missions "somehow" did not decline, but grew. Missionary heroism rose to a great height. Tears are still shed and eulogies still delivered for these heroes of the Christian faith. We remember how one labored long and hard and eventually died of malaria, how one gave his life while caring for a Chinese patient who had typhoid, how one (along with his wife) had to sleep in the wild, and how one ran out of money and still continued to preach in the mountains with only a shoulder bag and a walking stick. The result was that by the middle of the twentieth century, Protestant Christians in China reached 1 million.

After colonialism and civil war ended in China, following World War II, foreign missionaries were evicted, churches were closed, and religious activities were banned. Many people outside of China thought Christianity would be wiped out. But "somehow" the opposite happened. True, Christians were persecuted and many of them did die from starvation, banditry, torture, and execution; but some survived. They fled into the wilderness, lived in mountain caves, ate wild berries and herbs, and kept warm with sheep skins. They continued to worship God. In some cases, even government party members became Christians during this period of time.

Yes, the God of Esther has grew His church in China, which is now about 60 million strong. Despite suffering ongoing oppositions, the power of the gospel is "somehow" still at work in this land.

Ken Chan (Ph.D., biblical studies) is a linguist translator with SIL International serving in East Asia.

QUESTIONS

1. In what specific ways does Norton identify with Esther? How are their contexts and situations different?
2. Assess Bulkeley's comments on Mordecai. Could one make the case that male readers can readily identify with Mordecai?
3. What "lessons" would you draw from the book of Esther, based on your particular religious and political context? How do they compare to the "lessons" drawn by Marzouk?
4. In addition to the ones mentioned by Chan, what other "chance" occurrences in the book of Esther might one identify?

CHAPTER 27

DANIEL

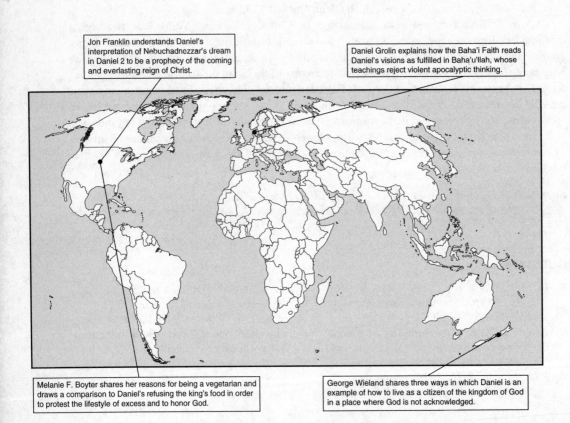

Jon Franklin understands Daniel's interpretation of Nebuchadnezzar's dream in Daniel 2 to be a prophecy of the coming and everlasting reign of Christ.

Daniel Grolin explains how the Baha'i Faith reads Daniel's visions as fulfilled in Baha'u'llah, whose teachings reject violent apocalyptic thinking.

Melanie F. Boyter shares her reasons for being a vegetarian and draws a comparison to Daniel's refusing the king's food in order to protest the lifestyle of excess and to honor God.

George Wieland shares three ways in which Daniel is an example of how to live as a citizen of the kingdom of God in a place where God is not acknowledged.

READINGS

Daniel in Babylon as an Example for Christians in New Zealand
George Wieland

Daniel's Diet and Vegetarianism
Melanie F. Boyter

Daniel's Prophecy of Christ's Future, Eternal Kingdom
Jon Franklin

Daniel and the Baha'i Faith
Daniel Grolin

DANIEL IN BABYLON AS AN EXAMPLE FOR CHRISTIANS IN NEW ZEALAND

George Wieland (New Zealand)

There are still those who insist that New Zealand is a "Christian country" but the claim is increasingly difficult to justify. The proportion of the population that describes itself as Christian has steadily declined over the past century from almost 90 percent to about 53 percent, with a particularly marked decrease during the last two decades. Only a small minority attend church services with any frequency.

In this context, Christians express a wide range of attitudes toward participation in national politics. Some want to seek political power by which they could try to reverse what they see as the deterioration of the nation's Christian identity and character. Political parties that claim to represent Christians and their values have emerged, but they have had very little electoral success, often competing with each other for the "Christian vote." Other Christians have questioned whether it is realistic or even right to claim a privileged place for the Christian religion in a nation that is increasingly diverse, but they attempt to exercise some Christian influence through participation in broadly based political parties. A number of Christians have attained political office in one or other of the main parties, but they must live with the constant tension between what they believe to be right and what they are required to support if they are to keep their place at the table. For many Christians, the solution seems to be to withdraw altogether from the political arena with its complexities and compromises and focus their energies on living Christian lives free from entanglement in secular politics.

Who is right? What does it mean to pray and work for the coming of the kingdom of God in this context? Those who aspire to make New Zealand a "Christian nation" cite Old Testament accounts of Israel prospering under godly rulers, who legislated and governed according to God's laws. In post- or sub- or simply non-Christian New Zealand, however, such a theocratic vision seems very remote from the reality. Worshippers of God have to recognize that the government, culture, norms, and attitudes of the society in which they live are not those of the kingdom of God into which Christ has called them. How do they live as citizens of that kingdom in a context where it is not acknowledged?

The book of Daniel engages such questions. Here the worshippers of God are not in a place where the faith that they hold is the basis for the society in which they live. They are exiles, marginalized members of a defeated people whose great days are in the past, living now under the domination of rulers and structures that give no recognition to the God whom they serve. The book is a narrative of political activity involving despotic rulers and their whims, government officials and their rivalries, manipulation of the legal system and behind-the-scenes plotting. Interspersed with all this are tempestuous visions of the rise and fall of kings and kingdoms.

As the narrative unfolds, we discover at least three modes of engagement of worshippers of God with a society that does not share their faith. First, we read of the appointment of Daniel and his three friends to high office and are astonished to find these Jewish exiles participating in the government of the Babylonian empire. This might encourage those who seek political power as a means of realizing God's kingdom in New Zealand. Throughout the book, however, authority remains with the successive kings and the activity of those believers in God who are appointed to various offices is in the service of the whole kingdom and its people, not expressly for the benefit of the believing community.

Second, we see the authenticity of the exiles' faith and their evident relationship with the God of Israel leading not only to appointment to specific roles but also to invitations to Daniel to speak in times of crisis to a succession of emperors. This might suggest that the most effective engagement is achieved through influence derived from spiritual and moral authority rather than mere political authority. Third, we observe first Shadrach, Meshach, and Abednego and then Daniel himself breaking ranks with their fellow governors and officials and showing themselves ready to surrender power, position, and even their lives, choosing faithful witness outside the system when whatever influence they might retain by remaining inside it would be at the cost of denying their allegiance to the God of Israel.

There is tension but not inconsistency between those modes of engagement. Coherence is found in what the book declares, demonstrates, and implies about the kingdom of God. The rule of God extends into an everlasting future, in which all peoples, nations, and languages will serve God's appointed king (7:13–14), and it is that rule, more than the transient reign of a mortal emperor, that the worshippers of God acknowledge and serve. It is as "servants of the Most High God" that they contribute their abilities and training in the service of the king and people of the land of their exile. Furthermore, while they look to a future realization of the kingdom of God in its fullness, there is evidence that God's rule is operative even there in Babylon. God not only hears and helps the faithful Jewish worshippers (2:20–23; 6:19–23), he also deals directly with the Babylonian kings through dreams and signs, revealing mysteries, humbling and restoring, and demonstrating that even in the present age God has the power to set leaders over human kingdoms and those rulers are accountable to him (2:28; 4:1–37; 5:18–28; 6:25–27). In its varying modes, the constant for those who seek God's kingdom while living in a human kingdom is to be faithful servants of God, whether this means serving the nation in which they find themselves with the abilities God has given them, or influencing the king and other officials by the integrity of their faith and lives, or by bearing courageous and costly witness that places them outside the norms and demands of that society.

How did the servants of God discern how faithfulness should be expressed as circumstances changed? Daniel models a deep spirituality of engagement. Refuting the dichotomy that is often assumed between people of prayer and people of action, between the way of quiet contemplation and the way of purposeful political involvement, Daniel's astonishingly effective political engagement was utterly inseparable from his life of prayer (2:17–23; 6:10–13; 9:3–23) and scripture-searching (9:1–2). Even people who did not share or understand his faith recognized Daniel to be "endowed with a spirit of the holy gods," which gave him a hearing at the royal court (4:9, 18; 5:11). Daniel was able to seek the kingdom of God in his place of exile. He found it in Babylon not only in visions of its eschatological fulfillment but also in its demands there and then for his own costly obedience and in the glimpses of the activity of God, who was present even in Babylon, dealing with its kings and through them affecting the nation.

Reading Daniel in a New Zealand that is no longer, if ever it was, a "Christian country," I am prompted to look for intimations of the rule of God even where God is not acknowledged; I am inspired to serve the people among whom I live with all the abilities that God gives, honed and developed through study and practice; I take encouragement in seeing that real influence is inextricably linked to integrity and authenticity; and I am challenged to bear the cost of a faithful witness that marginalizes the worshipper of God in a population whose devotion is to other gods.

George Wieland is Lecturer in New Testament and Director of Mission Research and Training at Carey Baptist College, Auckland, New Zealand.

DANIEL'S DIET AND VEGETARIANISM

Melanie F. Boyter (United States)

The Bible tells us that our body is a temple and that we should glorify God with our body; this idea seems to come up most commonly in reference to exercising, and tattoos, honestly. However, I believe vegetarianism is an effective means to glorify God through the body: first, by adhering to the diet originally intended for humankind and thereby putting less burden and strain on the earth and next, by refusing to promote a lifestyle of excess (through foods that require animal suffering/death). We can see this exemplified in the dietary practice of the prophet Daniel.

On February 12, 2009, our dog Lady passed away. She was 10 years old. She'd lived her entire life with severe allergies, even from grass, often licking and chewing her paws and scratching her ears until she bled. We had her on a regimen of Benadryl for a while, but eventually even that stopped working and we had to move to prednisone to keep her inflammation down. It helped, but as steroids tend to do, it also began to destroy her bones and, on that day in February, her body could no longer handle the strain.

On that very day I became a vegetarian. Watching her suffer through a life of discomfort made me keenly aware of the far-reaching ramifications of the original sin which resulted in expulsion from Eden, causing pain, toil, and death. So often, we only pay attention to the consequences of Adam and Eve's sin on humanity, and we fail to notice the innocent bystander who fell along with us through no fault of its own: the very creation itself. Lady caused me to realize that our sin caused her to have to live this life that she didn't deserve. Romans 8:22 says that "the whole creation groans and suffers the pains of childbirth together until now" (NASB). Creation awaits redemption with us, although it would never have needed it were it not for our transgression.

And thus, I decided to refrain from eating animals because of my conviction that they never would have had to die were it not for my sin. The original diet prescribed in Genesis was a wholly vegetarian one (Genesis 1:29–30). Thus, God's original plan for us was to live in harmony with creation, without need for bloodshed from human or animal alike. For me, the vegetarian lifestyle, at least on a small scale, is to live in a constant state of repentance for mankind's actions which separated creation from the Creator and to repent for the modern lifestyle of excess, which further damages the earth each day.

We turn now to Daniel. As a young man, he was part of a group of boys selected to be specially trained and educated to work in personal service to the king and, as such, the king directed them to eat from his "choice food" (1:5) so that they would be strong and fit to serve him. Today, "choice food" would probably be all-natural, organic, cage-free, and grass-fed; however, during Daniel's day, the king's "choice food" would be decadent, rich, and heavy and would focus largely on breads and meat which back then (just as it is now in non-first-world countries) were a sign of wealth. If these men were going to be in service of the king, they needed to become accustomed to the diet of the royal family. For the Jews among these "choice men," this was certainly a big change, as they would have been much more accustomed to the simple foods of the poor: vegetables, some grain and bread, and maybe meat if it was available and affordable. The idea of having meat and wine at every meal would have been totally foreign to Daniel.

Daniel could very easily have fallen into his new lifestyle and forgotten about his faith and his people, but instead, he chose to honor God by refraining from the king's "choice food." He even goes as far as claiming that to eat the king's food would be to "defile" himself (1:8). His use of the word "defile" brings a spiritual aspect to the decision; he would fail to honor God properly if he were to allow himself to fall into this lifestyle of excess and rich (animal) foods.

As a result, Daniel petitions one of the commanders to allow him to refrain from the king's meals and instead to have only vegetables and water—in essence, to return to the Edenic diet originally prescribed by God in Genesis. His decision serves two purposes: first, he protests the royal lifestyle of excess by keeping himself separate from it, and second, he honors God by adhering to his original instructions on how to properly use creation for food. The result? After ten days, he and his three companions, Shadrach, Mesach, and Abed-nego, were found to be much healthier than the other boys who'd eaten the king's "choice food" (1:15). This is proof not only of the validity of the vegetarian (or Edenic) diet, but is also proof that God honored their decision to glorify Him with their bodies by giving them greater strength than the other men.

Incidentally, Daniel's honoring God by adhering to a vegetarian diet may have benefitted him later; in Chapter 6 of the book of Daniel, Daniel is cast into the lion's den for, again, remaining true to God and praying to Him only. What would have been an immediate death for Daniel was, in reality, a night of peaceful slumber, as God took away the normally carnivorous instinct of the lions. Perhaps, for just one night, God allowed creation to exist as he'd originally intended, with man and beast peacefully sleeping together, without strife or violence. Perhaps, since Daniel honored God those years earlier through his faithfulness in diet, God honored Daniel—not just by protecting him from certain death at the hands of the lions but by allowing him to have a small glimpse into what creation was intended to be.

Melanie F. Boyter is a food blogger and has a Master's degree in multicultural literature and seeks to live out her faith in the everyday.

Daniel's Prophecy of Christ's Future, Eternal Kingdom

Jon Franklin (United States)

Daniel is one of the few Old Testament characters whose life was untarnished. Unlike Abraham, who lied twice about the identity of his wife; Jacob, the deceiver, who stole his brother's birthright; Moses, who killed a man; and King David, who was both a murderer and an adulterer, Daniel stands as one committed to personal integrity and resolute faith in the God of the Hebrews.

In 605 B.C. Daniel was carried off into Babylonian captivity. The key to understanding his character is found in Daniel 1:8. Although but a youth at the time of his capture, Daniel "purposed in his heart" (KJV) or "made up his mind" (NASB) that he would not defile himself. Daniel determined in advance that he would not compromise his principles and succumb to the corrupt and immoral philosophy or behavior of his Babylonian captors. He would remain faithful to the God of his fathers. He responded in the most adverse of circumstances with wisdom and grace. It is little wonder that Daniel was awarded a significant measure of authority in the Babylonian government. "God granted him favor" (1:9 NASB) and that favor surrounded him even in the lion's den some 70 years later.

Many other words and phrases provide insight into Daniel's character. When confronted with the defilement associated with eating the king's food, he "sought permission" to be excused and then suggested an alternative (1:8, 12–13). In 2:16 Daniel "requested" time; he prayed for God's compassion (2:18); he "blessed the God of heaven" (2:19); he thanked God privately (2:23); he acknowledged God publicly (2:28, 30); and when elevated to a position of authority, he did not forget his friends (2:49). Daniel is truly an Old Testament example of Christ-likeness.

Daniel's prophetic career was launched when King Nebuchadnezzar suffered a troubling dream and demanded of his "spiritual counselors" an interpretation. He, however, withheld information about the dream reasoning that if they could inform him of the contents, he could rely on the accuracy of their interpretation. In a night vision God disclosed Nebuchadnezzar's dream to Daniel, who specifically noted that God had revealed to Nebuchadnezzar things "that would take place in the future" (2:29).

Daniel 2:31–35 furnish the details of the dream and 2:36–45 unveil its interpretation. The great statue with its head of gold, chest and arms of silver, belly and thighs of bronze, and legs of iron represent four great kingdoms. Observe that the materials of this statue decrease in value from head to foot (gold is more expensive than iron) but increase in strength (the strongest weapons were made of iron).

Daniel announced to Nebuchadnezzar, "You are the head of gold" (2:38). Babylon fell to the Persians (silver), who were in turn conquered by the Greeks (bronze), and finally Rome (iron) dominated those empires and more. (Later in Daniel 7 when Nebuchadnezzar was succeeded by Belshazzar, Daniel in a vision saw four great beasts: a lion representing Babylon; a bear, Persia; a leopard, Alexander the Great and the swiftness with which he conquered; and the fourth beast, terrible and dreadful, symbolizing Rome.)

These prophecies of Daniel were so specifically fulfilled that many so-called scholars assign a much later date to the writings of Daniel, making it not prophecy but merely history.

The most significant and yet-to-be fulfilled part of Nebuchadnezzar's dream recorded in 2:35 reads "…the iron, the clay, the bronze, the silver and the gold were crushed…not a trace of them was found." In the interpretation, Daniels explains that "the God of heaven will set up a kingdom which will never be destroyed…it will crush and put an end to all other kingdoms, but it will itself endure forever" (2:44). This is God's future eternal kingdom, which, when instituted, will signal the termination of all other kingdoms. Further, in 7:18 Daniel states that "the saints of the Highest One will receive the kingdom and possess the kingdom forever, for all ages to come" (see 7:22 also).

Daniel is not alone in this concept of a future eternal kingdom. Five hundred years earlier the prophet Nathan informed David that while David's desire was to build an earthly, temporal structure for God, it was God's plan to establish the kingdom of David forever (2 Samuel 7:16). Who is the descendant of David who will sit on his throne forever and ever? Who is the king who will reign over this everlasting kingdom? Daniel describes him in 7:12–13 as "one like the Son of Man…and to Him was given dominion, glory and a kingdom…His dominion is an everlasting dominion which will not pass away and His kingdom is one which will not be destroyed." It was the angel Gabriel (8:16) who was sent by God to reveal to Daniel much of the mystery he had witnessed. So it is fitting that it was Gabriel who spoke the following words to Mary, the mother of Jesus: "He will be great and will be called the Son of the Most High; and the Lord God will give Him the throne of His father David; and He will reign over the house of Jacob forever, and His kingdom will have no end" (Luke 1:32–33).

Isaiah, in portraying the child who would be born of a virgin, declares that "the government shall rest upon His shoulders…there will be no end to the increase of His government….on the throne of David and over his kingdom" (Isaiah 9:6–7). Jesus, who often used the term "Son of Man" to identify Himself is quoted in Matthew 24:30 "and they will see the Son of Man coming on the clouds of the sky with power and great glory." Again in Revelation 5:12–13 we read, "Worthy is the Lamb that was slain…to Him who sits on the throne, and to the Lamb be blessing and honor and glory and dominion forever and ever."

The majority of Daniel's prophetic statements have come to pass; history has recorded them and his words were incredibly and undeniably accurate. Babylon is now barren and desolate, the

Medes and Persians have been buried in the desert sand, and the glory which belonged to Greece has faded away. The iron fist of Rome, once feared by all so that none dared to challenge it, has crumbled and imploded from within.

What remains of Daniel's prophecy is the second coming of the Son of Man and the establishment of His eternal kingdom. Indeed, Christ will soon return as a conquering King who will reign forever and ever over His eternal kingdom.

Jon Franklin (B.S., King's College) is a retired psychology, math, and Bible teacher.

DANIEL AND THE BAHA'I FAITH
Daniel Grolin (Denmark)

When I was quite young my mother explained that my name, Daniel, had been chosen because Daniel of the Bible had been a great prophet. As a Baha'i, her high regard for Daniel was probably more a reflection of his significance in that faith than in the biblical tradition. Indeed, for Baha'is Daniel is seen as pointing directly to the Baha'i revelation.

'Abdu'l-Baha, the son of Baha'u'llah (the founder of the Baha'i faith), has offered an interpretation of Daniel, published in English in a volume called *Some Answered Questions*. Here 'Abdu'l-Baha explains how Daniel's prophecies are fulfilled by Jesus and Baha'u'llah. For instance, 'Abdu'l-Baha, following other Christian thinkers, understands the 70 weeks of Daniel 9:24 to refer to the period between the rebuilding of Jerusalem and the crucifixion of Jesus. 'Abdu'l-Baha also has some interesting connections with the well-known Christian eschatological sect called the Millerites. The leader of this national movement, William Miller, declared that the second coming of Jesus Christ would happen in 1843. When that did not materialize, Miller predicted 1844. One of Miller's key arguments in this prediction derived from the number 2,300 from Daniel 8:14, which for him pointed to the year 1844. From a Baha'i point of view, Miller was in fact right about 1844, but he got the person wrong: it was not the return of Jesus, but rather the arrival of the Bab. The Bab was the precursor, the forerunner of Baha'u'llah, like John the Baptist was for Jesus Christ. The Bab declared his mission in 1844 and was thus the fulfillment of the prophecy. The Millerites were mistakenly looking for Jesus to descend from the sky in 1844, while he was in fact revealing himself in Shiraz in Persia in the person of the Bab.

Another number that 'Abdu'l-Baha interprets is 1,260, derived from Daniel 12:7, which has the unusual phrase "a time, times, and a half." This is understood as three and half years or 42 months, each 30 days (i.e., 42 times 30). Here 'Abdu'l-Baha notes that it is 1,260 years from the Hejira of Muhammad and until the coming of the Bab in 1844, which is also the year 1260 in the Muslim calendar. Furthermore, by that same calendar there are 1,290 years between the proclamation of the mission of Muhammad and the declaration of the mission of Baha'u'llah in 1863. This fulfills the prophecy of 1,290 years in Daniel 12:11. Not surprisingly, books about prophecy written by Baha'is often reiterate these interpretations—that is, they are biblical prophecies which are fulfilled by the life of Baha'u'llah.

Another way of looking at the book of Daniel from a Baha'i perspective is to reflect on what has been regarded as its apocalyptic message. In apocalyptic literature, the powers of evil prevail over the powers of good in this present age; for God has withdrawn from the world. But in the age to come, so apocalyptic thinking goes, God will once again enter the world and defeat the powers of darkness. This seems to be the thinking undergirding the book of Daniel. While the rest of the prophets of the Hebrew Bible appear to be advocates of action and reform, the book of Daniel is very much an advocate of piety and quietism. This quietism goes hand-in-hand with the belief of God's future violent (apocalyptic) intervention into human affairs. "Wait," the message seems to say: "You do not need to fight the impossible battle. God will reach into the world and gloriously undo all the forces of evil."

Century after century, in Jewish, Christian, and Muslim tradition, this apocalyptic vision has rallied believers. When worldly forces have seemed insurmountable, believers have turned to the hope that supernatural powers will set things right where conventional means have failed. Hopeful souls suffering oppression of one type or another have proclaimed that the end was near.

The teachings of Baha'u'llah reject this sort of apocalyptic hope; it rejects the idea of a violent God, or that God directly interferes in the human course of history. God, Baha'u'llah teaches, is transcendent and no eye can behold His glory or hear the sweetness of His voice, save through His prophets. There is no apocalyptic end. The end of oppression does not come through the violence of God, but through the guidance of His prophets. It is not a mythical fight between monstrous figures of light and darkness, but humans aligning themselves with the will of God. The reign of God, while glorious as Daniel proclaims, wins through choices made by human hearts. Apocalyptic thinking removes responsibility from humanity and places it in nonhuman agencies, but the Baha'i faith rejects this. The world is what humanity has made of it, both good and bad. For justice and prosperity to reach those wronged and downtrodden, humanity must unite and eschew prejudices between religions, races, and sexes. It must promote education and the eradication of extreme poverty and wealth.

Because of these perspectives, Baha'is, like some Church Fathers before them, do not follow the common apocalyptic understanding of the text. 'Abdu'l-Baha refashions the apocalyptic language by making the nonapocalyptic arrival of the Bab and Baha'u'llah the fulfillment of Daniel's visions. Rather than a violent fulfillment, which defeats the wicked, the Bab and Baha'u'llah preach a message of unity and peace: "It has been prophesied that in the time of these two Manifestations [the Bab and Baha'u'llah] the earth will be transformed, the world of existence will be renewed, and beings will be clothed in new garments. Justice and truth will encompass the world; enmity and hatred will disappear; all causes of division among peoples, races and nations will vanish; and the cause of union, harmony and concord will appear."

Daniel Grolin (Masters of Computer Engineering, University of Southern Denmark) is an Information Technology Architect, journal editor (Baha'i Studies Review), *and author* (Jesus and Early Christianity in the Gospels: A New Dialogue).

QUESTIONS

1. How do people with religious commitments engage the government and politics in your context? How does it compare to Wieland's proposal?

2. Evaluate the reasons for Boyter's vegetarianism. Is her connection to Daniel's diet compelling?

3. Why is it important for Franklin to read Daniel 2 as "prophecy" and not history as "so-called scholars" do?

4. Are you convinced by 'Abdu'l-Baha's interpretations of the numbers in Daniel's visions, as Grolin explains? If not, how would you interpret them?

CHAPTER 28

EZRA AND NEHEMIAH

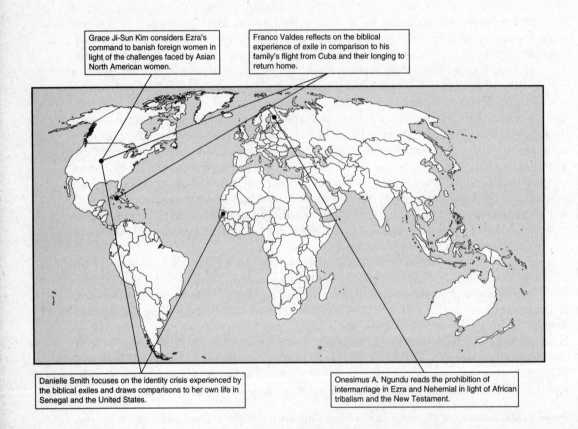

Grace Ji-Sun Kim considers Ezra's command to banish foreign women in light of the challenges faced by Asian North American women.

Franco Valdes reflects on the biblical experience of exile in comparison to his family's flight from Cuba and their longing to return home.

Danielle Smith focuses on the identity crisis experienced by the biblical exiles and draws comparisons to her own life in Senegal and the United States.

Onesimus A. Ngundu reads the prohibition of intermarriage in Ezra and Nehemial in light of African tribalism and the New Testament.

READINGS

Asian North American Women and the Banishment of Foreign Wives
Grace Ji-Sun Kim

Intermarriage in Ezra-Nehemiah, Africa, and Christianity
Onesimus A. Ngundu

A Cuban Reflection on the Biblical Experience of Exile
Franco Valdes

Personal Thoughts on the Identity Crisis of Biblical Exiles
Danielle Smith

ASIAN NORTH AMERICAN WOMEN AND THE
BANISHMENT OF FOREIGN WIVES

Grace Ji-Sun Kim (United States)

When Nehemiah chastises the Jews who had married foreign women, he reminds them that Solomon's foreign wives turned his heart away from the Lord and caused him to sin despite the great favor he received from God (1 Kings 11). In Ezra 9, Shecaniah suggests they make a covenant with God and send the foreign women away. Ezra makes the elders of Israel swear to do as they had said originally, and he sends messengers to inform all the returnees that they must appear in Jerusalem within three days or face confiscation of all property and excommunication from the congregation. Three days later, the whole congregation arrives and sits trembling in the rain waiting for Ezra to address them. Rebuking them for their unfaithfulness, he commands them to separate from "the peoples of the land and from the foreign women." When the meeting concludes they establish a commission, and three months later 113 men send away their wives.

In the Bible, foreign women and wives become pawns to be negotiated or dismissed by various peoples—men, religious leaders, even other women. Perhaps the story of Abraham sending away Hagar and her son can be viewed as a justification to dismiss the foreign wives and their children. Foreign women in the biblical narratives were often discriminated against both racially and religiously. They were identified as pagan, non-Jewish women whose idolatrous practices would draw the returnees back into the very sin that had precipitated the Exile. Thus, the foreign women became the scapegoats. Rather than the failings of the political leadership, the foreign women were blamed for Jahweh's anger. Ezra 9 exposes some of the horror of the casting away of foreign women, which had great consequences for the family, community, and the nation. These women had little control over their circumstances and often found themselves as expendable commodities.

This image of casting away "undesirable" women has perpetuated the continuous domination and scapegoating of women. They are viewed as inferior and simply as "the Other," which has allowed terrible acts of violence, dominance, sexual objectification, and slavery. Scapegoating was literally a tradition in Jewish culture—a goat would take on the sins of the people on the Day of Atonement and be cast away. The goat is an innocent creature blamed and punished for the sins, and often distracts attention from the real causes to problems. Likewise, the foreign women in Ezra are seen as creatures to take on the sins of the people, one of which is the issue of purity. The female body represents the abject (hopeless, miserable) which must be expelled, and everything maternal and female are represented as unclean. In many ways, knowingly or not, this is still occurring in our context today.

The history of Asian North American immigration involves more than 100 years in North America and much of this was plagued with hardship, turmoil, difficulties, and perseverance. Coming to North America is a difficult transition for many immigrants who face the challenge of living with a new culture, language, and religion. From the beginning of immigration, Asian North American women have been viewed as the foreign wives of Ezra's assessment, polluting the pure strain and angering God.

As immigrants came into the United States, the white Europeans were treated differently from Asians or people of color. Europeans entered the United States through Ellis Island in New York, which was essentially a processing center. Immigrants simply had their identification checked by officials and then they were registered to enter America. Asians, on the other hand, came through Angel Island in San Francisco Bay, which was essentially a prison. While European immigrants at Ellis Island waited a couple of hours or overnight before they were allowed to enter the land of milk and honey, Asian immigrants at Angel Island had to wait weeks, months, or even years. Whereas 2 percent of Europeans who applied for entry were sent back, Asians were sent back at more than 10 times that rate. The difference in treatment toward these two groups of people was race. It was not that European immigrants were any healthier or smarter than Asian immigrants; it was rather a difference of color. The Japanese government actually did their best to send only the smartest, most educated, and healthiest to America. However, this did not matter in the eyes of white immigration officials who already had negative views of Asians.

While white European immigrant women are able to quickly assimilate into the dominant Western culture, Asian immigrant women are obviously foreign. It does not matter how many generations they live in North America, their "yellow" skin will continue to mark them as a "foreigner." The portrayal of Asian North American women as the perpetual foreigner leads to racism, subordination, objectification, and discrimination. Since they experience a double discrimination as "foreign" and "women," they are easily cast away as unimportant members of society. Their experiences of racism and sexism often go unnoticed and therefore ignored by others.

Discrimination still continues in interracial marriages. During and after the Korean War, there were many American GIs who married Korean women. This interracial marriage was viewed negatively by the Korean society as impure, thus violating the pure Korean society. To add to this problem, when the American GIs returned to the United States, these wives were often ostracized and isolated from the rest of the American community. There was a sense of disdain by both the American society and the Korean immigrant community. Thus these wives became triply despised by three different social groups. To make things worse, some of these Korean women were abandoned by their GI husbands as the men eventually found Caucasian American women to remarry back in the United States. Many still used the purity code to justify this discrimination.

It is necessary to move beyond the way Ezra 9 dealt with these very pertinent issues. The question of foreign women and intermarriage is essentially about hybridity and purity. It is crucial to recognize that everyone is a hybrid and to rejoice in the differences. Hybridity brings together and fuses while at the same time maintaining separation: If one is a North American Korean woman, she is both North American and Korean, and therefore different—in a positive way—from North American women. Hybridity brings insight into analyzing the notion of the foreign women in Ezra 9. The foreign women of Ezra's day, just like Asian North American immigrant women, were living lives of hybridity as they were bordering on different religions, cultures, and heritages. Rather than banishing these women as the scapegoats of our issues, we need to embrace, welcome, and celebrate diversity, and find a richer way of being together in community.

Grace Ji-Sun Kim (Ph.D.) is Associate Professor of Doctrinal Theology at Moravian Theological Seminary, Bethlehem, Pennsylvania, United States.

Intermarriage in Ezra-Nehemiah, Africa, and Christianity

Onesimus A. Ngundu (Zimbabwe)

The books of Ezra and Nehemiah are a narrative about the return of the Israelites from Babylonian captivity. Some years later, after Ezra and company had arrived back in Jerusalem and completed rebuilding the Temple, a problem emerged: some of the priests and Levites and leaders had married women from the neighbouring peoples, referred to in Ezra 9:2 as "the peoples of the lands." Instead of referring to the women involved as "the daughters of the peoples of the lands" they are called "foreign women" (Ezra 10:2). In the Hebrew Bible, "foreigners" are people who came from elsewhere with no intention of staying permanently with the Jewish community. Foreigners, in short, are wicked and dangerous.

Before the introduction of Western civilization, industrialization, and Christianity, traditional Africans maintained strict tribal boundaries which strongly discouraged inter-tribal marriages. For example, no intermarriages are known to have taken place between the Kikuyu and Akamba tribes of Kenya, the Zulus and Xhosas of South Africa, or the Shona and the Ndebele of Zimbabwe. Marriages were contracted only within each tribal group because people of each ethnic group considered themselves linguistically different, ethnically and socially separate. While inter-tribal marriages are usually shunned in rural African society where people are still grouped together according to their family lines and tribes, they have become less of an issue among African urban people because cities have become a melting pot of people from different tribes and races. Nonetheless, African young people working in cities are always mindful of their own parents and family values when considering a marriage partner. Ideally, they would prefer to marry someone who speaks their mother-tongue and who is accepted by their parents. This is because in African society, a marriage contract is essentially an agreement between two families in which the individual interests of the groom and bride, though implicitly or formally recognized, are but a subordinate element to the wider dominating interests of their families. As in the bible, the African concept of a marriage relationship involves other family members. It is much less individualistic than the Western view of marriage.

Today, many single Africans living, studying, or working abroad end up marrying people from completely different cultures and races. This can create certain challenges. For instance, if a Western woman moves to Africa with their husband, she will often find it socially, economically, and relationally difficult to adjust. For example, while it is quite acceptable and even admirable in Western culture for couples to show their affection in public, such a practice, especially in the presence of the relatives, is taboo in traditional African society. In African society, men spend time with other men, women with other women, and children with other children; this is difficult for Western women who expect a husband to spend time with his wife. Unfortunately, many Western women who join their African husbands in Africa are not aware of, and sometimes less sensitive to some of these cultural differences and African family dynamics. In most cases, Western women find it very difficult to remain in Africa with their husbands, and they often choose to return to their homeland.

While Western women today may choose voluntarily to leave their African husbands, such choice was not part of the equation in the days of Ezra and Nehemiah. There the "foreign women" were sent away, banished, along with their children (Ezra 10; Neh. 13). From my perspective as a Christian, this presents a serious challenge: how could God condone divorce—even require it? Indeed, marriage is a divinely ordained estate (Genesis 2:24), and divorce is contrary to the intention of God as Jesus made it clear when he disapproved of it (Matthew 5:32; 19:3-9; Mark 10:2-9), as also did his Apostle Paul (1 Corinthians 7:10-17).

How then can we understand the actions of Ezra and Nehemiah who sanctioned and encouraged divorce? Intermarriage with foreign women was one of the most notoriously detestable sins (Leviticus 18: 22, 26-27, 30), and such "detestable practices" or "abominations" were centered in idolatry which included the pagan rites and sacrifices that accompanied such false worship (Deuteronomy 20:18; Jeremiah 16:18; Ezekiel 7:20). The concern, then, in Ezra and Nehemiah, is not intermarriage with non-Jewish women per se, but intermarriage with foreign women who wished to keep their identity as foreigners, including their pagan worship of false gods (cf. Solomon's foreign wives in 1 Kings 11:4-8).

Yes, the foreign women in Ezra and Nehemiah appear to have married Jewish men while continuing to cling on to their foreign identity, including their heathen beliefs and worship. In Ezra 9:1, some Jewish leaders lamented that those who had intermarried "have not separated themselves from the peoples of the lands, who live according to *their detestable practices*." Nehemiah is characteristically more direct in stating the matter, noting that some of the children out of these unions with foreign women "were not able to understand or speak the Jewish language" but "spoke the language of Ashdod" (Neh. 13:24). The mothers of these children had not rejected their foreign identities (including the worship of false gods) after marrying Jewish men. Thus it is not unexpected that the people of Ezra and Nehemiah's day had to make the unfortunate choice between remaining married to foreign women and divorcing them (Ezra 10:2-3).

Therefore, there is no real conflict between what Ezra and Nehemiah did and the advice that Paul gave to the Christians at Corinth (1 Corinthians 7:12-17) about marriage unions that had existed before they became Christians. Such marriages were not to be dissolved by the Christian partners as long as the unbelieving partners were willing to maintain the marriage bond. However, Paul discouraged people who were already Christians from entering into a marriage relationship with unbelievers. In principle, the Bible is not against inter-racial marriages, rather it warns against mixed marriages—that is, marriage unions between Christians and non-Christians.

Biblically, then, God is not against inter-tribal and inter-racial marriages. Jewish men like Moses, Joseph, Boaz, and David married non Jewesses. In fact, God struck Miriam, Moses' sister, with leprosy when she spoke against his marriage to a Cushite woman (Numbers 12:1-16). The main criterion is religious affiliation. For Christians that means we are to marry someone who is also a Christian. But if a believer knowingly and deliberately chooses to marry an unbeliever, the Bible says such a Christian is yoked together with a "foreigner" or an "outsider" (2 Corinthians 6:14-16). And that can be a dangerous thing.

Onesimus A. Ngundu (Ph.D., University of Cambridge; Th.D., Dallas Theological Seminary) is currently a Research Assistant at the University of Cambridge, England.

A CUBAN REFLECTION ON THE BIBLICAL EXPERIENCE OF EXILE

Franco Valdes (Cuba, United States)

The Cuban American people mostly reside in South Florida, the place I call Home. Even now, that I live elsewhere, South Florida remains my "Home," the place I was born and raised. This thought is one that is embedded in Cuban Americans today, even more so in Cubans who have immigrated to the United States in the last 30 years and are now even American citizens. This feeling of Home is a very strong sentiment to Cubans; their small Cuban neighborhood, their friends, and their families all play part to this significant attachment.

Before we continue, it is important to have an abridged history lesson of both the political revolution in Cuba and the biblical one in Jerusalem. Cuba, backed by the United States, was under control of a communist government ruled by Fulgencio Batista. Attacks against Batista started in 1953 on Moncada Barracks in Santiago and ended in 1959 when Batista finally fled the country. During these six years of war people began to understand the inevitable future of the country. Many of them fled Cuba and came to the United States before it was too late. Today, the doors remain closed, and the thousands of now South Floridians have no choice but to accept their new residence, away from their real Home.

At the end of the year 2012, Cuba will have served over 53 years under Fidel Castro and his administration and many more under a communist government, including Batista's reign. That is over five decades of poverty, hunger, suffering, and hardship that the Cuban people have had to cope with. Still, the Cuban people residing in South Florida do not call the United States their Home. My father, who came to the United States in 1984, is now an American citizen and even receives help from the U.S. government; in conversation he will still attest to Cuba being his real home and only residing here temporarily: "I live here and I have family here, but this is not my country." That view will never change.

Traveling back in history many centuries we come to read about the Assyrian empire, ruling the Middle East from 900 B.C.E. to 607 B.C.E. The Kingdom of Judah was client to this vast territory. After a few years of war, the Babylonians overthrew the Assyrian Empire in 599 B.C.E. and two years later, the city of Judah fell as well and was destroyed by the Babylonian ruler Nebuchadnezzar. Nebuchadnezzar appointed Zedekiah to be king of the territory not knowing that he would revolt against him in the future. Zedekiah entered into an alliance with the Egyptian Pharaoh Hophra and attempted to take back Judah. Nebuchadnezzar once again succeeded and in 587 B.C.E. destroyed the city walls, Temple, and the houses of the most important citizens. During this time many people fled to avoid the destruction, seeking refuge in neighboring cities such as Moab, Ammon, and Edom.

The thought of leaving behind everything you have ever known is a very difficult decision. Leaving your family, your home, your job, your security, your values, and anything else you own is a decision that every person in exile has made. Each situation may be different but the feeling is always the same. It is tough to know the specific conditions in which people left Judah, but as a Cuban American, I know the conditions in which people have left Cuba. My father, mother, uncles, and aunts have all shared with me their stories of escape. Speaking to my mother about this brings her to tears; she misses Home deeply and painfully. She left everything to come to the United States and avoid the cruel world inside Cuba. Although she does not regret her decision, she feels as though she has lost her identity and has completely disconnected herself from her past, her memories, and her family who still remain in Cuba.

In theory both moments in history, Israelite and Cuban, have many similarities. Both, for example, coincide with a lack of democracy and a lack of freedom. There is a crucial difference, however. Nehemiah 1 and 2 feature a theme that not a single Cuban American can relate to: returning Home, rebuilding, and rejoicing. This part of the story has not yet been written for Cuba and the Cuban American people. This longing for Home in the Cuban American people's hearts is persistent. We hope that one day—before our time on this earth is done—that part of the story will take place. This hope is what keeps so many of them so close. South Florida is not only a safe haven for these people, but it is also a very close geographical location to their Home. One day they hope to be able to go Home and experience the joy of the returning Israelites: the end of hardship and the establishing of a new country, the regaining of their identity and rejoining a community that they were forced to leave years ago, the rejoicing in and reconstructing of their past and their memories. This possibility, tragically, remains far away for Cuban Americans. Times only get tougher in Cuba, making a place so beautiful and so close feel yet so distant and destroyed.

Franco Valdes (B.A., Latin American History, University of Virginia) is a first-generation Cuban American from Miami.

PERSONAL THOUGHTS ON THE IDENTITY CRISIS
OF BIBLICAL EXILES

Danielle Smith (Senegal, United States)

The books of Ezra and Nehemiah are essentially a story about an identity crisis, one in which the Israelites struggle to define who they are as a people. Are they defined by their past as the nation of Israel? Are they defined by their present as a part of the Persian Empire? Or is it a common faith that binds them, regardless of their political and national status and geographic location? Having grown up in a missionary family and lived in various African cultures, I can relate to this struggle. There is a constant battle between the American roots of my family and birthplace, and my African heritage, as I had spent the majority of my childhood in Africa. While residing in America I was in the racial and religious majority and yet I thought in ways that were culturally different; whereas, in Africa, I was distinctly in a racial and religious minority but found I was more culturally attune to the African way of living. Each location required a thoughtful reflection on who I was. When seen through these cultural dynamics, Ezra's actions are those of a servant of God who is attempting to unite the Israelites through the rebuilding of their Temple—a Temple that served as a symbol of their faith and the very heart of what brought them together as a nation in the first place. In the final analysis he is seeking to bring an identity to a dispossessed people whom God was returning to the Promise Land and the faith of their fathers.

King Cyrus allowed the Israelites to return to Jerusalem in order to rebuild the temple which had been destroyed previously by King Nebuchadnezzar. Therefore, the heads of the Israelite families prepared their things and moved to Jerusalem and the surrounding towns in hopes of renewing their covenant with God as they attempted to reestablish the destroyed temple. As the "newcomers" struggled with moving and starting such a great task, however, they met opposition from hostile people around them.

To me this recalls my first year in an African school. As the only white person in the entire school and not knowing any French at all, I was definitely a misfit in their eyes, as well as in my own. They did not understand me or why I was so different and they could not relate to me or my ways. Consequently, I remember the seemingly endless days of students pulling at my hair because it was long, blonde, and so different from their own, or kids always begging for money with the assumption that every white person was wealthy. It wasn't until many months later that the kids began to warm up to the idea of having a foreigner amongst them. Much like the era of Ezra, in African societies, racial identity often assumes religious affiliation. For example, the Wolof of Senegal will assume that any fellow Wolof is a Muslim and therefore anyone seeking to integrate into their community will come under intense pressure to espouse Islam. Similarly with the Jews, surrounding areas did not welcome them as they brought their own traditions and history with them. They sought to rebuild something unique to their own culture amongst the people of an entirely different one. What is important to remember is that the resistance they met was created by their attempt to be faithful to God; we, too, can expect similar hostility until God gives us a clear direction on how to engage with those around us.

As time went on and the Israelites became more accustomed to their surroundings, they started assimilating with the people around them. They began intermarrying and following the foreign customs of their neighbors. Just before my freshman year of high school, my family left Senegal indefinitely and moved back to America. I was faced with a new home, a new school, and a culture with which I was not very familiar. My first reaction was to push away from conforming to the cookie-cutter American image because of my loyalty to my African roots. However, being different can be exhausting, especially as a young teenager, and I soon found that I just wanted to be "normal." I began dressing, talking, and acting like what I thought was the typical American. It was not simply an outward appearance with which I was struggling, but an inner perception.

Throughout the book of Ezra, we see a fundamental struggle of identity amongst the Israelites who were tired of being oppressed and whose tendency was, just like me, to blend in with the society surrounding them. All who have ever experienced the process of cultural adaptation understand the challenges of integrating into a new environment without assimilating. Integration means to become a participant in the new society but assimilation occurs when one surrenders their very identity in the pursuit of being accepted by their new neighbors. At the core of this decision is the question of personal beliefs, personal faith. How far will one go just to fit in?

Unlike Nehemiah, who focused on political restoration, the heart of Ezra's message was the spiritual restoration of the people of God. Ezra sought to bring the Israelites' focus back to their faith and God thus making it the essence of their identity. There were practical consequences concerning intermarriage and enculturation with the surrounding nations. It is a stark reminder that faith does impact daily life. While the New Testament does not espouse a racial bloodline from Abraham, the Good News does declare that the bloodline of Jesus will cause separation from the world when it seeks to alter our identity in Christ.

When God is at the center of our worldview it affects our practical decisions. Like the Israelites, who we marry and what we build (the Temple) are expressions of our faith. Every generation has to make the critical choice of conforming to the world around them or being transformed by the truth of God's Word. Whether in Africa or in America, the day-to-day decisions I make are part of the worldview that God is instilling in me. In Ezra's time, God was seeking a people no longer held in captivity by alien beliefs or influences; rather their identity was to be in the God of Abraham, Isaac, and Jacob. The same can be said today: God is still seeking a people who live according to their identity in Christ and not that of the culture around them. It is the most practical form of the concept called holiness.

Danielle Smith spent her early life in Senegal and is currently studying cultural anthropology in the United States.

QUESTIONS

1. Explain and evaluate Ji-Sun Kim's point that "everyone is a hybrid" and that one should "rejoice in the differences."

2. What is your assessment of and reaction to Ngundu's views that the Bible is opposed to interreligious marriages (if not inter interracial and intertribal ones)?

3. In addition to the ones mentioned by Valdes, what are some other similarities and differences between the Cuban and Israelite contexts?

4. How does your cultural context compare to that of Smith and Ezra-Nehemiah in terms of associating racial identity with religious affiliation?

CREDITS

Chapter 1: p. 2; Fang Li (ed.). *Imperial Readings of the Taiping Era*, 977–983; p. 7; Desmond Tutu. *No Future without Forgiveness* [2000]. Image.

Chapter 2: pp. 11–12; Saint Ambrose. *Hexaemeron*; p. 14; Ludwig Feuerbach. *The Essence of Christianity* [New York: Harper and Row, 1957], 287.

Chapter 3: p. 21; *The Intrareligious Dialogue* [New York: Mahwah/Paulist Press, 1978], 2 ; p. 26; STAROBSERVER.AU

Chapter 4: p. 21; Abdullah Yusuf Ali. *An English Interpretation of the Holy Quran* [Lushena Books, 2001]; p. 32; Excerpt from p. 108 from ABRAHAM: A JOURNEY TO THE HEART OF THREE FAITHS by BRUCE FEILER. Copyright © 2002 by Bruce Feiler. Reprinted with permission of HarperCollins Publishers ; Julia Ward Howe's *Mother's Day Proclamation*, 1870.

Chapter 5: p. 33; pearson Education; p. 40; *New Revised Standard Version Bible*, copyright 1989, Division of Christian Education of the National Council of the Churches of Christ in the United States of America. Used by permission. All rights reserved.

Chapter 7: p. 57; *New Revised Standard Version Bible*, copyright 1989, Division of Christian Education of the National Council of the Churches of Christ in the United States of America. Used by permission. All rights reserved.

Chapter 8: p. 70; "Familism and Ancestor Veneration: A Look at Chinese Funeral Rites," *Missiology* 24 O [1996]: 516.

Chapter 11: p. 94; *New Revised Standard Version Bible*, copyright 1989, Division of Christian Education of the National Council of the Churches of Christ in the United States of America. Used by permission. All rights reserved.

Chapter 12: p. 100; Chris White (ed.). *Nineteenth Century Writings on Homosexuality: A Sourcebook* [London: Routledge, 1999]; pp. 100, 102; *New Revised Standard Version Bible*, copyright 1989, Division of Christian Education of the National Council of the Churches of Christ in the United States of America. Used by permission. All rights reserved.

Chapter 13: p. 111; *New Revised Standard Version Bible*, copyright 1989, Division of Christian Education of the National Council of the Churches of Christ in the United States of America. Used by permission. All rights reserved; p. 112; Jesse Russell and Ronald Cohn. *Vayu Purana* [Books on Demand, 2012]; p. 112; Mahatma Jyatorao Foole, *Gulamgiri*, 1873.

Chapter 15: pp. 124; *New Revised Standard Version Bible*, copyright 1989, Division of Christian Education of the National Council of the Churches of Christ in the United States of America. Used by permission. All rights reserved.

Chapter 16: pp. 132 ; *New Revised Standard Version Bible*, copyright 1989, Division of Christian Education of the National Council of the Churches of Christ in the United States of America. Used by permission. All rights reserved.

Chapter 18: p. 149 ; *New Revised Standard Version Bible*, copyright 1989, Division of Christian Education of the National Council of the Churches of Christ in the United States of America. Used by permission. All rights reserved ; p. 152, 153; Courtesy of Amy Lambert.

Chapter 19: pp. 160, 162; *New Revised Standard Version Bible*, copyright 1989, Division of Christian Education of the National Council of the Churches of Christ in the United States of America. Used by permission. All rights reserved.

Chapter 20: p. 168; Adarsh Mumbai News and Feature Agency ; pandita Ramabai, *A Testimony of our Inexhaustible Treasure.* (American Council of the Ramabai Mukti Mission, 1977) ; p. 170; Nubaek Choi. Praise of Lady Yum.

Chapter 21: p. 178; *New Revised Standard Version Bible, copyright 1989*, Division of Christian Education of the National Council of the Churches of Christ in the United States of America. Used by permission. All rights reserved.

Chapter 22: p. 189; *New Revised Standard Version Bible*, copyright 1989, Division of Christian Education of the National Council of the Churches of Christ in the United States of America. Used by permission. All rights reserved.

Chapter 23: pp. 194, 195, 196; *New Revised Standard Version Bible*, copyright 1989, Division of Christian Education of the National Council of the Churches of Christ in the United States of America. Used by permission. All rights reserved.

Chapter 24: pp. 203, 204; *New Revised Standard Version Bible*, copyright 1989, Division of Christian Education of the National Council of the Churches of Christ in the United States of America. Used by permission. All rights reserved.